Shojo Beat

Absolute Boyfriend

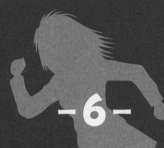

-6-

Story & Art by
Yuu Watase

Absolute Boyfriend

CAST

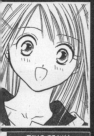
RIIKO IZAWA

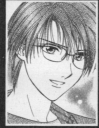
SOSHI ASAMOTO

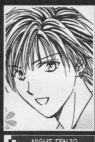
NIGHT TENJO

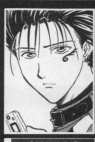
GAKU NAMIKIRI

STORY

LONELY RIIKO GOT MORE THAN SHE BARGAINED FOR
WHEN SHE BOUGHT A LOVER FIGURE FROM A MYSTERIOUS
WEBSITE. HER NEW "BOYFRIEND" TURNED OUT TO BE A
WALKING, TALKING (AND KISSING) ANDROID NAMED NIGHT.
LIFE WITH NIGHT IS FILLED WITH UNEXPECTED CHALLENGES,
BUT WHEN HE GETS RECALLED, RIIKO SUDDENLY REALIZES
JUST HOW MUCH SHE CARES FOR HIM. NIGHT MANAGES TO
ESCAPE KRONOS HEAVEN AND RETURNS TO RIIKO, BUT THE
COMPANY SENDS ANOTHER 01 MODEL TO BRING HIM BACK.
A SUPERHUMAN BATTLE ENSUES, AND NIGHT EMERGES
TRIUMPHANT. HE AND RIIKO EMBRACE IN THE RAIN,
PROMISING TO STAY TOGETHER FOREVER...

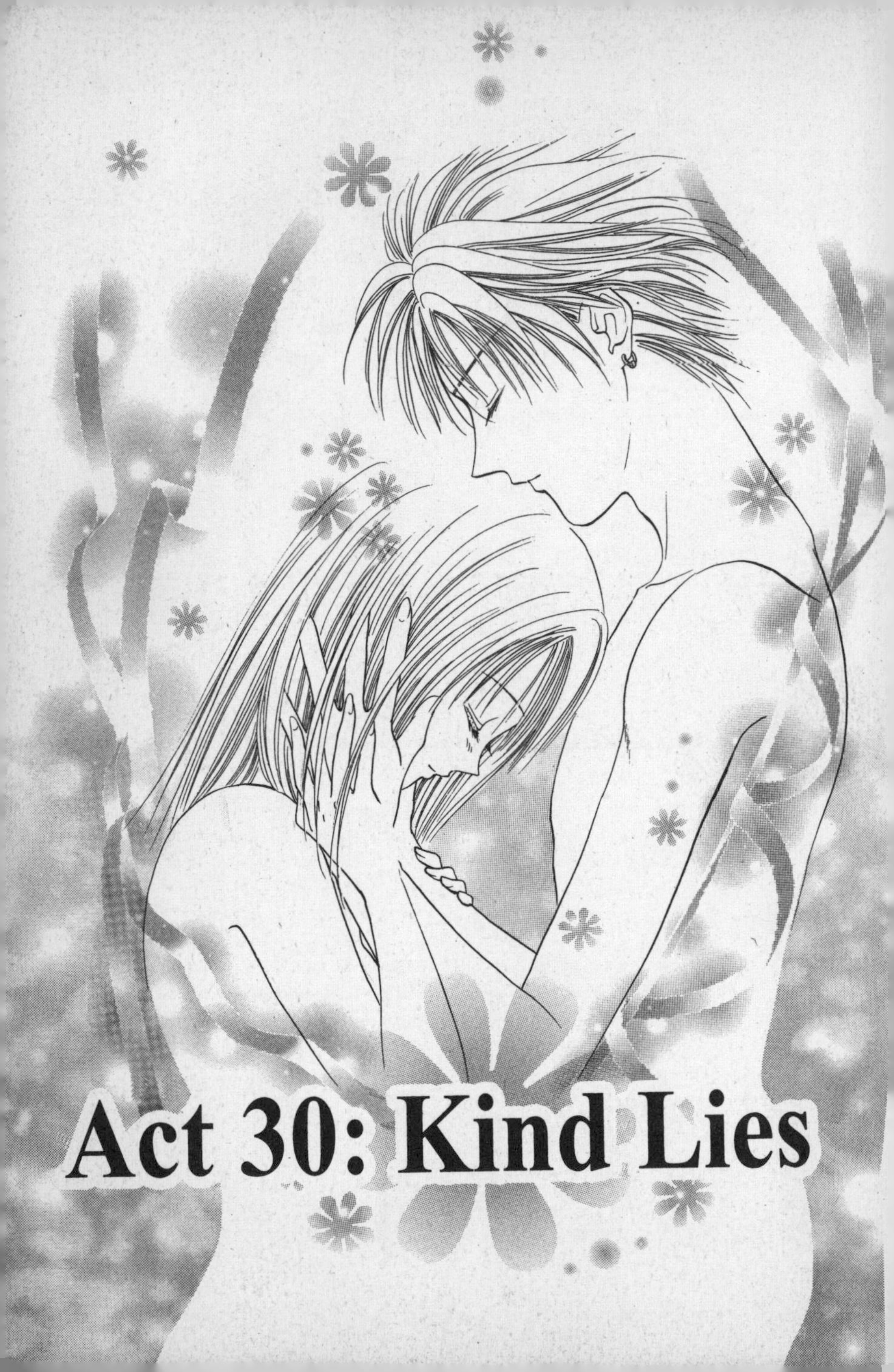

Act 30: Kind Lies

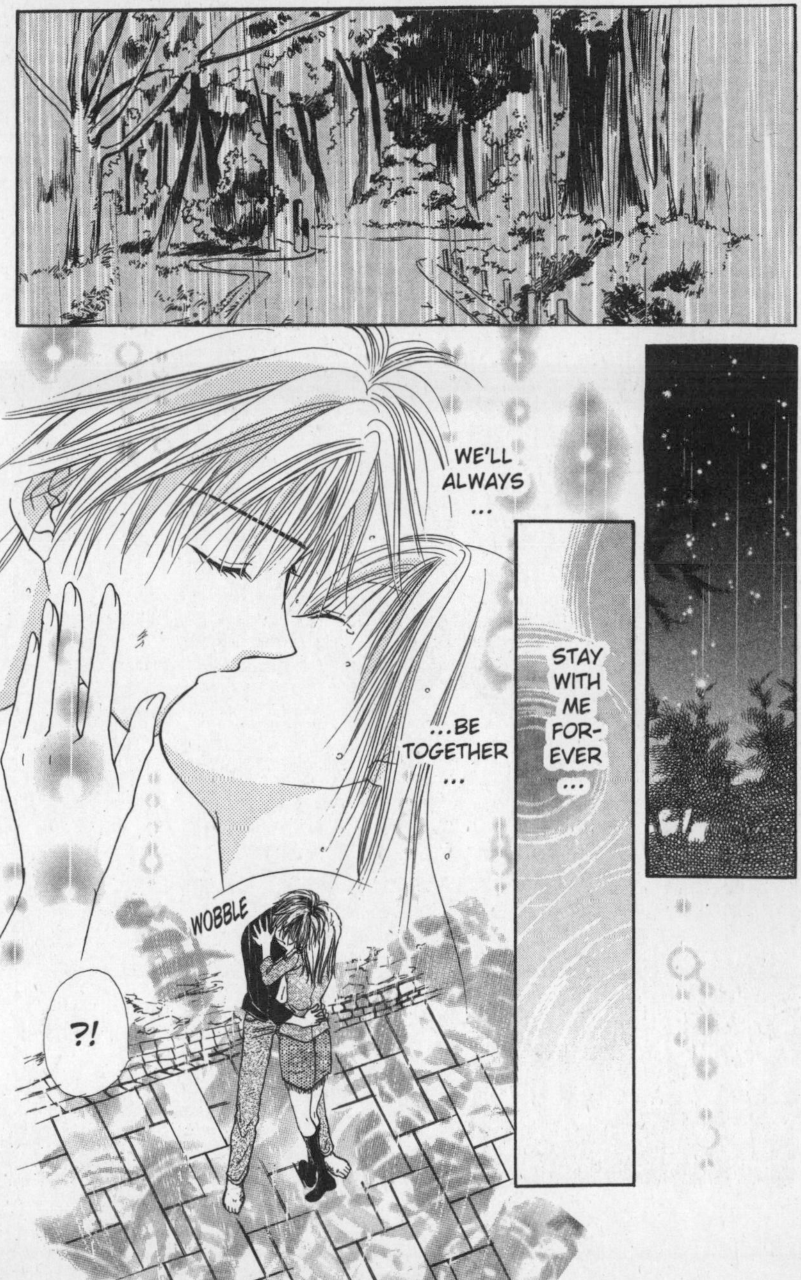
STAY WITH ME FOR- EVER ...
WE'LL ALWAYS ...
...BE TOGETHER ...
WOBBLE
?!

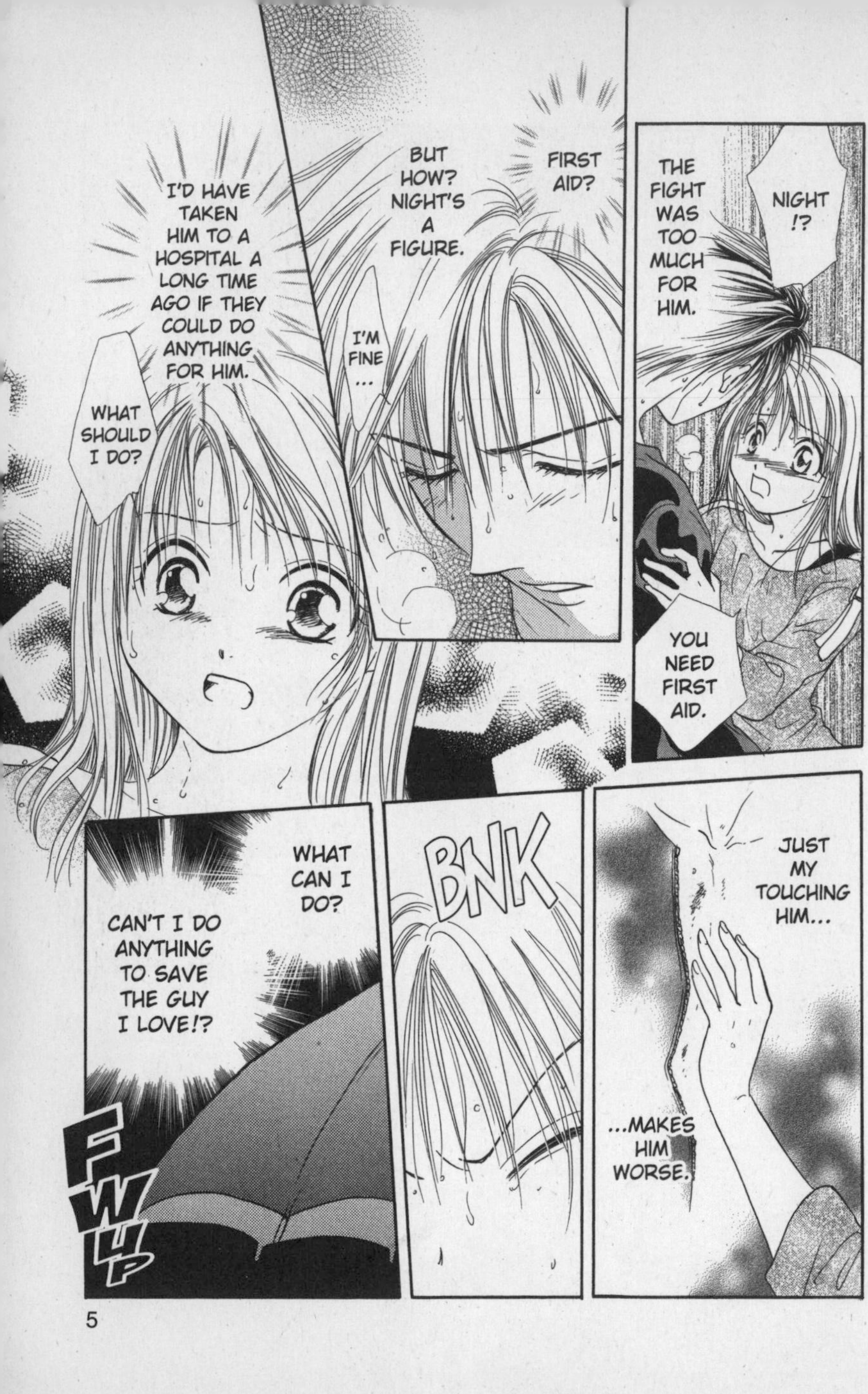
NIGHT !?
THE FIGHT WAS TOO MUCH FOR HIM.
YOU NEED FIRST AID.
FIRST AID?
BUT HOW? NIGHT'S A FIGURE.
I'M FINE ...
I'D HAVE TAKEN HIM TO A HOSPITAL A LONG TIME AGO IF THEY COULD DO ANYTHING FOR HIM.
WHAT SHOULD I DO?
JUST MY TOUCHING HIM...
...MAKES HIM WORSE.
BNK
WHAT CAN I DO?
CAN'T I DO ANYTHING TO SAVE THE GUY I LOVE!?
FWUP

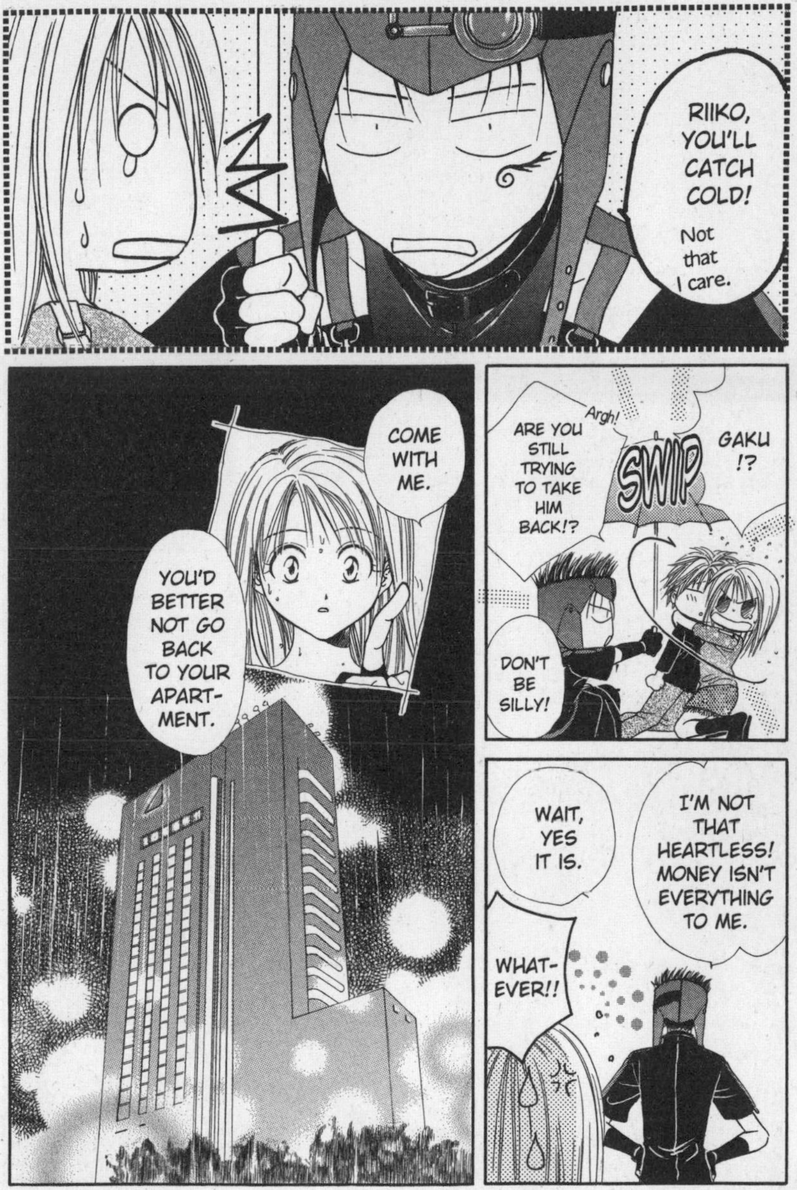
RIIKO, YOU'LL CATCH COLD!
Not that I care.
GAKU !?
Argh!
SWIP
ARE YOU STILL TRYING TO TAKE HIM BACK!?
DON'T BE SILLY!
I'M NOT THAT HEARTLESS! MONEY ISN'T EVERYTHING TO ME.
WAIT, YES IT IS.
WHAT-EVER!!
COME WITH ME.
YOU'D BETTER NOT GO BACK TO YOUR APART-MENT.

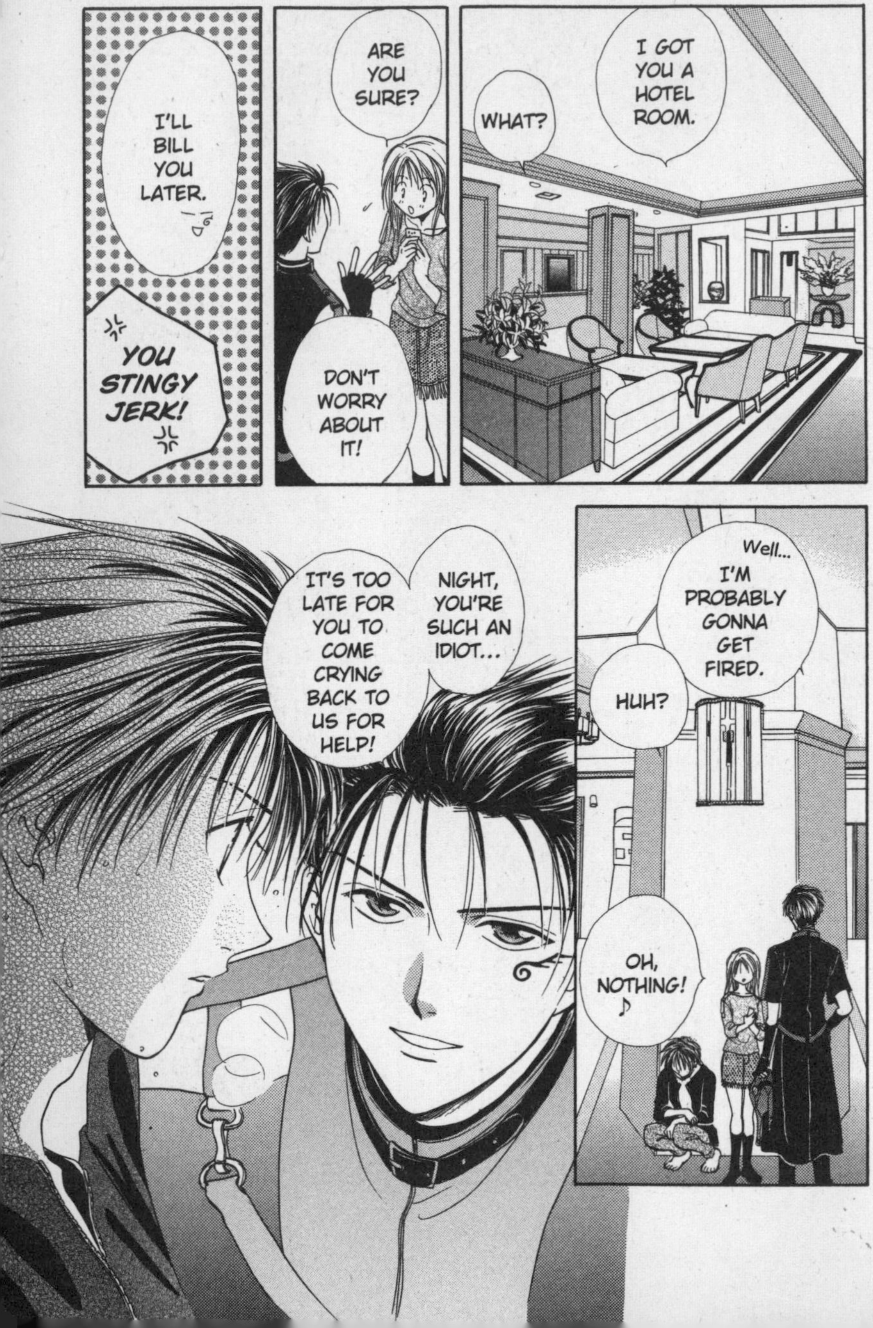
I GOT YOU A HOTEL ROOM.
WHAT?
ARE YOU SURE?
DON'T WORRY ABOUT IT!
I'LL BILL YOU LATER.
YOU STINGY JERK!
Well... I'M PROBABLY GONNA GET FIRED.
HUH?
OH, NOTHING! ♪
NIGHT, YOU'RE SUCH AN IDIOT...
IT'S TOO LATE FOR YOU TO COME CRYING BACK TO US FOR HELP!

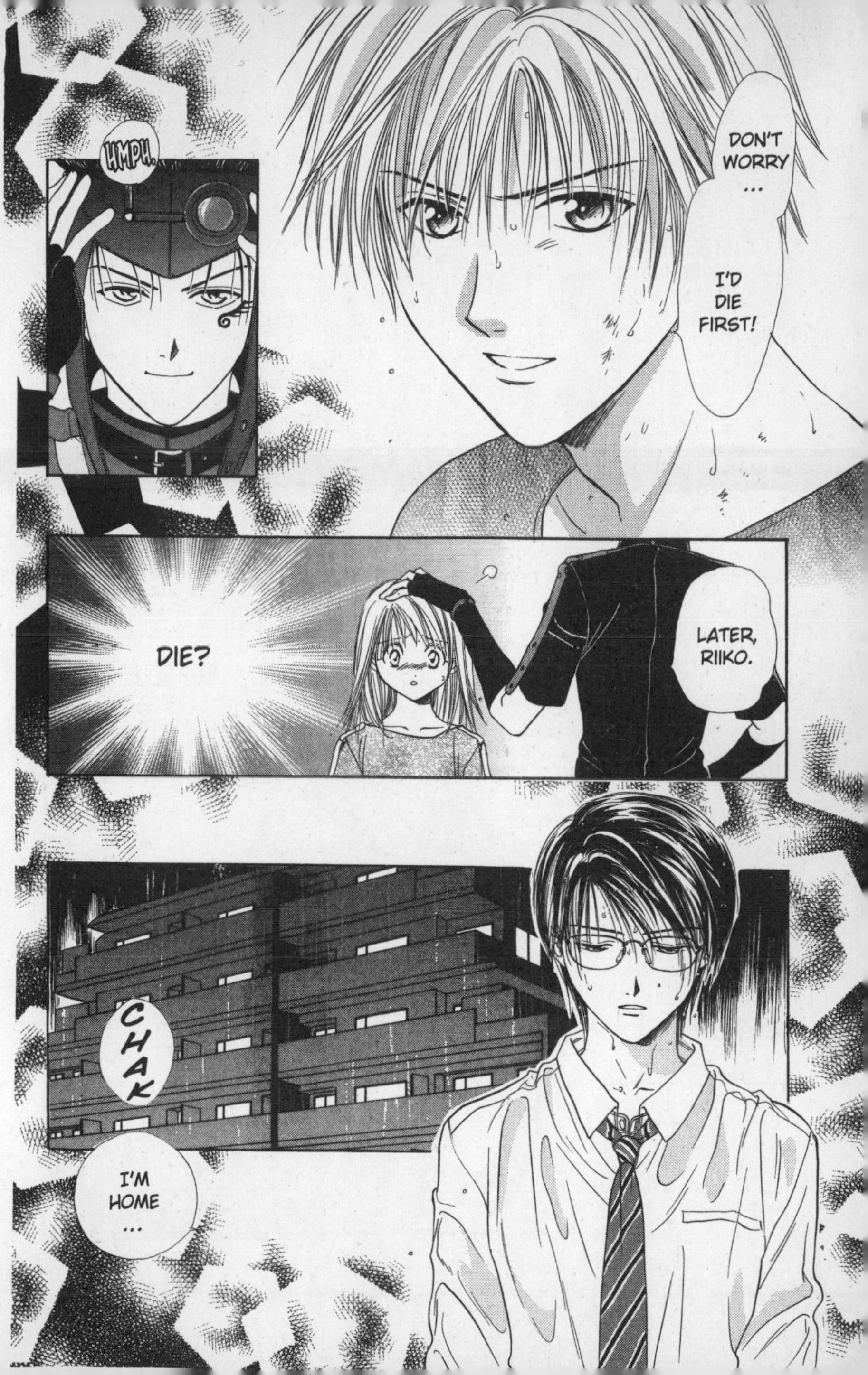
DON'T WORRY ...
I'D DIE FIRST!
HMPH.
LATER, RIIKO.
DIE?
CHAK
I'M HOME ...

SOSHI, GOOD TIMING ...
HEY, YOU'RE SOAKING WET!
I'LL GET YOU A TOWEL!
HERE, TAKE THE PHONE!
PLUP
?
HELLO?
HELLO, SOSHI?
DAD ?!

Hello! *Absolute Boyfriend* has safely reached its final volume! Thank you so much for staying with me to the end. Please enjoy.

I debated until the last minute whether to have Riiko end up with Night or with Soshi. You usually make it clear somewhere in the middle of the story, but I liked both of them so much. (smile) Riiko's indecision was a reflection of my own, I guess. Anyway, after agonizing for some time, I came up with this ending.

Romantic stories are tough, especially for me because I don't particularly like writing about romance. But then, I don't hate it either. I think it's because I don't need to be in a relationship to feel good about myself. Of course, it's nice to experience love. You discover feelings you never knew you had, and it makes you grow as a person. But I don't need a man in my life all the time. There are plenty of other fun things to fill my life, so I don't really understand people who are desperate to find someone. Though I do get lonely sometimes.

Some people want to be popular and love attention, but that's not me. I just want the person I love to love me back. Nobody else matters. The idea that a relationship is everything seems so limiting to me. So this story was hard for me because I don't really share Riiko's obsession. But I guess most women are more like her. Obviously, my least favorite movies are romances. But it's not that I hate them, and I have seen a few that I liked. Stop waffling!

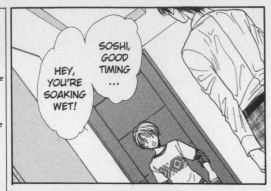

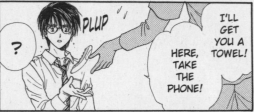

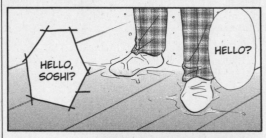

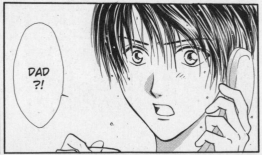

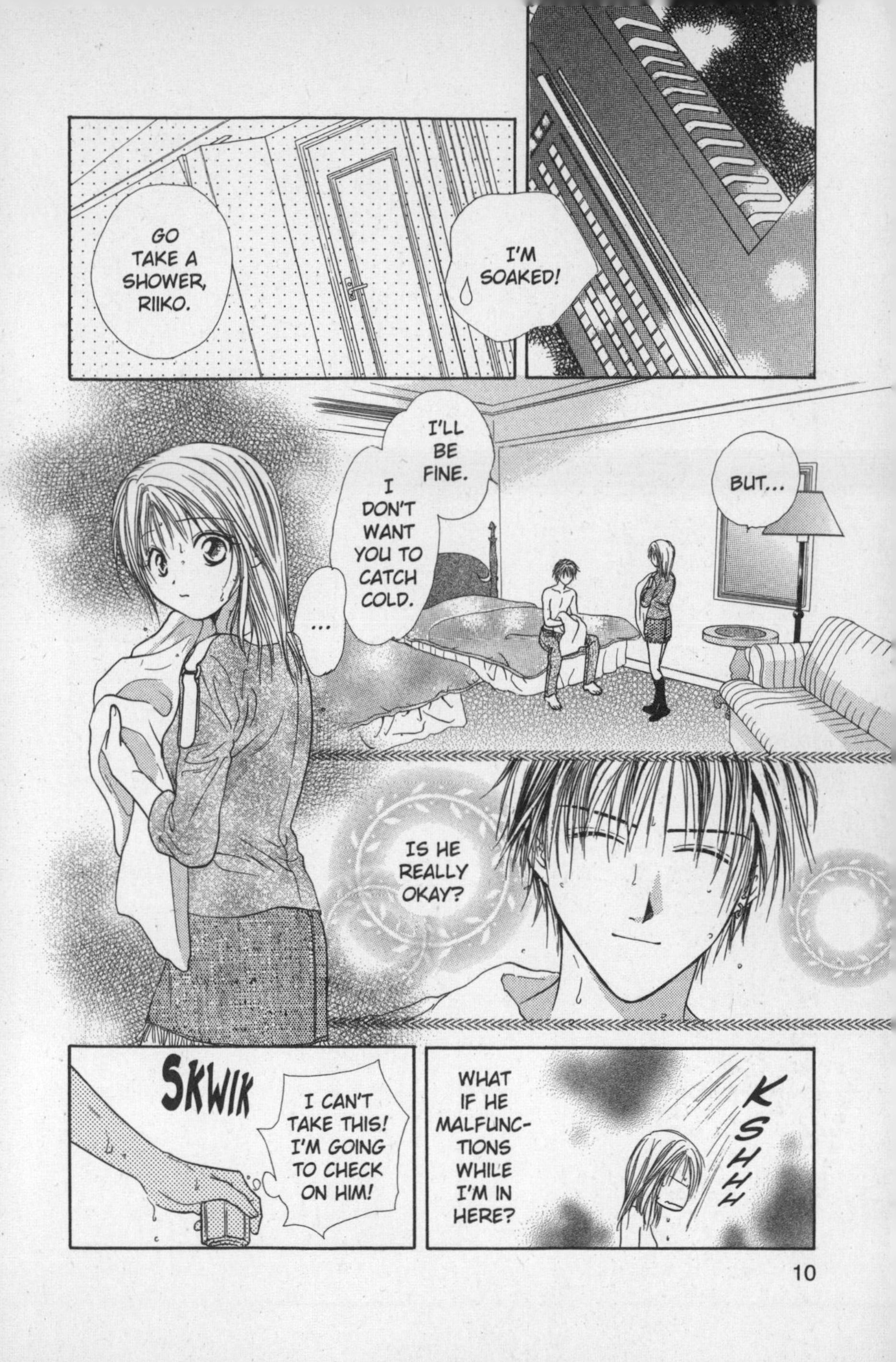
I'M SOAKED!
GO TAKE A SHOWER, RIIKO.
BUT...
I'LL BE FINE.
I DON'T WANT YOU TO CATCH COLD.
...
IS HE REALLY OKAY?
KSHHH
WHAT IF HE MALFUNCTIONS WHILE I'M IN HERE?
SKWIK
I CAN'T TAKE THIS! I'M GOING TO CHECK ON HIM!

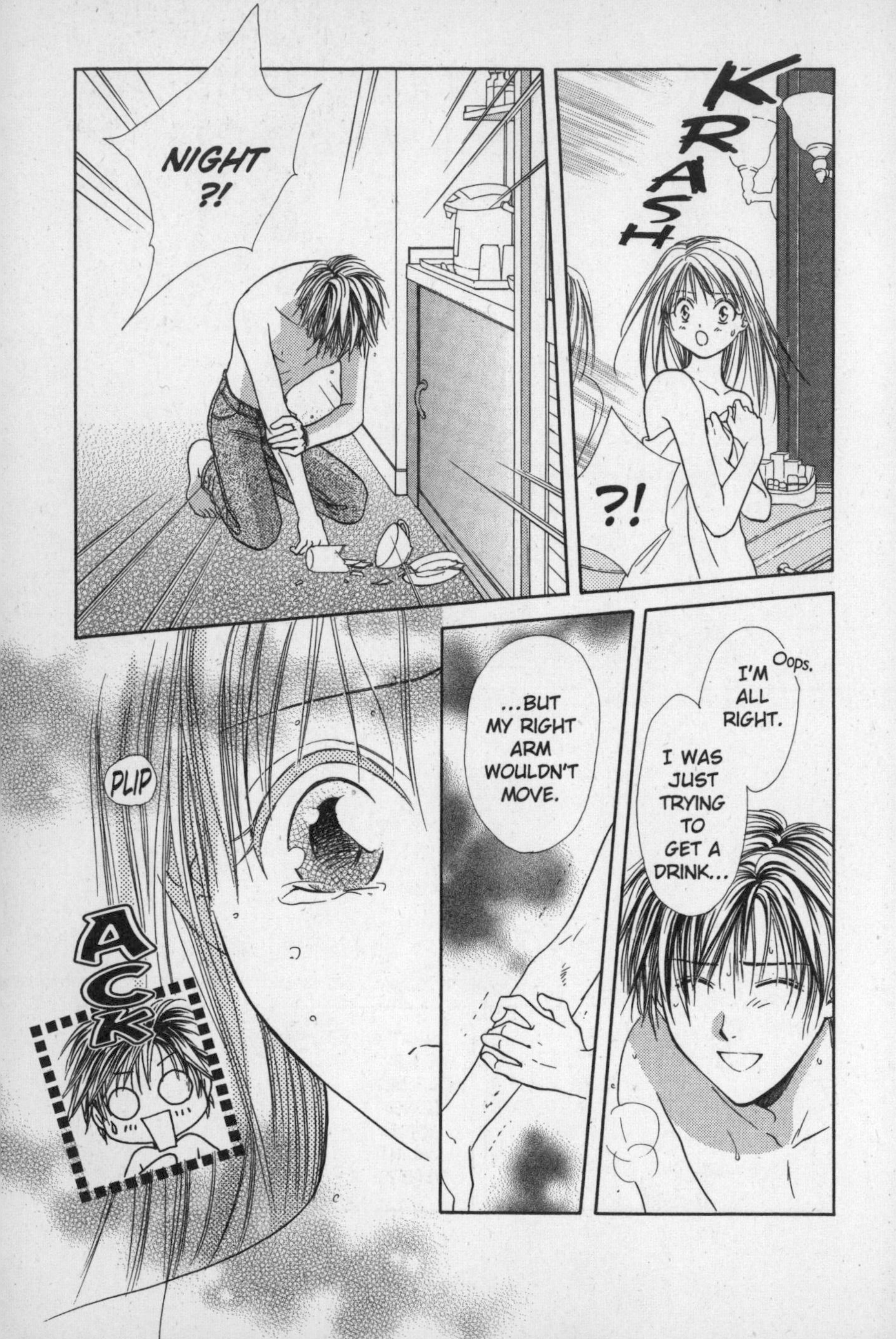
KRASH
?!
NIGHT ?!
Oops.
I'M ALL RIGHT.
I WAS JUST TRYING TO GET A DRINK...
...BUT MY RIGHT ARM WOULDN'T MOVE.
PLIP
ACK

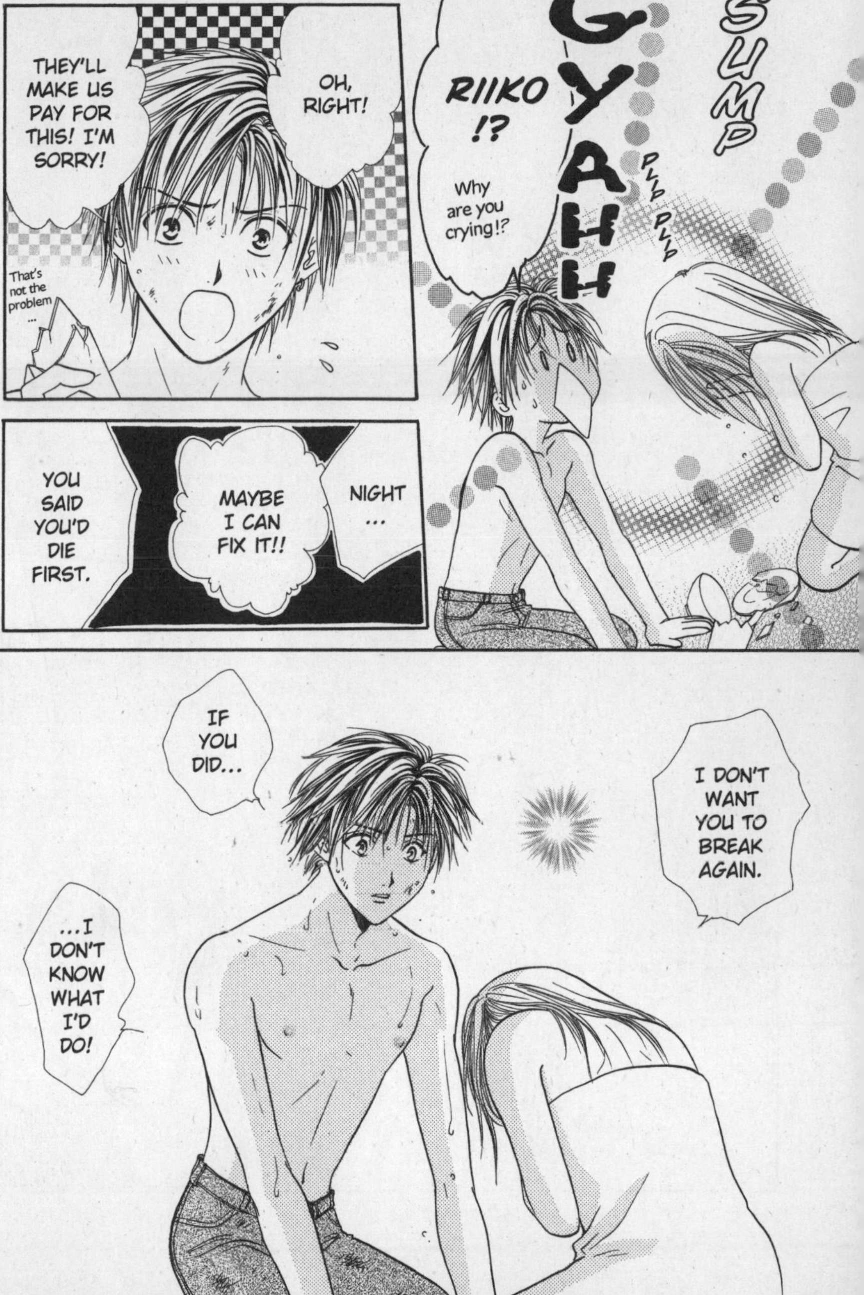
SUMP
GYAHH
RIIKO!?
Why are you crying!?
PLIP PLIP
OH, RIGHT!
THEY'LL MAKE US PAY FOR THIS! I'M SORRY!
That's not the problem ...
NIGHT ...
MAYBE I CAN FIX IT!!
YOU SAID YOU'D DIE FIRST.
I DON'T WANT YOU TO BREAK AGAIN.
IF YOU DID...
...I DON'T KNOW WHAT I'D DO!

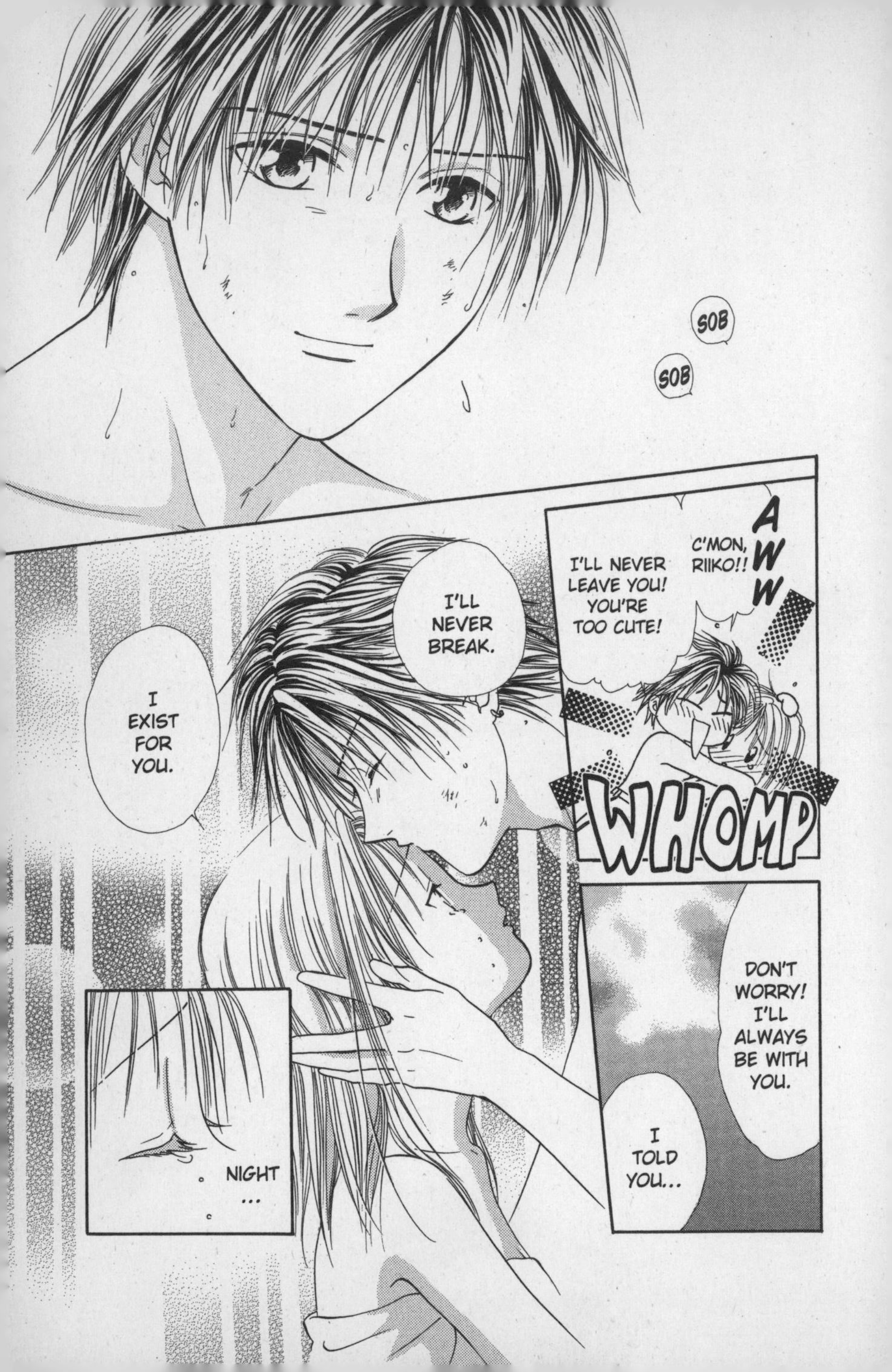
SOB
SOB
AWW
C'MON, RIIKO!!
I'LL NEVER LEAVE YOU! YOU'RE TOO CUTE!
WHOMP
I'LL NEVER BREAK.
I EXIST FOR YOU.
DON'T WORRY! I'LL ALWAYS BE WITH YOU.
I TOLD YOU...
NIGHT ...

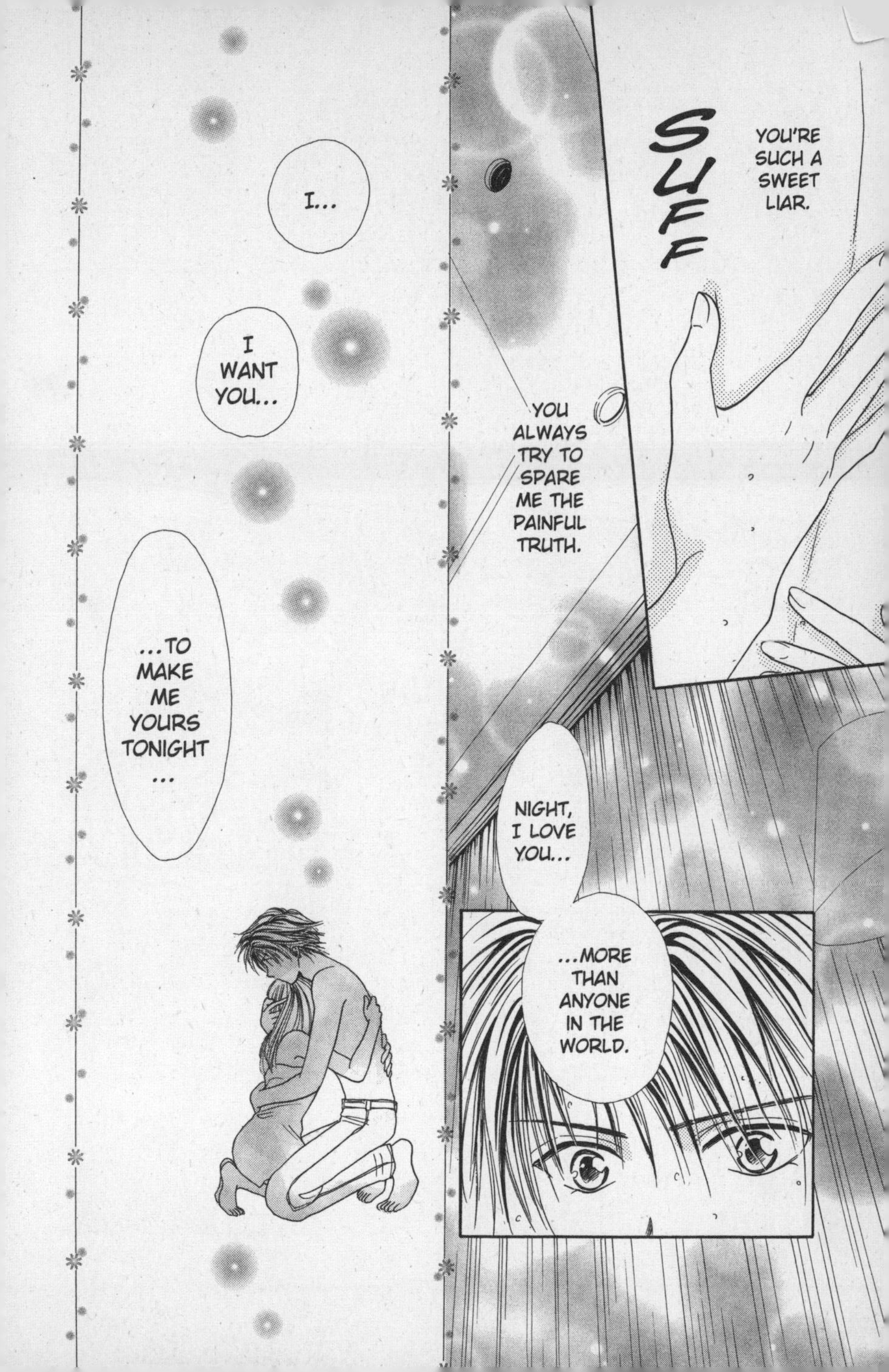
YOU'RE SUCH A SWEET LIAR.
SUFF
YOU ALWAYS TRY TO SPARE ME THE PAINFUL TRUTH.
NIGHT, I LOVE YOU...
...MORE THAN ANYONE IN THE WORLD.
I...
I WANT YOU...
...TO MAKE ME YOURS TONIGHT...

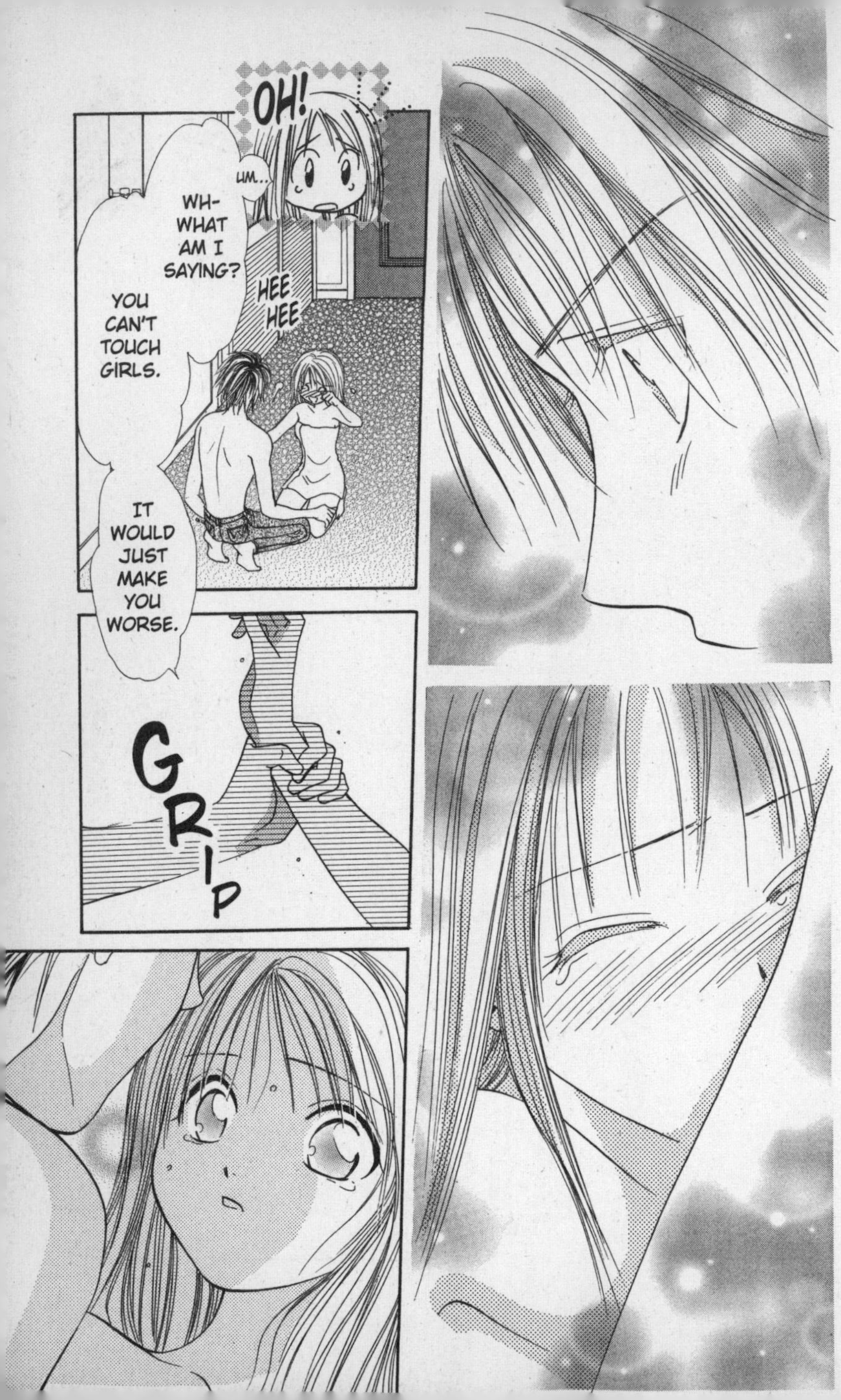
OH!
UM...
WH- WHAT AM I SAYING?
HEE HEE
YOU CAN'T TOUCH GIRLS.
IT WOULD JUST MAKE YOU WORSE.
GRIP

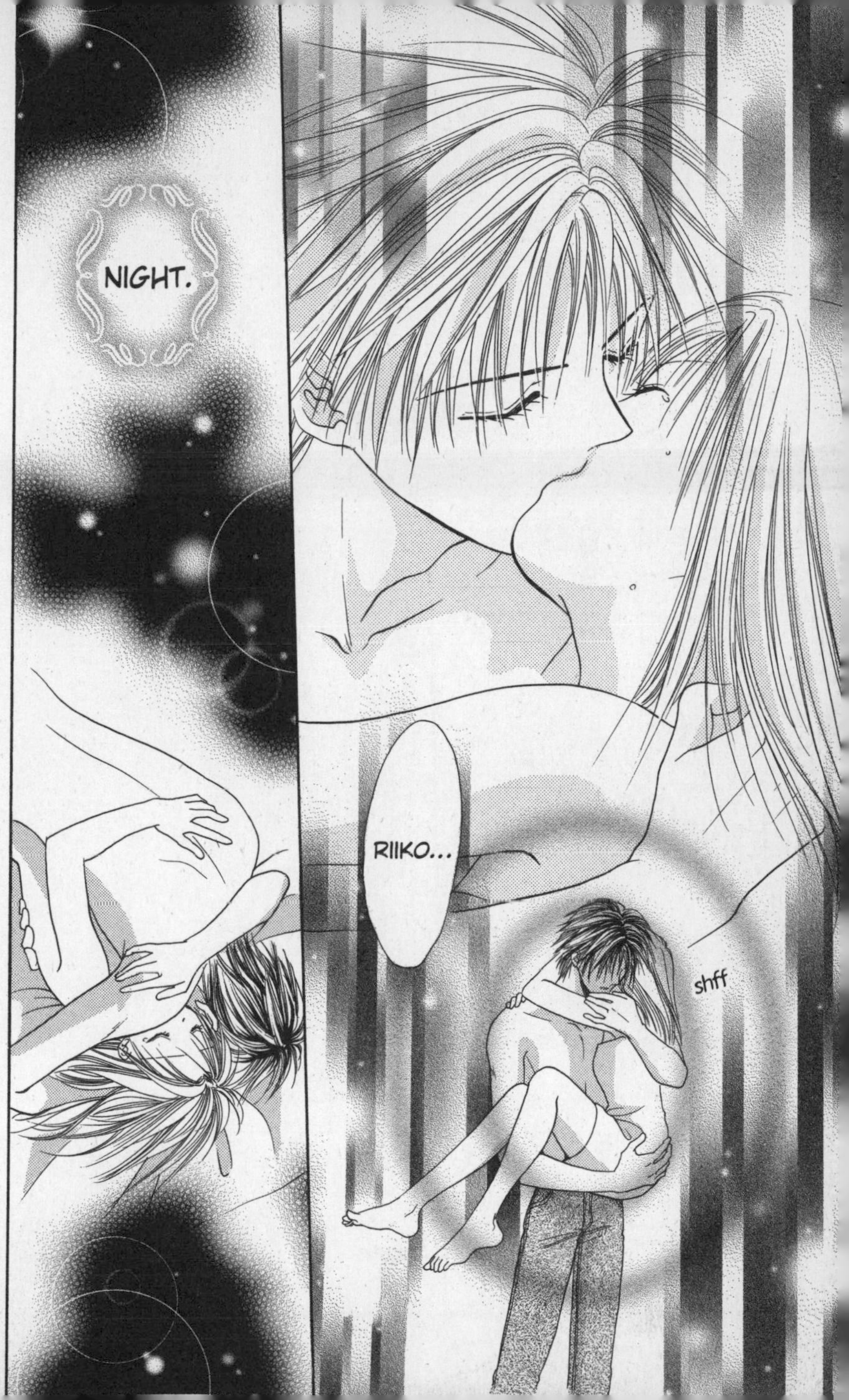
RIIKO...
shff
NIGHT.

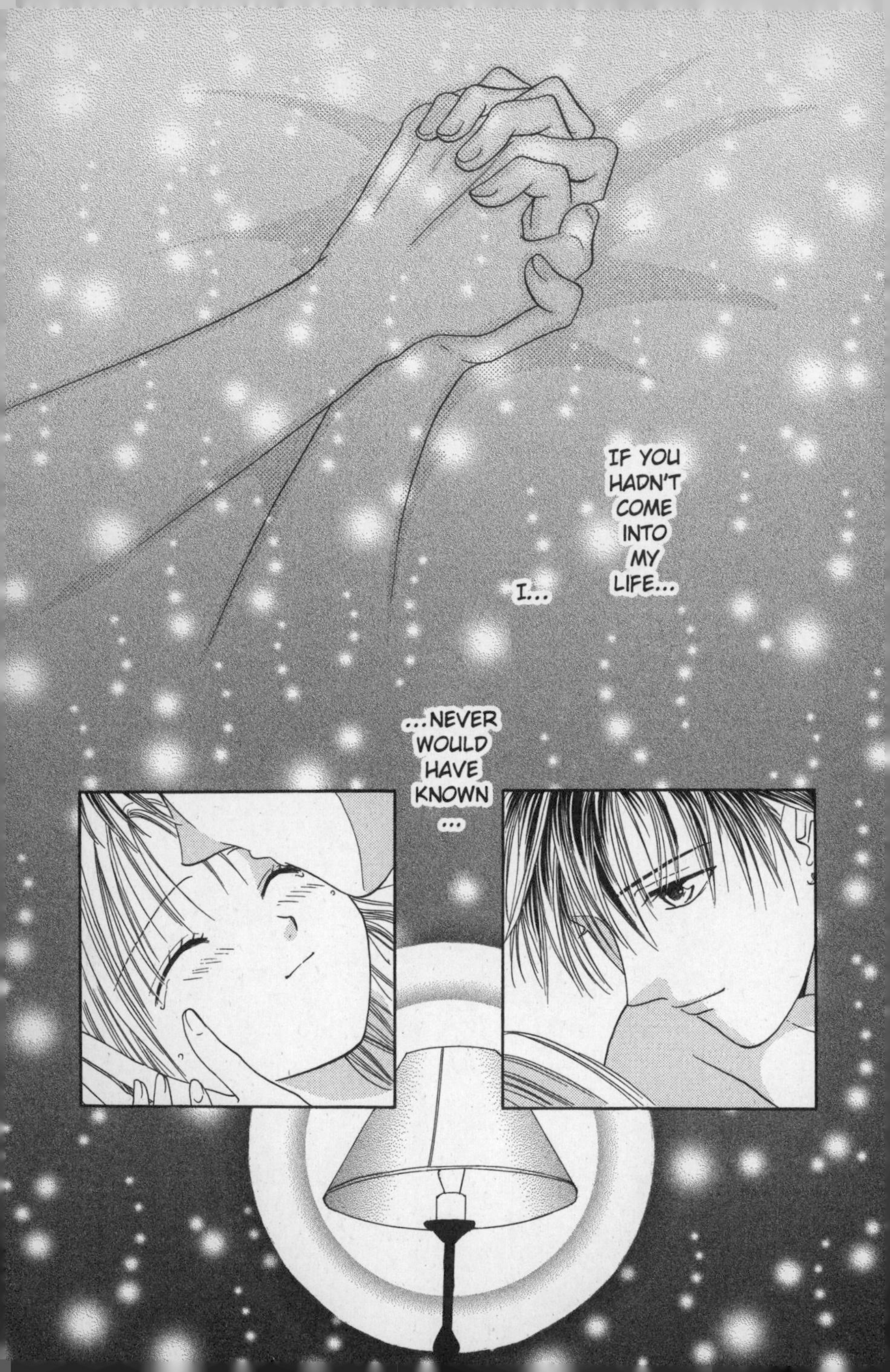
IF YOU HADN'T COME INTO MY LIFE...
I...
...NEVER WOULD HAVE KNOWN...

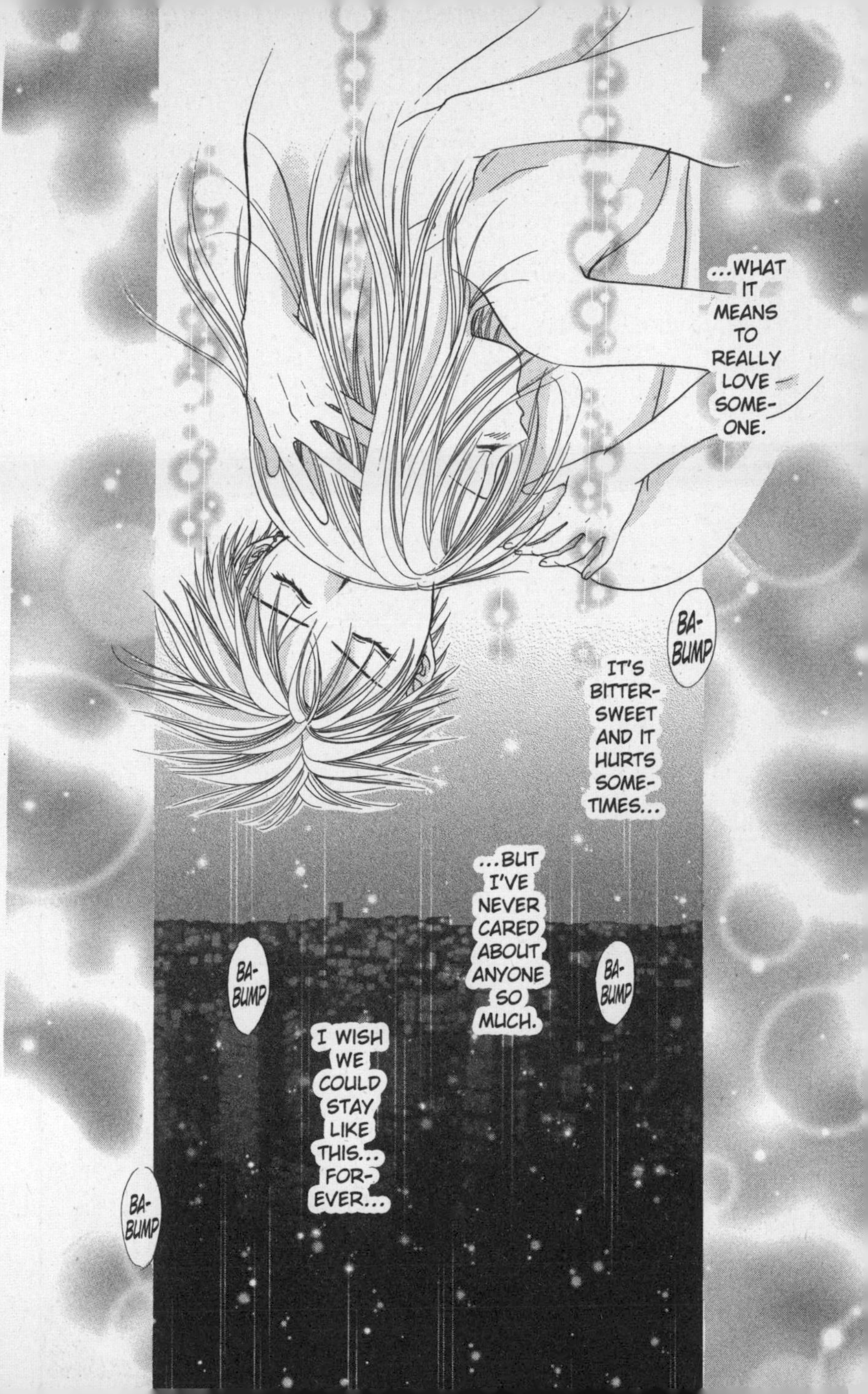
...WHAT IT MEANS TO REALLY LOVE SOME-ONE.
BA-BUMP
IT'S BITTER-SWEET AND IT HURTS SOME-TIMES...
...BUT I'VE NEVER CARED ABOUT ANYONE SO MUCH.
BA-BUMP
BA-BUMP
I WISH WE COULD STAY LIKE THIS... FOR-EVER...
BA-BUMP

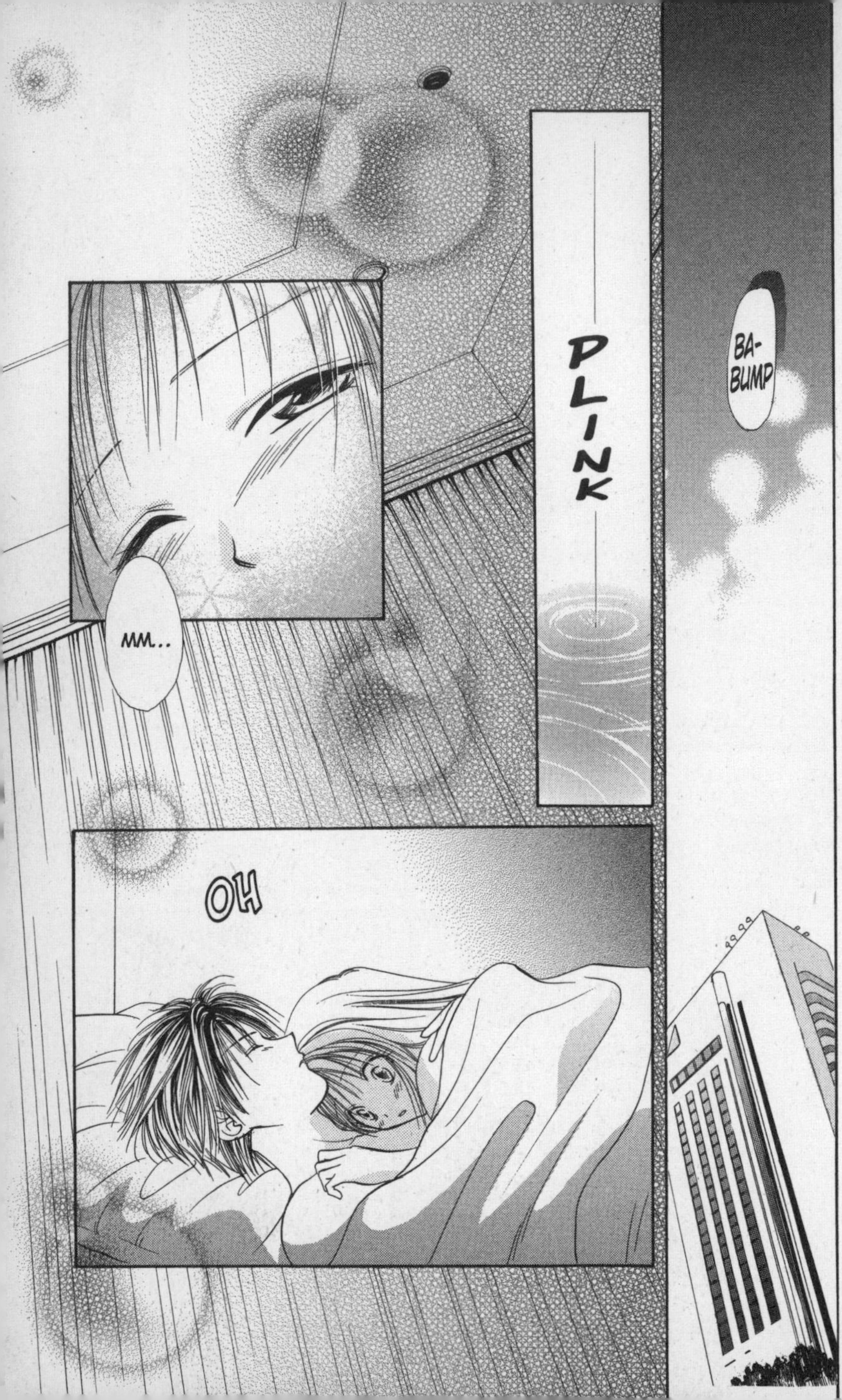
BA-BUMP
PLINK
MM...
OH

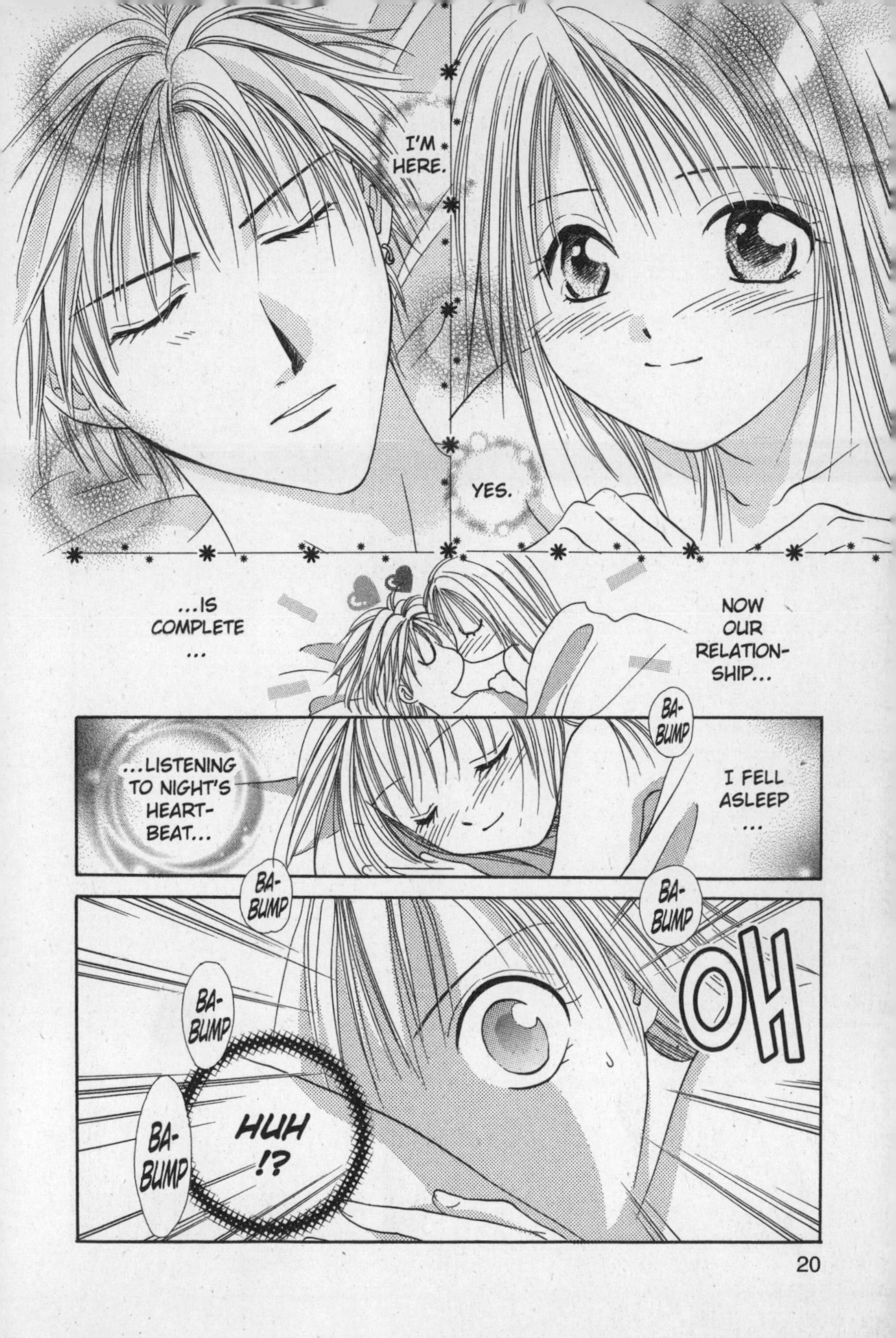
I'M HERE.
YES.
NOW OUR RELATION-SHIP...
...IS COMPLETE...
BA-BUMP
I FELL ASLEEP...
...LISTENING TO NIGHT'S HEART-BEAT...
BA-BUMP
BA-BUMP
OH
BA-BUMP
BA-BUMP
HUH!?

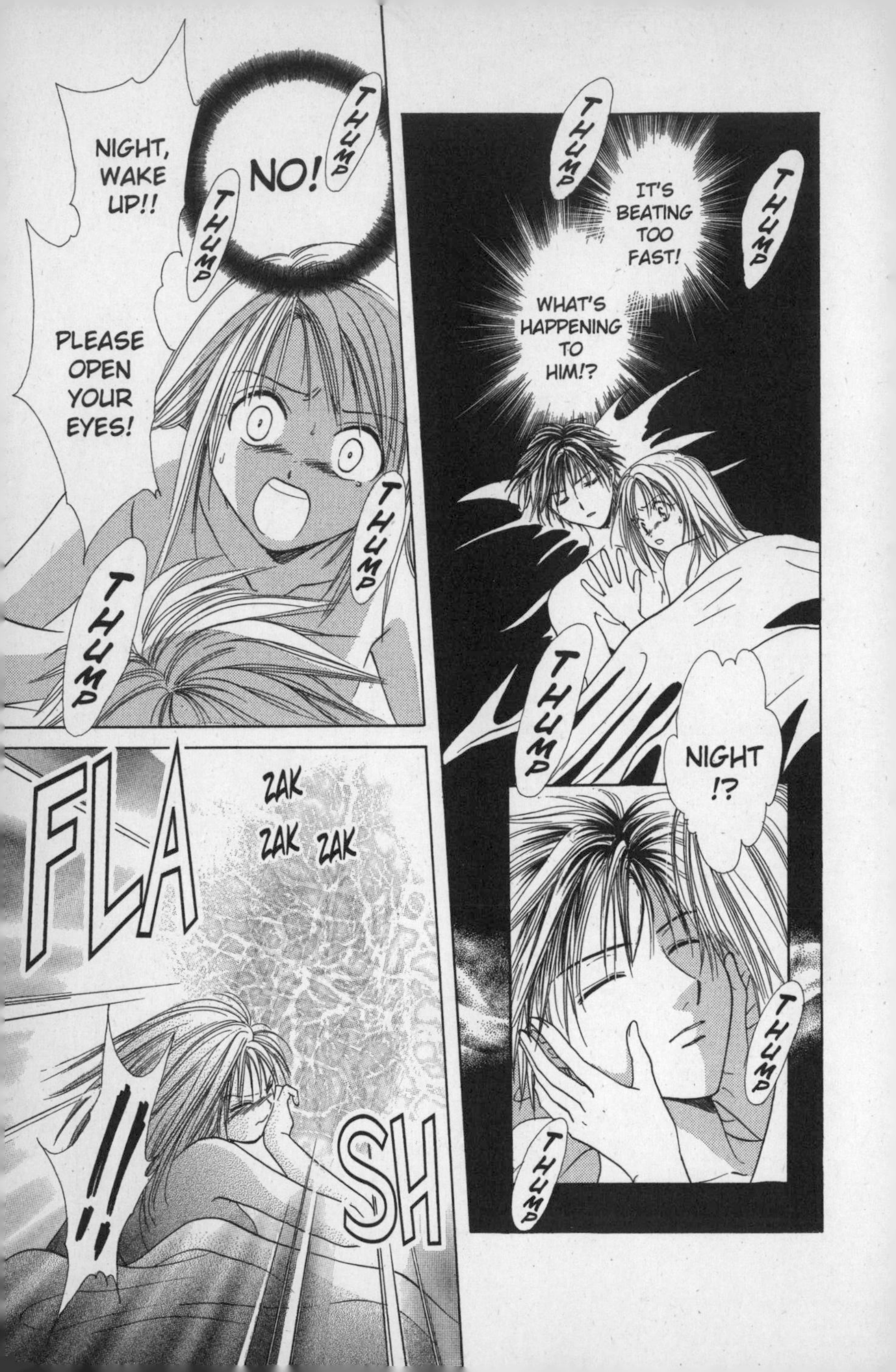
THUMP
THUMP
IT'S BEATING TOO FAST!
WHAT'S HAPPENING TO HIM!?
THUMP
NIGHT !?
THUMP
THUMP
THUMP
NO!
THUMP
NIGHT, WAKE UP!!
PLEASE OPEN YOUR EYES!
THUMP
THUMP
ZAK
ZAK ZAK
FLASH
!!

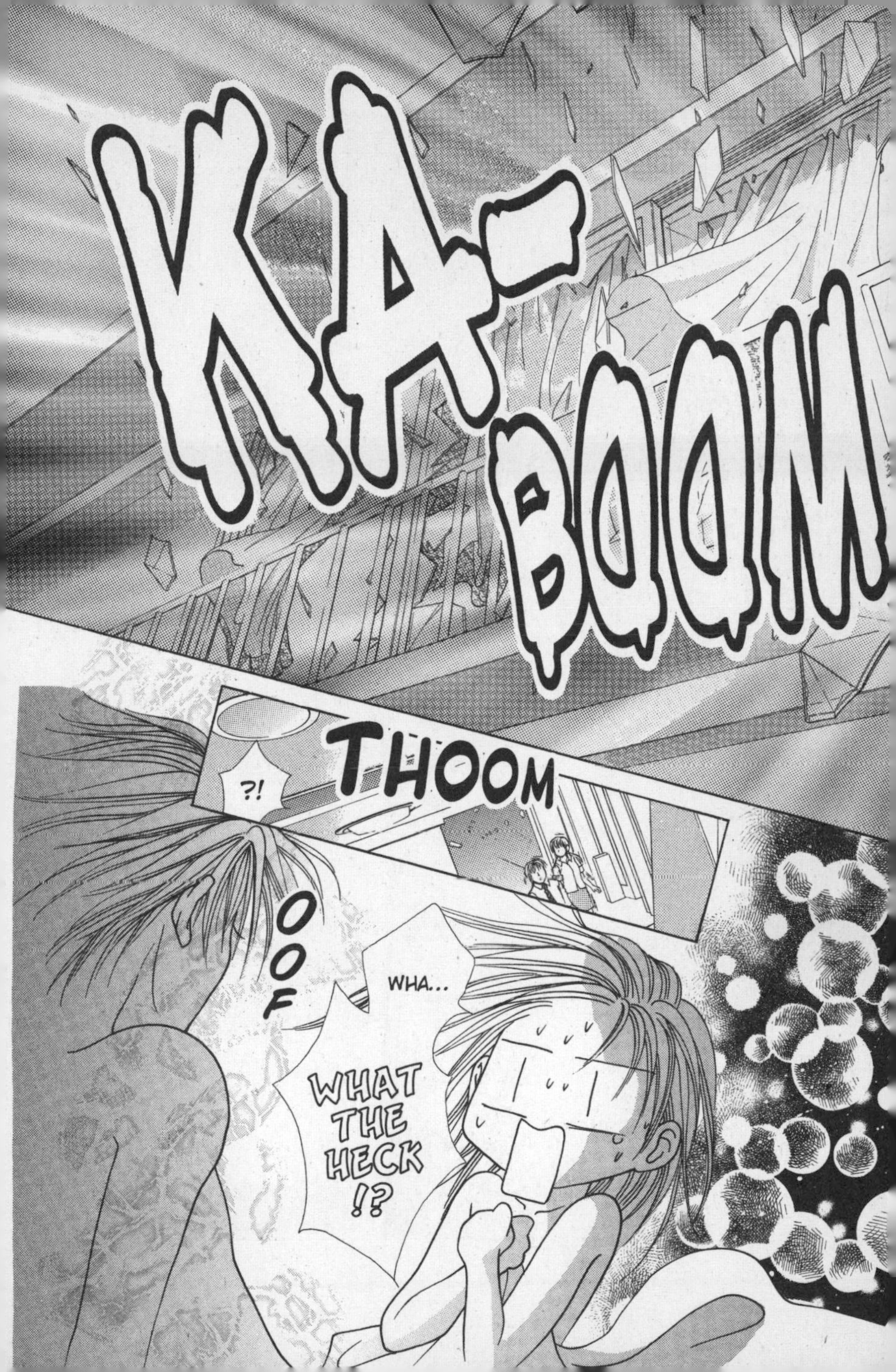
KA-BOOM
THOOM
?!
WHA...
WHAT THE HECK !?
OOOF

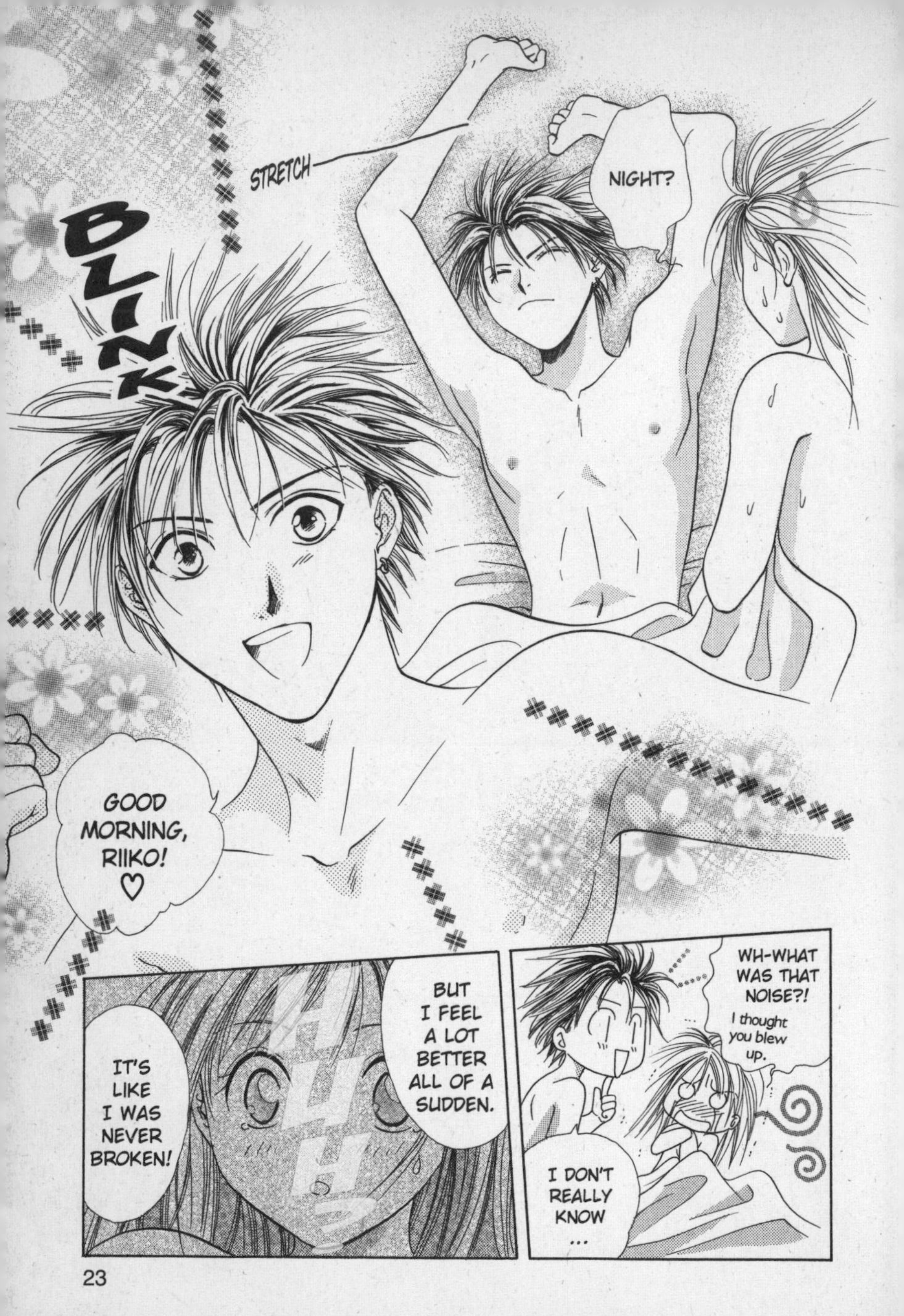
NIGHT?
STRETCH
BLINK
GOOD MORNING, RIIKO! ♡
WH-WHAT WAS THAT NOISE?!
I thought you blew up.
I DON'T REALLY KNOW ...
BUT I FEEL A LOT BETTER ALL OF A SUDDEN.
IT'S LIKE I WAS NEVER BROKEN!

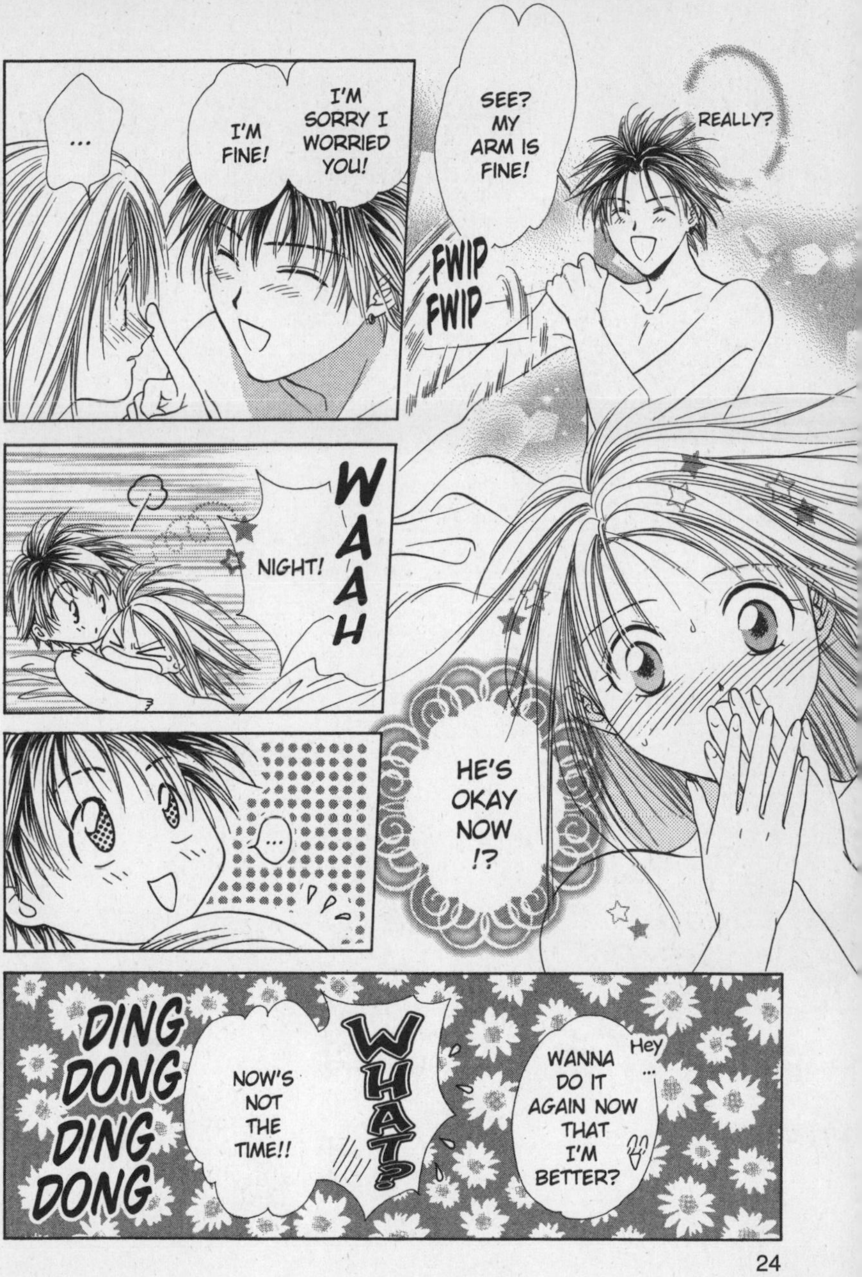
REALLY?
SEE? MY ARM IS FINE!
FWIP FWIP
HE'S OKAY NOW !?
I'M SORRY I WORRIED YOU!
I'M FINE!
...
WAAAH
NIGHT!
...
Hey ...
WANNA DO IT AGAIN NOW THAT I'M BETTER?
WHAT?
NOW'S NOT THE TIME!!
DING DONG DING DONG

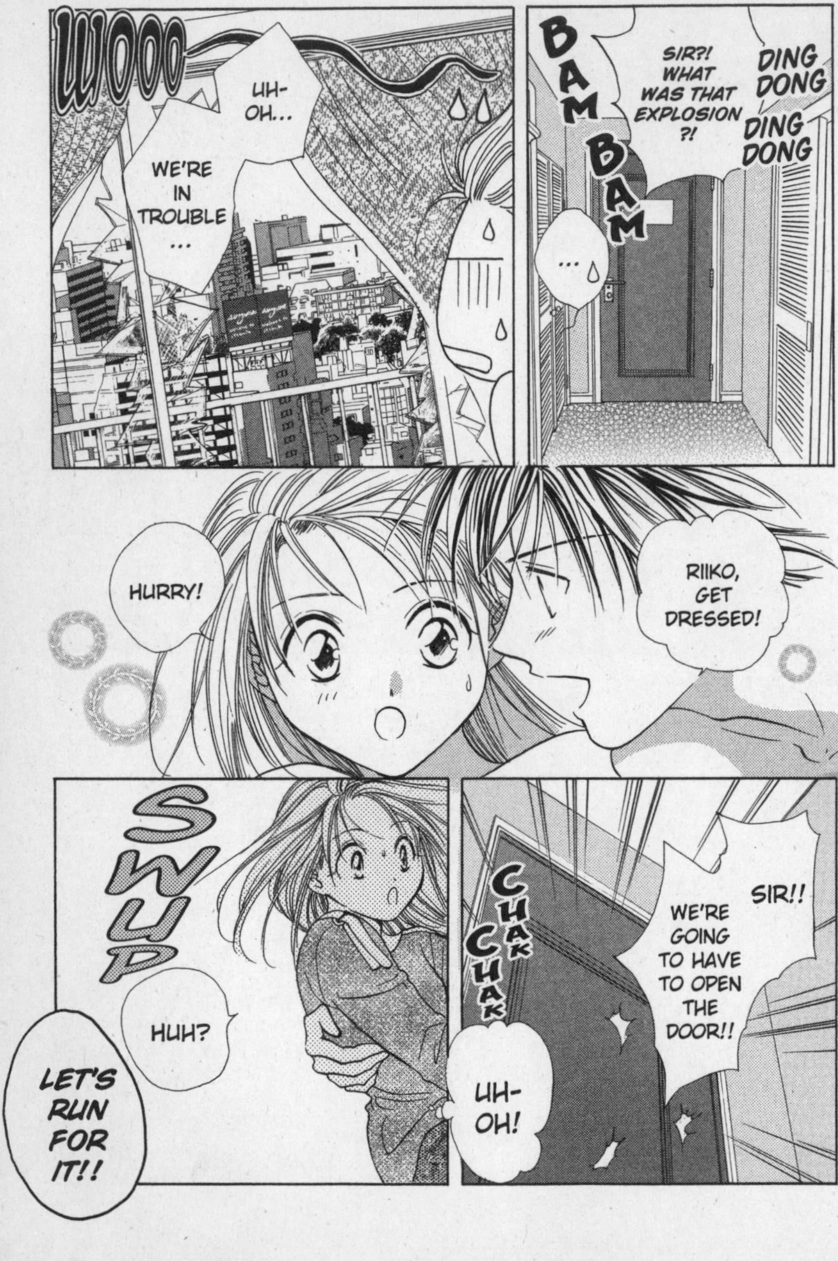
DING DONG
DING DONG
SIR?! WHAT WAS THAT EXPLOSION ?!
BAM BAM
...
WOOO
UH-OH...
WE'RE IN TROUBLE ...
RIIKO, GET DRESSED!
HURRY!
SIR!!
WE'RE GOING TO HAVE TO OPEN THE DOOR!!
CHAK CHAK
UH-OH!
SWUP
HUH?
LET'S RUN FOR IT!!

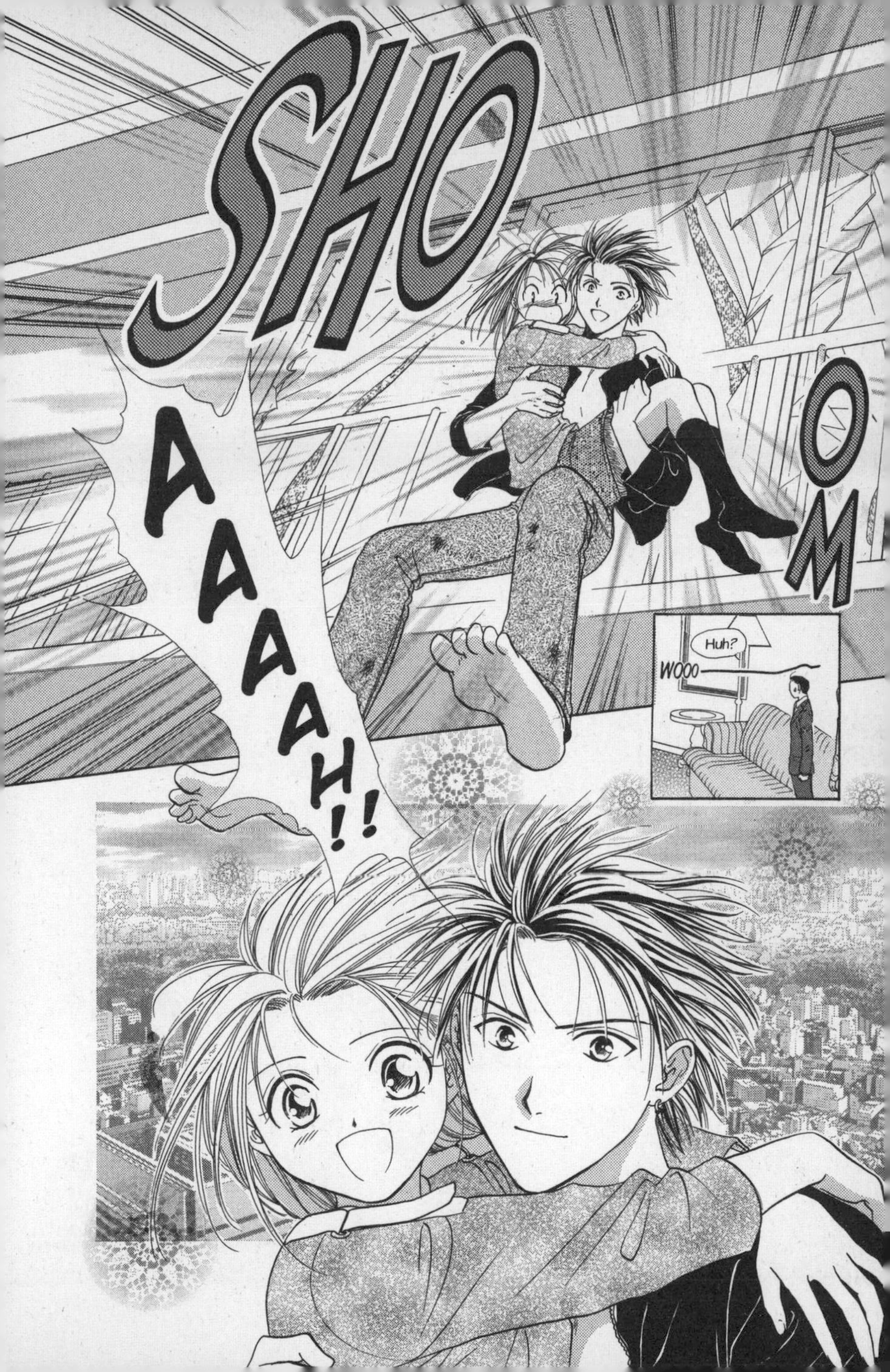
SHO
OM
Huh?
WOOO
AAAAAH!!

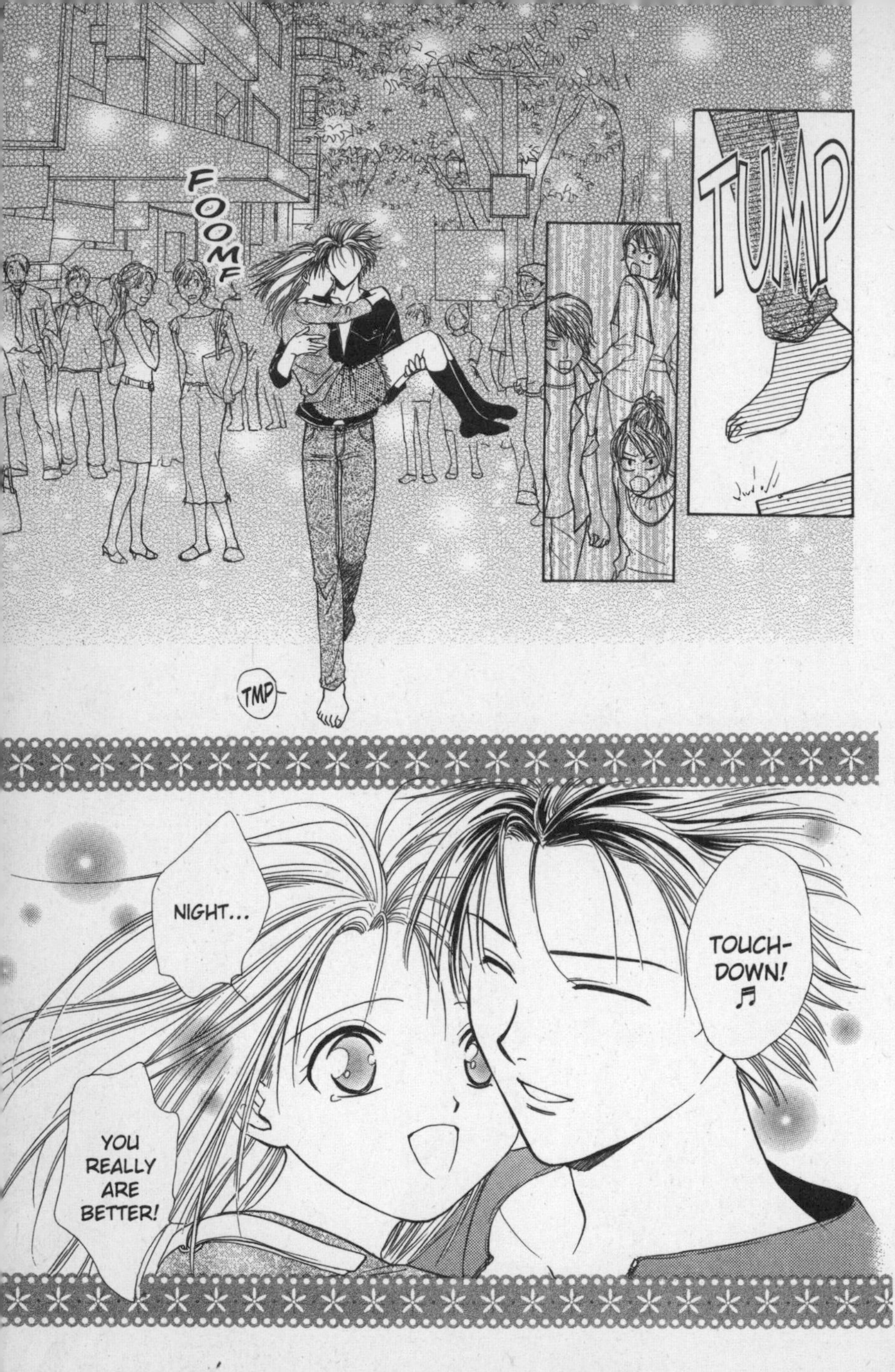
TUMP
FOOMF
TMP
TOUCH-DOWN! ♬
NIGHT...
YOU REALLY ARE BETTER!

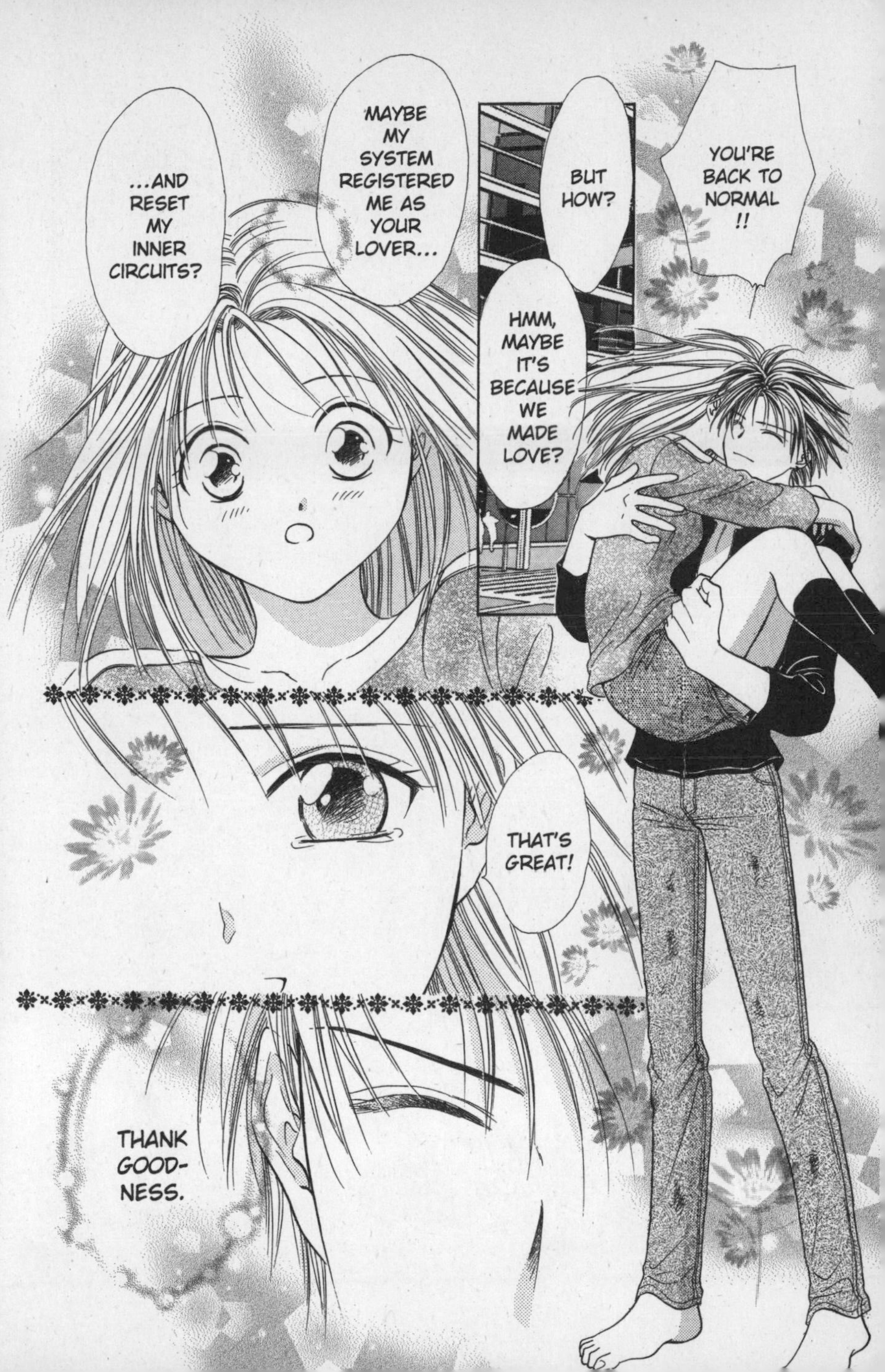
YOU'RE BACK TO NORMAL !!
BUT HOW?
HMM, MAYBE IT'S BECAUSE WE MADE LOVE?
MAYBE MY SYSTEM REGISTERED ME AS YOUR LOVER...
...AND RESET MY INNER CIRCUITS?
THAT'S GREAT!
THANK GOOD-NESS.

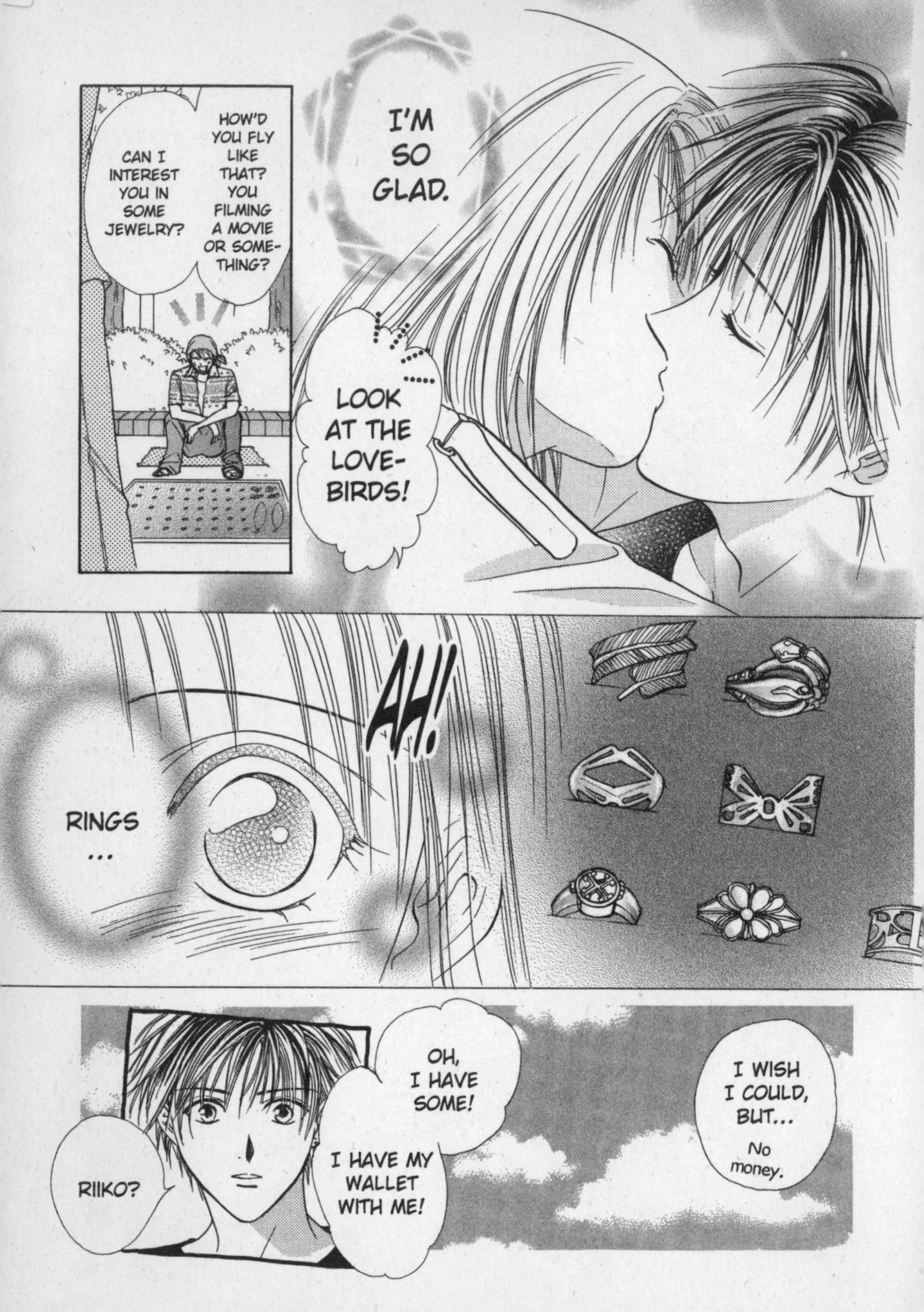
I'M SO GLAD.
......LOOK AT THE LOVE-BIRDS!
HOW'D YOU FLY LIKE THAT? YOU FILMING A MOVIE OR SOME-THING?
CAN I INTEREST YOU IN SOME JEWELRY?
AH!
RINGS ...
I WISH I COULD, BUT...
No money.
OH, I HAVE SOME!
I HAVE MY WALLET WITH ME!
RIIKO?

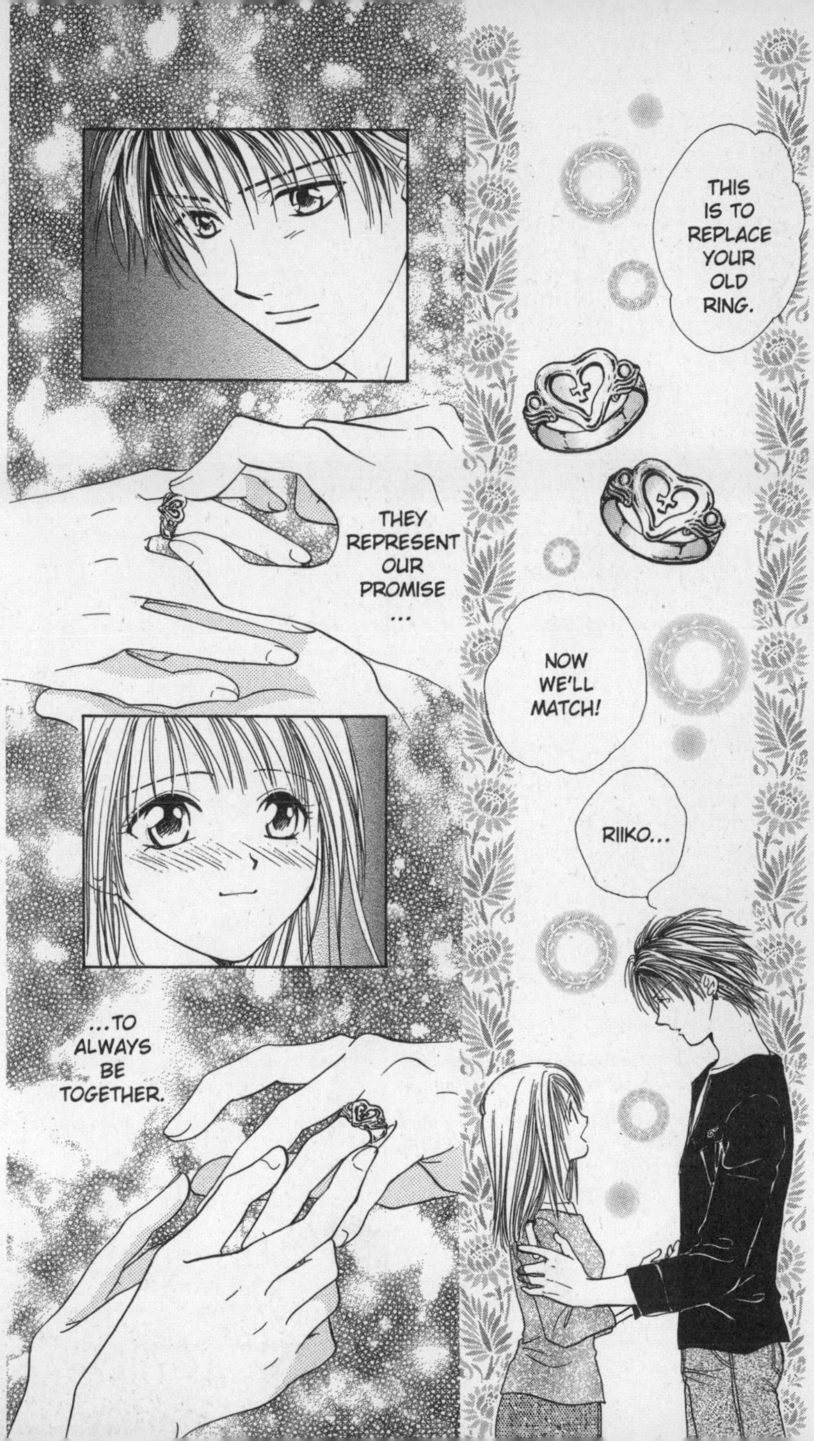
THIS IS TO REPLACE YOUR OLD RING.
NOW WE'LL MATCH!
RIIKO...
THEY REPRESENT OUR PROMISE ...
...TO ALWAYS BE TOGETHER.

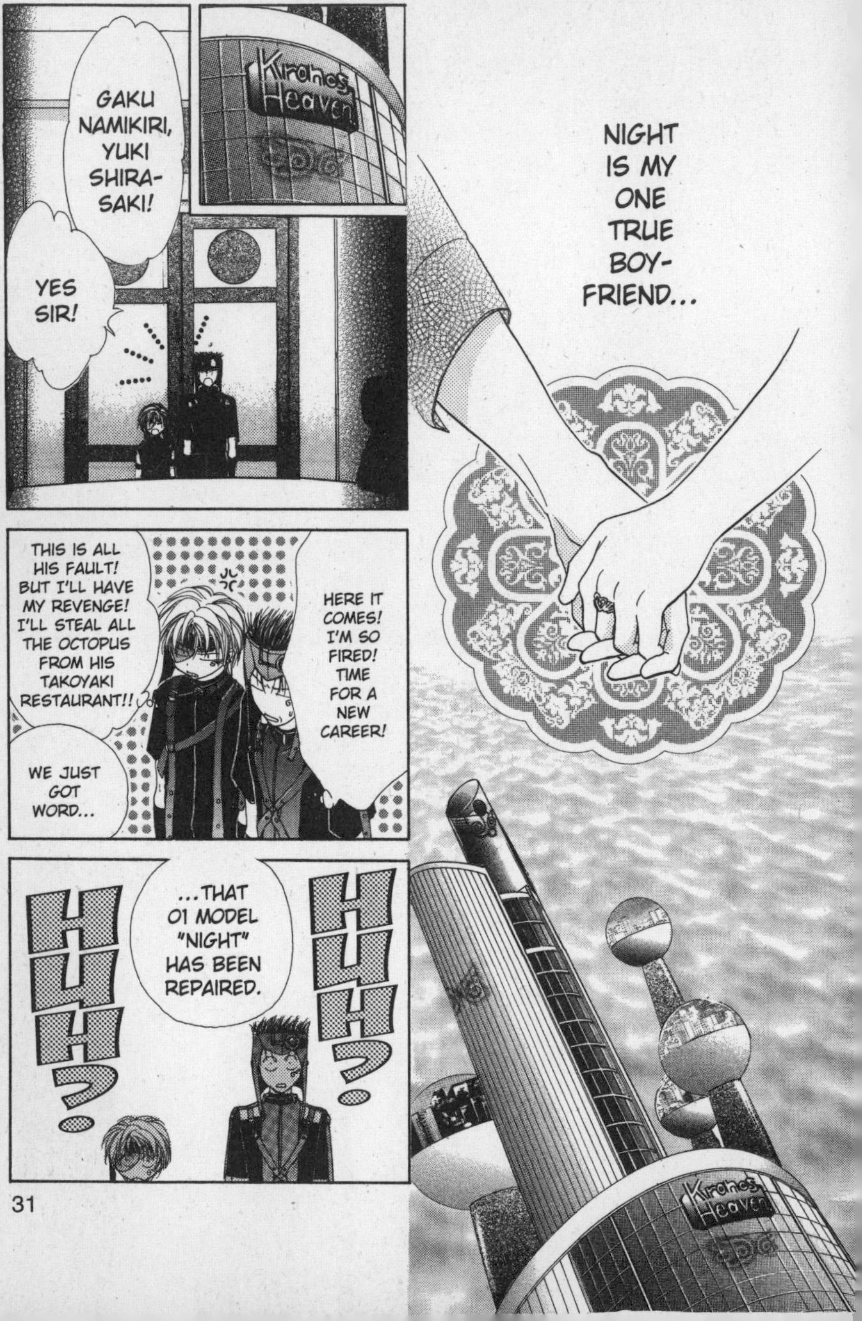
NIGHT IS MY ONE TRUE BOY-FRIEND...
Kiranos Heaven
Kiranos Heaven
GAKU NAMIKIRI, YUKI SHIRA-SAKI!
YES SIR!
HERE IT COMES! I'M SO FIRED! TIME FOR A NEW CAREER!
THIS IS ALL HIS FAULT! BUT I'LL HAVE MY REVENGE! I'LL STEAL ALL THE OCTOPUS FROM HIS TAKOYAKI RESTAURANT!!
WE JUST GOT WORD...
...THAT 01 MODEL "NIGHT" HAS BEEN REPAIRED.
HUH?!
HUH?!

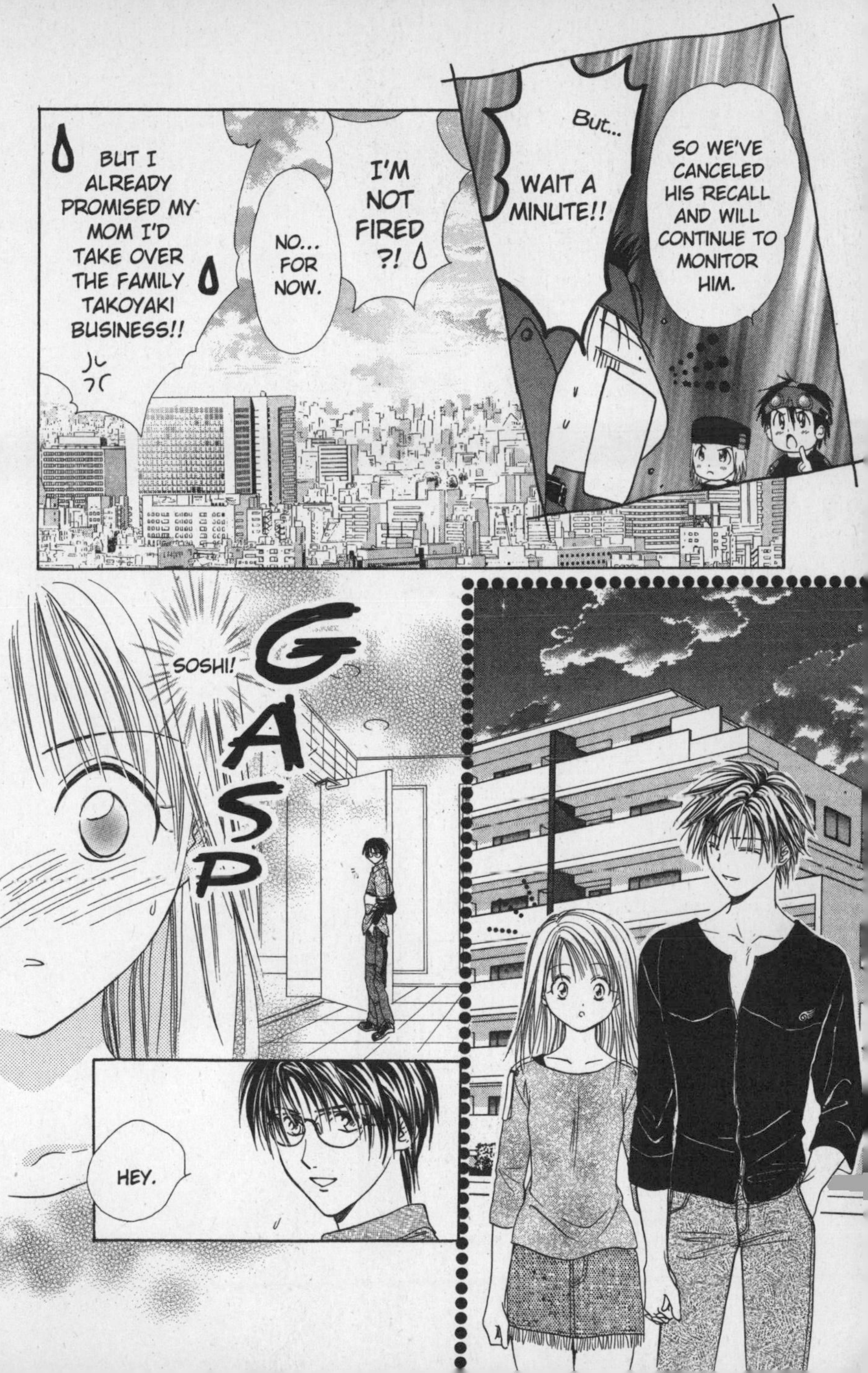
SO WE'VE CANCELED HIS RECALL AND WILL CONTINUE TO MONITOR HIM.
But...
WAIT A MINUTE!!
I'M NOT FIRED ?!
NO... FOR NOW.
BUT I ALREADY PROMISED MY MOM I'D TAKE OVER THE FAMILY TAKOYAKI BUSINESS!!
.....
SOSHI!
GASP
HEY.

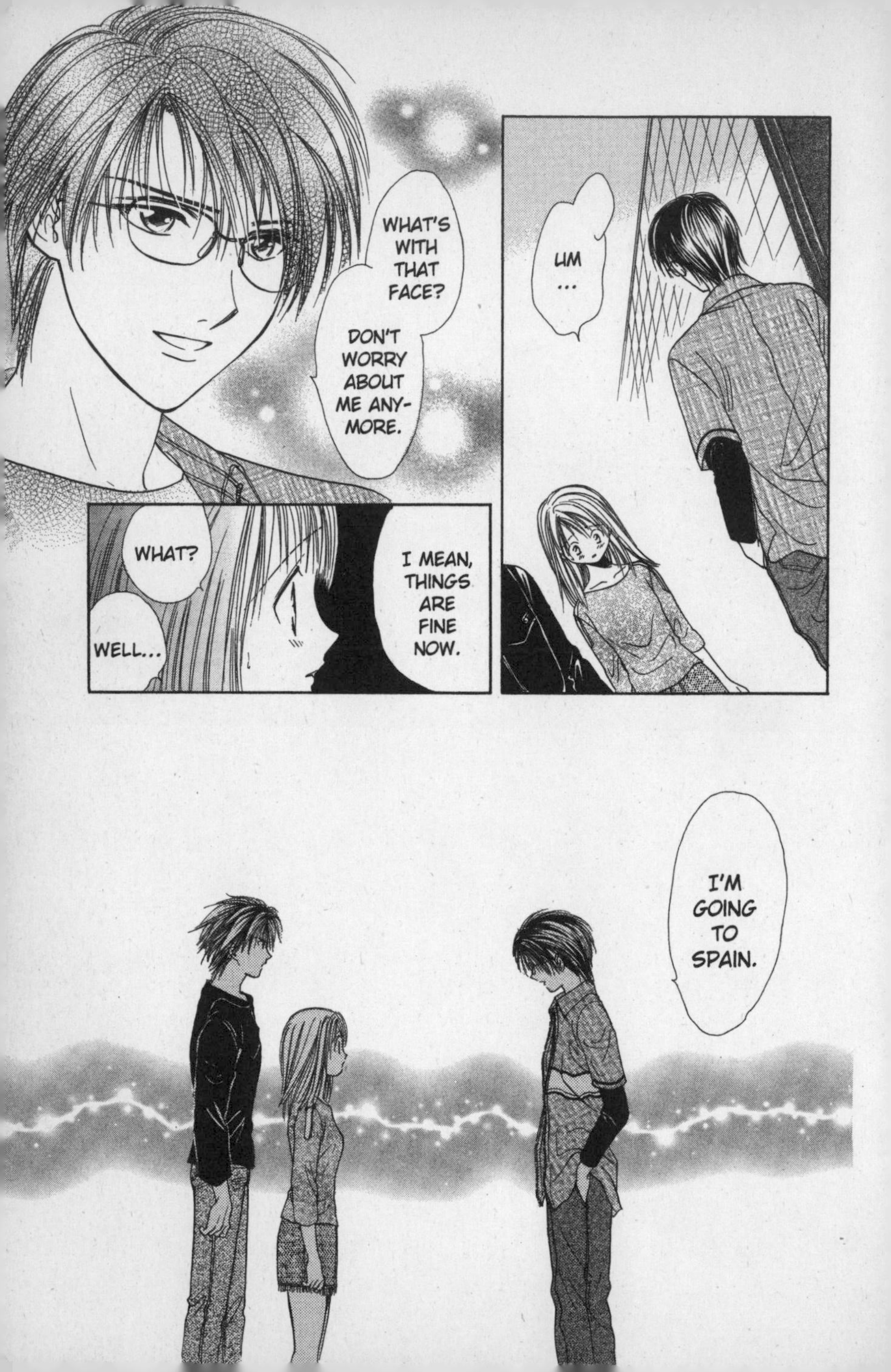
UM ...
WHAT'S WITH THAT FACE?
DON'T WORRY ABOUT ME ANY-MORE.
I MEAN, THINGS ARE FINE NOW.
WHAT?
WELL...
I'M GOING TO SPAIN.

Absolute
Boyfriend

Act 31: Someday

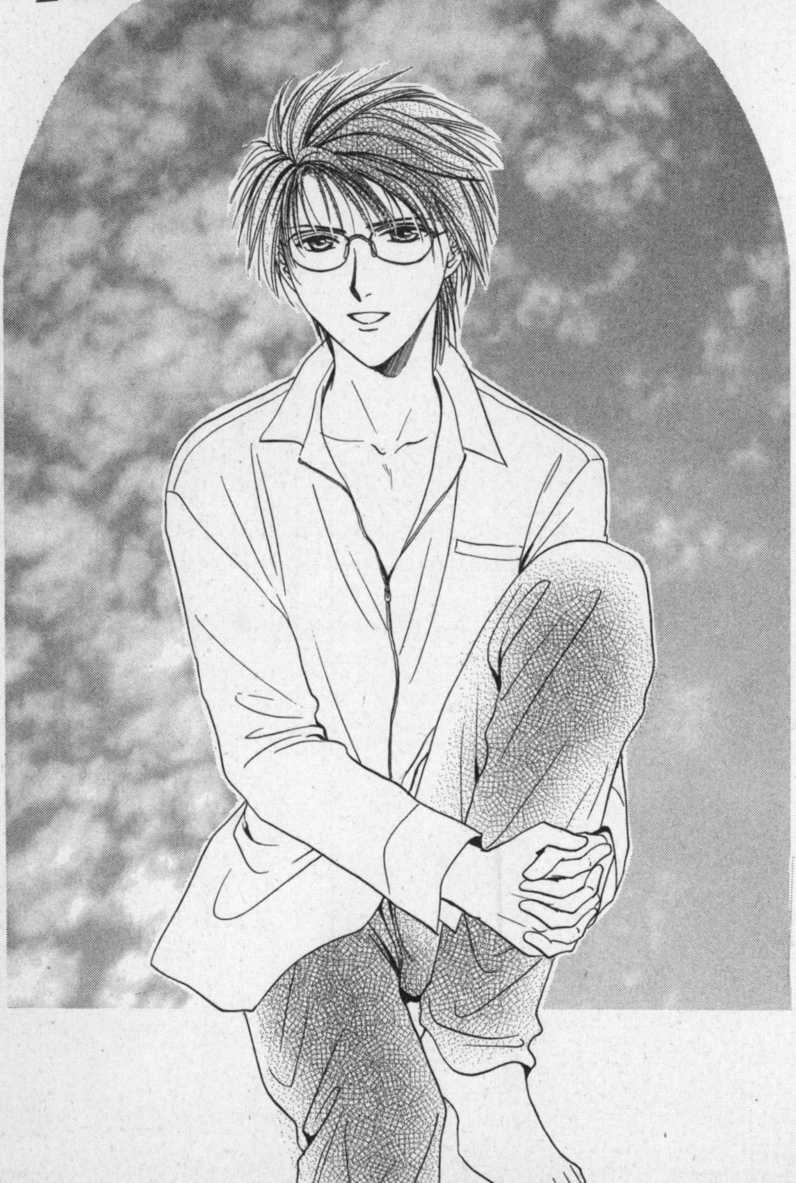

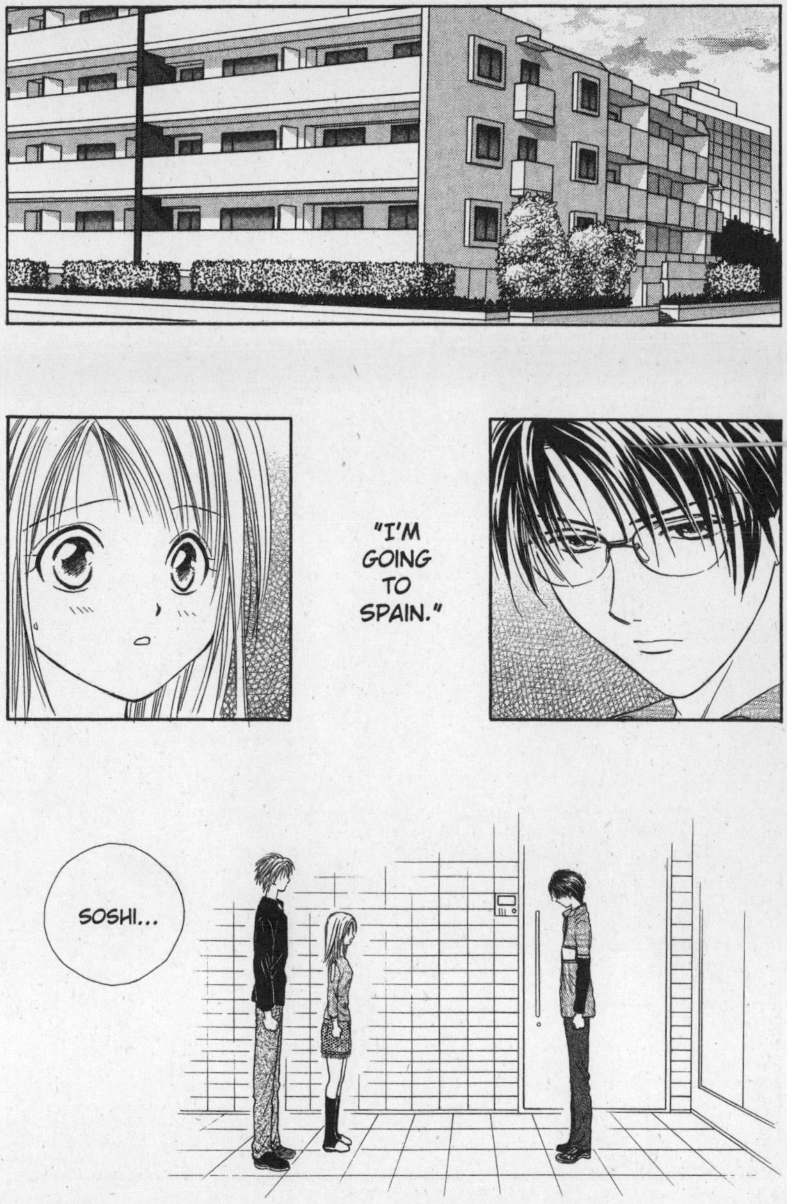
"I'M GOING TO SPAIN."
SOSHI...

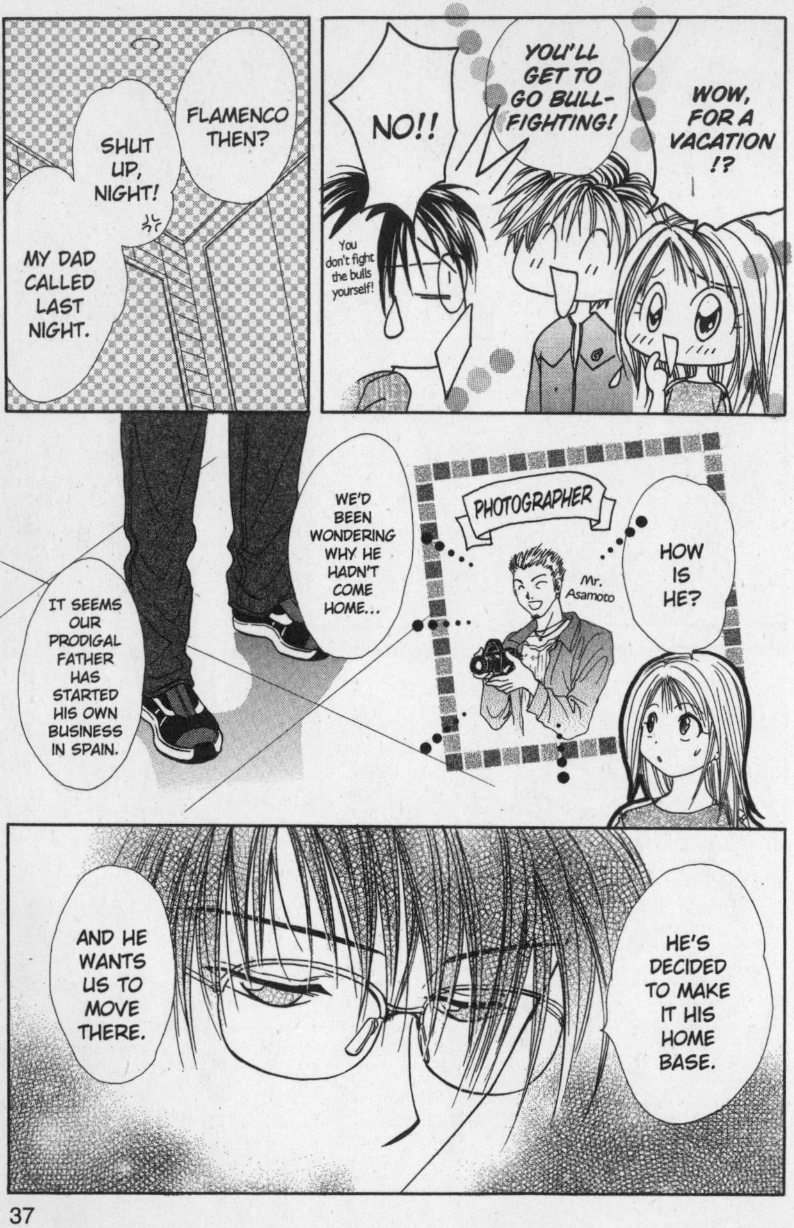
WOW, FOR A VACATION !?
YOU'LL GET TO GO BULL-FIGHTING!
NO!!
You don't fight the bulls yourself!
FLAMENCO THEN?
SHUT UP, NIGHT!
MY DAD CALLED LAST NIGHT.
HOW IS HE?
PHOTOGRAPHER
Mr. Asamoto
WE'D BEEN WONDERING WHY HE HADN'T COME HOME...
IT SEEMS OUR PRODIGAL FATHER HAS STARTED HIS OWN BUSINESS IN SPAIN.
HE'S DECIDED TO MAKE IT HIS HOME BASE.
AND HE WANTS US TO MOVE THERE.

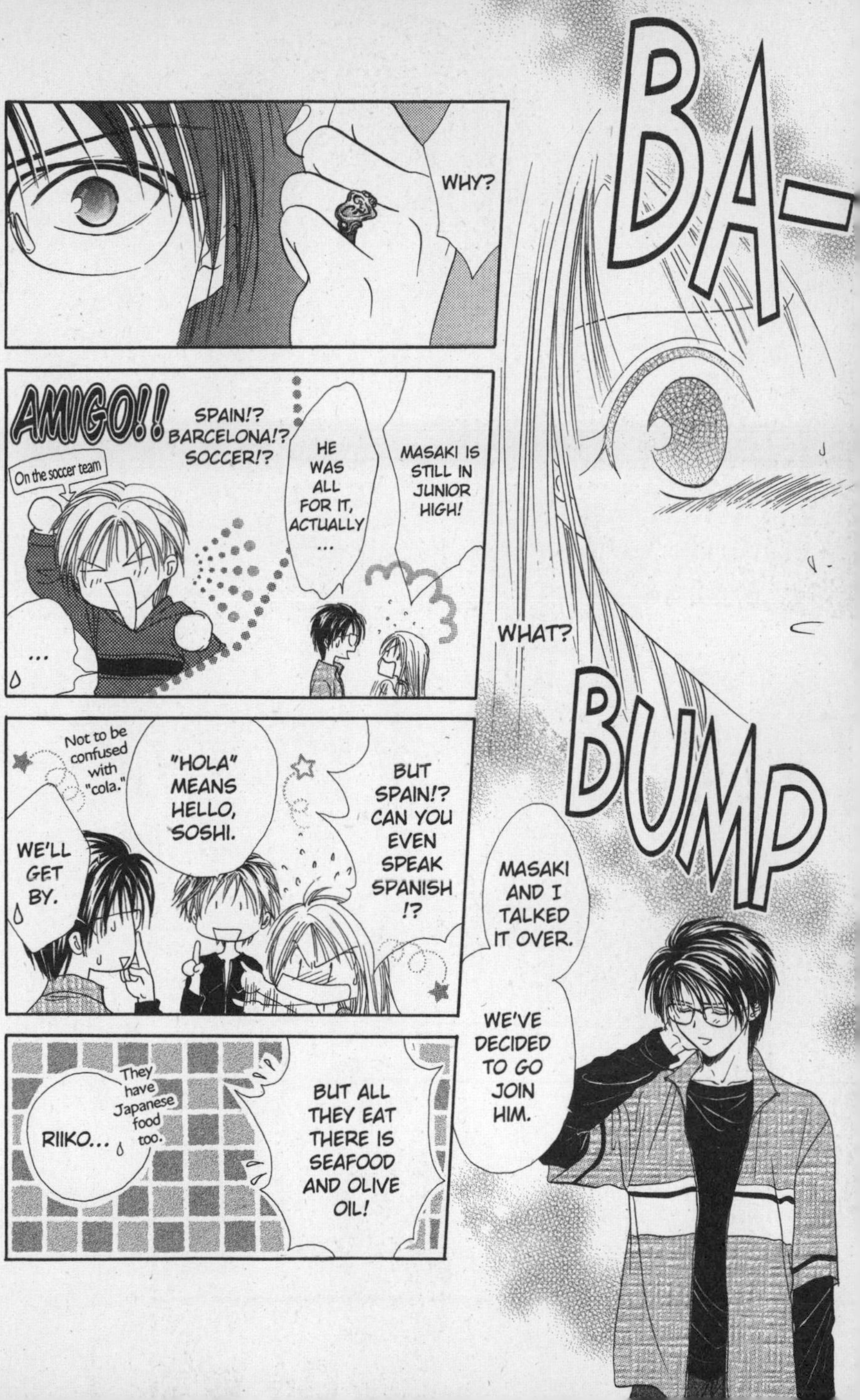
BA-
WHAT?
BUMP
MASAKI AND I TALKED IT OVER.
WE'VE DECIDED TO GO JOIN HIM.
WHY?
MASAKI IS STILL IN JUNIOR HIGH!
HE WAS ALL FOR IT, ACTUALLY...
SPAIN!? BARCELONA!? SOCCER!?
AMIGO!!
On the soccer team
...
BUT SPAIN!? CAN YOU EVEN SPEAK SPANISH!?
"HOLA" MEANS HELLO, SOSHI.
Not to be confused with "cola."
WE'LL GET BY.
BUT ALL THEY EAT THERE IS SEAFOOD AND OLIVE OIL!
They have Japanese food too.
RIIKO...

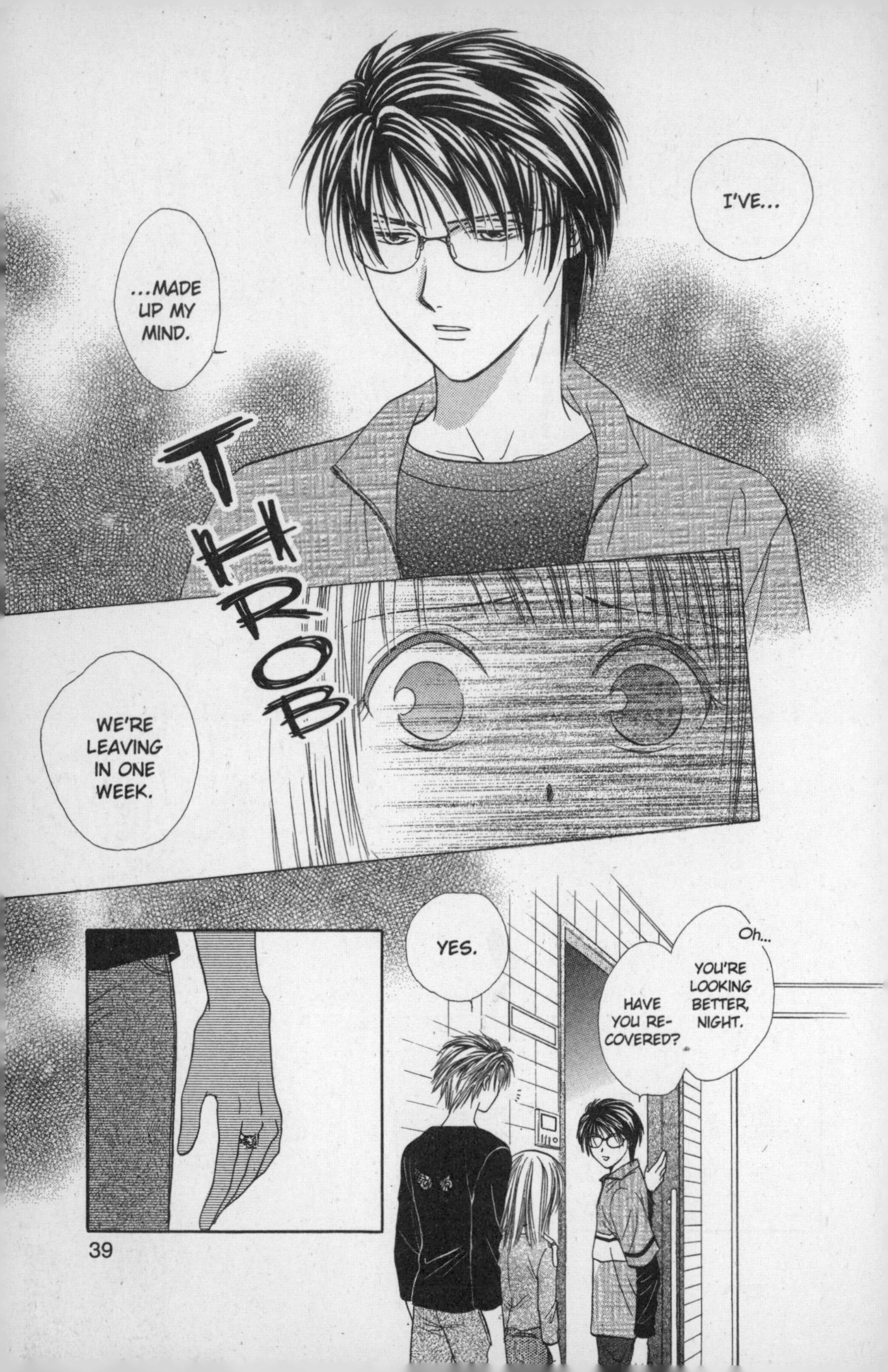
I'VE...
...MADE UP MY MIND.
THROB
WE'RE LEAVING IN ONE WEEK.
Oh...
YOU'RE LOOKING BETTER, NIGHT.
HAVE YOU RE-COVERED?
YES.

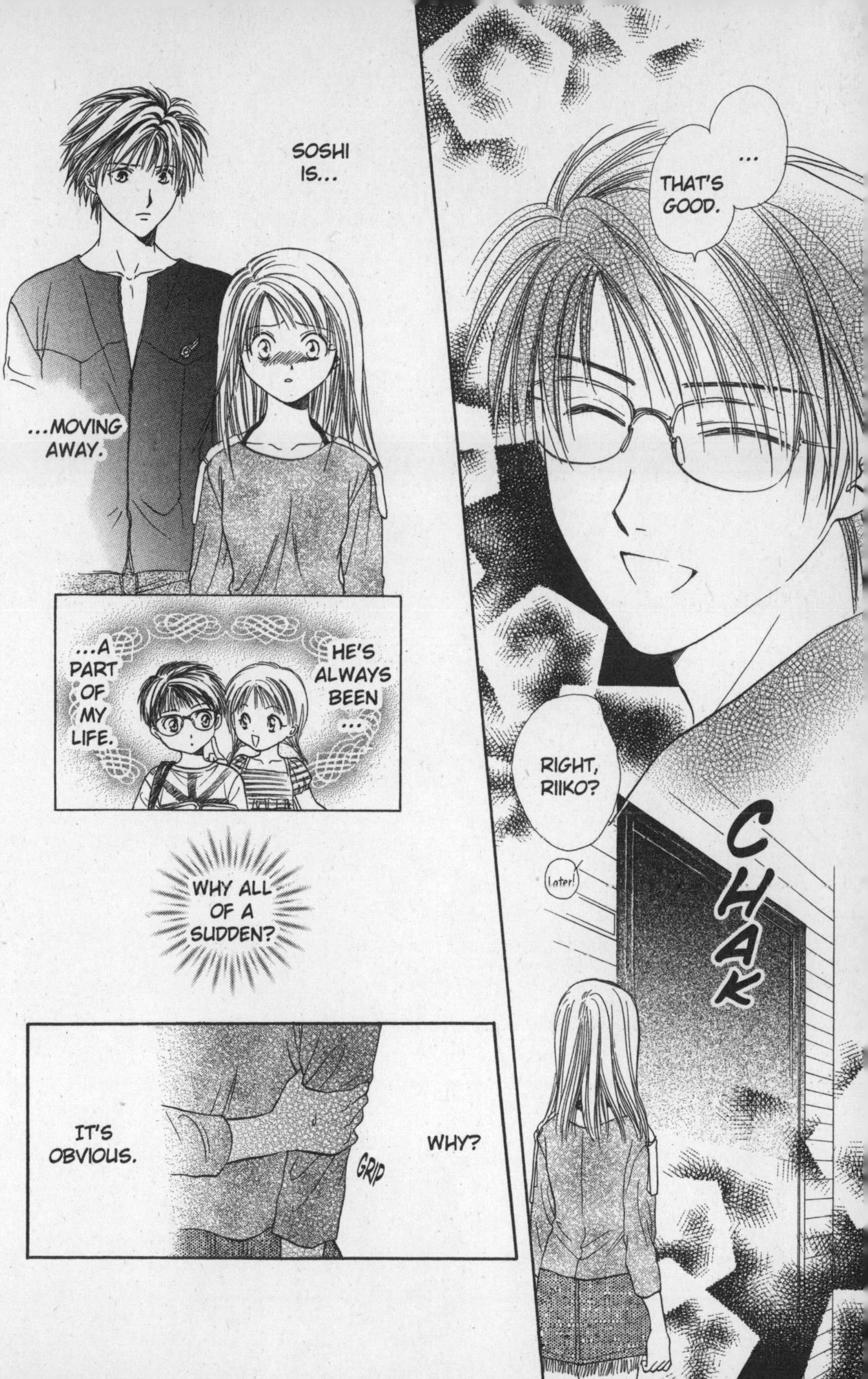
... THAT'S GOOD.
RIGHT, RIIKO?
Later!
CHAK
SOSHI IS...
...MOVING AWAY.
HE'S ALWAYS BEEN ...
...A PART OF MY LIFE.
WHY ALL OF A SUDDEN?
WHY?
GRIP
IT'S OBVIOUS.

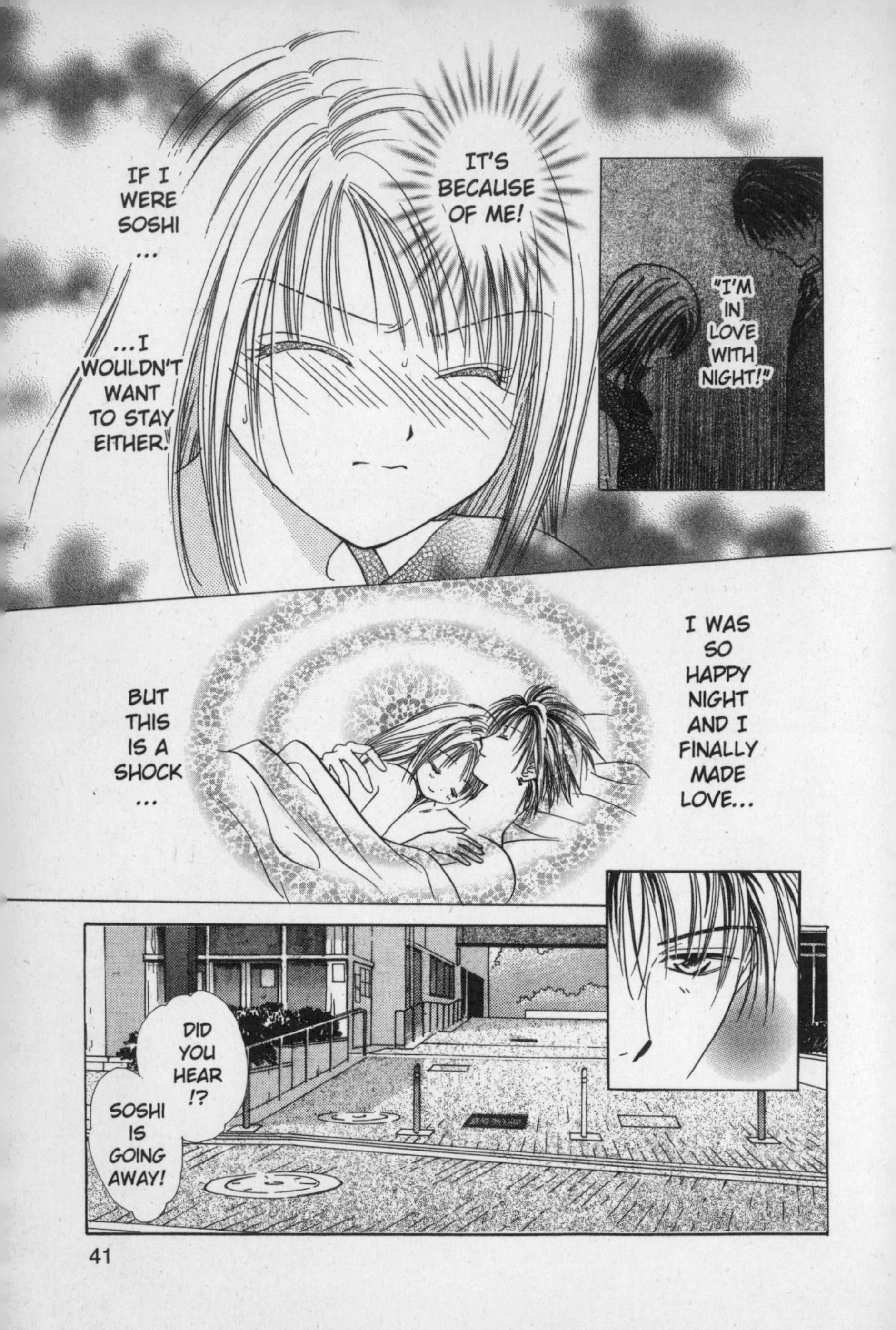
"I'M IN LOVE WITH NIGHT!"
IT'S BECAUSE OF ME!
IF I WERE SOSHI ...
...I WOULDN'T WANT TO STAY EITHER!
I WAS SO HAPPY NIGHT AND I FINALLY MADE LOVE...
BUT THIS IS A SHOCK ...
DID YOU HEAR !?
SOSHI IS GOING AWAY!

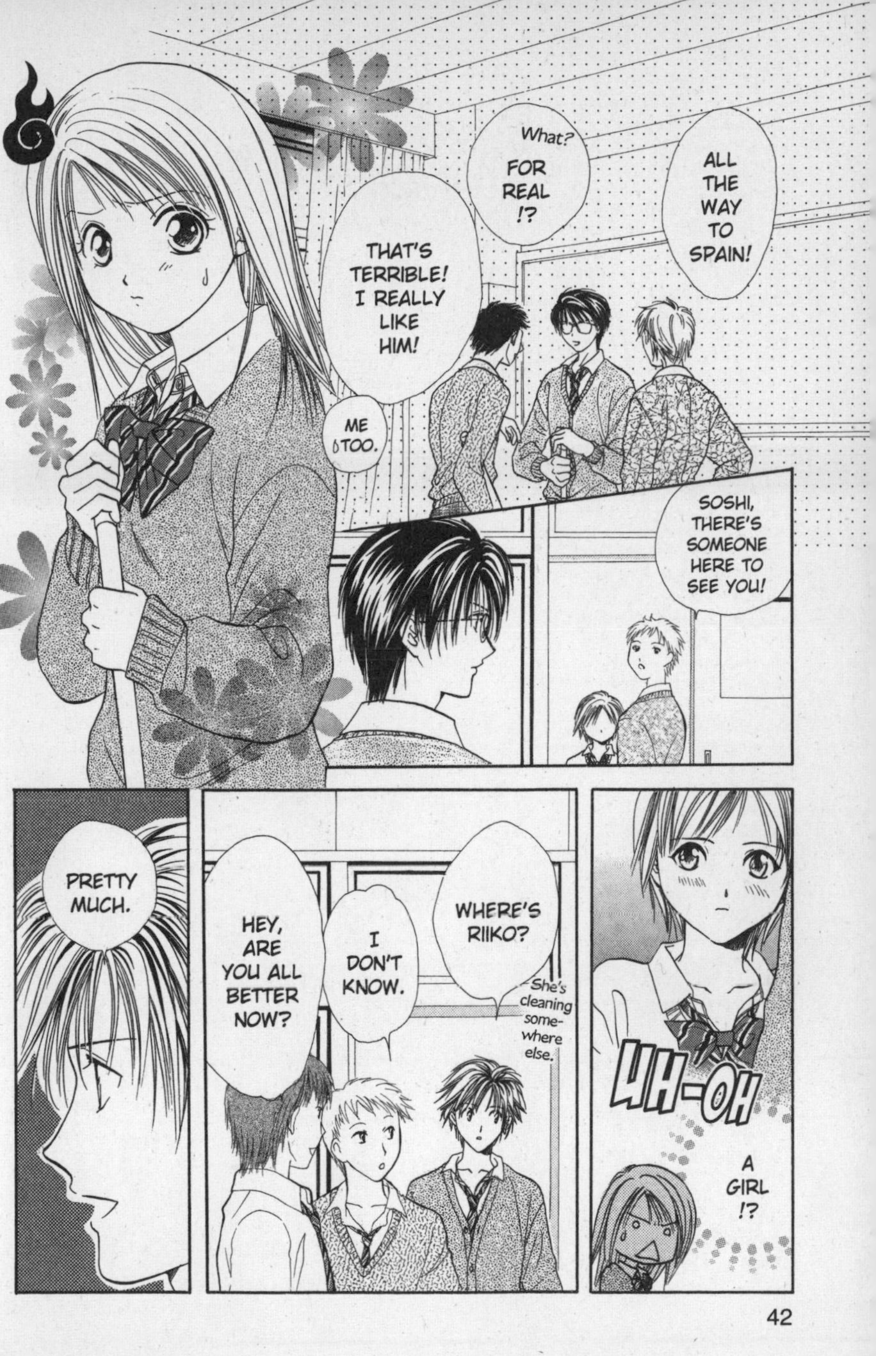
ALL THE WAY TO SPAIN!
What? FOR REAL!?
THAT'S TERRIBLE! I REALLY LIKE HIM!
ME TOO.
SOSHI, THERE'S SOMEONE HERE TO SEE YOU!
UH-OH
A GIRL!?
WHERE'S RIIKO?
—She's cleaning some-where else.
I DON'T KNOW.
HEY, ARE YOU ALL BETTER NOW?
PRETTY MUCH.

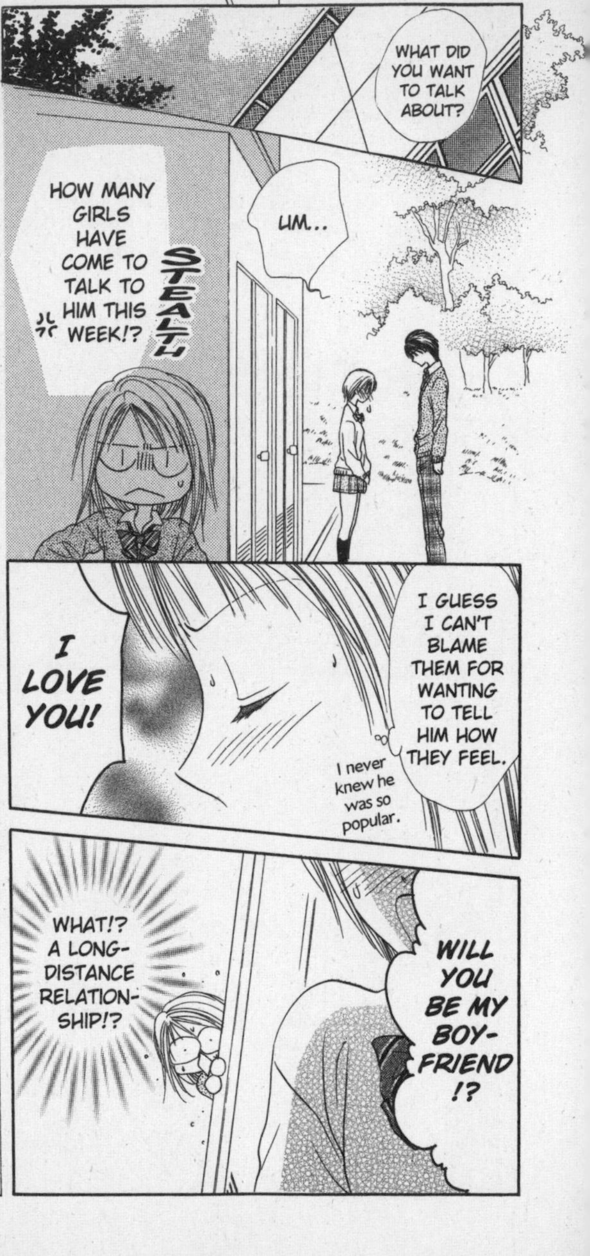
WHAT DID YOU WANT TO TALK ABOUT?
UM...
HOW MANY GIRLS HAVE COME TO TALK TO HIM THIS WEEK!?
STEALTH
I GUESS I CAN'T BLAME THEM FOR WANTING TO TELL HIM HOW THEY FEEL.
I never knew he was so popular.
I LOVE YOU!
WILL YOU BE MY BOY-FRIEND!?
WHAT!? A LONG-DISTANCE RELATION-SHIP!?

Shojo manga are all about romance today. But when I was a kid, I liked manga that wasn't just about cute girls and handsome heroes and romance. I preferred manga that had other themes as well. And I cared more about the stories than the art. I liked stories that really made you think. Those are the ones I still remember even now. Romance just added a little spice to the stories, and that's what I've tried to do with my own titles. (That was my intention, anyway.)

But to be honest, I haven't read much shojo manga at all. I think the last time was when I was in 7th grade. I browsed through the big hits that everyone was talking about when they got passed around at school, but I haven't really kept up with it for the past ten years. I only read a few seinen (for adult men) and shonen manga these days. This isn't good. I have to read more manga!

I'm more interested in anime. I never had much of an allowance, so I grew up watching anime on TV. I think I learned more from anime than manga. But I only watch the movies now. Maybe I just don't get into the kid stuff. I really should watch more. (This is turning into a soul-searching session.)

Oops, I got too caught up in the "Kinpachi-sensei" show! It makes me cry! These socially-aware stories are the best. Friendship is a crucial element! And so is a tiny bit of love. (smile) There are plenty of manga artists who are better at romance than I. A little romance is all I can handle.

Sensei! I'm gonna cry! (I've got to stop writing while I watch this show!)

Hot guys are the meat and potatoes of shojo manga! But the guys I think are cool aren't the popular mainstream ones.

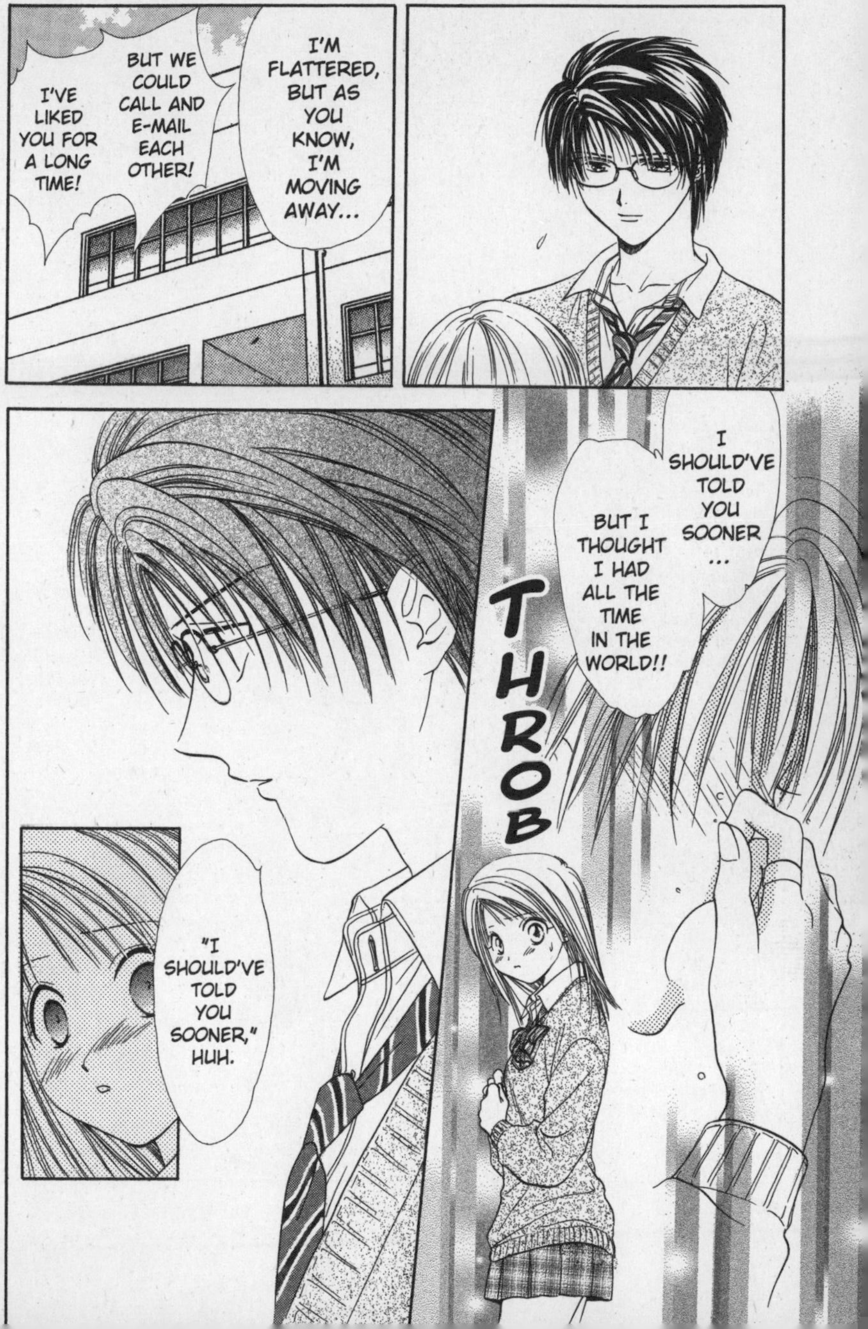
I'M FLATTERED, BUT AS YOU KNOW, I'M MOVING AWAY...
BUT WE COULD CALL AND E-MAIL EACH OTHER!
I'VE LIKED YOU FOR A LONG TIME!
I SHOULD'VE TOLD YOU SOONER...
BUT I THOUGHT I HAD ALL THE TIME IN THE WORLD!!
THROB
"I SHOULD'VE TOLD YOU SOONER," HUH.

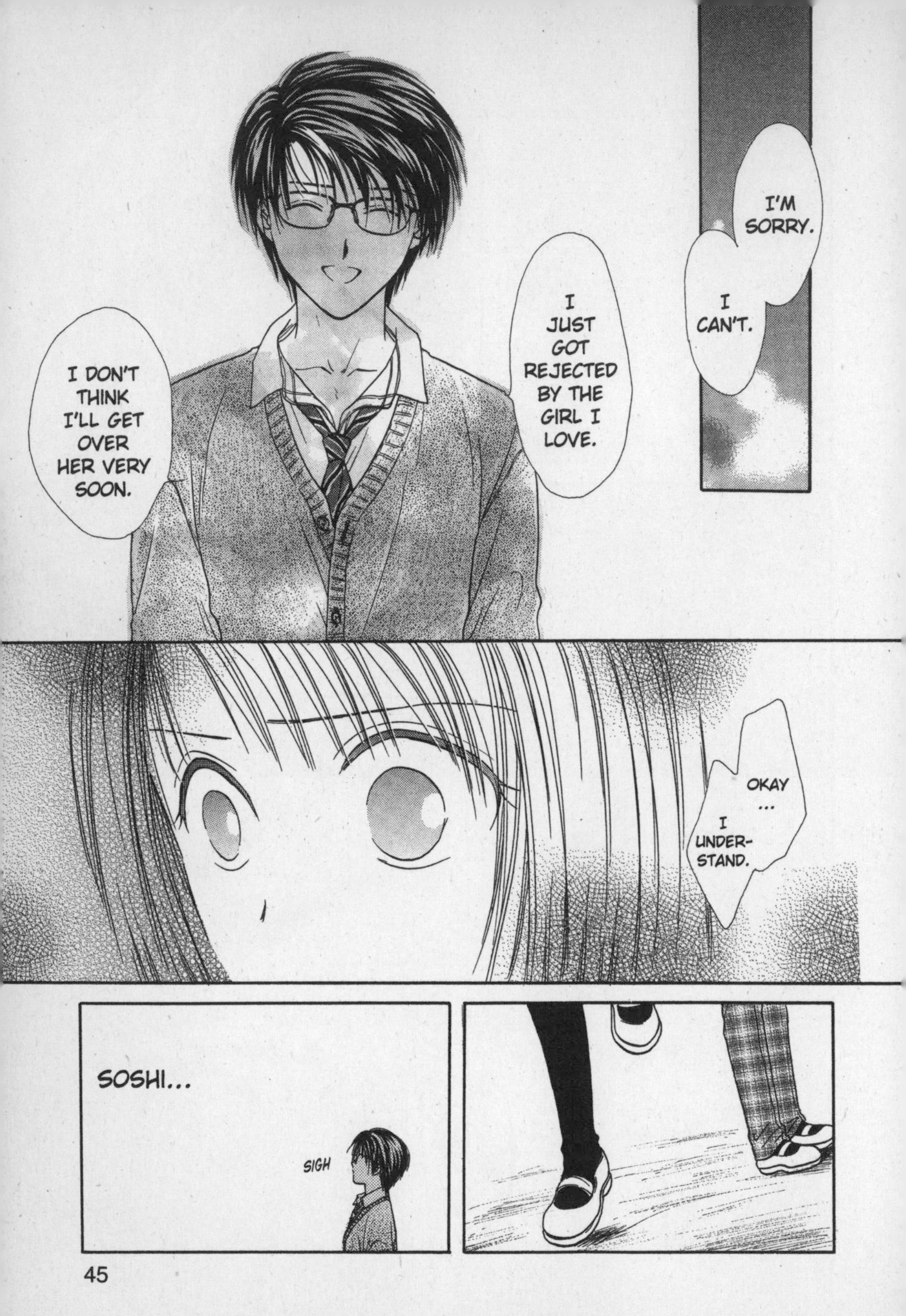
I'M SORRY.
I CAN'T.
I JUST GOT REJECTED BY THE GIRL I LOVE.
I DON'T THINK I'LL GET OVER HER VERY SOON.
OKAY... I UNDERSTAND.
SOSHI...
SIGH

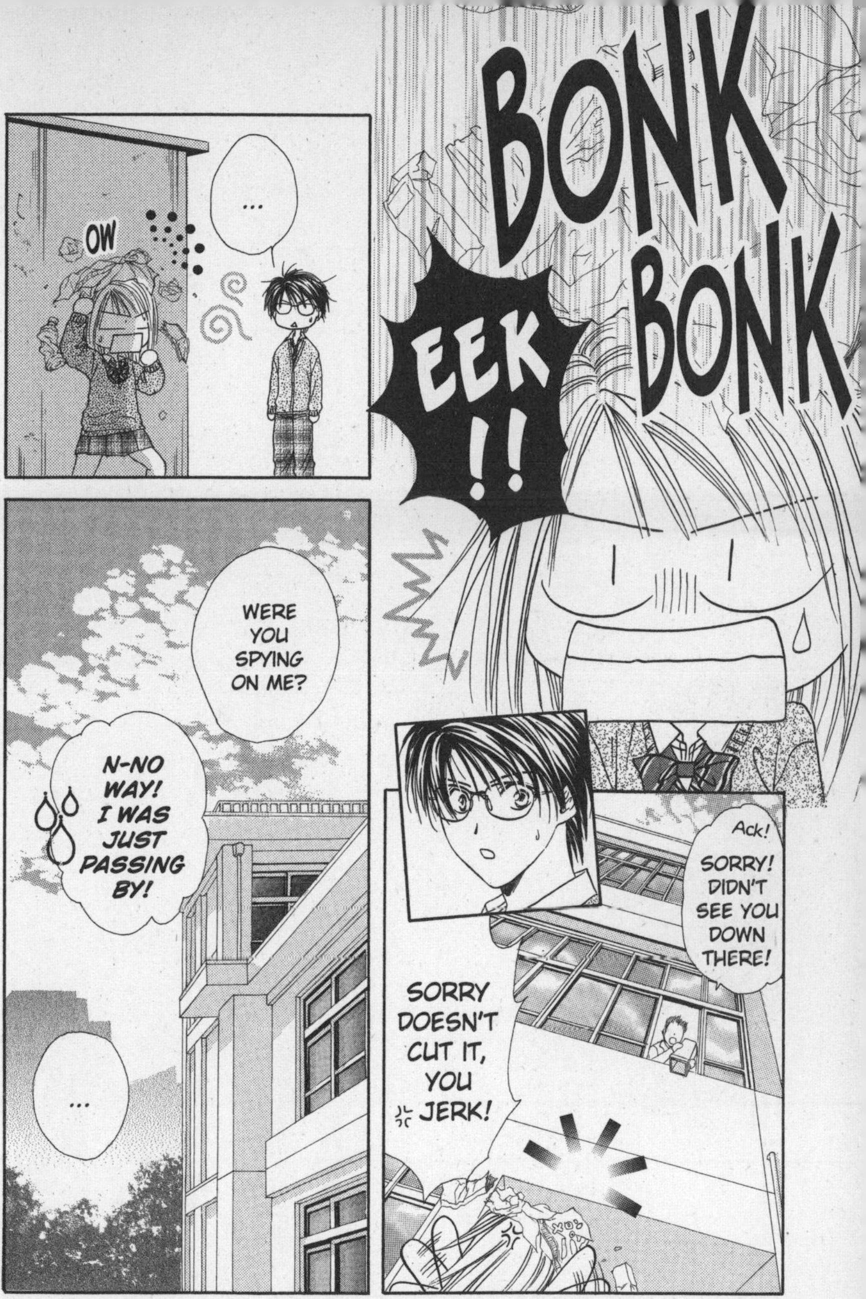
BONK
BONK
EEK!!
Ack!
SORRY! DIDN'T SEE YOU DOWN THERE!
SORRY DOESN'T CUT IT, YOU JERK!
...
OW
WERE YOU SPYING ON ME?
N-NO WAY! I WAS JUST PASSING BY!
...

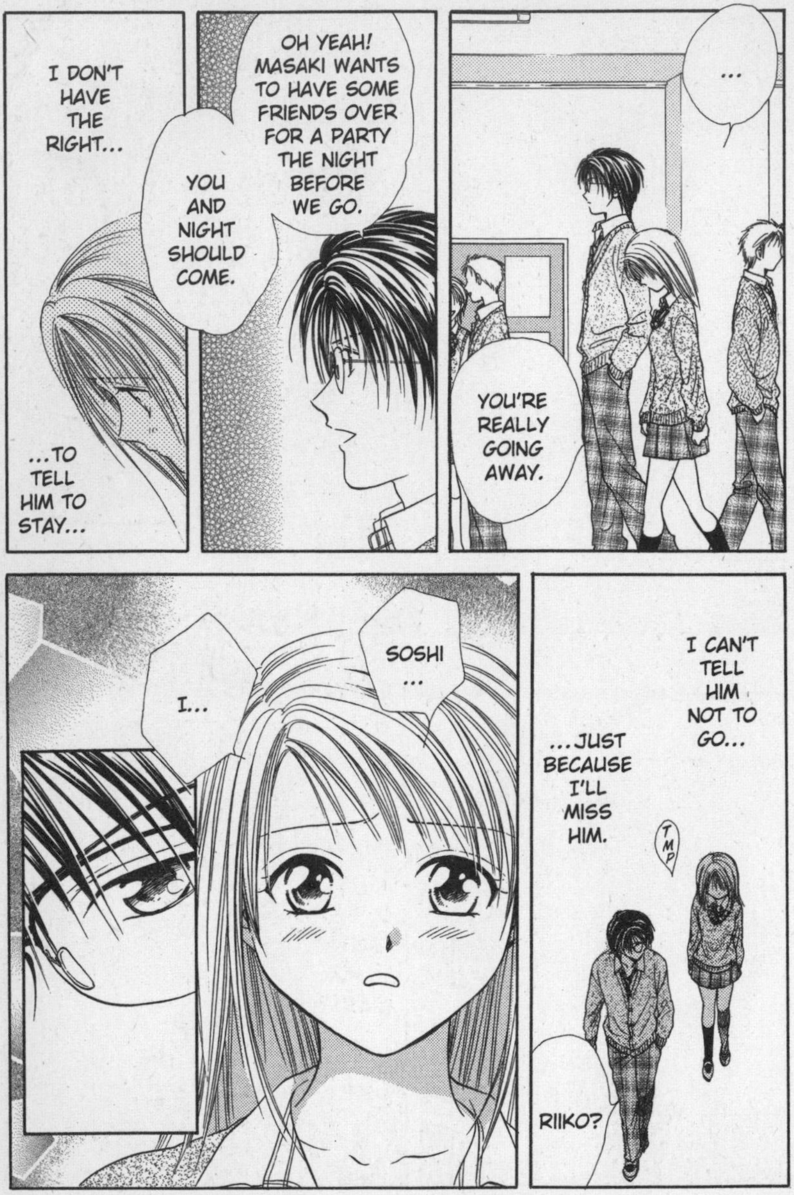
...
YOU'RE REALLY GOING AWAY.
OH YEAH! MASAKI WANTS TO HAVE SOME FRIENDS OVER FOR A PARTY THE NIGHT BEFORE WE GO.
YOU AND NIGHT SHOULD COME.
I DON'T HAVE THE RIGHT...
...TO TELL HIM TO STAY...
I CAN'T TELL HIM NOT TO GO...
...JUST BECAUSE I'LL MISS HIM.
TMP
RIIKO?
SOSHI ...
I...

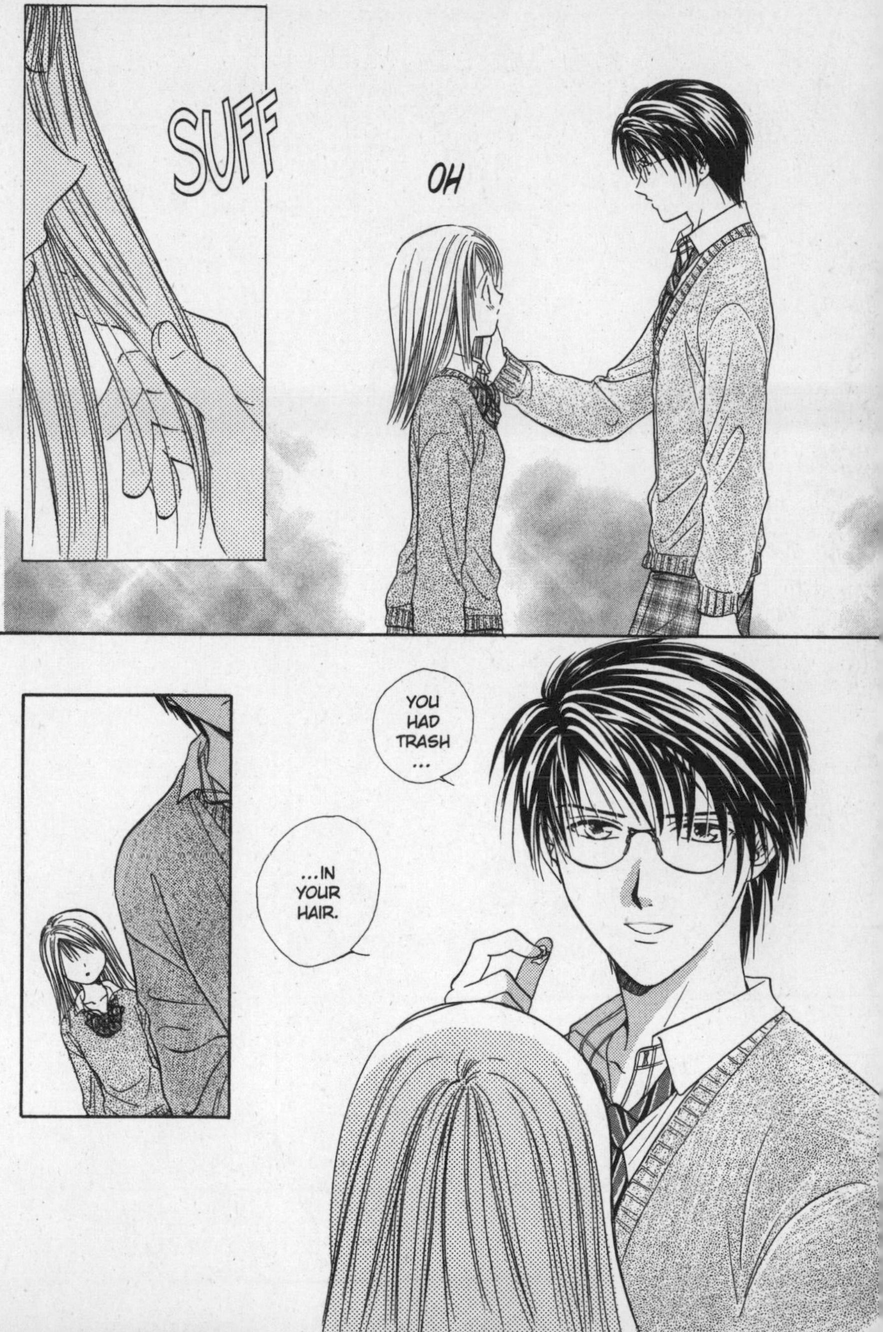
OH
SUFF
YOU HAD TRASH...
...IN YOUR HAIR.

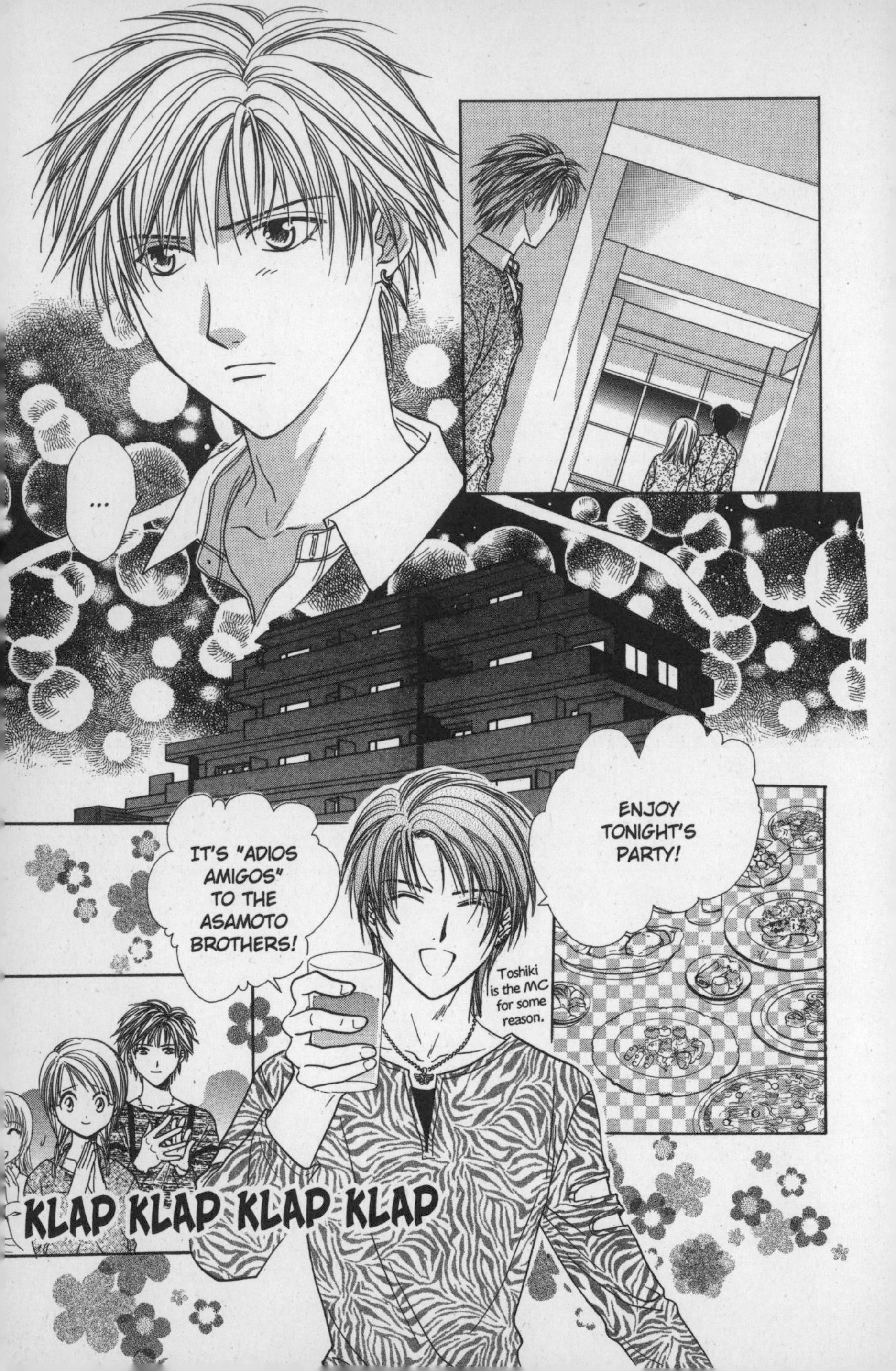
...
ENJOY TONIGHT'S PARTY!
IT'S "ADIOS AMIGOS" TO THE ASAMOTO BROTHERS!
Toshiki is the MC for some reason.
KLAP KLAP KLAP KLAP

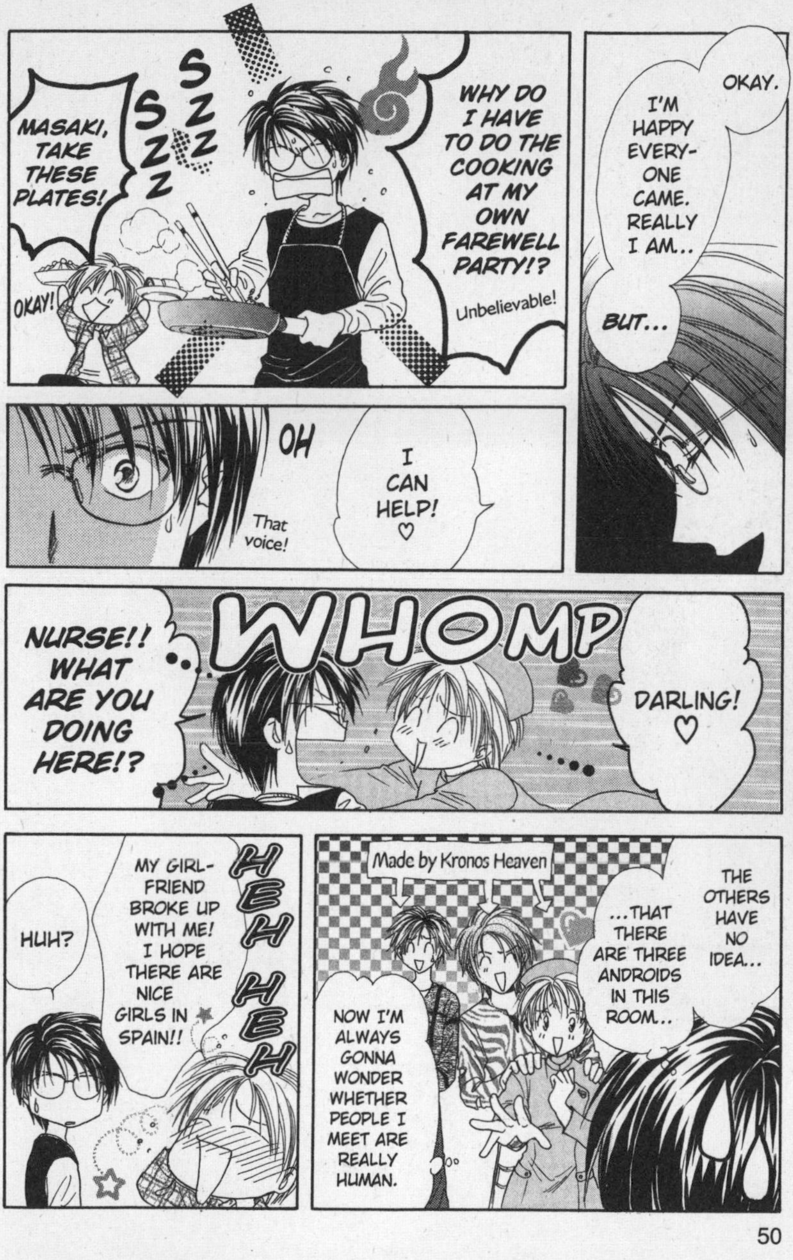

OKAY.
I'M HAPPY EVERYONE CAME. REALLY I AM...
BUT...
WHY DO I HAVE TO DO THE COOKING AT MY OWN FAREWELL PARTY!?
Unbelievable!
SZZ SZZ
MASAKI, TAKE THESE PLATES!
OKAY!
I CAN HELP! ♡
OH
That voice!
DARLING! ♡
WHOMP
NURSE!! WHAT ARE YOU DOING HERE!?
THE OTHERS HAVE NO IDEA...
...THAT THERE ARE THREE ANDROIDS IN THIS ROOM...
Made by Kronos Heaven
NOW I'M ALWAYS GONNA WONDER WHETHER PEOPLE I MEET ARE REALLY HUMAN.
HEH HEH HEH
MY GIRLFRIEND BROKE UP WITH ME! I HOPE THERE ARE NICE GIRLS IN SPAIN!!
HUH?

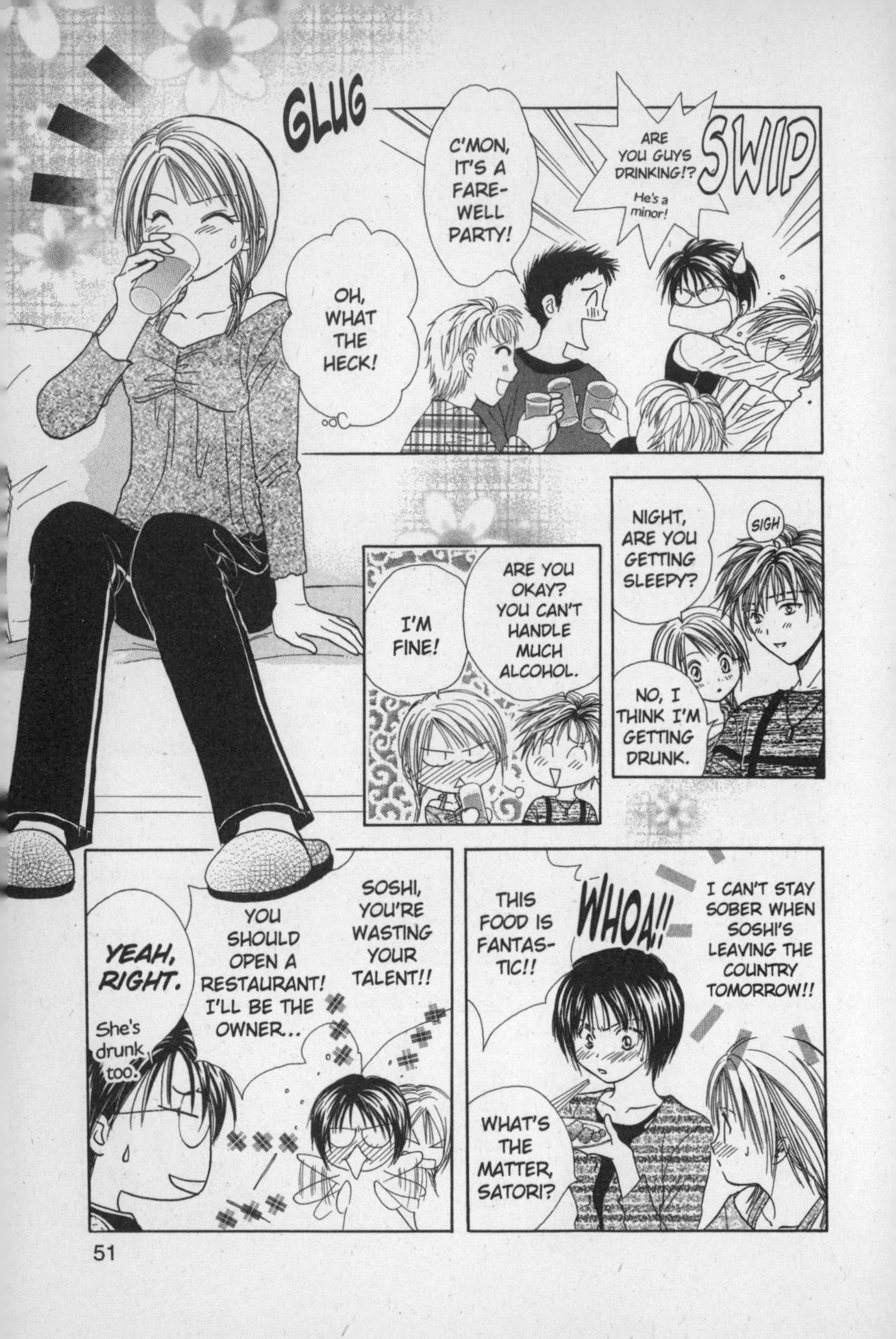

SWIP
ARE YOU GUYS DRINKING!?
He's a minor!
C'MON, IT'S A FARE-WELL PARTY!
GLUG
OH, WHAT THE HECK!
NIGHT, ARE YOU GETTING SLEEPY?
SIGH
NO, I THINK I'M GETTING DRUNK.
ARE YOU OKAY? YOU CAN'T HANDLE MUCH ALCOHOL.
I'M FINE!
I CAN'T STAY SOBER WHEN SOSHI'S LEAVING THE COUNTRY TOMORROW!!
WHOA!!
THIS FOOD IS FANTAS-TIC!!
WHAT'S THE MATTER, SATORI?
SOSHI, YOU'RE WASTING YOUR TALENT!!
YOU SHOULD OPEN A RESTAURANT! I'LL BE THE OWNER...
YEAH, RIGHT.
She's drunk too.

ALAS, HIS ABSENCE WILL BE DEEPLY FELT!
MR. MUYAI, I'M NOT DEAD.
WHY DID I INVITE HIM?
TIME FOR PARTY TRICKS!! I'M GONNA TAKE MY ARM OFF!!
OOH
DO IT!
BUT THAT'S AN INDUSTRIAL SECRET!!
TOSHIKI, STOP!
NIGHT, SPIN YOUR HEAD AROUND !!
This isn't The Exorcist!
MY TURN! I'M GONNA TAKE MY CLOTHES OFF! ♡
OOH
STOP!!
KLINK
SHEESH ...

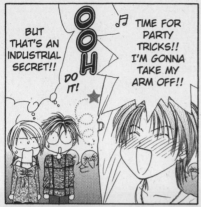

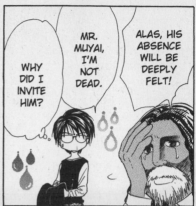

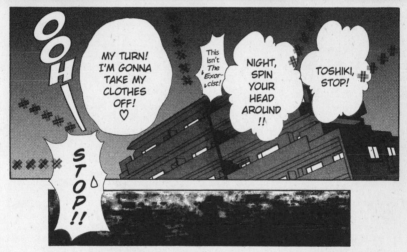

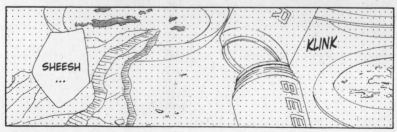

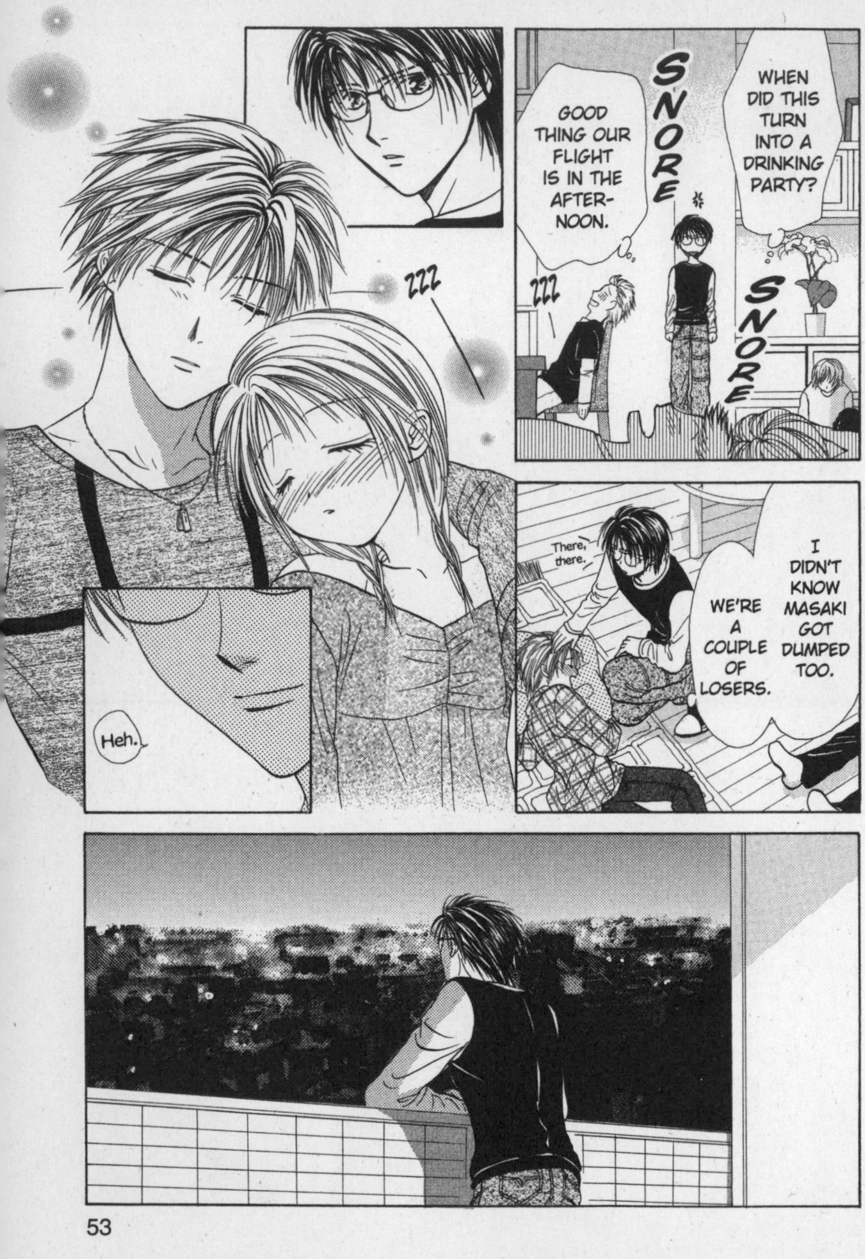
WHEN DID THIS TURN INTO A DRINKING PARTY?
SNORE
GOOD THING OUR FLIGHT IS IN THE AFTERNOON.
SNORE
ZZZ
I DIDN'T KNOW MASAKI GOT DUMPED TOO.
WE'RE A COUPLE OF LOSERS.
There, there.
ZZZ
Heh.

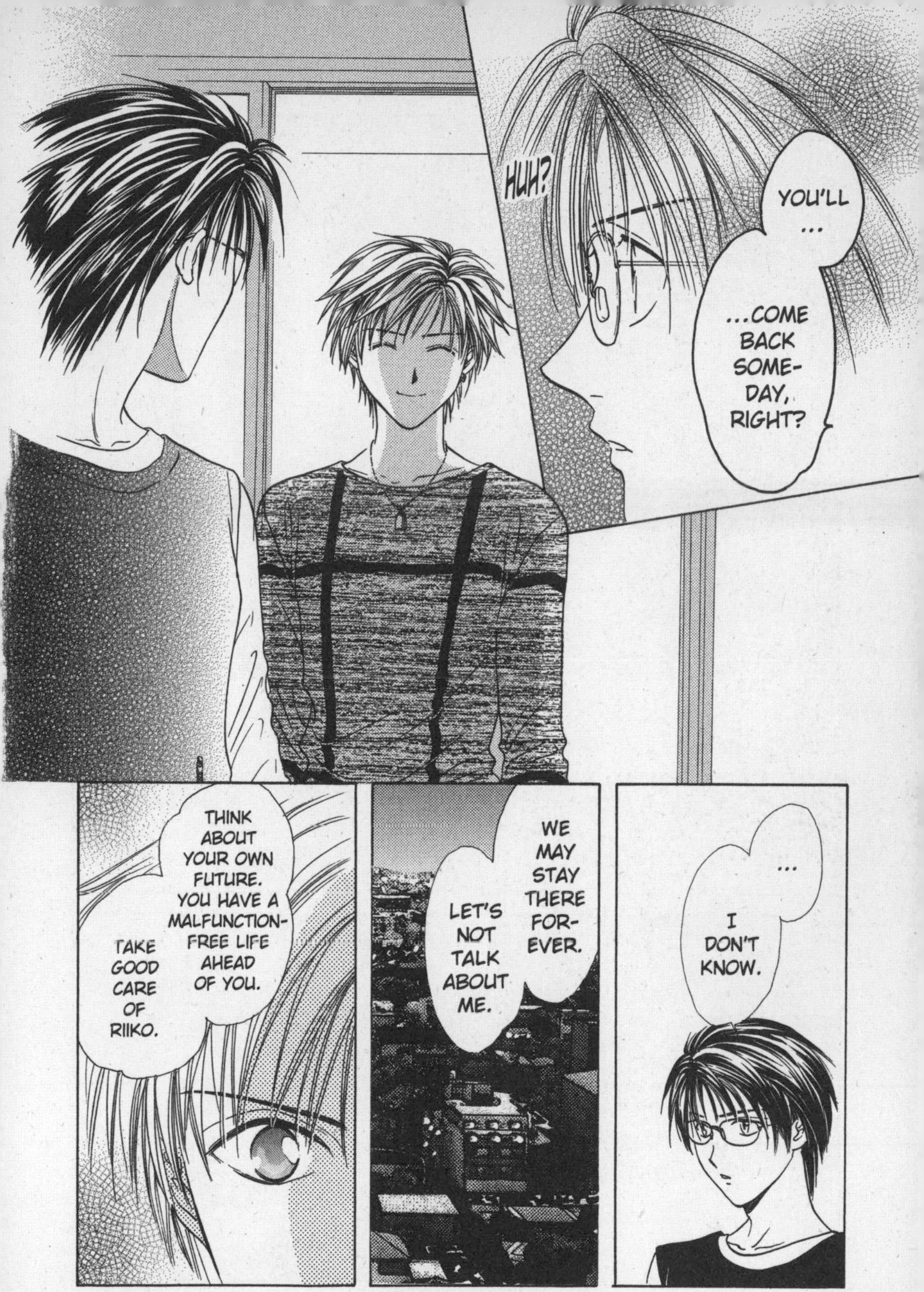
YOU'LL ...
HUH?
...COME BACK SOME-DAY, RIGHT?
...
I DON'T KNOW.
WE MAY STAY THERE FOR-EVER.
LET'S NOT TALK ABOUT ME.
THINK ABOUT YOUR OWN FUTURE. YOU HAVE A MALFUNCTION-FREE LIFE AHEAD OF YOU.
TAKE GOOD CARE OF RIIKO.

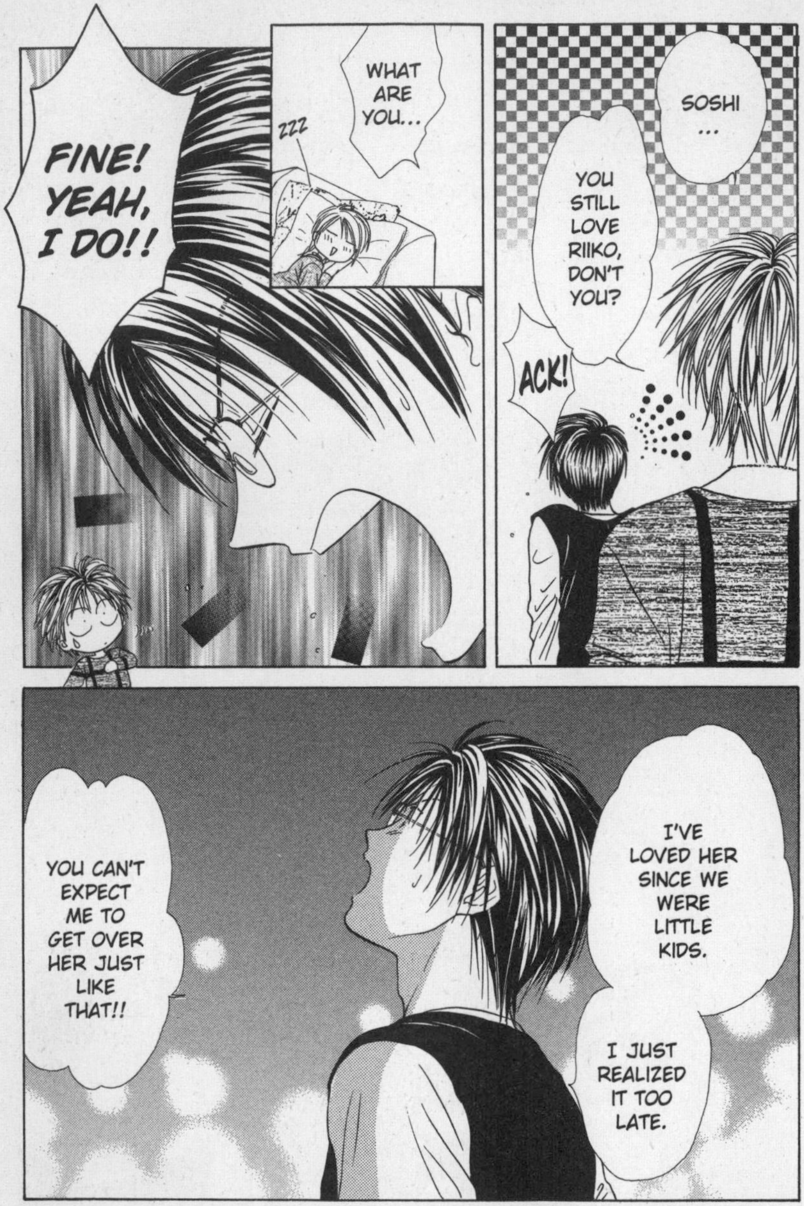
SOSHI ...
YOU STILL LOVE RIIKO, DON'T YOU?
ACK!
WHAT ARE YOU...
ZZZ
FINE! YEAH, I DO!!
I'VE LOVED HER SINCE WE WERE LITTLE KIDS.
I JUST REALIZED IT TOO LATE.
YOU CAN'T EXPECT ME TO GET OVER HER JUST LIKE THAT!!

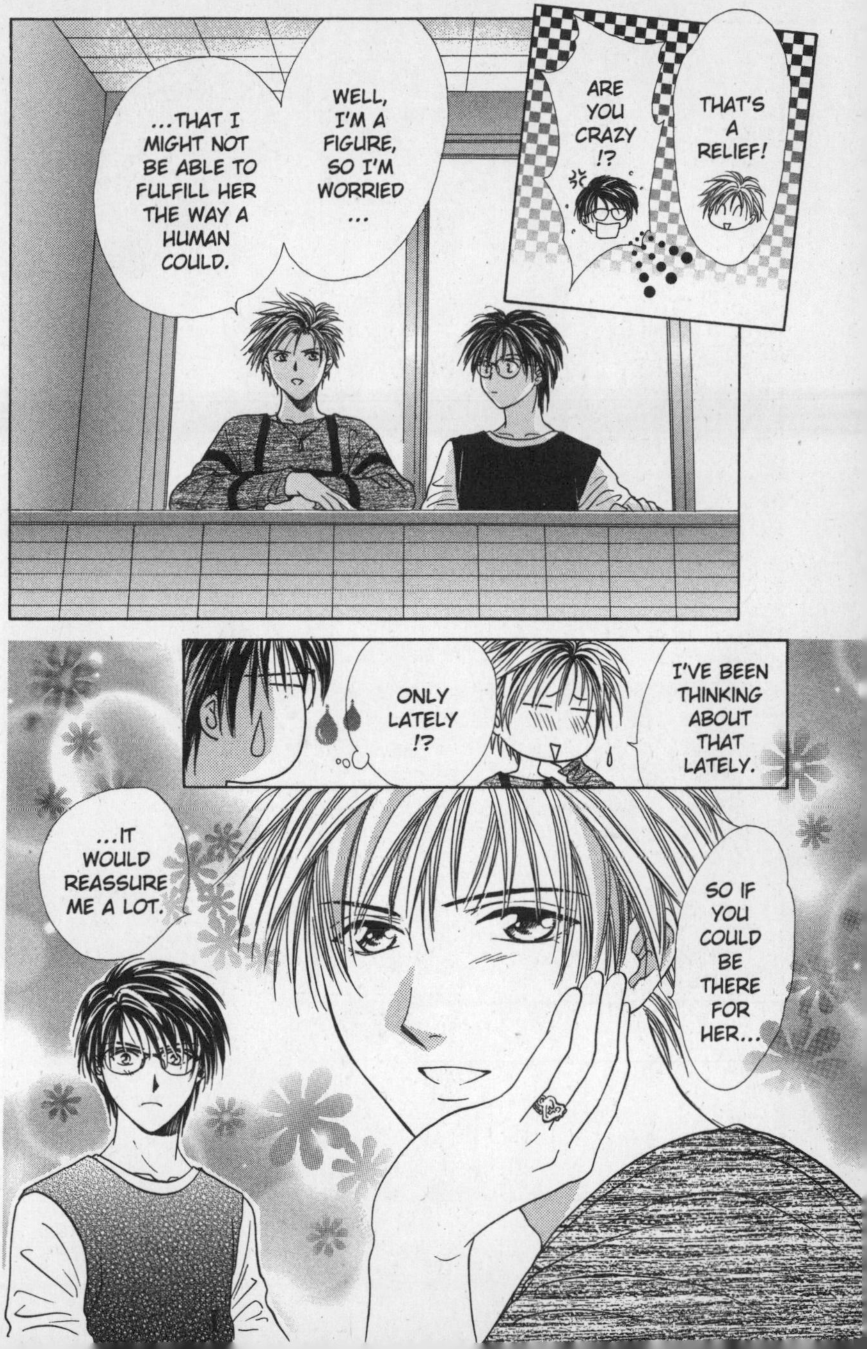
THAT'S A RELIEF!
ARE YOU CRAZY !?
WELL, I'M A FIGURE, SO I'M WORRIED ...
...THAT I MIGHT NOT BE ABLE TO FULFILL HER THE WAY A HUMAN COULD.
I'VE BEEN THINKING ABOUT THAT LATELY.
ONLY LATELY !?
SO IF YOU COULD BE THERE FOR HER...
...IT WOULD REASSURE ME A LOT.

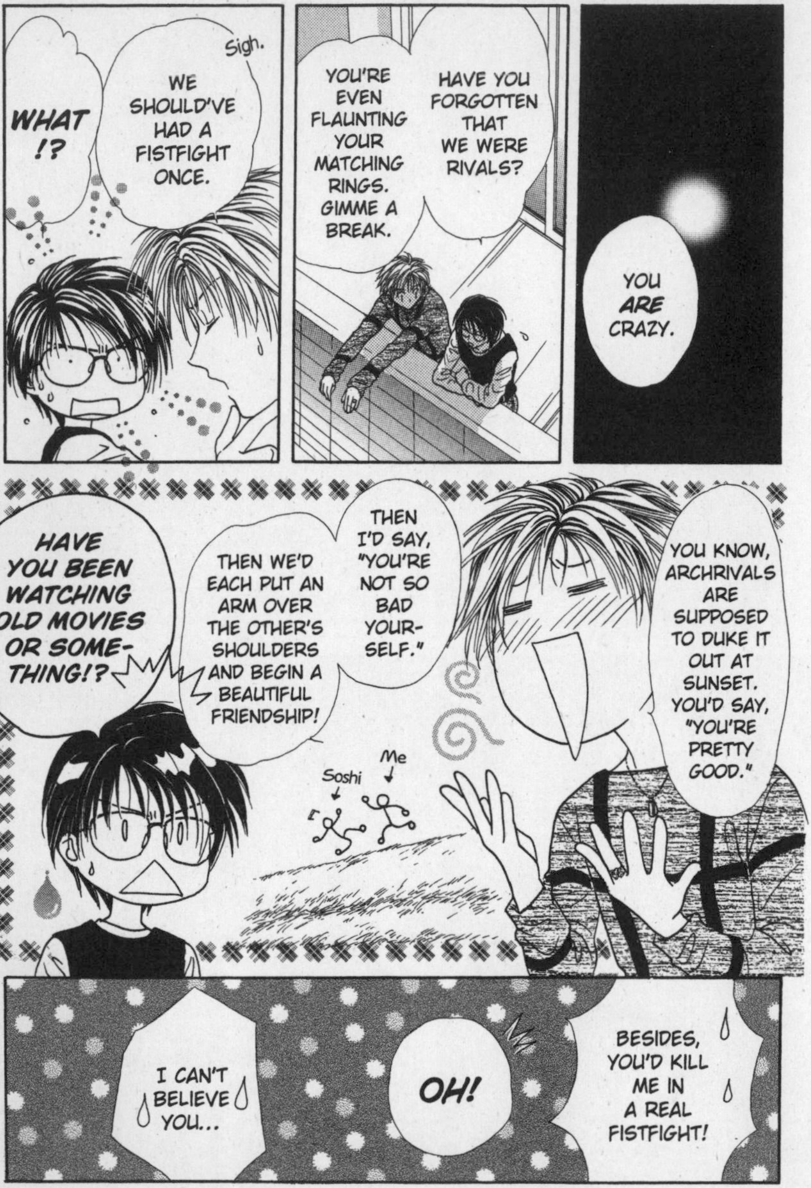
YOU ARE CRAZY.
HAVE YOU FORGOTTEN THAT WE WERE RIVALS?
YOU'RE EVEN FLAUNTING YOUR MATCHING RINGS. GIMME A BREAK.
Sigh.
WE SHOULD'VE HAD A FISTFIGHT ONCE.
WHAT!?
YOU KNOW, ARCHRIVALS ARE SUPPOSED TO DUKE IT OUT AT SUNSET. YOU'D SAY, "YOU'RE PRETTY GOOD."
THEN I'D SAY, "YOU'RE NOT SO BAD YOURSELF."
THEN WE'D EACH PUT AN ARM OVER THE OTHER'S SHOULDERS AND BEGIN A BEAUTIFUL FRIENDSHIP!
Me
Soshi
HAVE YOU BEEN WATCHING OLD MOVIES OR SOMETHING!?
BESIDES, YOU'D KILL ME IN A REAL FISTFIGHT!
OH!
I CAN'T BELIEVE YOU...

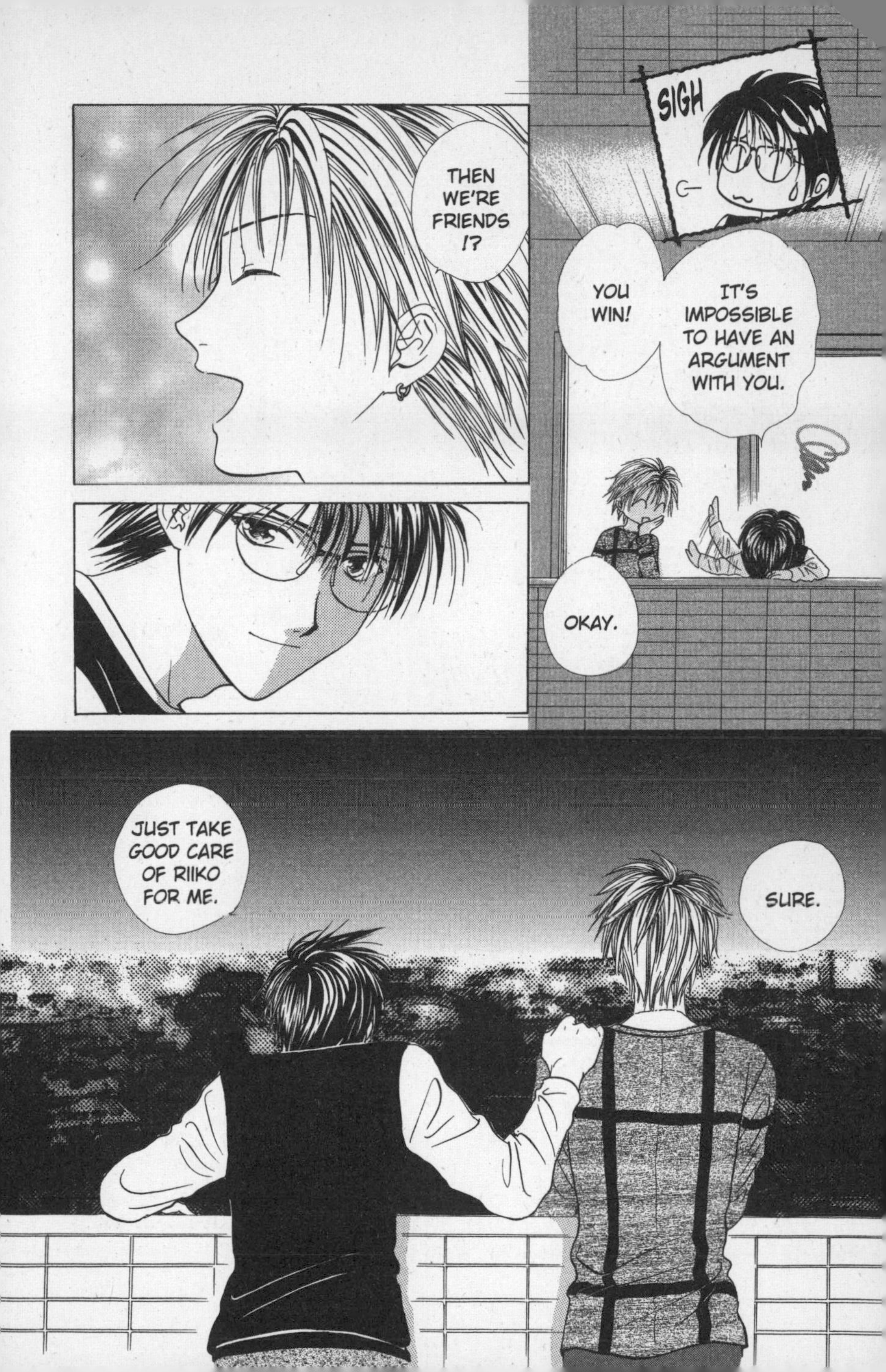
SIGH
IT'S IMPOSSIBLE TO HAVE AN ARGUMENT WITH YOU.
YOU WIN!
OKAY.
THEN WE'RE FRIENDS !?
JUST TAKE GOOD CARE OF RIIKO FOR ME.
SURE.

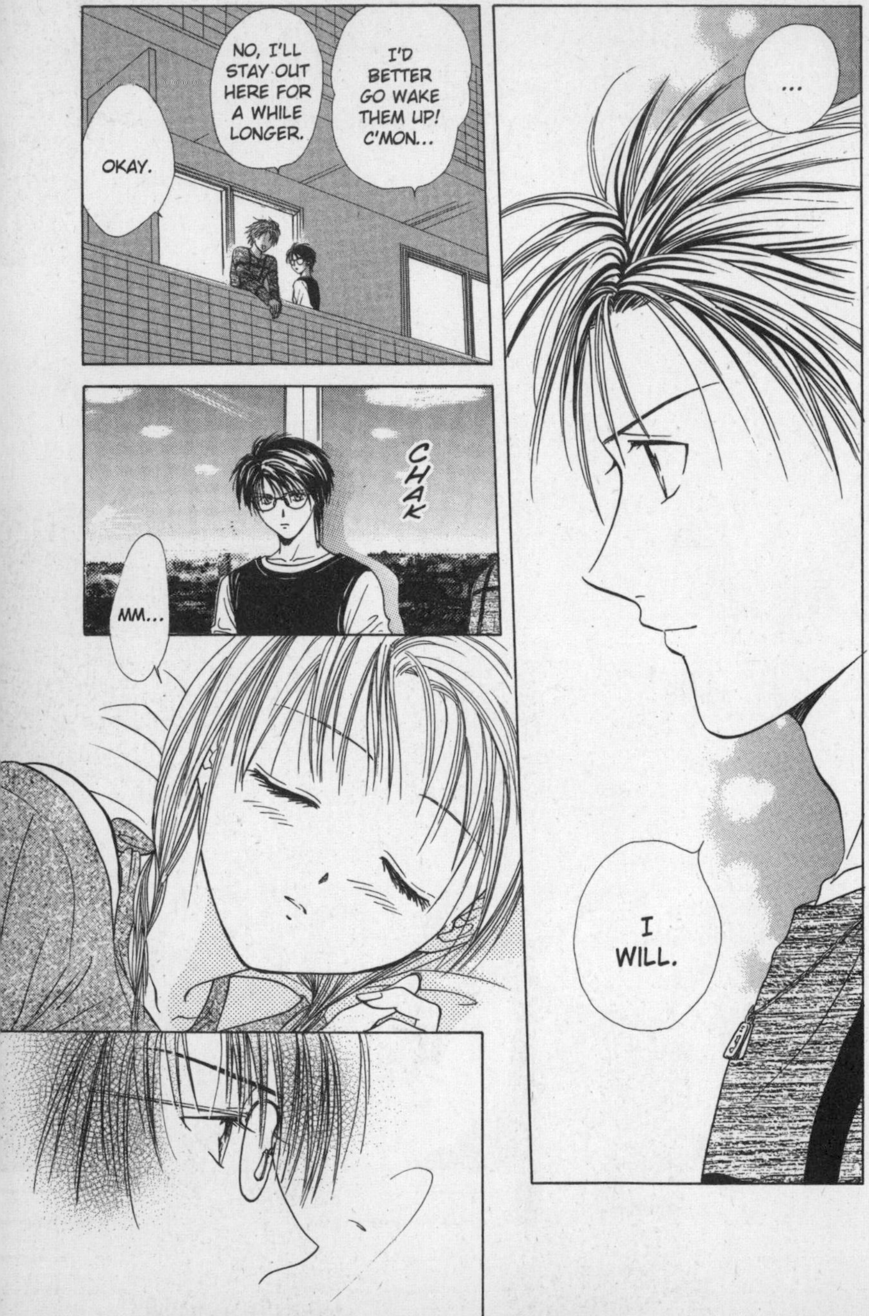
...
I WILL.
I'D BETTER GO WAKE THEM UP! C'MON...
NO, I'LL STAY OUT HERE FOR A WHILE LONGER.
OKAY.
CHAK
MM...

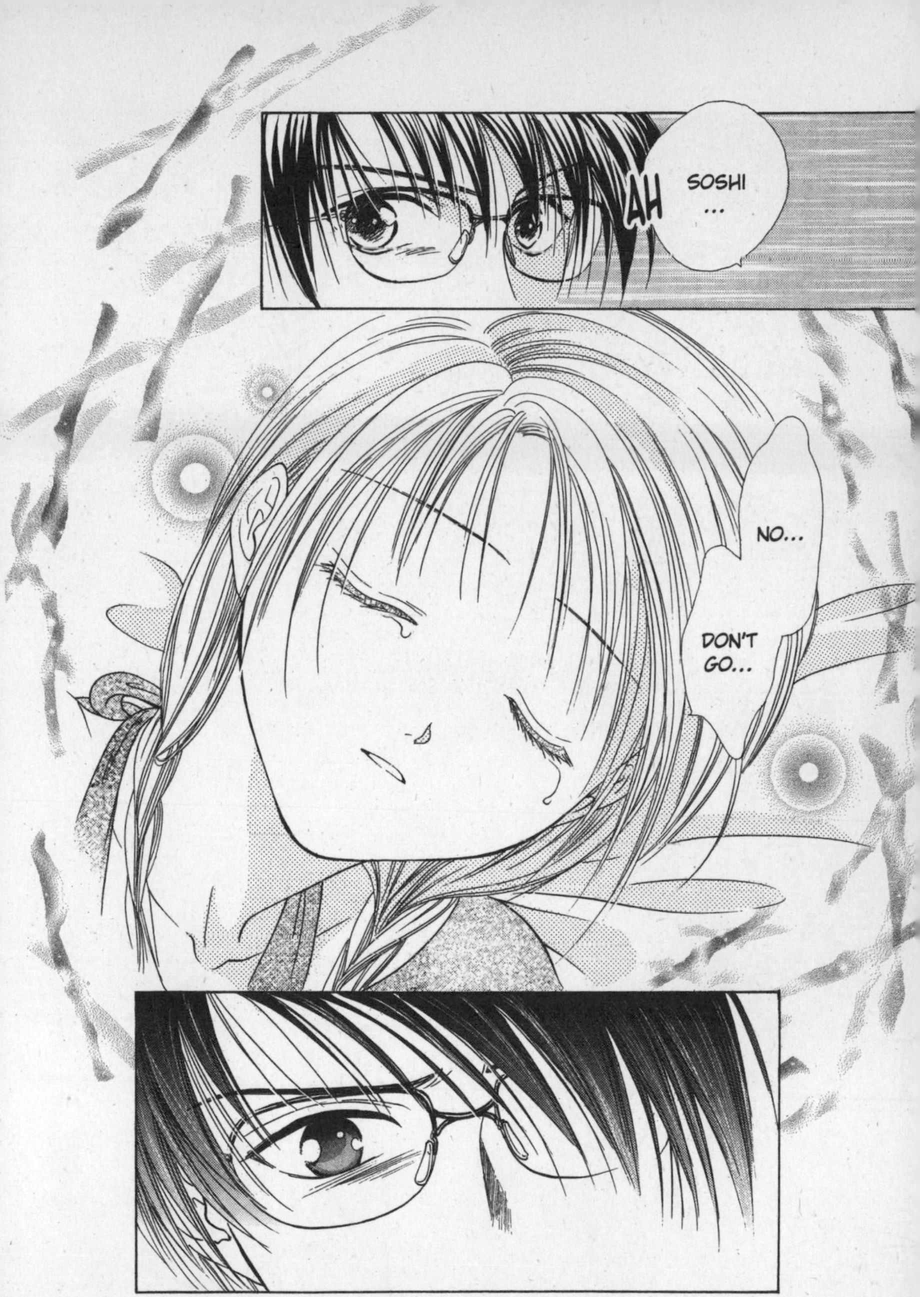
AH
SOSHI ...
NO...
DON'T GO...

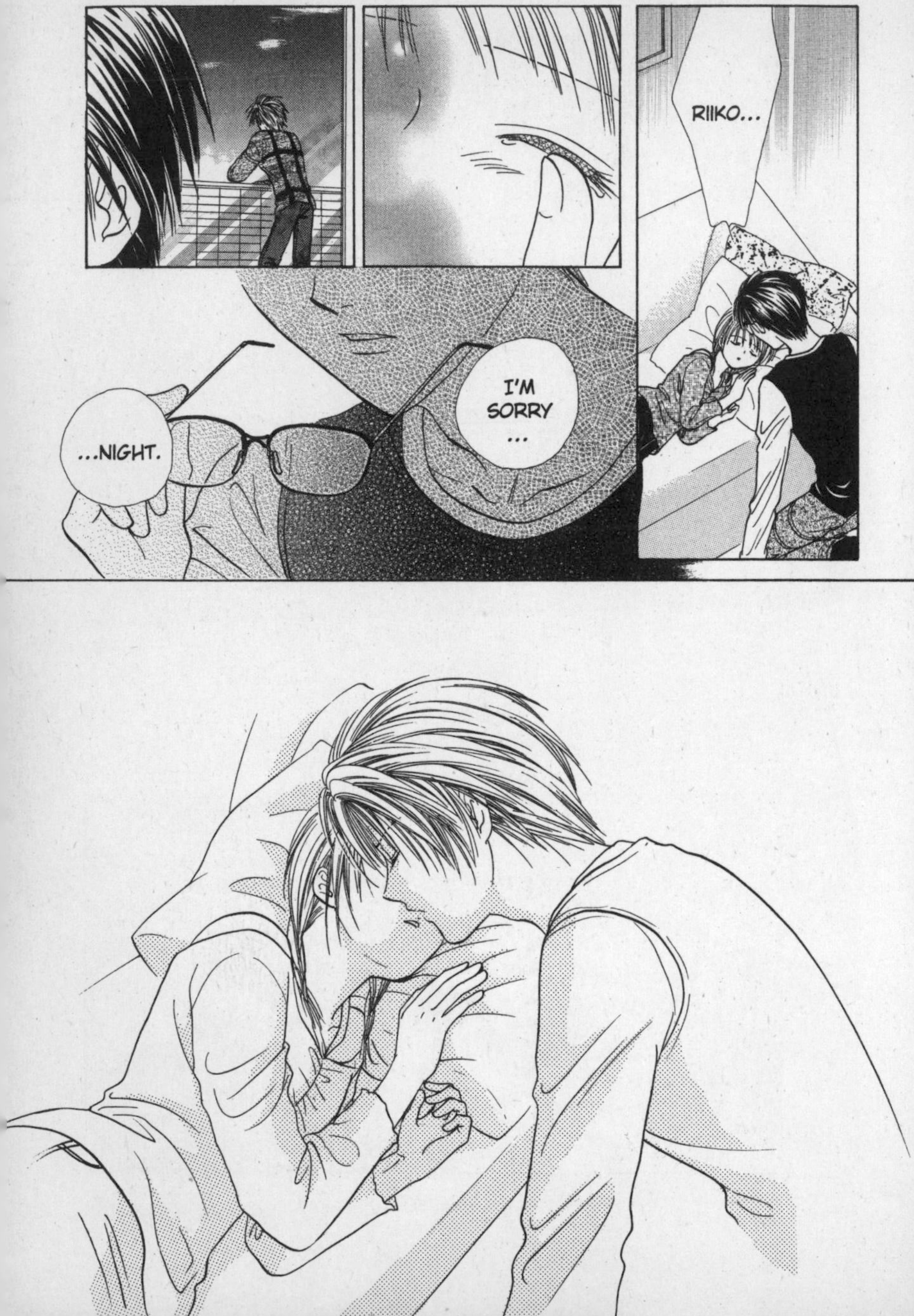
RIIKO...
I'M SORRY ...
...NIGHT.

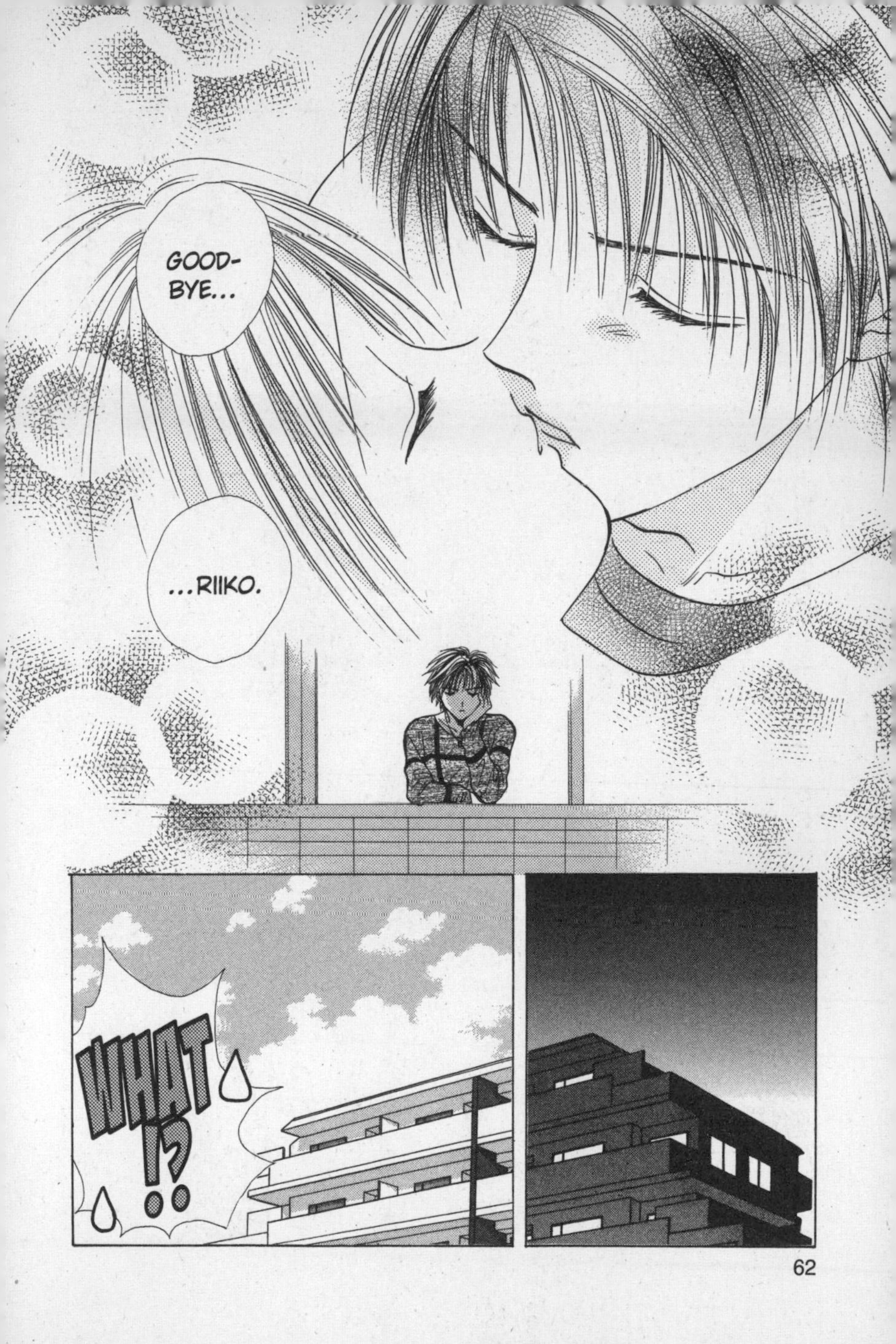
GOOD-BYE...
...RIIKO.
WHAT!?

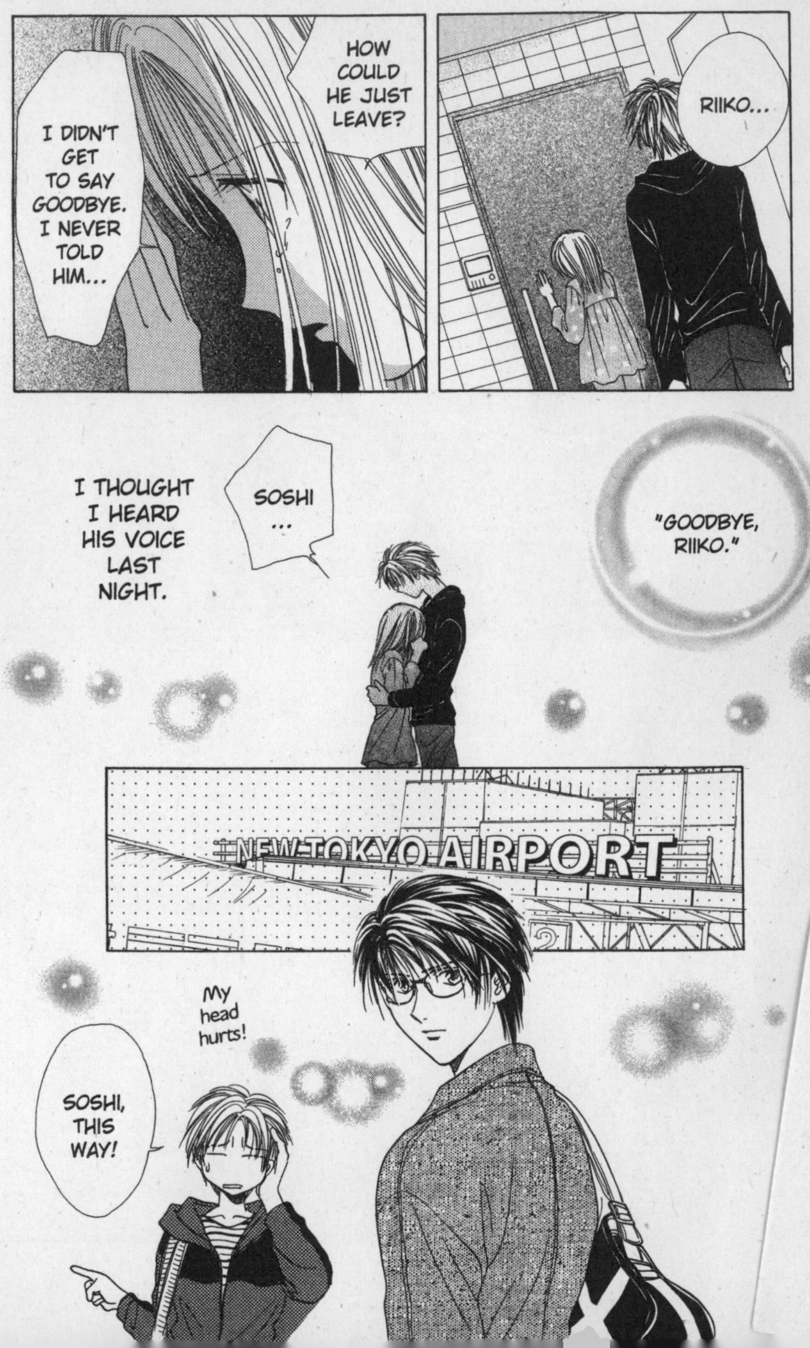
RIIKO...
HOW COULD HE JUST LEAVE?
I DIDN'T GET TO SAY GOODBYE. I NEVER TOLD HIM...
"GOODBYE, RIIKO."
SOSHI ...
I THOUGHT I HEARD HIS VOICE LAST NIGHT.
NEW TOKYO AIRPORT
My head hurts!
SOSHI, THIS WAY!

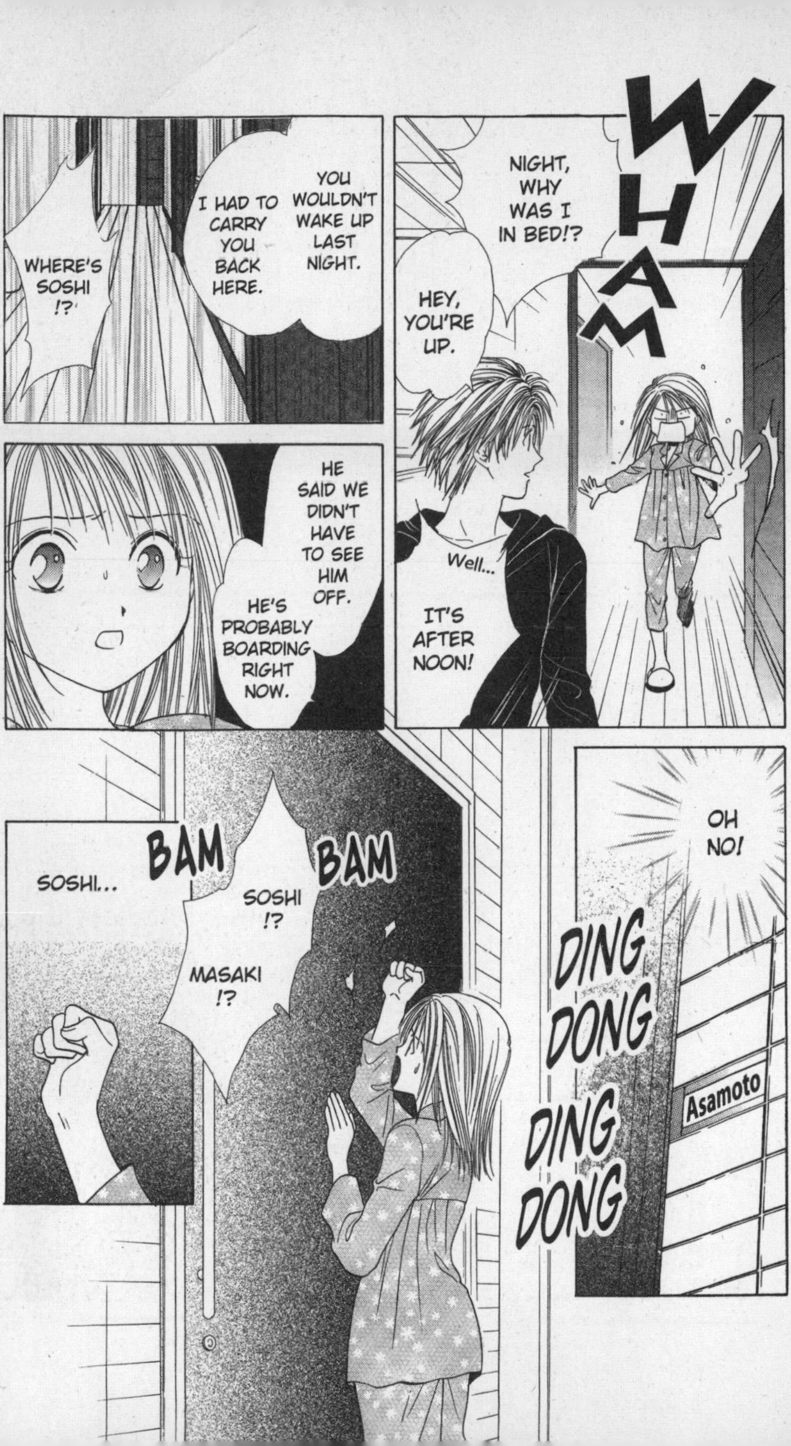

WHAM
NIGHT, WHY WAS I IN BED!?
HEY, YOU'RE UP.
Well...
IT'S AFTER NOON!
YOU WOULDN'T WAKE UP LAST NIGHT.
I HAD TO CARRY YOU BACK HERE.
WHERE'S SOSHI !?
HE SAID WE DIDN'T HAVE TO SEE HIM OFF.
HE'S PROBABLY BOARDING RIGHT NOW.
OH NO!
DING DONG DING DONG
Asamoto
BAM BAM
SOSHI !?
MASAKI !?
SOSHI...

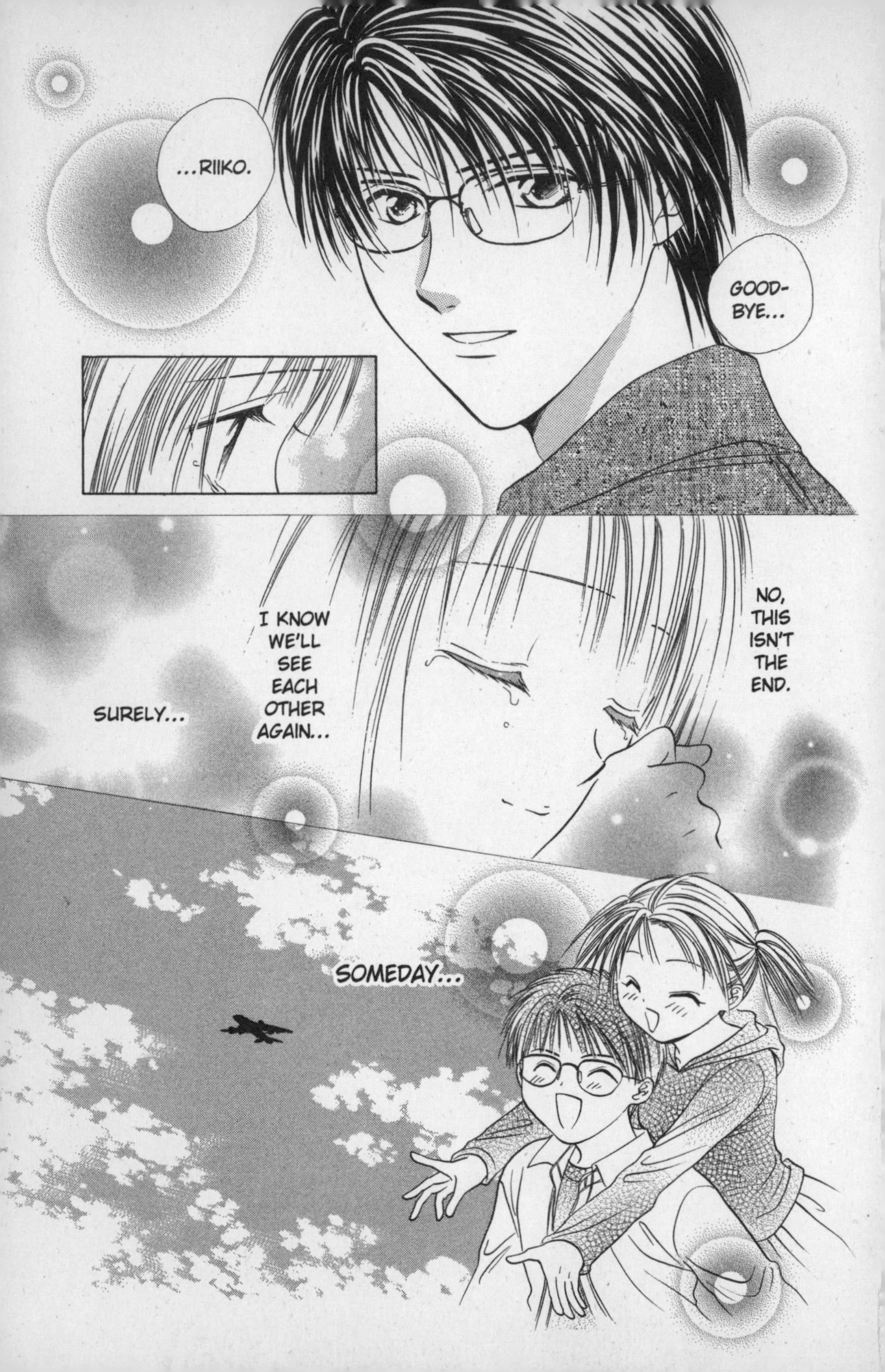
...RIIKO.
GOOD-BYE...
NO, THIS ISN'T THE END.
I KNOW WE'LL SEE EACH OTHER AGAIN...
SURELY...
SOMEDAY...

Absolute Boyfriend

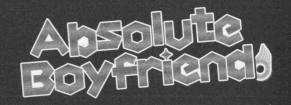

The Final Act: Eternal Boyfriend

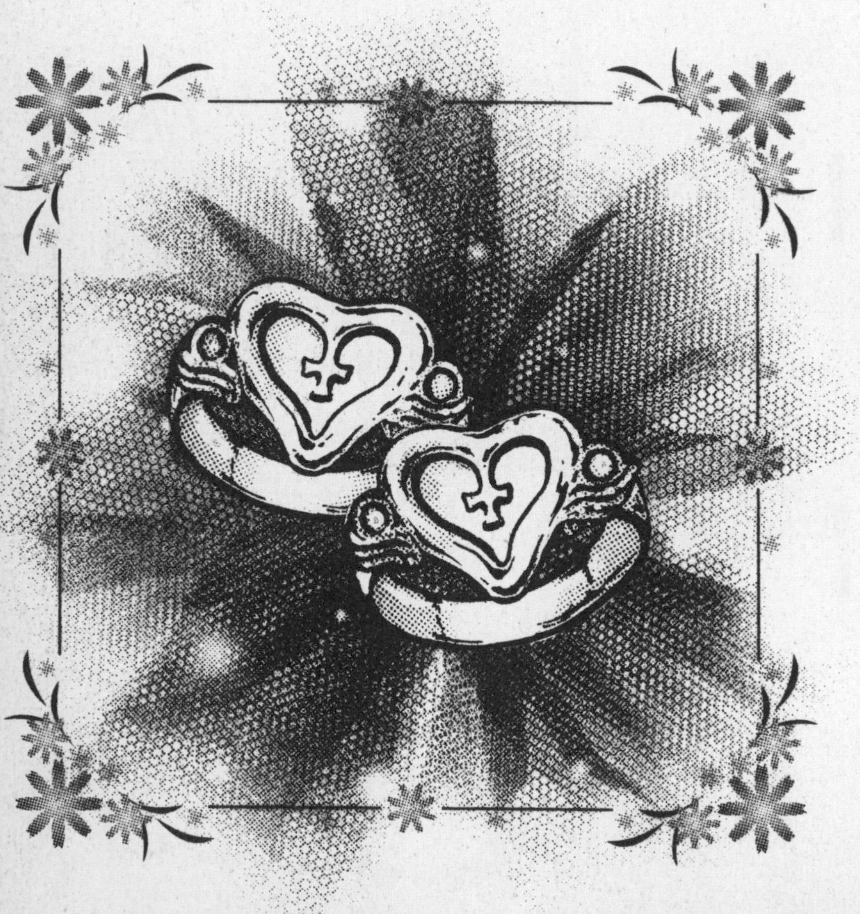

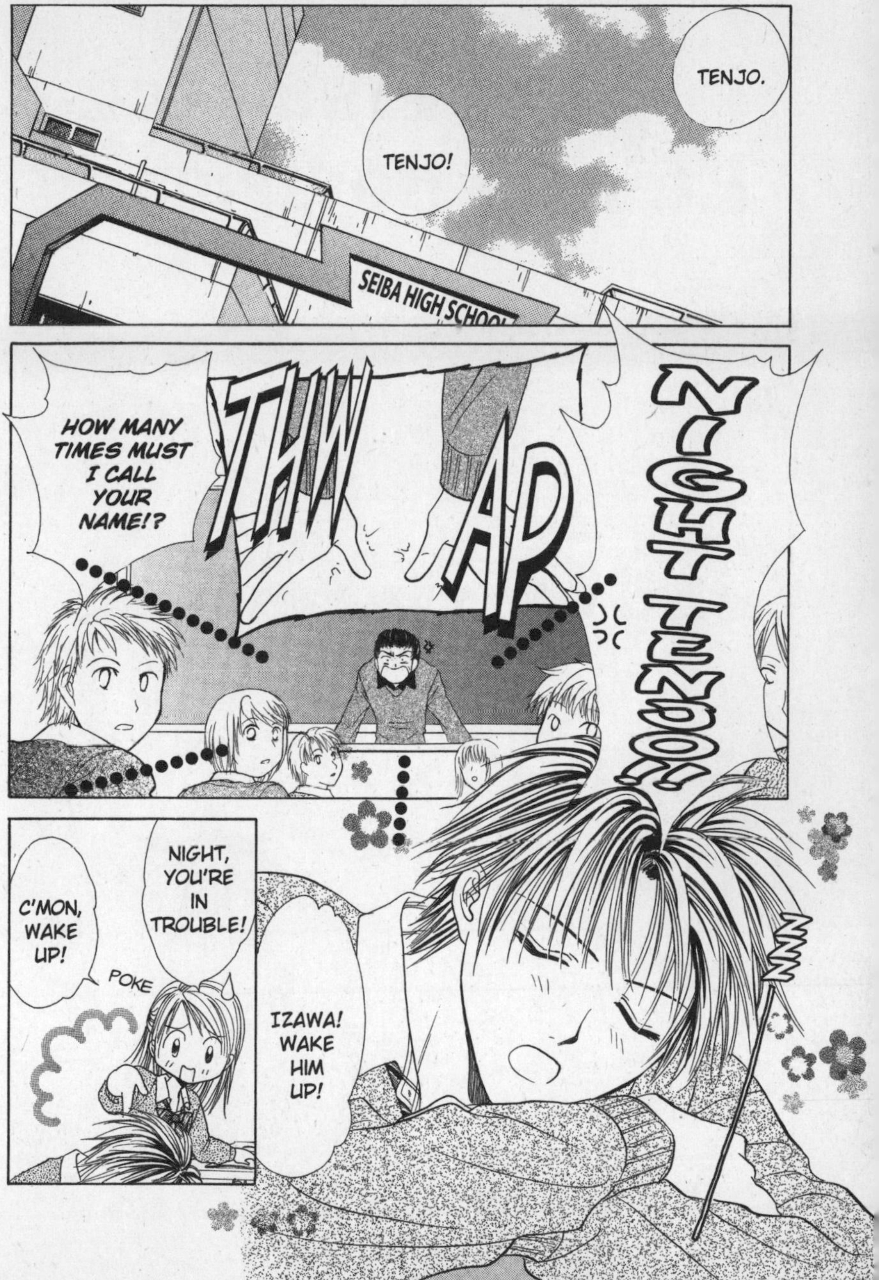
TENJO.
TENJO!
SEIBA HIGH SCHOO
NIGHT TENJO!
THWAP
HOW MANY TIMES MUST I CALL YOUR NAME!?
ZZZ
IZAWA! WAKE HIM UP!
NIGHT, YOU'RE IN TROUBLE!
C'MON, WAKE UP!
POKE

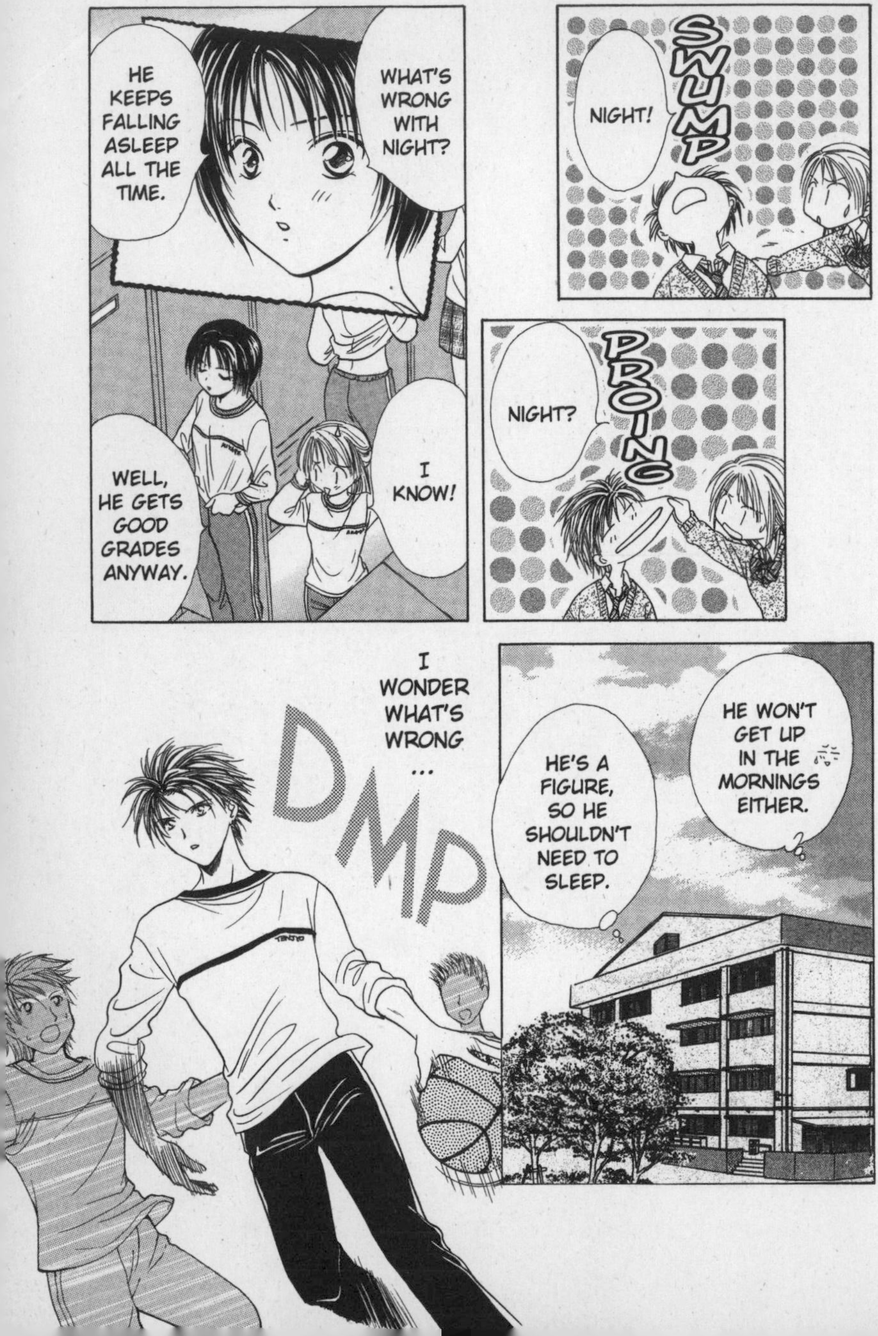
SWUMP
NIGHT!
PROING
NIGHT?
WHAT'S WRONG WITH NIGHT?
HE KEEPS FALLING ASLEEP ALL THE TIME.
I KNOW!
WELL, HE GETS GOOD GRADES ANYWAY.
HE WON'T GET UP IN THE MORNINGS EITHER.
HE'S A FIGURE, SO HE SHOULDN'T NEED TO SLEEP.
I WONDER WHAT'S WRONG...
DMP

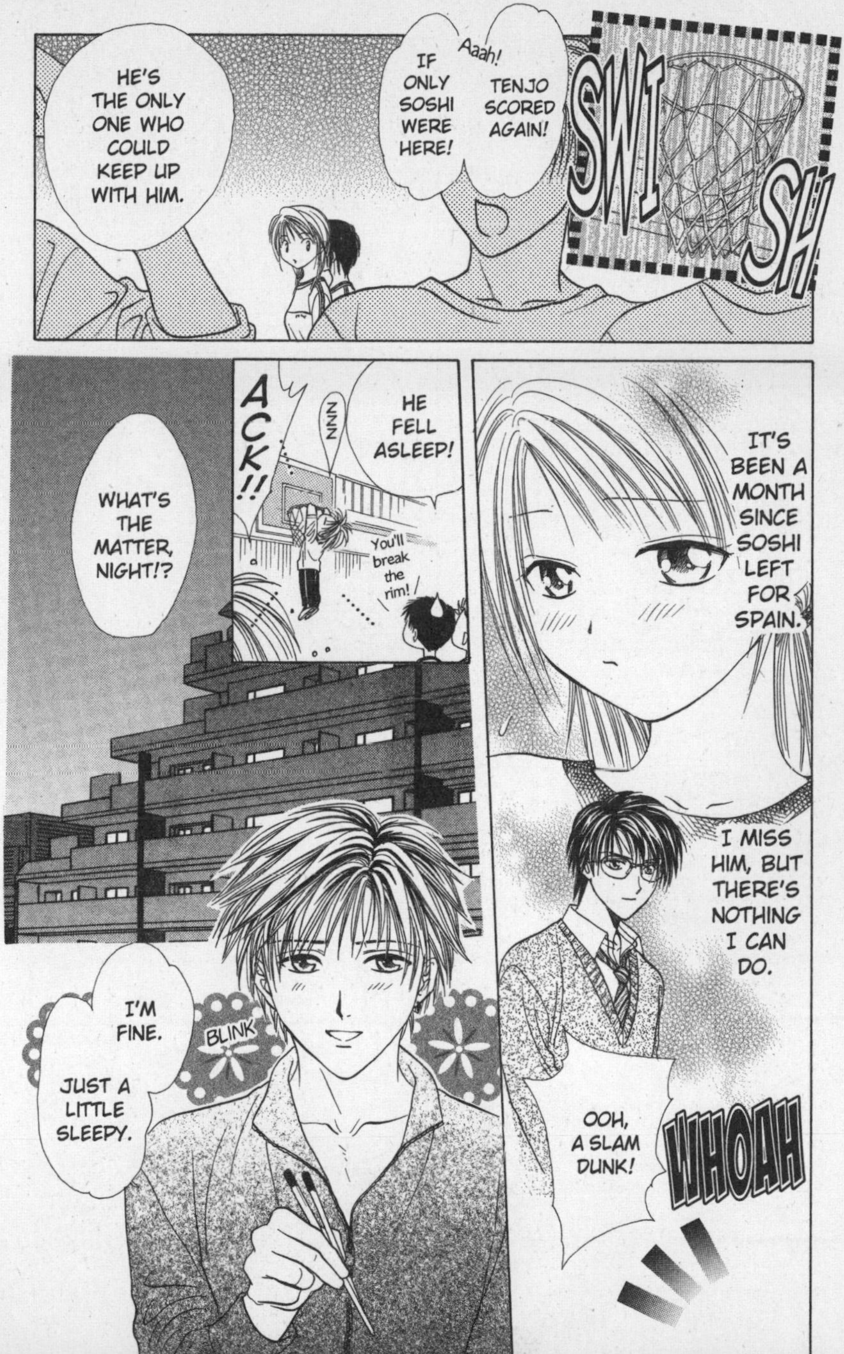
SWISH
Aaah!
TENJO SCORED AGAIN!
IF ONLY SOSHI WERE HERE!
HE'S THE ONLY ONE WHO COULD KEEP UP WITH HIM.
IT'S BEEN A MONTH SINCE SOSHI LEFT FOR SPAIN.
I MISS HIM, BUT THERE'S NOTHING I CAN DO.
OOH, A SLAM DUNK!
WHOAH
ACK!!
HE FELL ASLEEP!
ZZZ
You'll break the rim!
WHAT'S THE MATTER, NIGHT!?
I'M FINE.
BLINK
JUST A LITTLE SLEEPY.

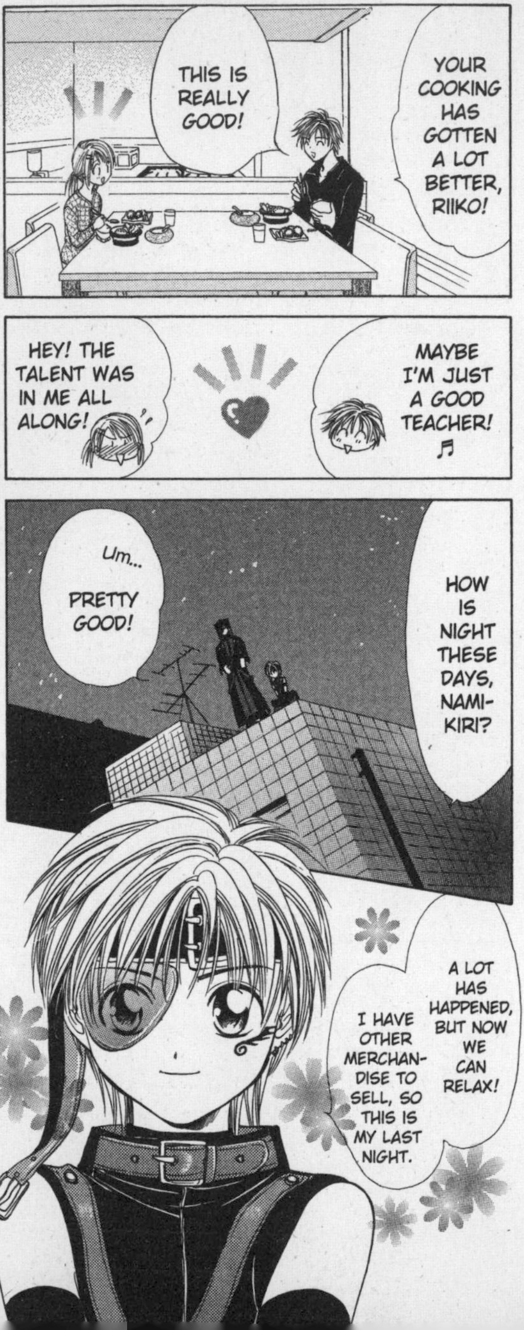

YOUR COOKING HAS GOTTEN A LOT BETTER, RIIKO!
THIS IS REALLY GOOD!
MAYBE I'M JUST A GOOD TEACHER! ♬
HEY! THE TALENT WAS IN ME ALL ALONG!
HOW IS NIGHT THESE DAYS, NAMIKIRI?
Um...
PRETTY GOOD!
A LOT HAS HAPPENED, BUT NOW WE CAN RELAX!
I HAVE OTHER MERCHANDISE TO SELL, SO THIS IS MY LAST NIGHT.

Speaking of "Kinpachi-sensei," my assistant K told me her junior high was short-listed as a location for the show, but the principal said no. Oh well.

I got the name Namikiri from Namikiri Hall, where I used to live! I heard there were fewer attendees for last year's festival because it didn't fall on the usual holiday. People said they should move the festival date to coincide with the holiday. I wonder what'll happen this year?

By the way, this scene on the right in which Night says he's been giving Riiko cooking lessons was meant to show that he was thinking about her future. In my opinion, true love doesn't seek anything in return. Everything Night said and did in this final volume was from deep and pure love, not programmed infatuation. He was a figure, but I think he's become truly human.

On the other hand, there are humans who act truly inhuman at times.

All of my works have different moods, dictated by the worlds in which they take place, so it may seem like they all have different themes. But really, I only ever use one theme--that the heart is the most important thing. I'm sure I'll keep saying that in all my future works, whatever the genre.

I don't really have any real-life models for my characters. I just draw whatever vague ideas come to mind. (Even if I had models, I wouldn't be able to make my characters look like them.) But I had trouble drawing Soshi's glasses, so I sketched out Smile from "Ping Pong" (the movie based on the manga by Taiyo Matsumoto). (smile) That was a great movie. I love stories about friendship. My friend made photocopies of those sketches and took them home. (smile)

Thank you for your continued support. See you again in my next work!

January 2005

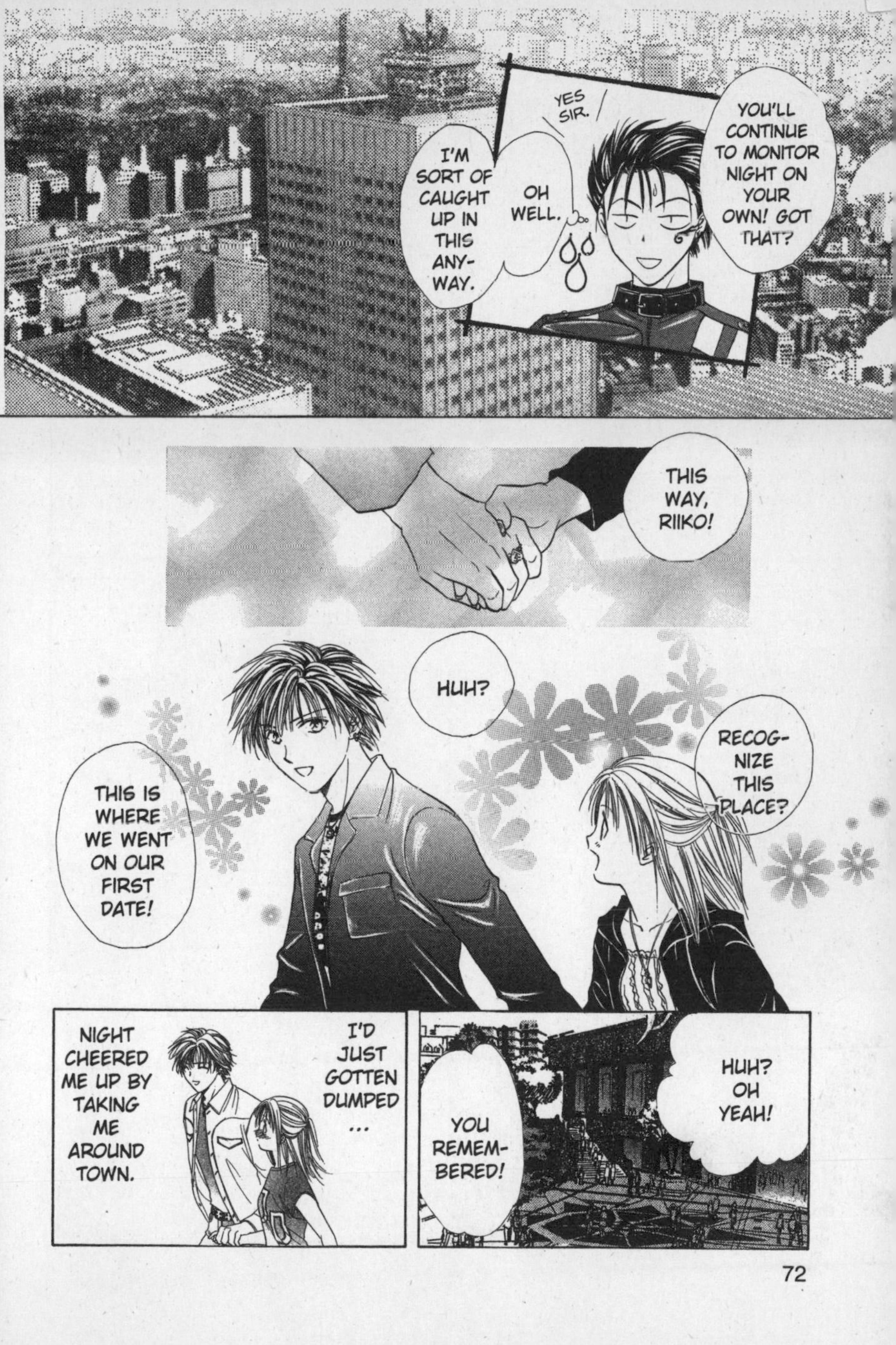
YOU'LL CONTINUE TO MONITOR NIGHT ON YOUR OWN! GOT THAT?
YES SIR.
OH WELL.
I'M SORT OF CAUGHT UP IN THIS ANYWAY.
THIS WAY, RIIKO!
HUH?
RECOGNIZE THIS PLACE?
THIS IS WHERE WE WENT ON OUR FIRST DATE!
HUH? OH YEAH!
YOU REMEMBERED!
I'D JUST GOTTEN DUMPED...
NIGHT CHEERED ME UP BY TAKING ME AROUND TOWN.

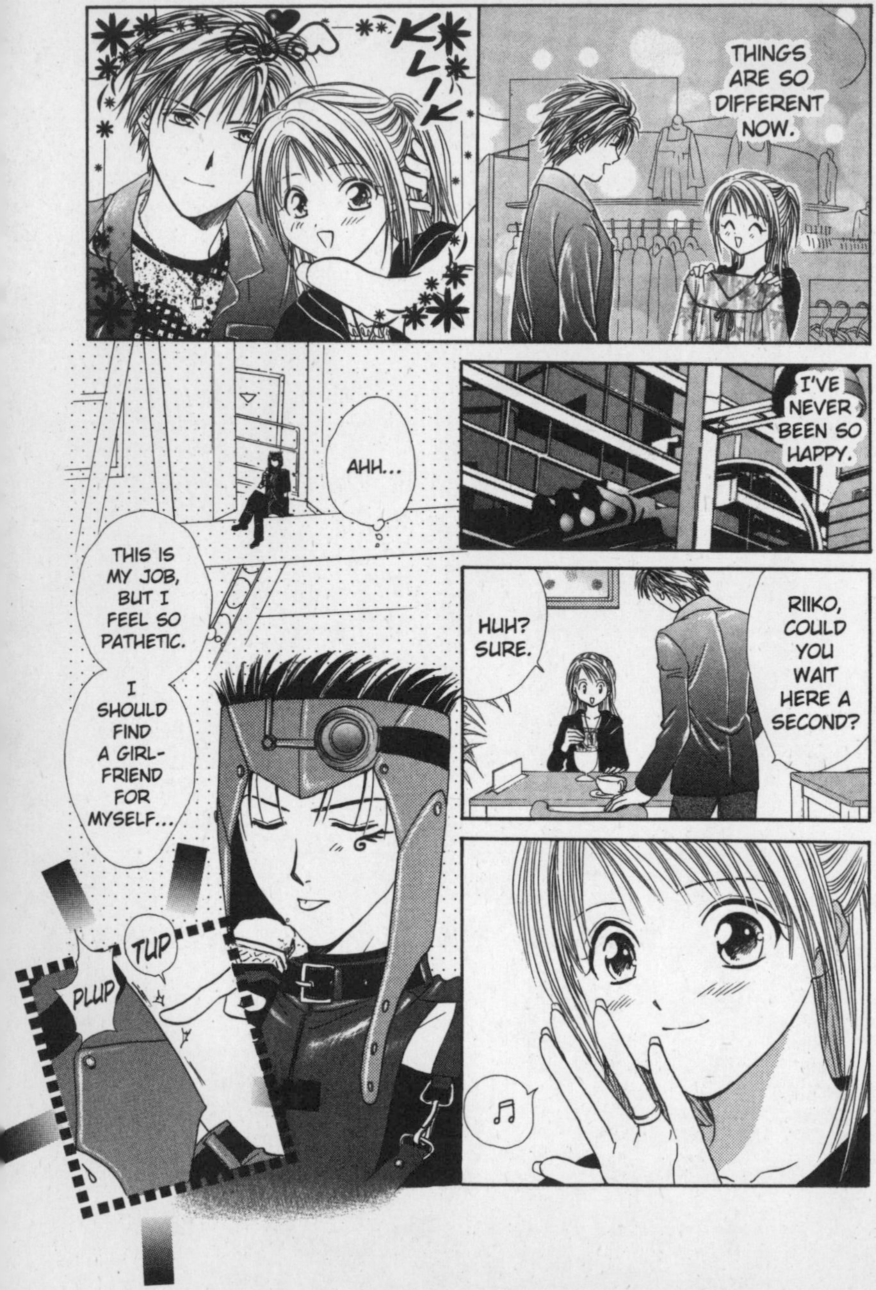
THINGS ARE SO DIFFERENT NOW.
I'VE NEVER BEEN SO HAPPY.
RIIKO, COULD YOU WAIT HERE A SECOND?
HUH? SURE.
♪
AHH...
THIS IS MY JOB, BUT I FEEL SO PATHETIC.
I SHOULD FIND A GIRL-FRIEND FOR MYSELF...
TUP
PLUP

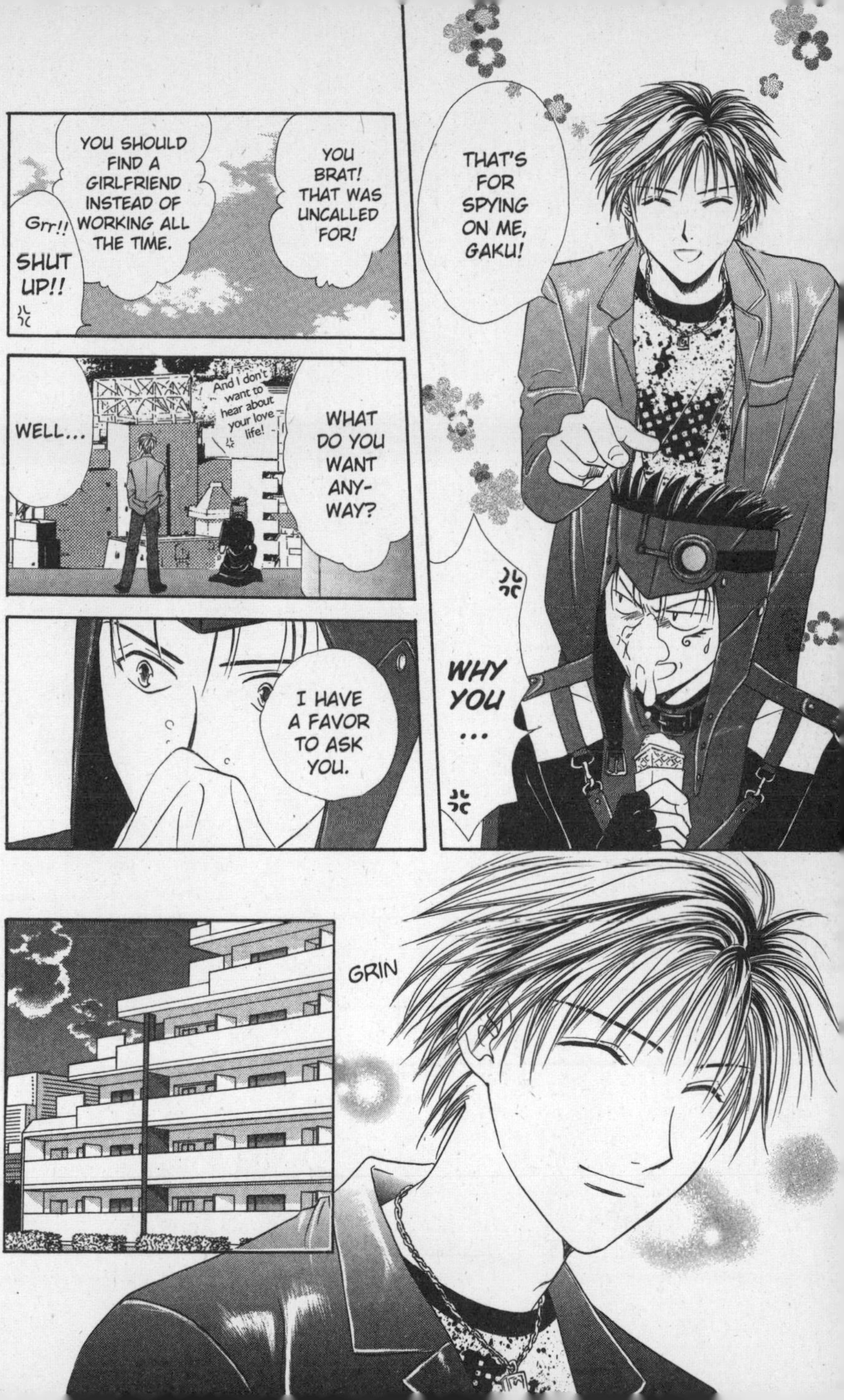
THAT'S FOR SPYING ON ME, GAKU!
WHY YOU ...
YOU BRAT! THAT WAS UNCALLED FOR!
YOU SHOULD FIND A GIRLFRIEND INSTEAD OF WORKING ALL THE TIME.
Grr!!
SHUT UP!!
WHAT DO YOU WANT ANY-WAY?
And I don't want to hear about your love life!
WELL...
I HAVE A FAVOR TO ASK YOU.
GRIN

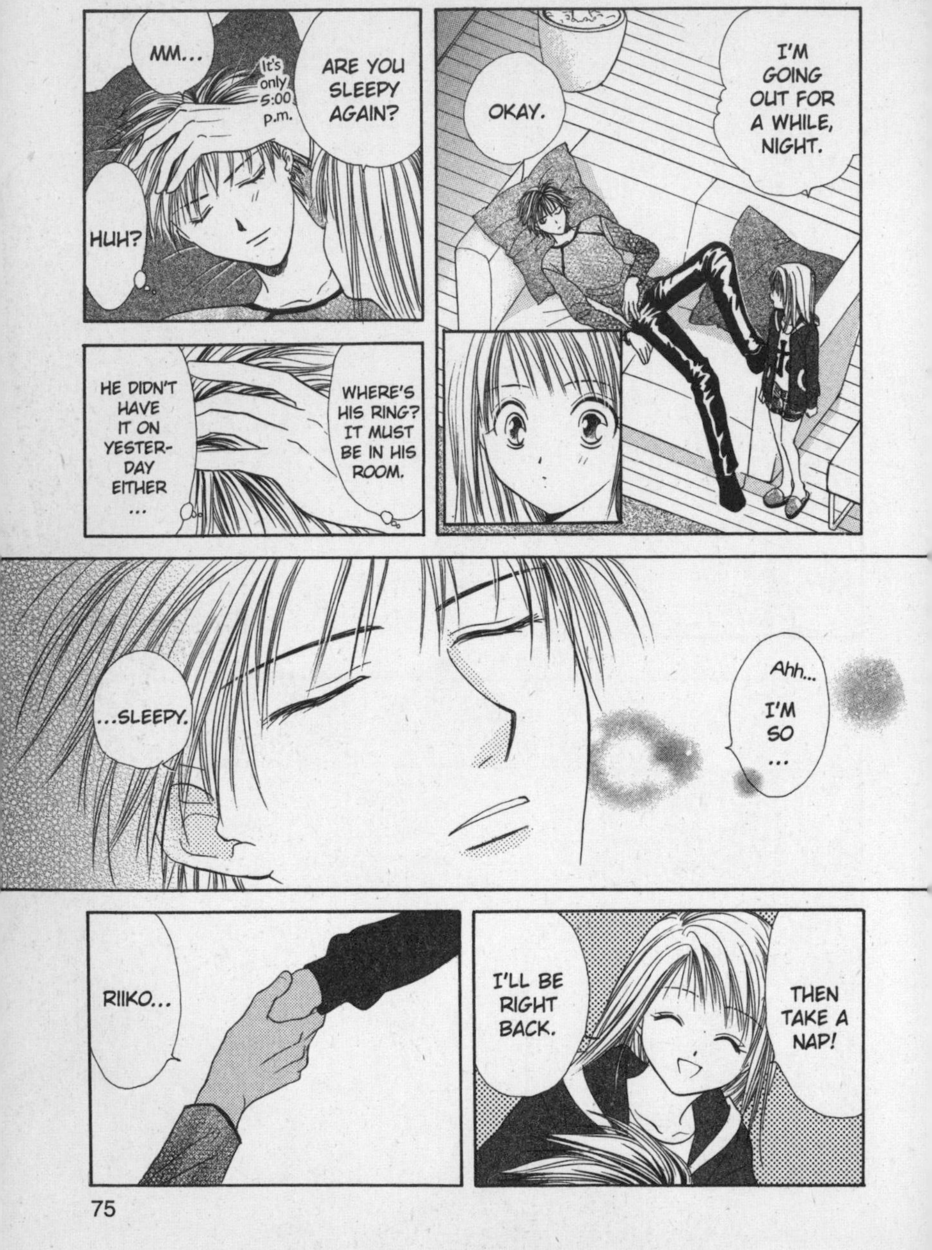
I'M GOING OUT FOR A WHILE, NIGHT.
OKAY.
ARE YOU SLEEPY AGAIN?
It's only 5:00 p.m.
MM...
HUH?
WHERE'S HIS RING? IT MUST BE IN HIS ROOM.
HE DIDN'T HAVE IT ON YESTERDAY EITHER...
Ahh... I'M SO...
...SLEEPY.
THEN TAKE A NAP!
I'LL BE RIGHT BACK.
RIIKO...

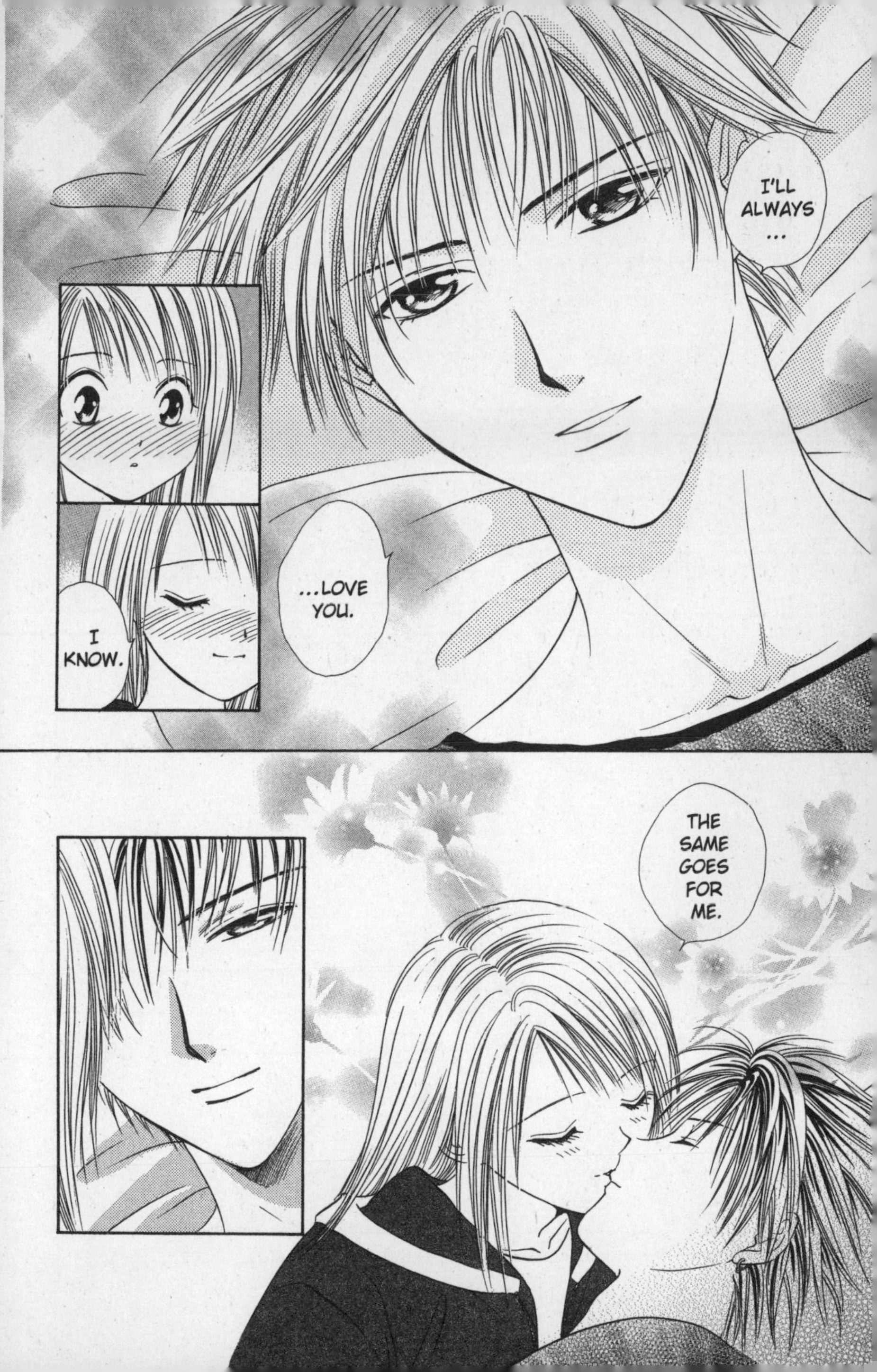
I'LL ALWAYS ...
...LOVE YOU.
I KNOW.
THE SAME GOES FOR ME.

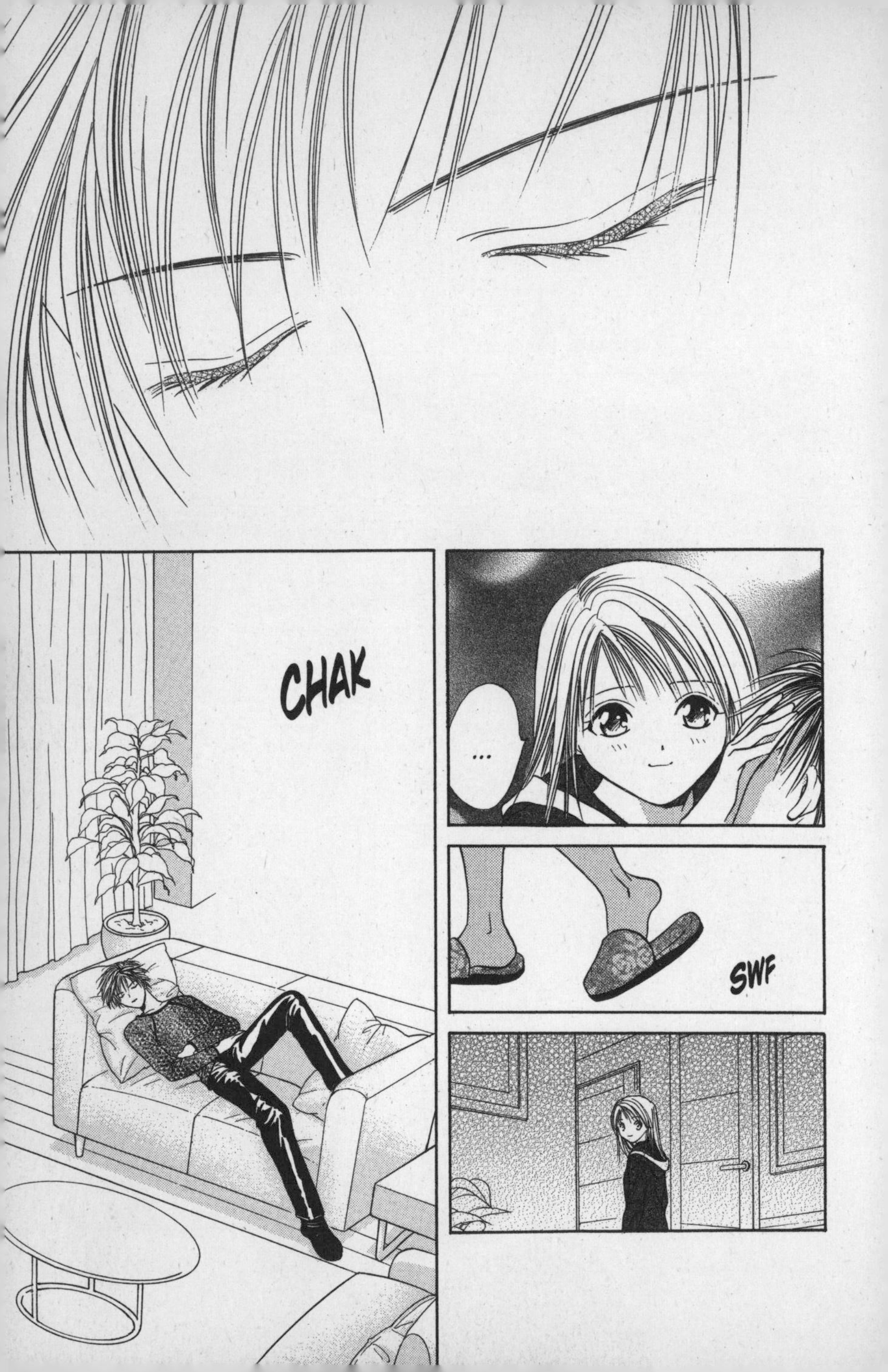
...
SWF
CHAK

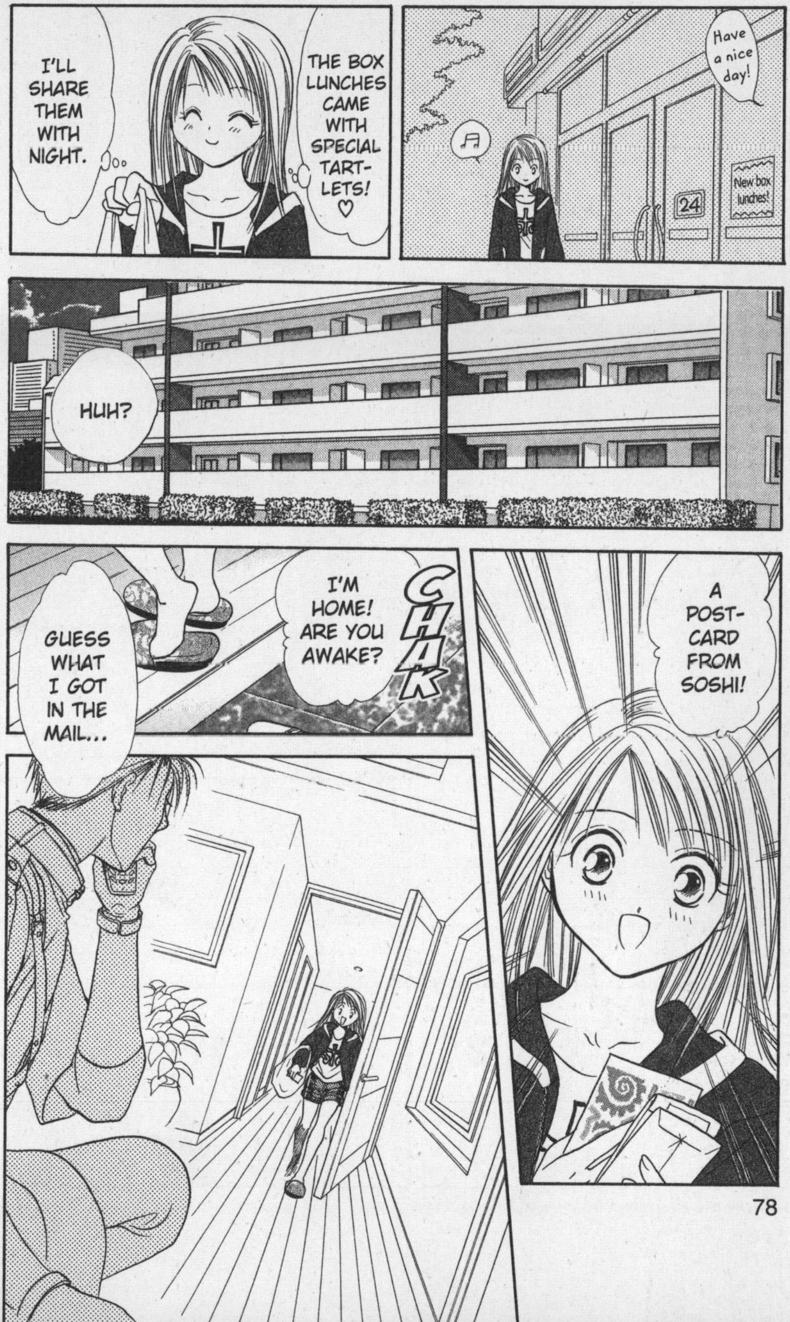
Have a nice day!
New box lunches!
24
THE BOX LUNCHES CAME WITH SPECIAL TART-LETS! ♡
I'LL SHARE THEM WITH NIGHT.
HUH?
A POST-CARD FROM SOSHI!
CHAK
I'M HOME! ARE YOU AWAKE?
GUESS WHAT I GOT IN THE MAIL...

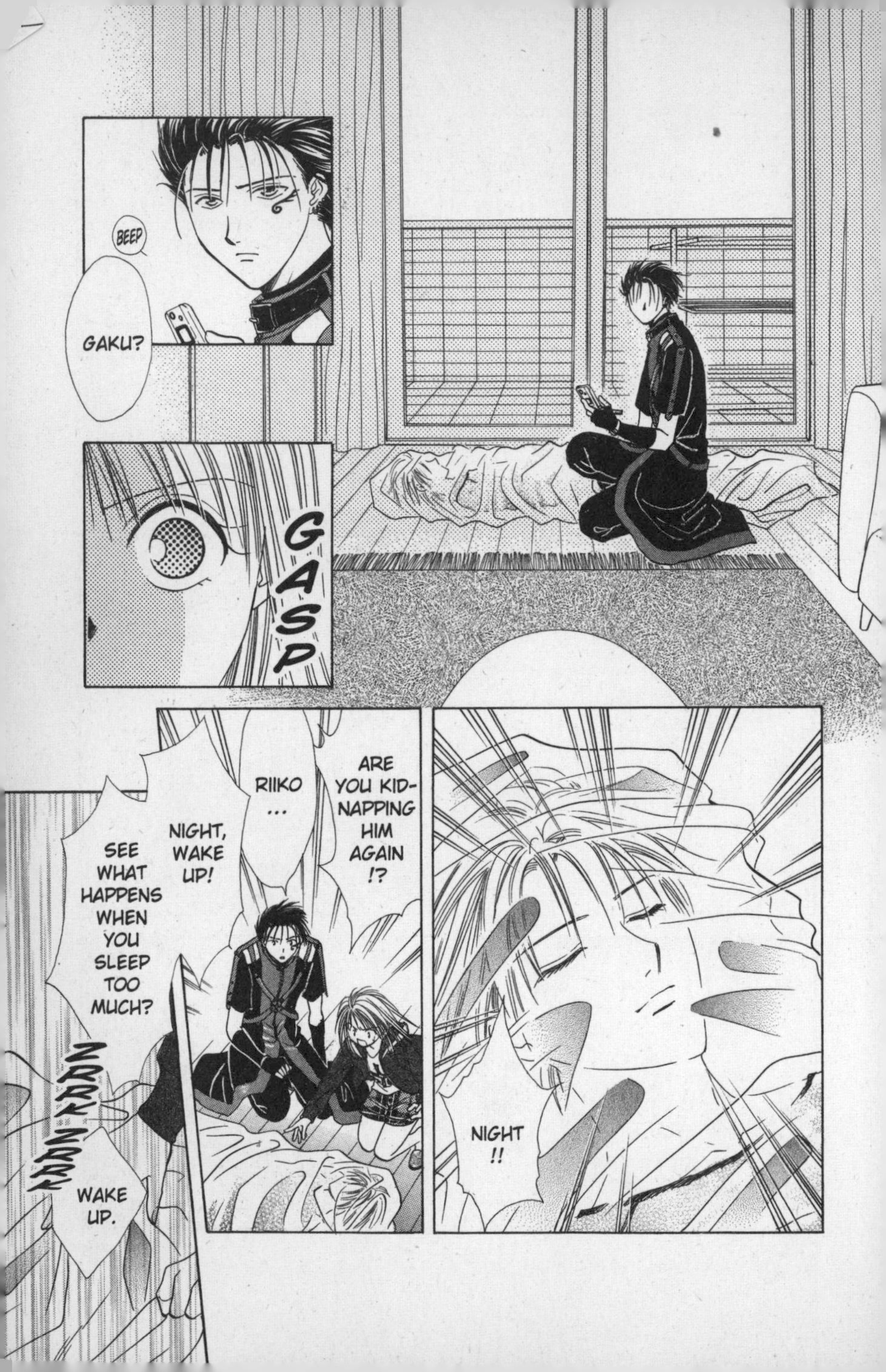
BEEP
GAKU?
GASP
NIGHT!!
ARE YOU KID-NAPPING HIM AGAIN!?
RIIKO...
NIGHT, WAKE UP!
SEE WHAT HAPPENS WHEN YOU SLEEP TOO MUCH?
WAKE UP.

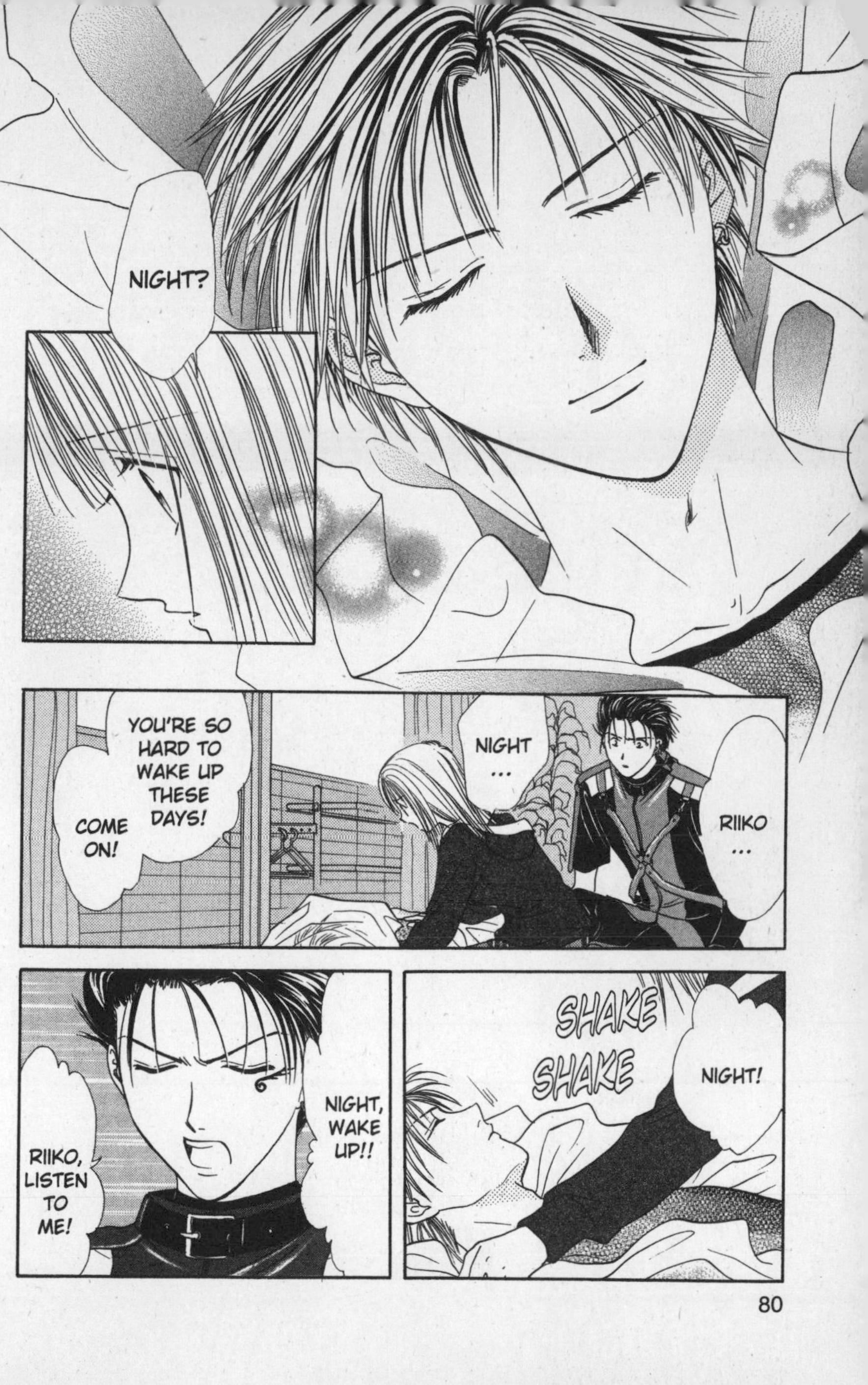
NIGHT?
RIIKO ...
NIGHT ...
YOU'RE SO HARD TO WAKE UP THESE DAYS!
COME ON!
NIGHT!
SHAKE SHAKE
NIGHT, WAKE UP!!
RIIKO, LISTEN TO ME!

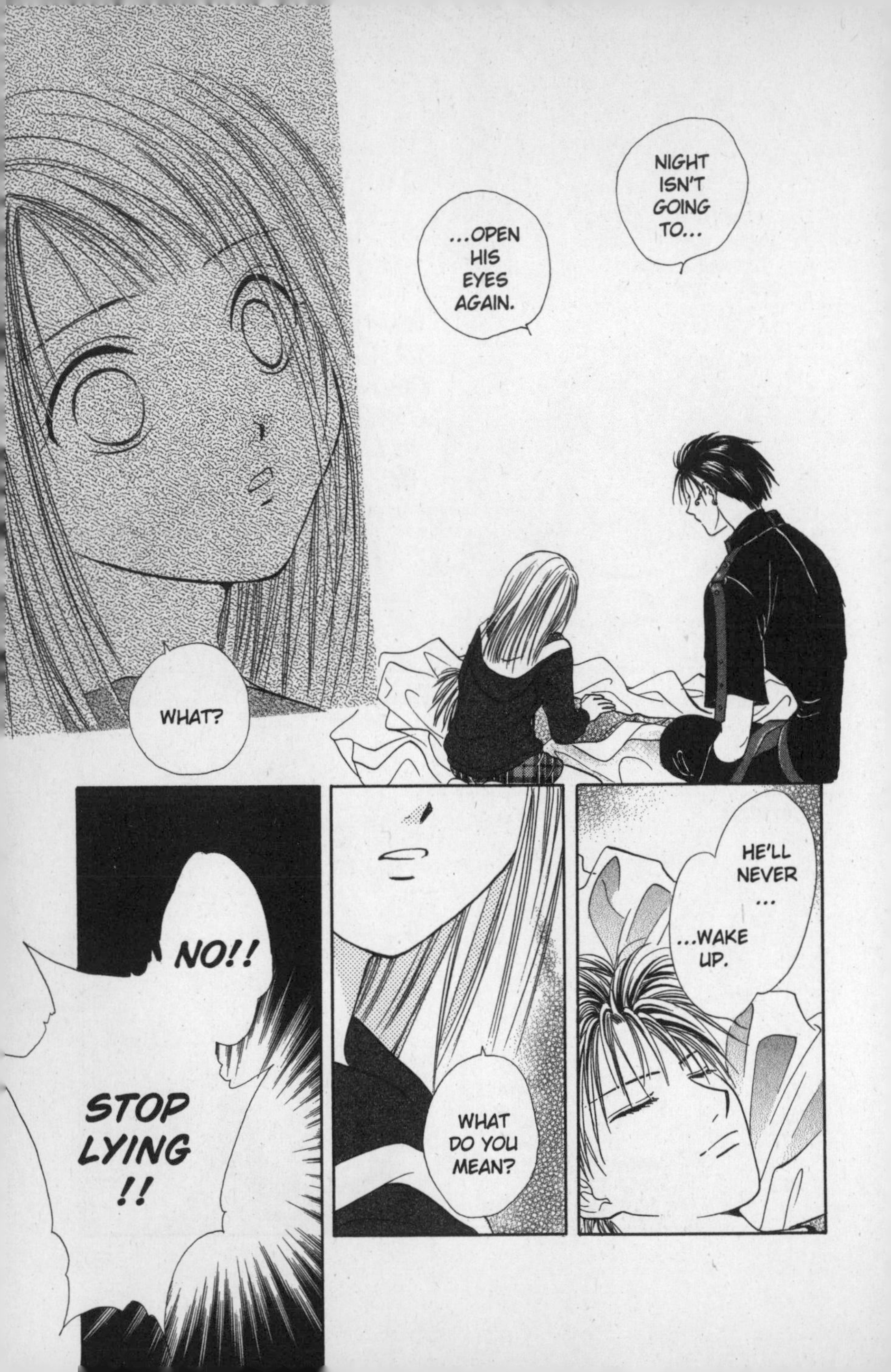
NIGHT ISN'T GOING TO...
...OPEN HIS EYES AGAIN.
WHAT?
HE'LL NEVER ...
...WAKE UP.
WHAT DO YOU MEAN?
NO!!
STOP LYING !!

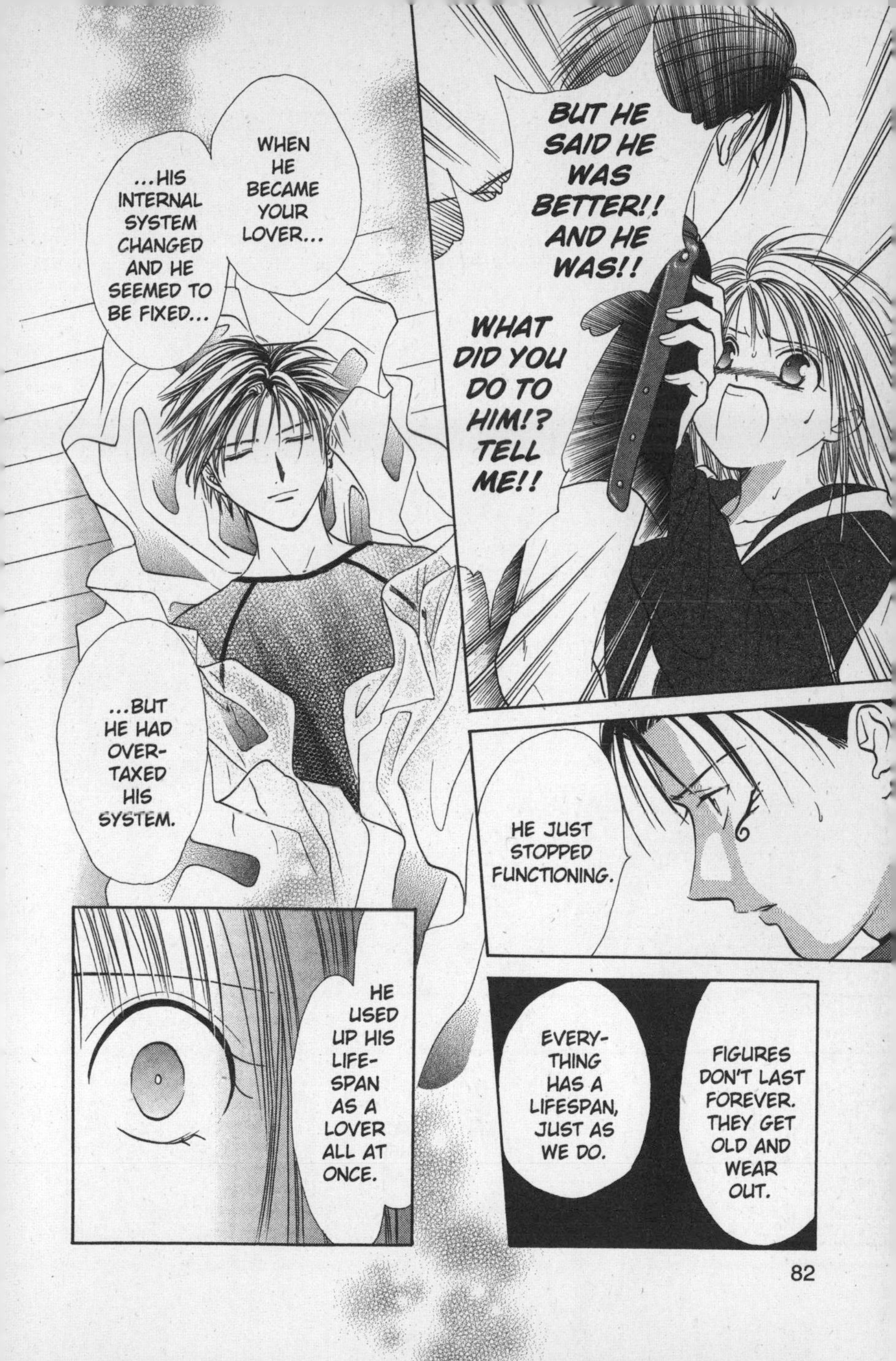
BUT HE SAID HE WAS BETTER!! AND HE WAS!!
WHAT DID YOU DO TO HIM!? TELL ME!!
HE JUST STOPPED FUNCTIONING.
WHEN HE BECAME YOUR LOVER...
...HIS INTERNAL SYSTEM CHANGED AND HE SEEMED TO BE FIXED...
...BUT HE HAD OVER-TAXED HIS SYSTEM.
FIGURES DON'T LAST FOREVER. THEY GET OLD AND WEAR OUT.
EVERY-THING HAS A LIFESPAN, JUST AS WE DO.
HE USED UP HIS LIFE-SPAN AS A LOVER ALL AT ONCE.

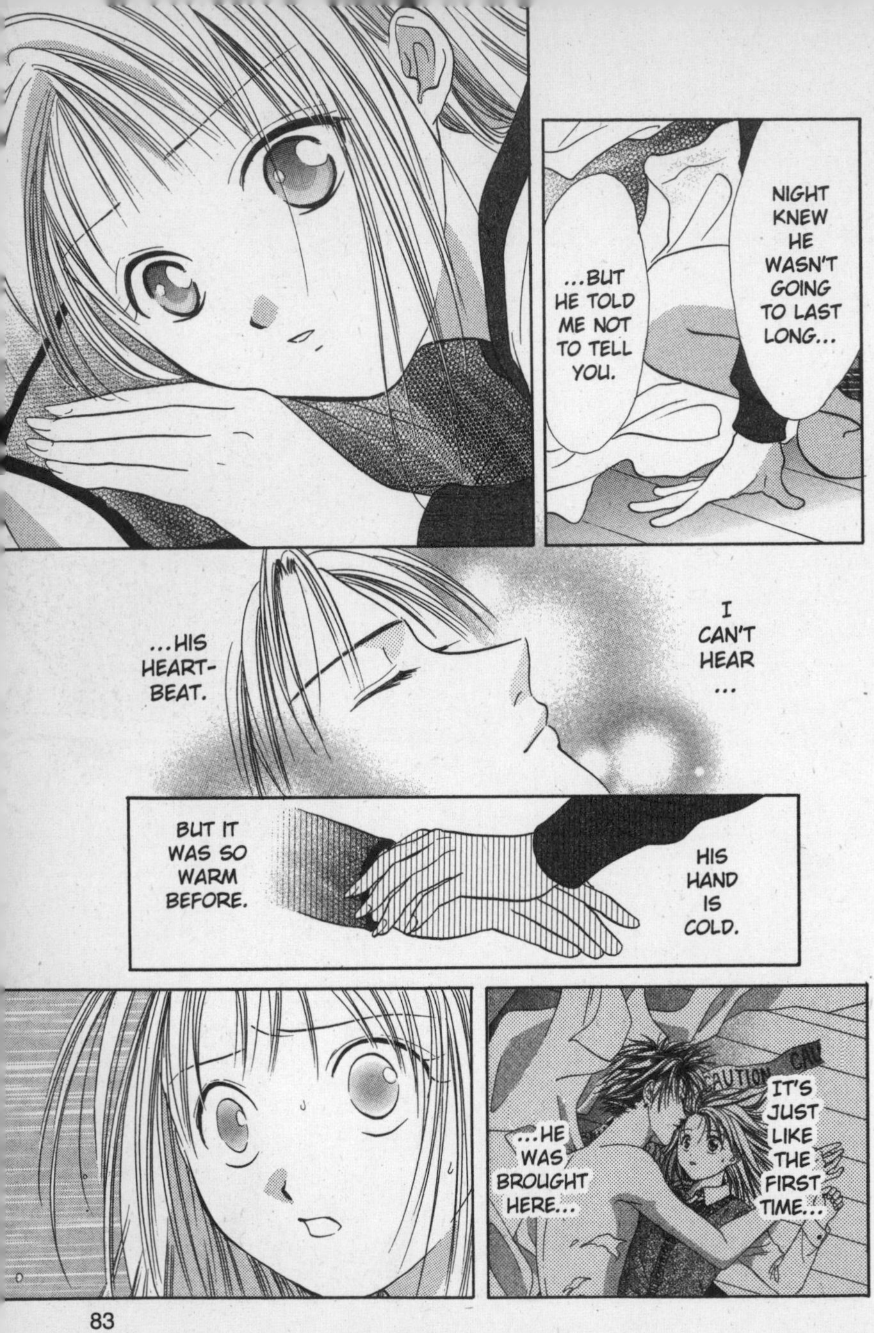
NIGHT KNEW HE WASN'T GOING TO LAST LONG...
...BUT HE TOLD ME NOT TO TELL YOU.
I CAN'T HEAR ...
...HIS HEART-BEAT.
HIS HAND IS COLD.
BUT IT WAS SO WARM BEFORE.
CAUTION
IT'S JUST LIKE THE FIRST TIME...
...HE WAS BROUGHT HERE...

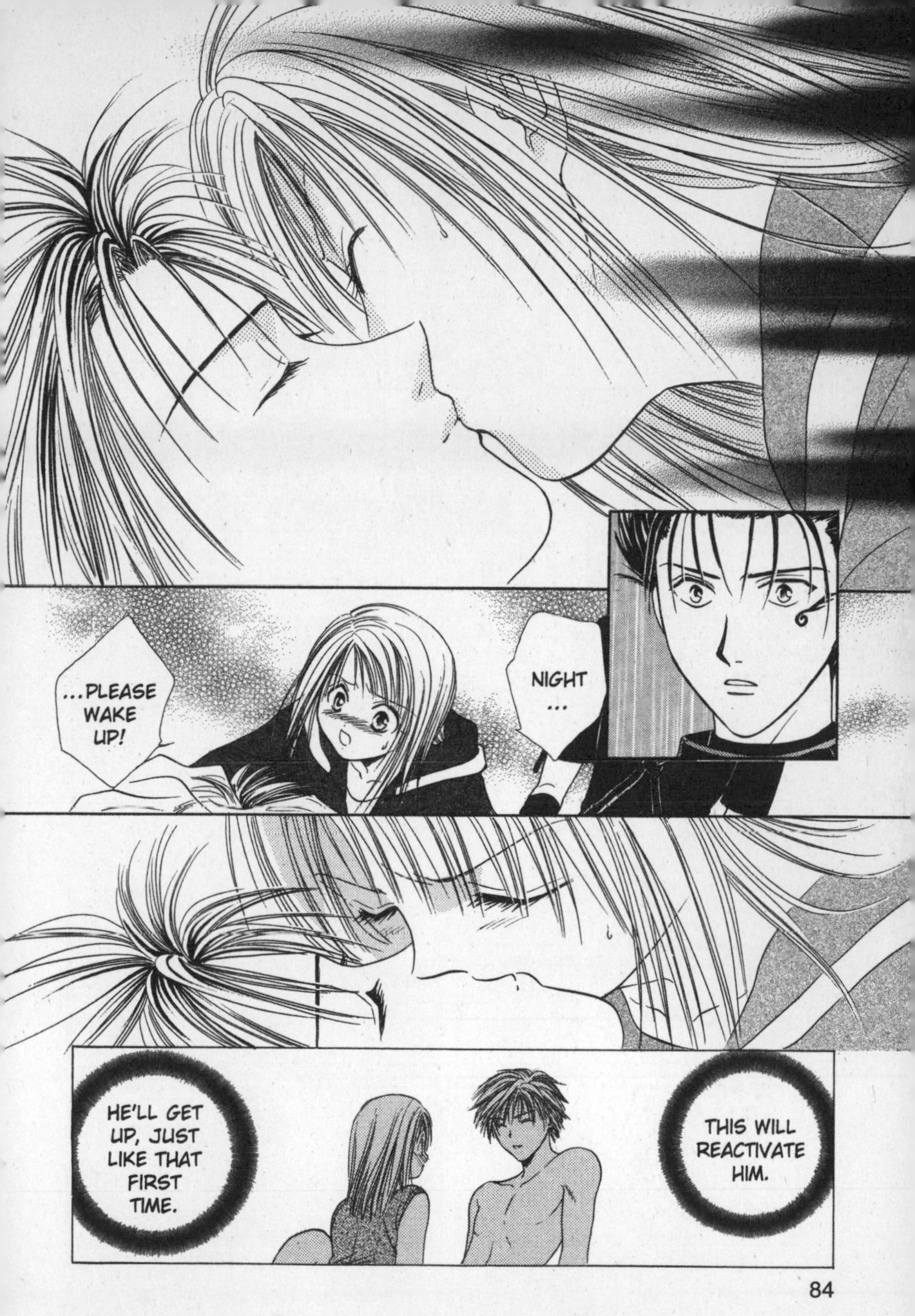
NIGHT...
...PLEASE WAKE UP!
THIS WILL REACTIVATE HIM.
HE'LL GET UP, JUST LIKE THAT FIRST TIME.

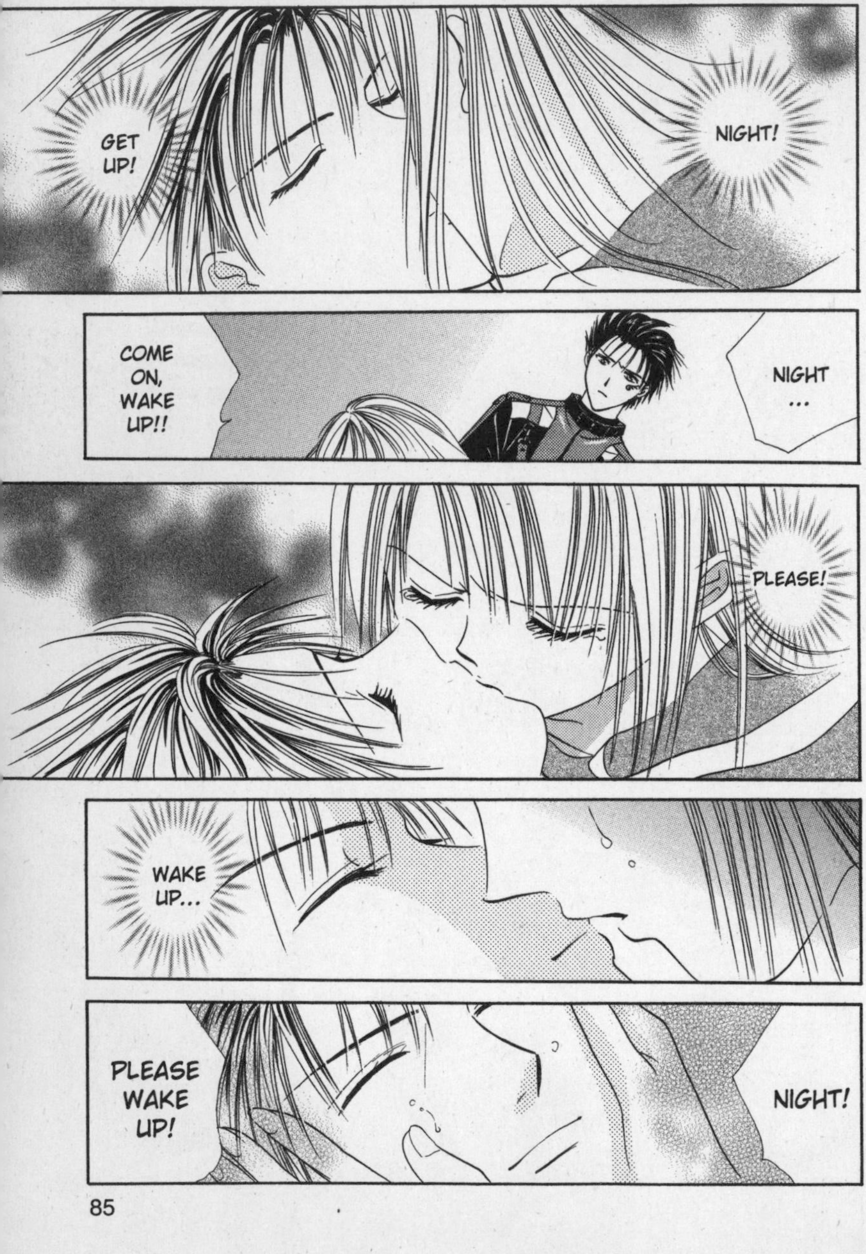
NIGHT!
GET UP!
NIGHT...
COME ON, WAKE UP!!
PLEASE!
WAKE UP...
NIGHT!
PLEASE WAKE UP!

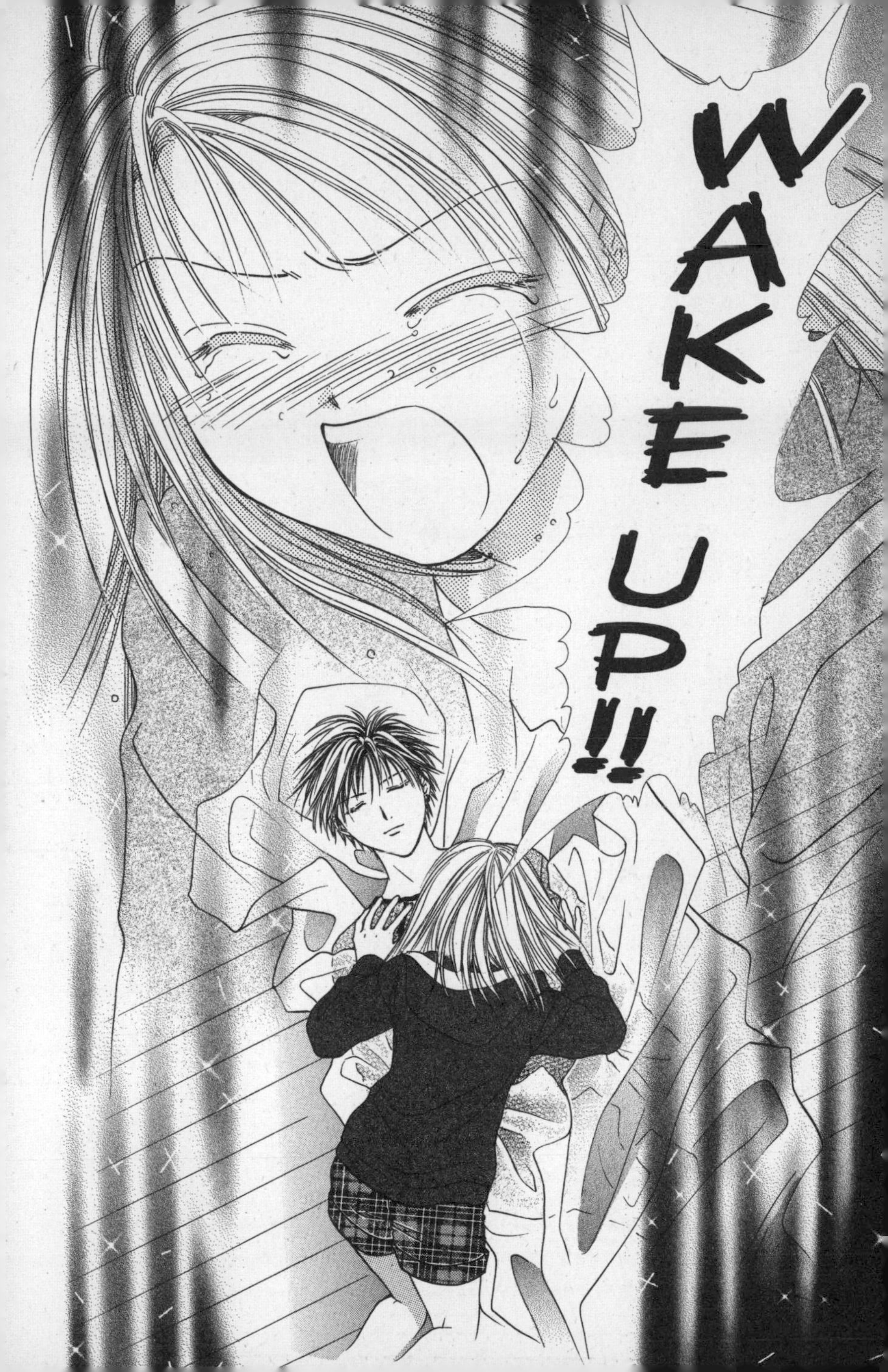
WAKE UP!!

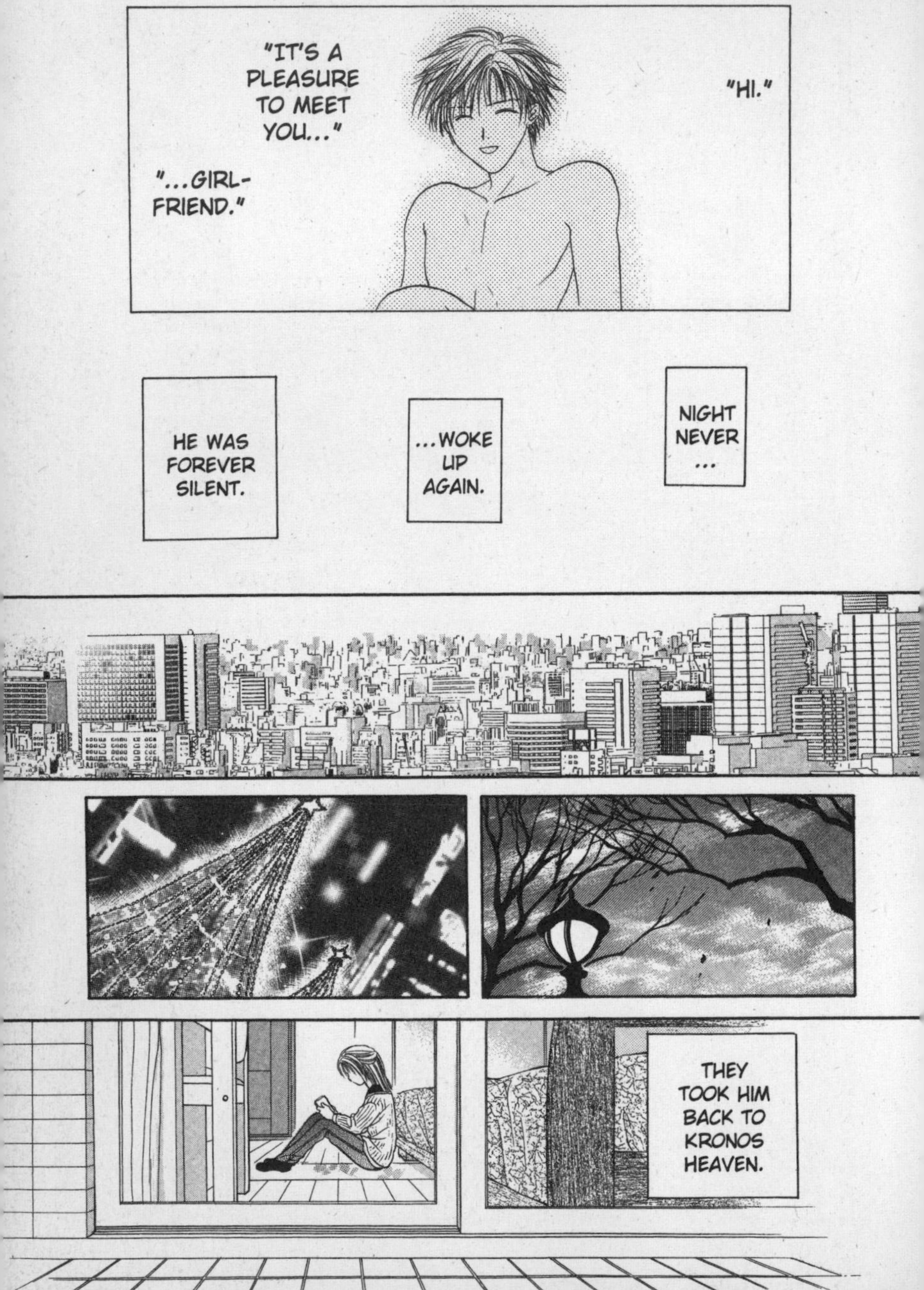
"HI."
"IT'S A PLEASURE TO MEET YOU..."
"...GIRL-FRIEND."
NIGHT NEVER ...
...WOKE UP AGAIN.
HE WAS FOREVER SILENT.
THEY TOOK HIM BACK TO KRONOS HEAVEN.

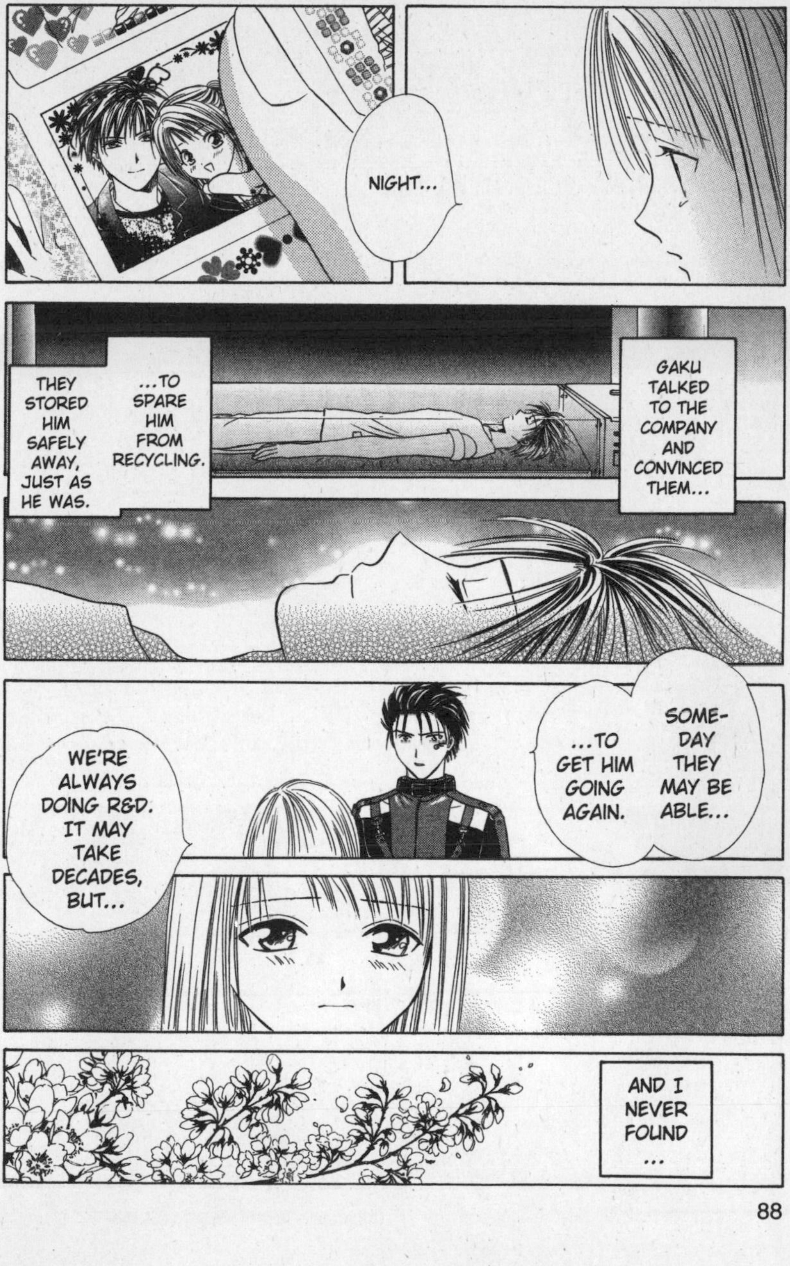

NIGHT...
GAKU TALKED TO THE COMPANY AND CONVINCED THEM...
...TO SPARE HIM FROM RECYCLING.
THEY STORED HIM SAFELY AWAY, JUST AS HE WAS.
SOME-DAY THEY MAY BE ABLE...
...TO GET HIM GOING AGAIN.
WE'RE ALWAYS DOING R&D. IT MAY TAKE DECADES, BUT...
AND I NEVER FOUND ...

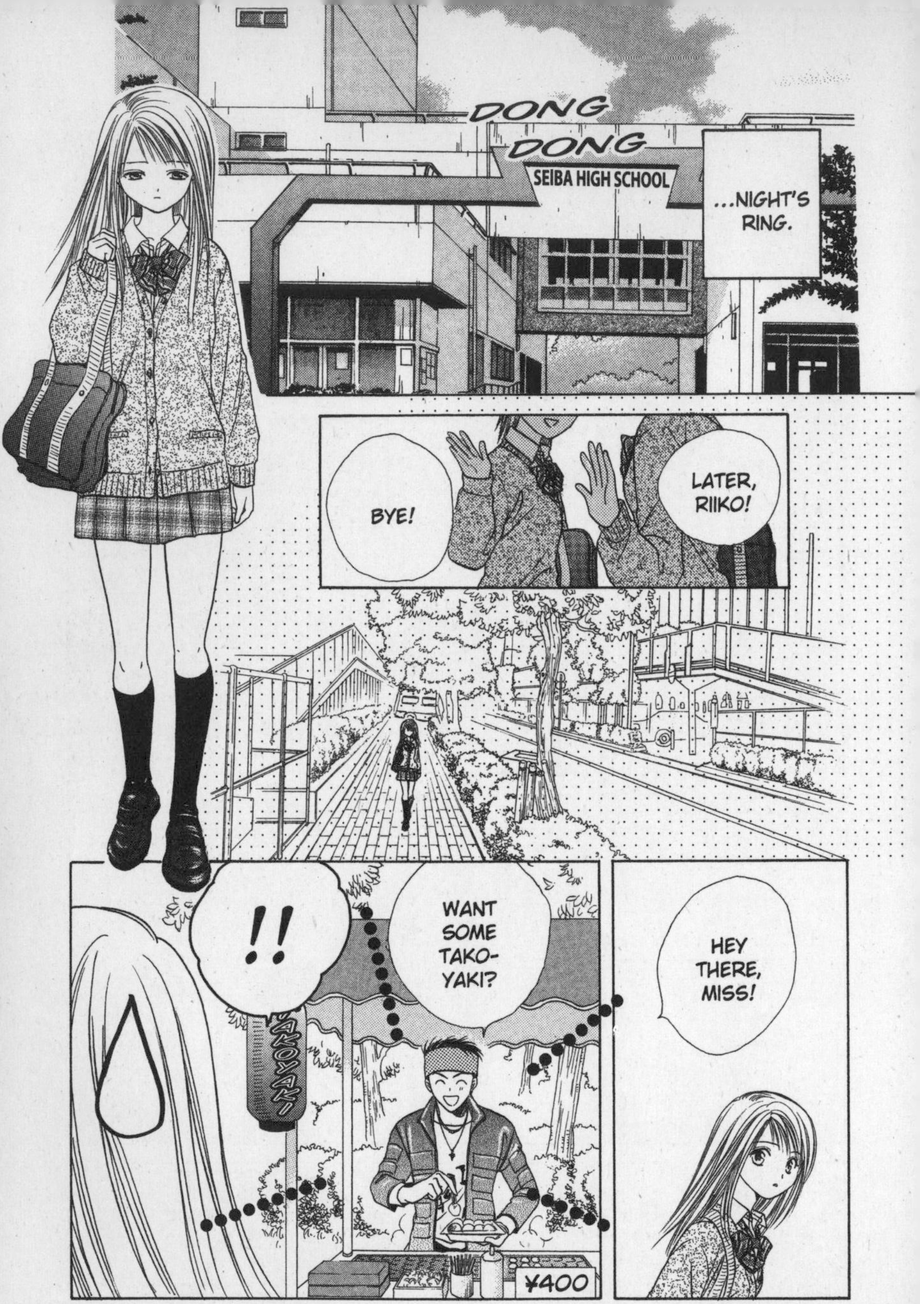
...NIGHT'S RING.
DONG DONG
SEIBA HIGH SCHOOL
LATER, RIIKO!
BYE!
HEY THERE, MISS!
WANT SOME TAKO-YAKI?
TAKOYAKI
¥400
!!

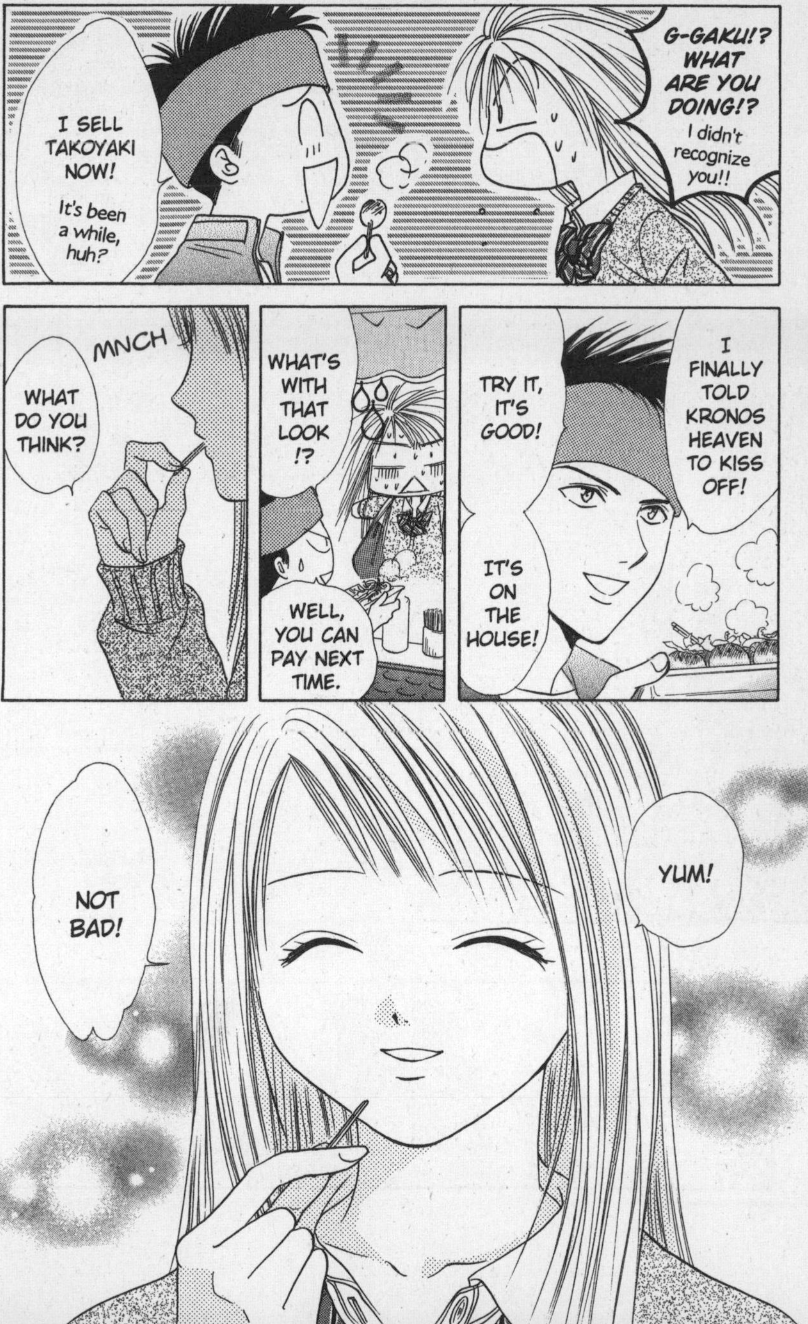
G-GAKU!? WHAT ARE YOU DOING!? I didn't recognize you!!
I SELL TAKOYAKI NOW! It's been a while, huh?
I FINALLY TOLD KRONOS HEAVEN TO KISS OFF!
TRY IT, IT'S GOOD!
IT'S ON THE HOUSE!
WHAT'S WITH THAT LOOK!?
WELL, YOU CAN PAY NEXT TIME.
MNCH
WHAT DO YOU THINK?
YUM!
NOT BAD!

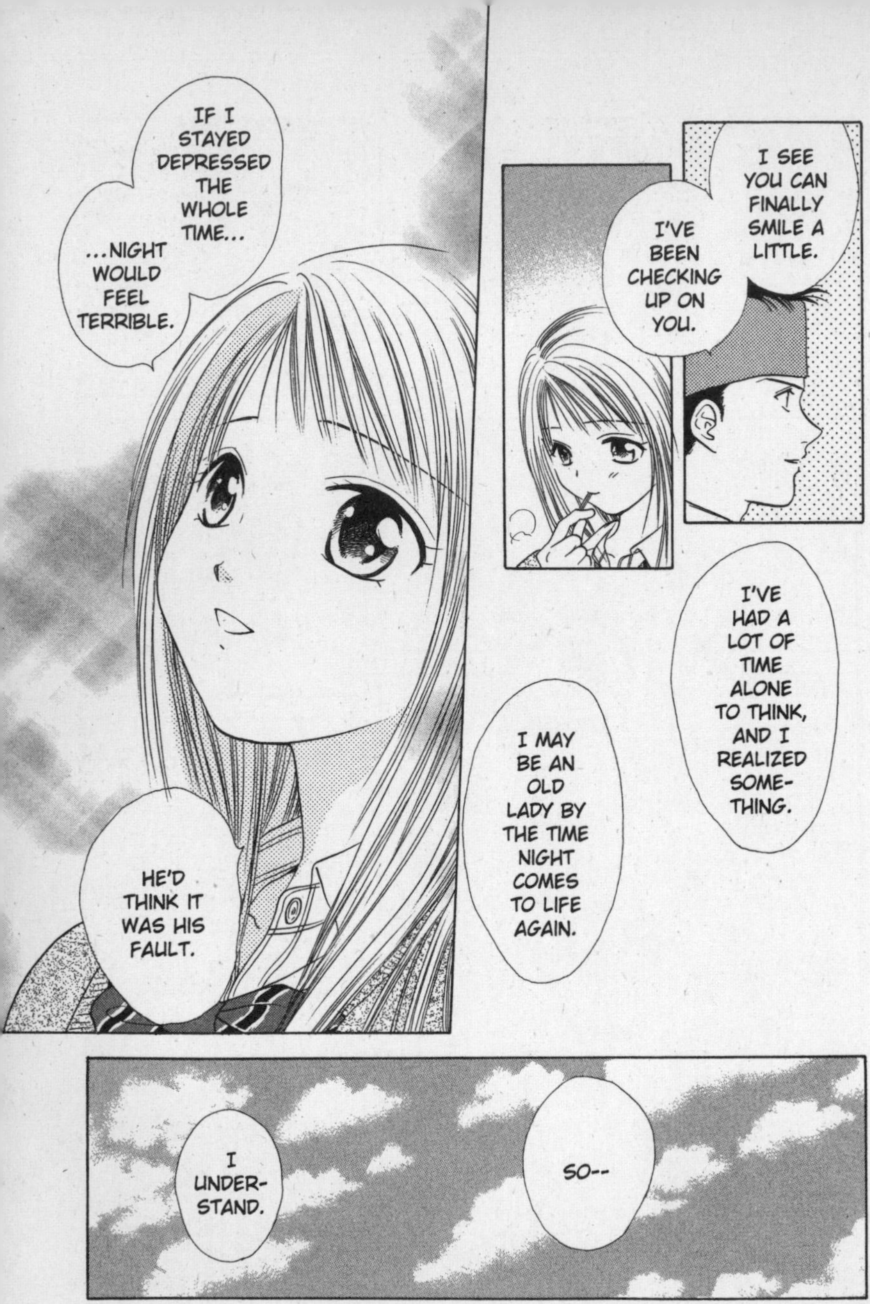
I SEE YOU CAN FINALLY SMILE A LITTLE.
I'VE BEEN CHECKING UP ON YOU.
I'VE HAD A LOT OF TIME ALONE TO THINK, AND I REALIZED SOME-THING.
I MAY BE AN OLD LADY BY THE TIME NIGHT COMES TO LIFE AGAIN.
IF I STAYED DEPRESSED THE WHOLE TIME...
...NIGHT WOULD FEEL TERRIBLE.
HE'D THINK IT WAS HIS FAULT.
SO--
I UNDER-STAND.

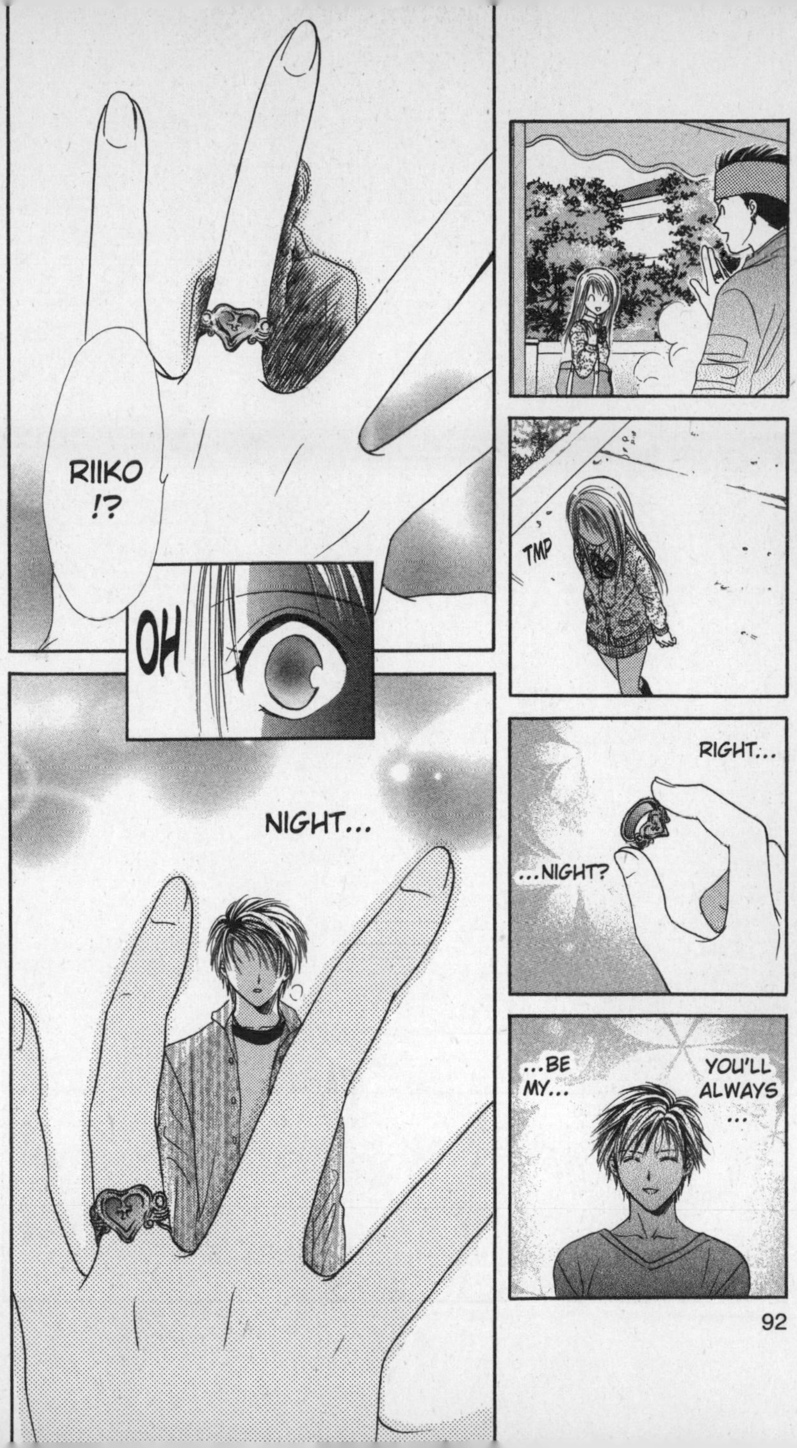
TMP
RIGHT...
...NIGHT?
YOU'LL ALWAYS ...
...BE MY...
RIIKO !?
OH
NIGHT...

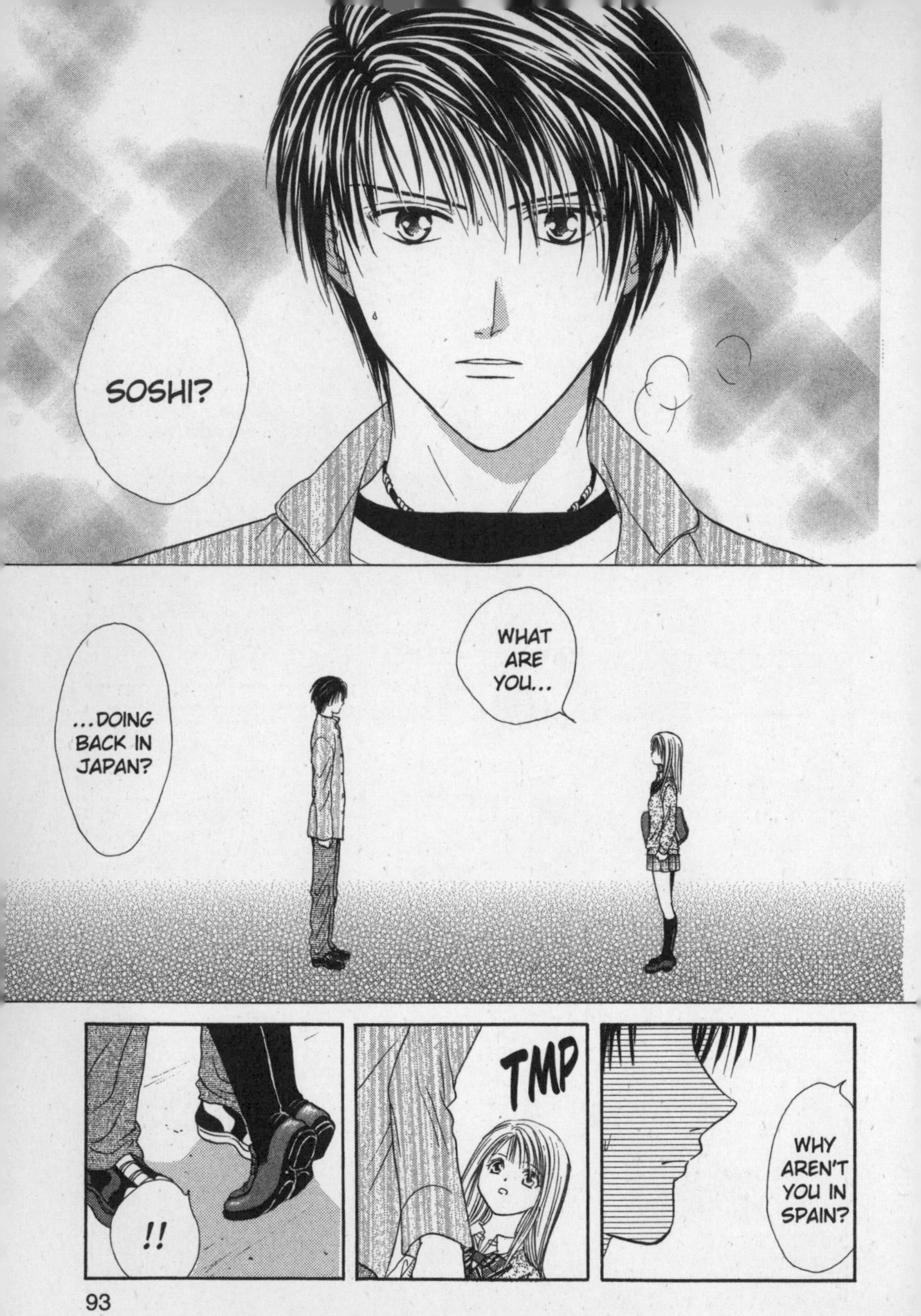
SOSHI?
WHAT ARE YOU...
...DOING BACK IN JAPAN?
WHY AREN'T YOU IN SPAIN?
TMP
!!

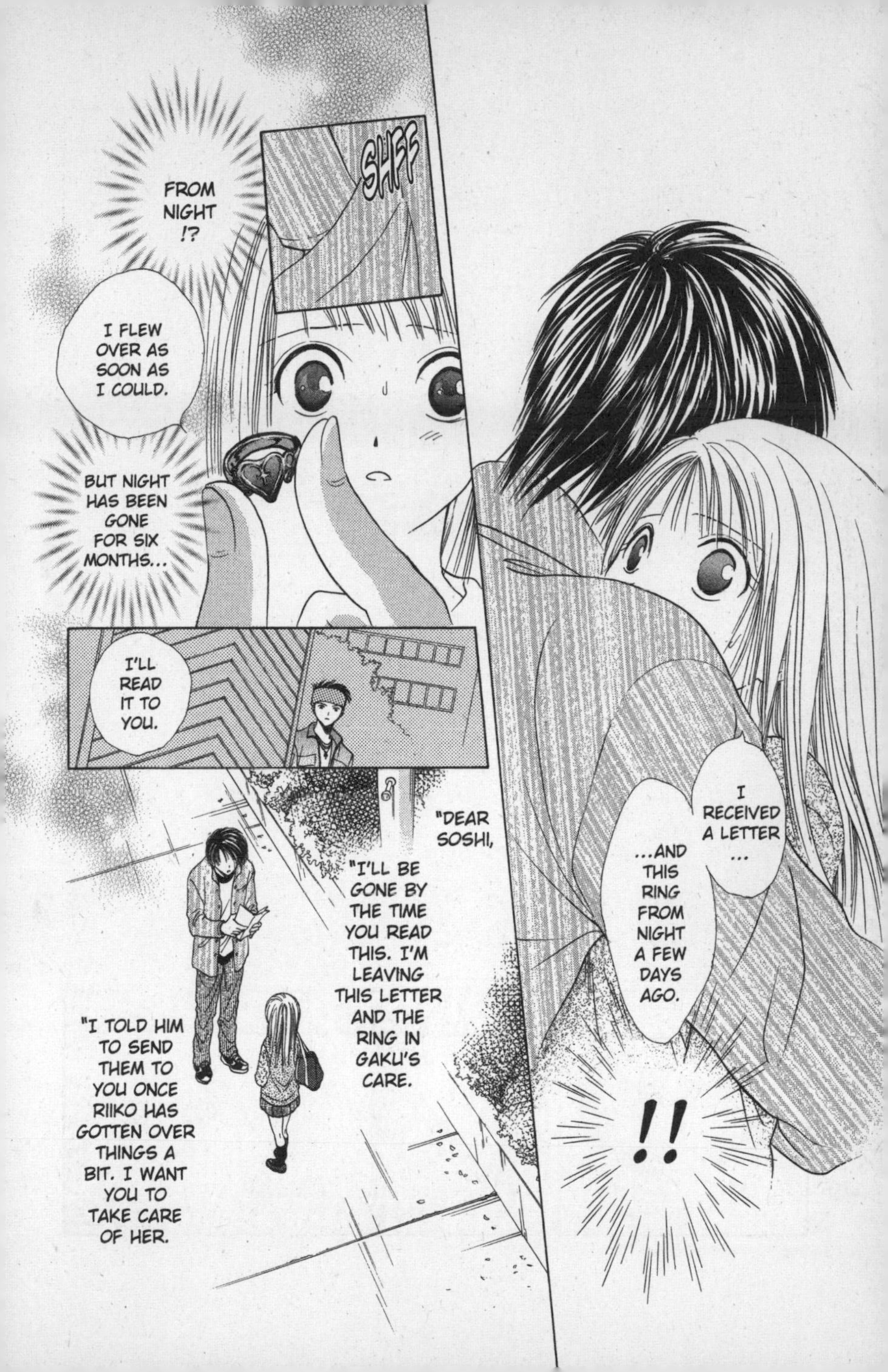
I RECEIVED A LETTER ...
...AND THIS RING FROM NIGHT A FEW DAYS AGO.
!!
SHFF
FROM NIGHT !?
I FLEW OVER AS SOON AS I COULD.
BUT NIGHT HAS BEEN GONE FOR SIX MONTHS...
I'LL READ IT TO YOU.
"DEAR SOSHI,
"I'LL BE GONE BY THE TIME YOU READ THIS. I'M LEAVING THIS LETTER AND THE RING IN GAKU'S CARE.
"I TOLD HIM TO SEND THEM TO YOU ONCE RIIKO HAS GOTTEN OVER THINGS A BIT. I WANT YOU TO TAKE CARE OF HER.

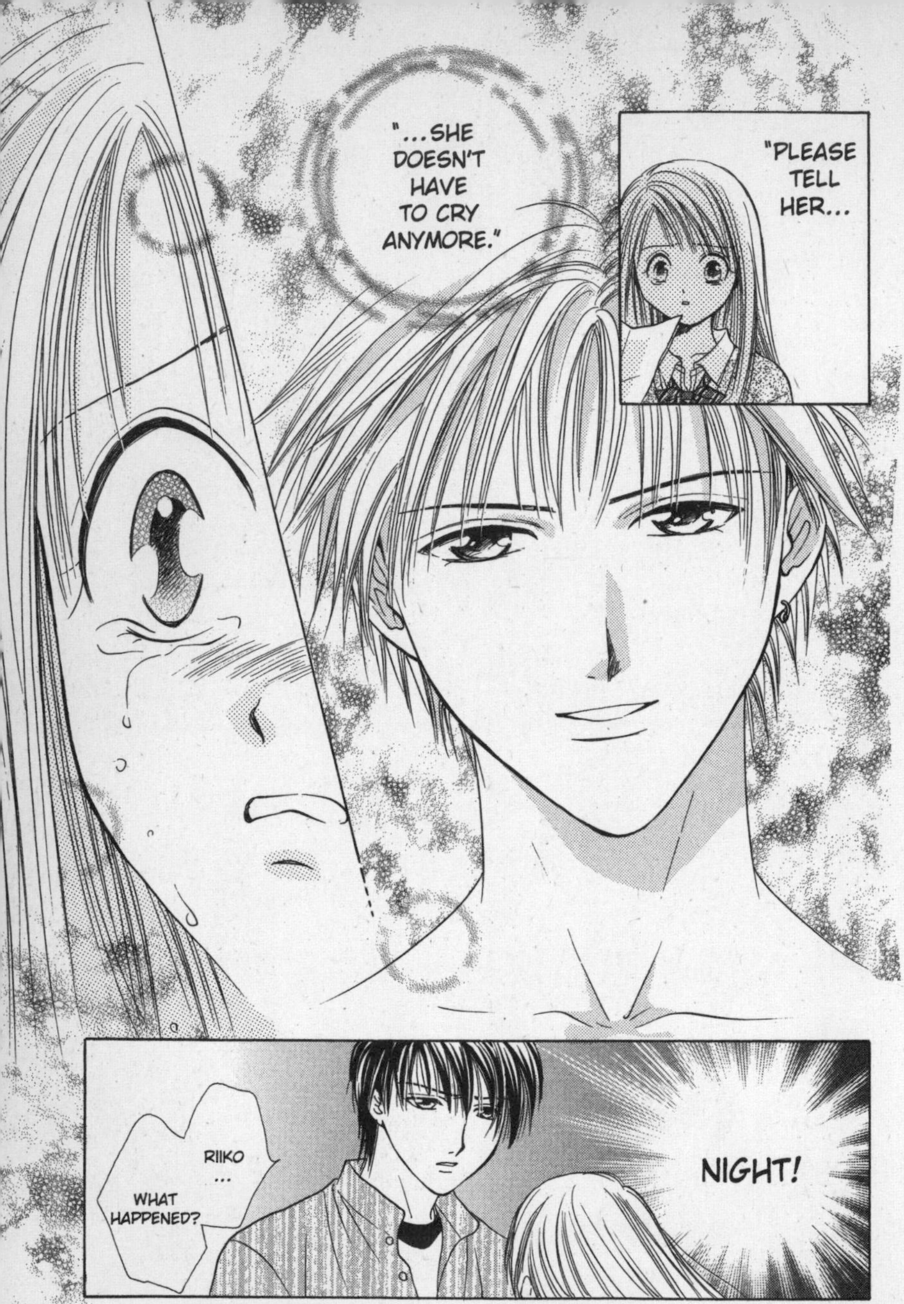
"PLEASE TELL HER...
"...SHE DOESN'T HAVE TO CRY ANYMORE."
NIGHT!
RIIKO ...
WHAT HAPPENED?

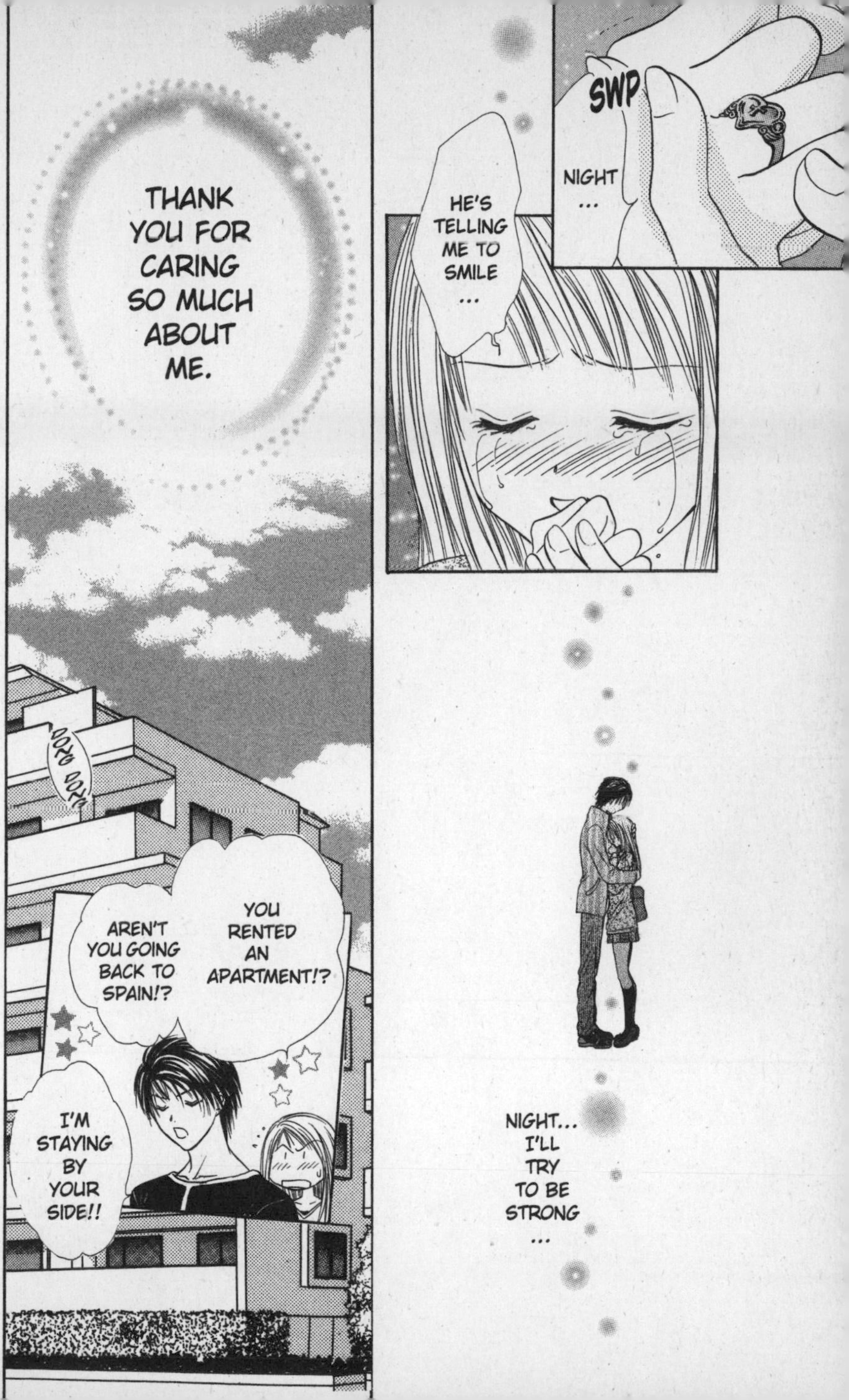
SWP
NIGHT ...
HE'S TELLING ME TO SMILE ...
NIGHT... I'LL TRY TO BE STRONG ...
THANK YOU FOR CARING SO MUCH ABOUT ME.
DONG DONG
YOU RENTED AN APARTMENT!?
AREN'T YOU GOING BACK TO SPAIN!?
I'M STAYING BY YOUR SIDE!!

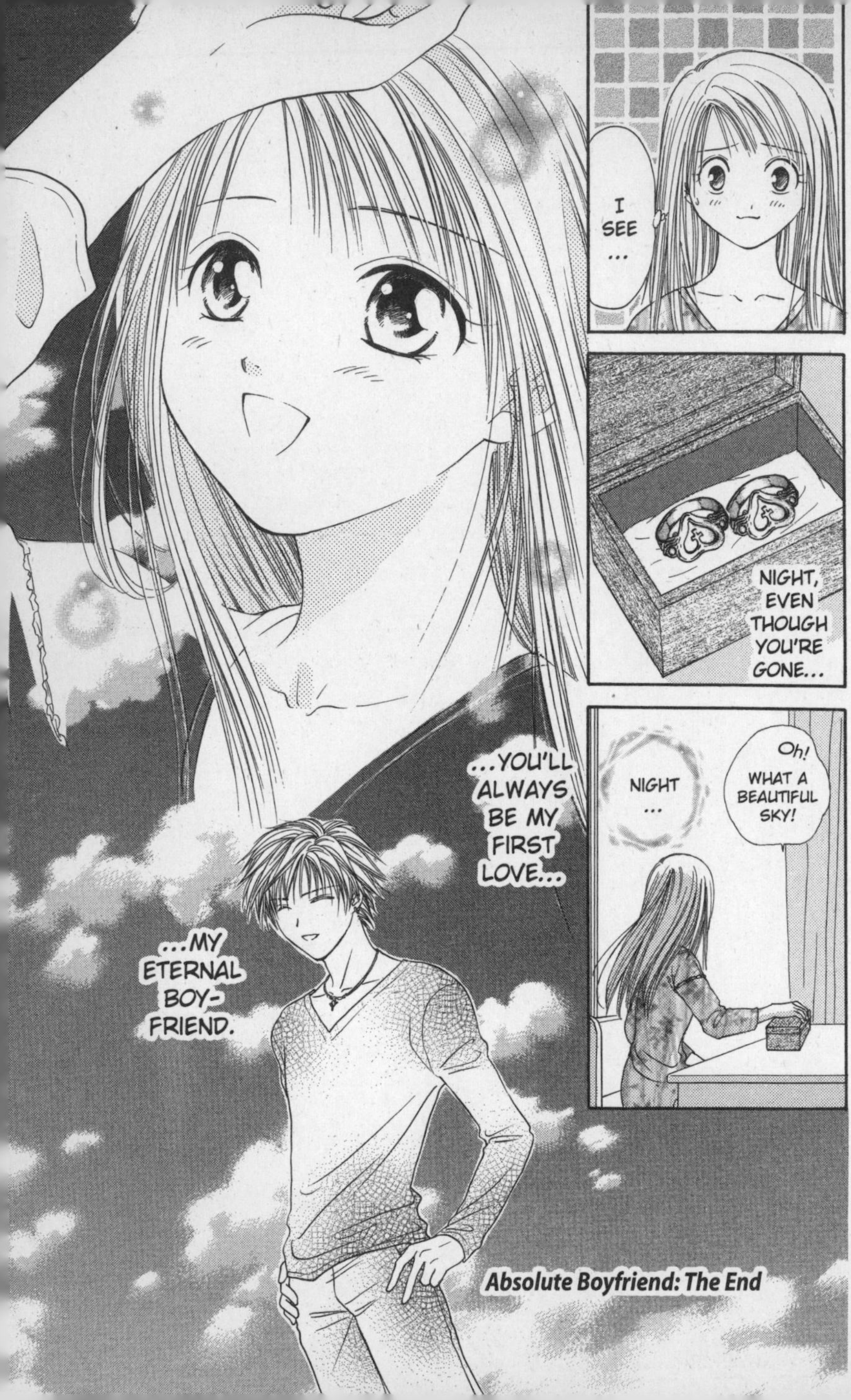
I SEE...
NIGHT, EVEN THOUGH YOU'RE GONE...
Oh! WHAT A BEAUTIFUL SKY!
NIGHT...
...YOU'LL ALWAYS BE MY FIRST LOVE...
...MY ETERNAL BOY-FRIEND.
Absolute Boyfriend: The End

Absolute Boyfriend

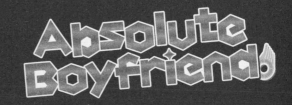

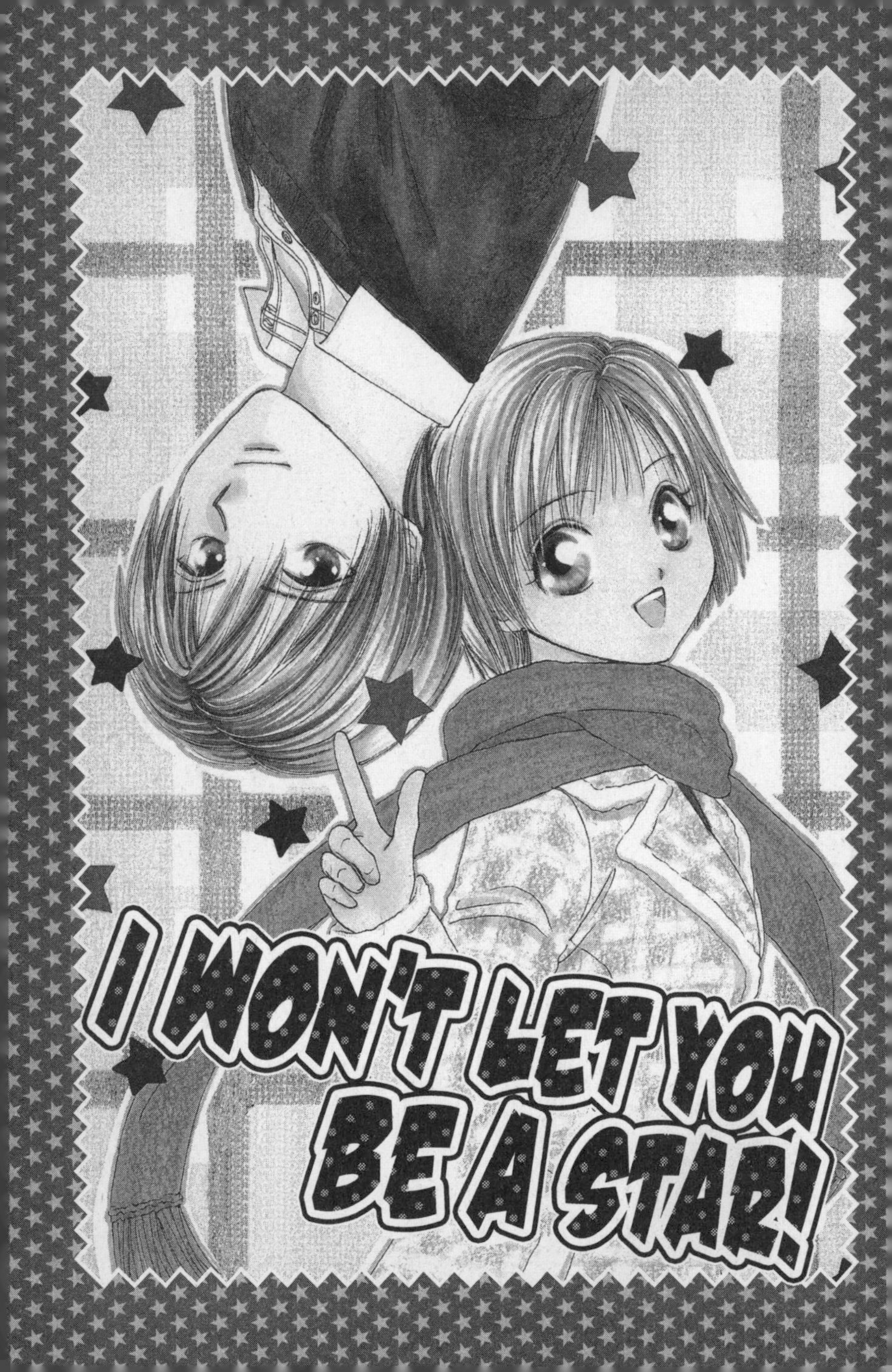
I WON'T LET YOU BE A STAR!

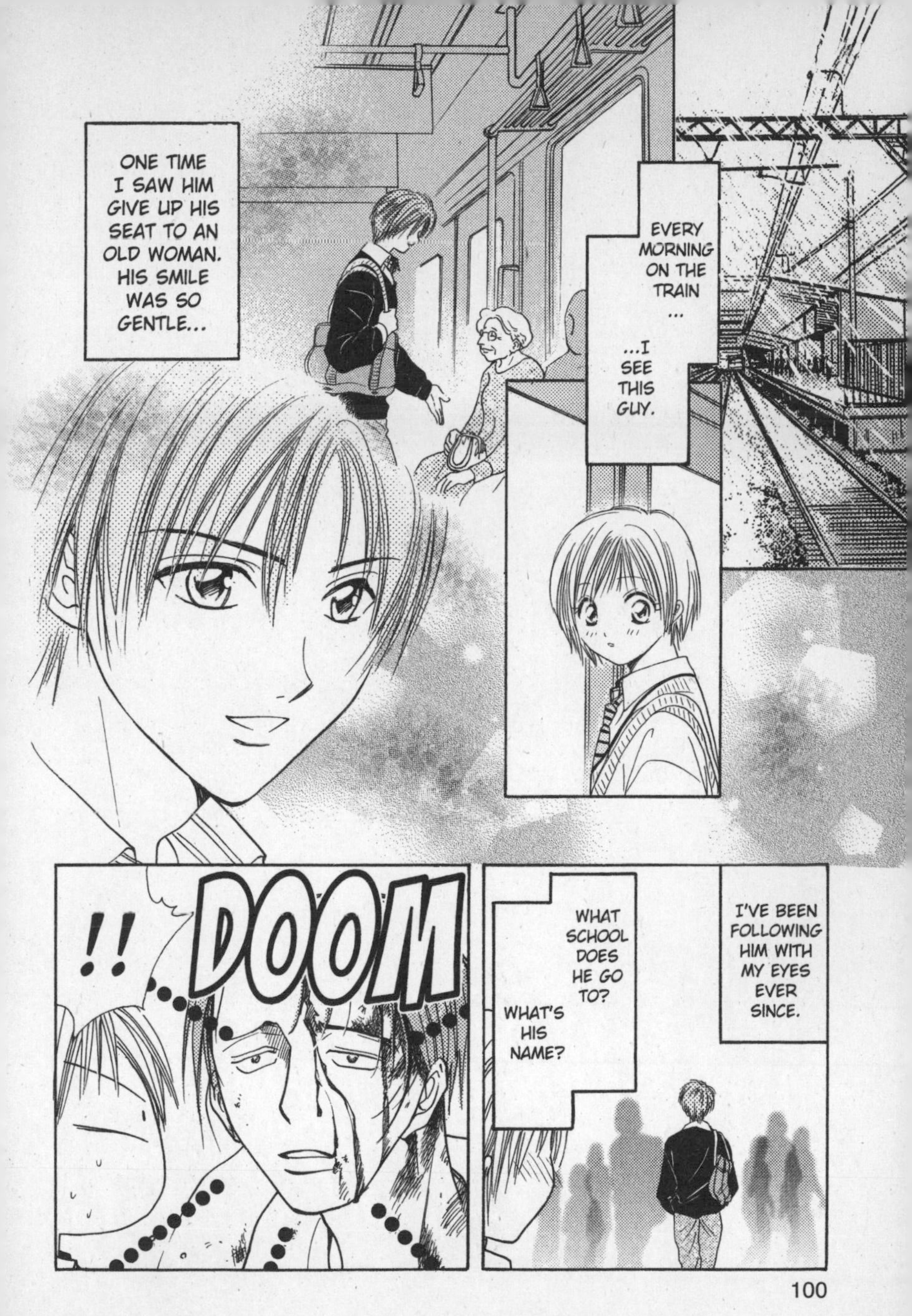
EVERY MORNING ON THE TRAIN ...
...I SEE THIS GUY.
ONE TIME I SAW HIM GIVE UP HIS SEAT TO AN OLD WOMAN. HIS SMILE WAS SO GENTLE...
I'VE BEEN FOLLOWING HIM WITH MY EYES EVER SINCE.
WHAT SCHOOL DOES HE GO TO?
WHAT'S HIS NAME?
DOOM
!!

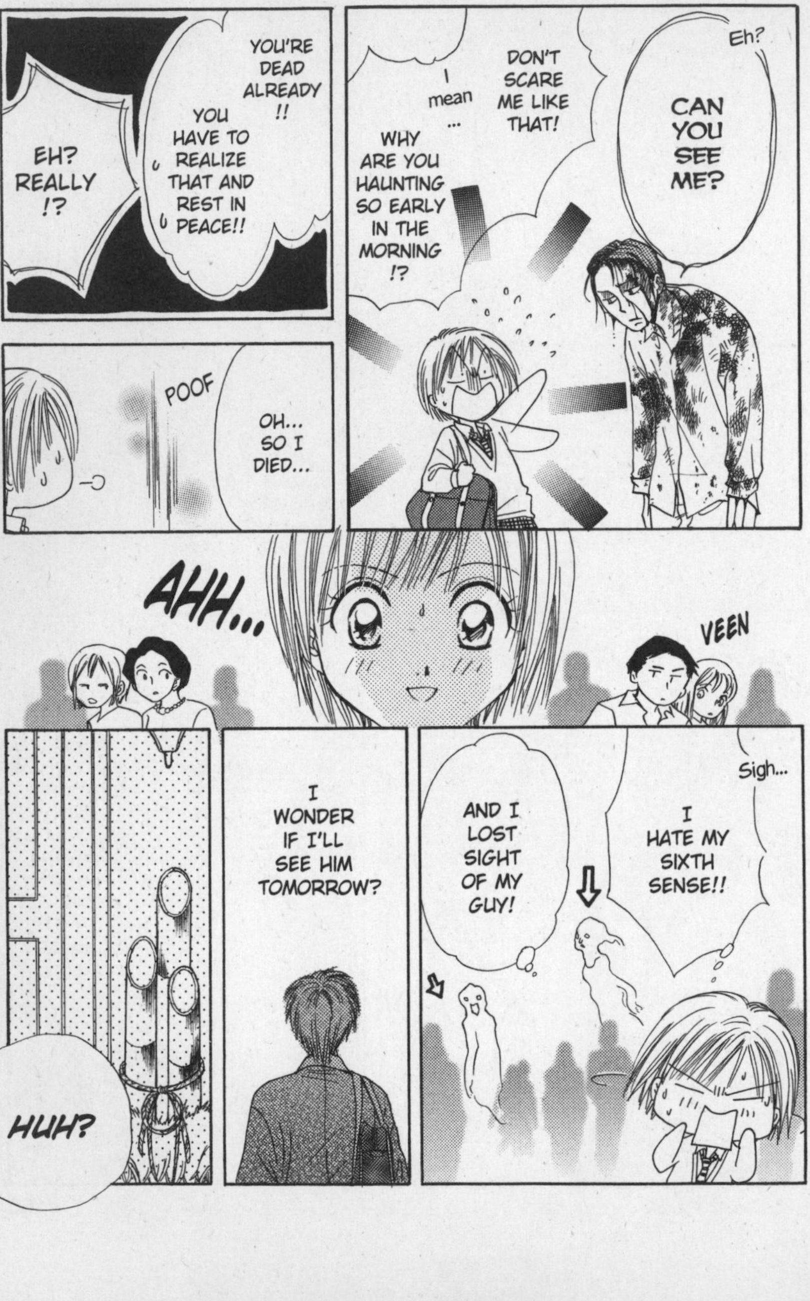

Eh?
CAN YOU SEE ME?
DON'T SCARE ME LIKE THAT!
I mean ...
WHY ARE YOU HAUNTING SO EARLY IN THE MORNING !?
YOU'RE DEAD ALREADY !!
YOU HAVE TO REALIZE THAT AND REST IN PEACE!!
EH? REALLY !?
OH... SO I DIED...
POOF
VEEN
AHH...
Sigh...
I HATE MY SIXTH SENSE!!
AND I LOST SIGHT OF MY GUY!
I WONDER IF I'LL SEE HIM TOMORROW?
HUH?

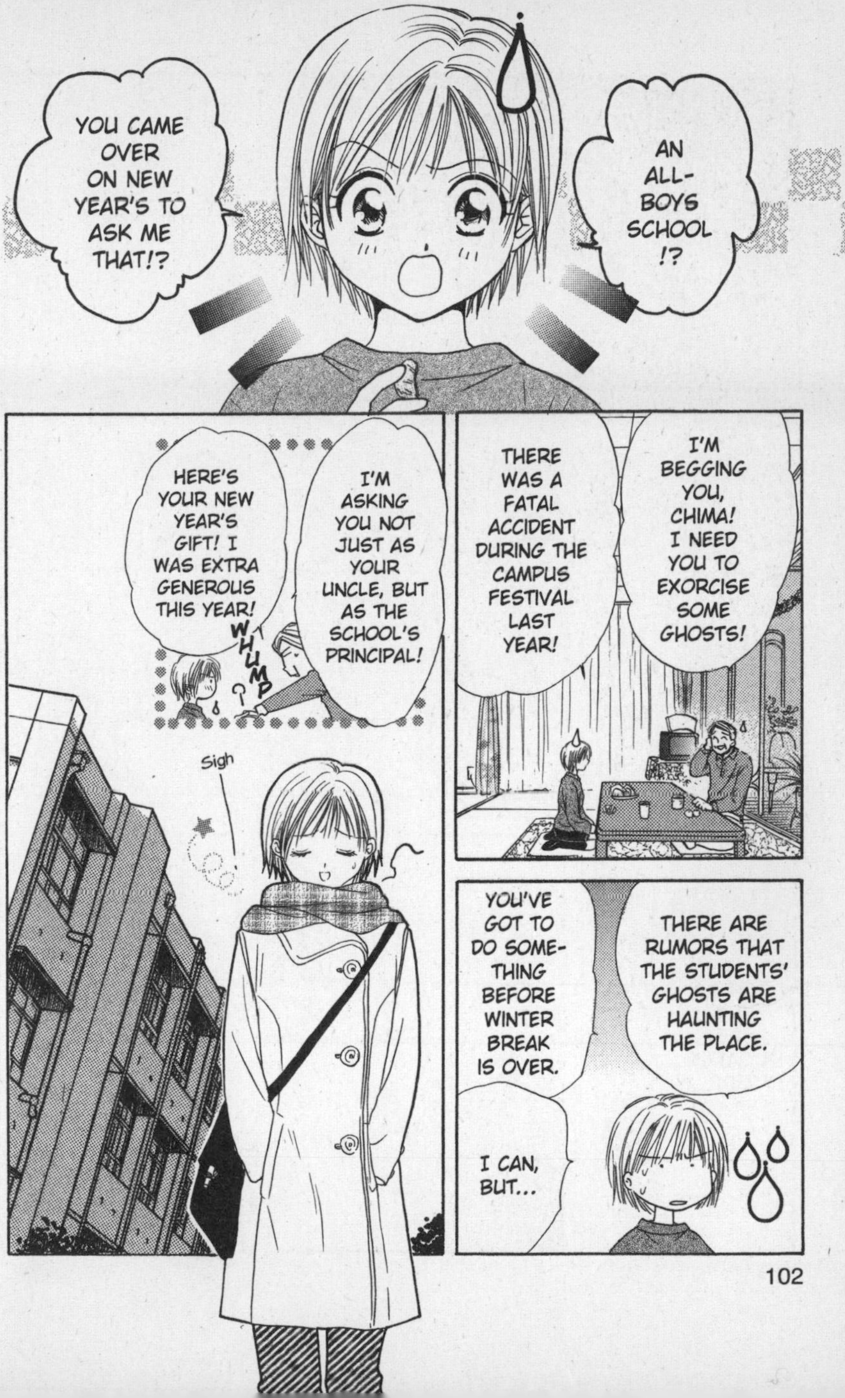
AN ALL-BOYS SCHOOL!?
YOU CAME OVER ON NEW YEAR'S TO ASK ME THAT!?
I'M BEGGING YOU, CHIMA! I NEED YOU TO EXORCISE SOME GHOSTS!
THERE WAS A FATAL ACCIDENT DURING THE CAMPUS FESTIVAL LAST YEAR!
THERE ARE RUMORS THAT THE STUDENTS' GHOSTS ARE HAUNTING THE PLACE.
YOU'VE GOT TO DO SOME-THING BEFORE WINTER BREAK IS OVER.
I CAN, BUT...
I'M ASKING YOU NOT JUST AS YOUR UNCLE, BUT AS THE SCHOOL'S PRINCIPAL!
HERE'S YOUR NEW YEAR'S GIFT! I WAS EXTRA GENEROUS THIS YEAR!
WHUMP
Sigh

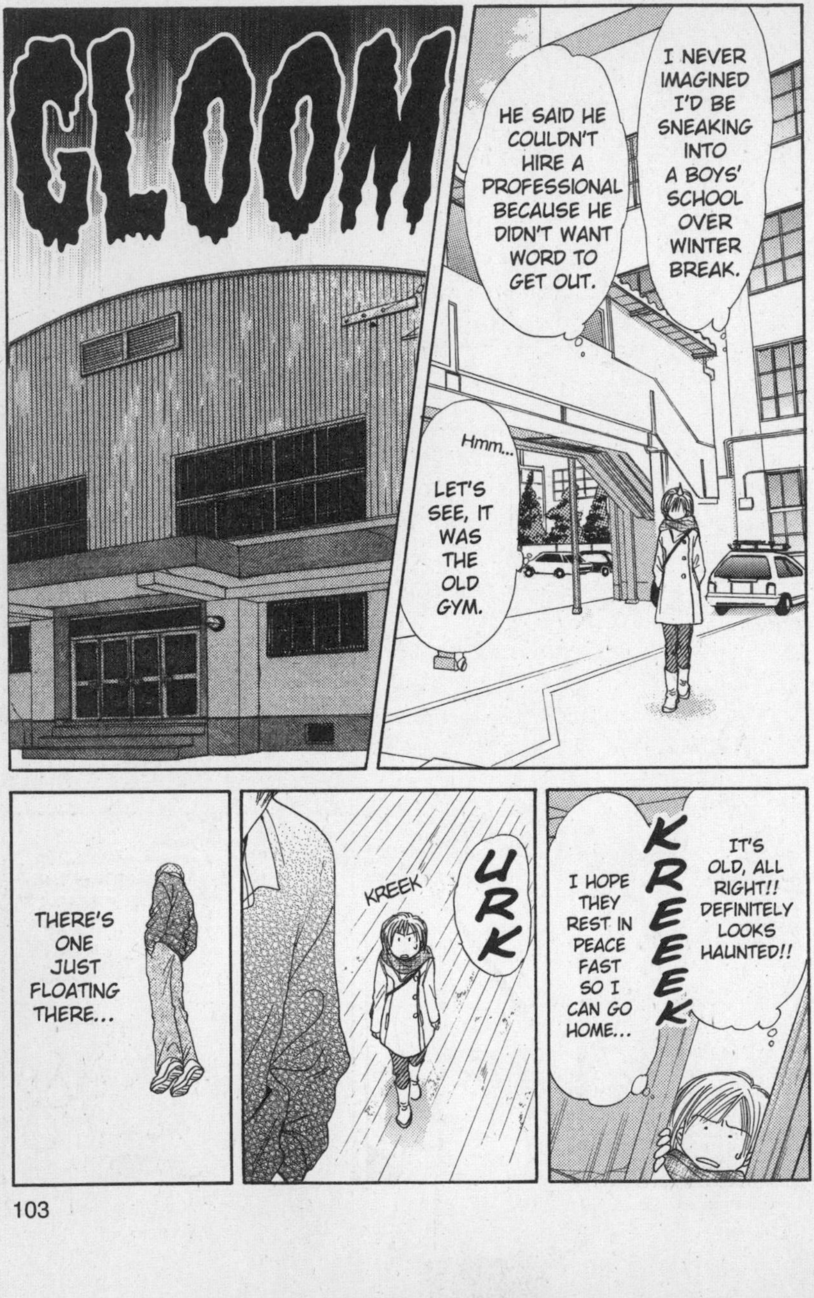
I NEVER IMAGINED I'D BE SNEAKING INTO A BOYS' SCHOOL OVER WINTER BREAK.
HE SAID HE COULDN'T HIRE A PROFESSIONAL BECAUSE HE DIDN'T WANT WORD TO GET OUT.
Hmm...
LET'S SEE, IT WAS THE OLD GYM.
GLOOM
IT'S OLD, ALL RIGHT!! DEFINITELY LOOKS HAUNTED!!
KREEEK
I HOPE THEY REST IN PEACE FAST SO I CAN GO HOME...
URK
KREEK
THERE'S ONE JUST FLOATING THERE...

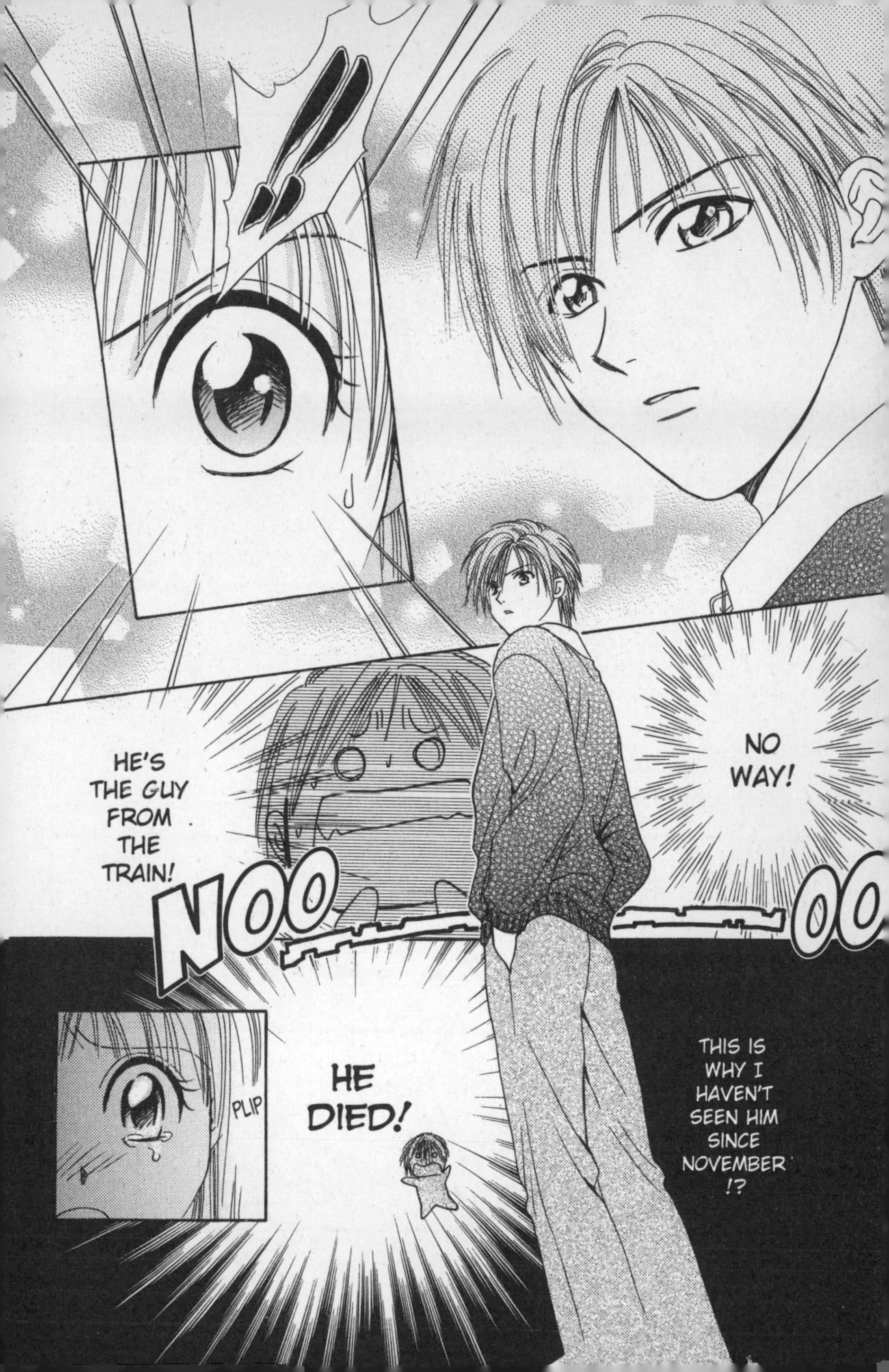
NO WAY!
HE'S THE GUY FROM THE TRAIN!
NOOOO
THIS IS WHY I HAVEN'T SEEN HIM SINCE NOVEMBER!?
HE DIED!
PLIP

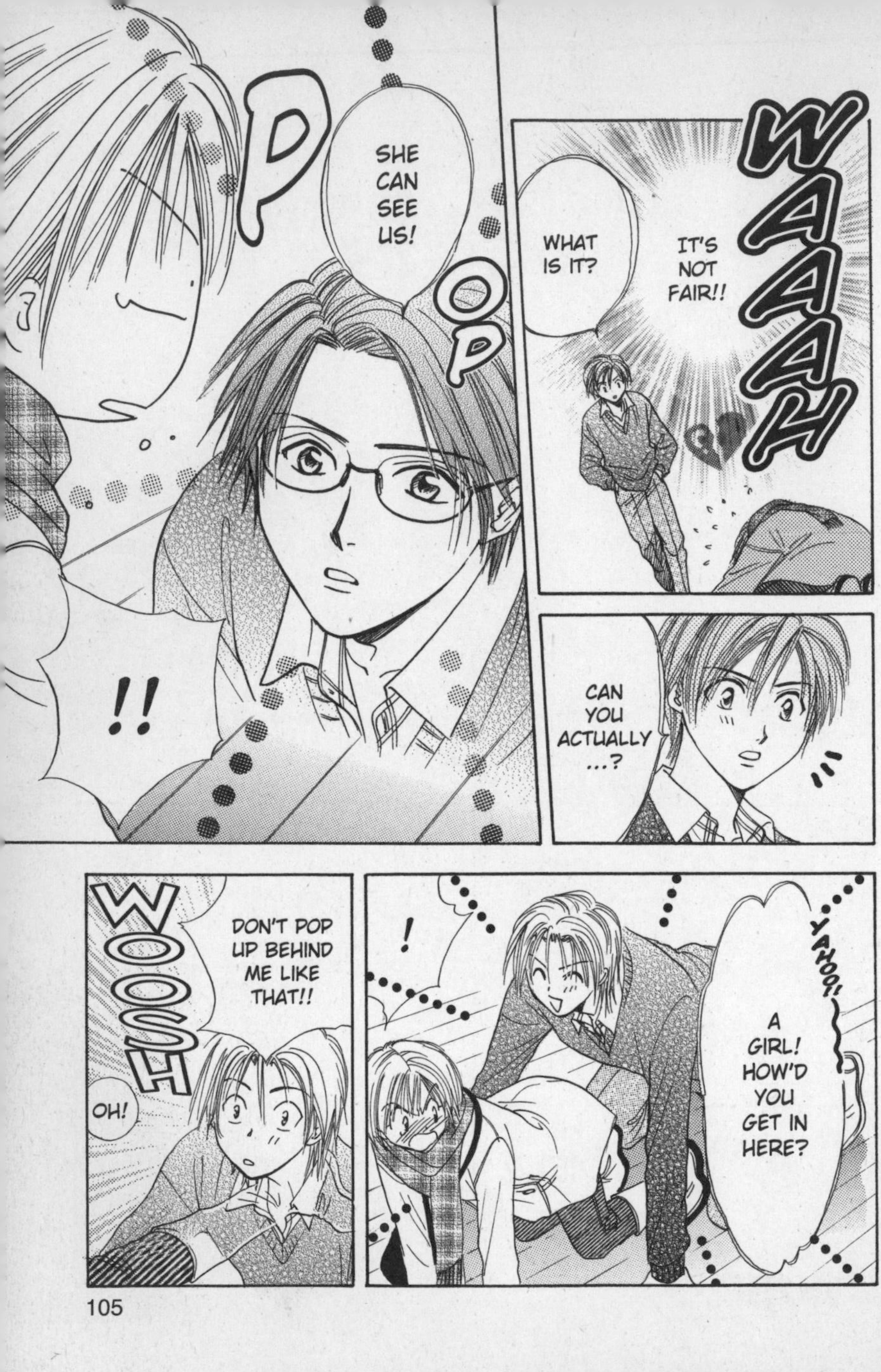

WAAAAH
IT'S NOT FAIR!!
WHAT IS IT?
CAN YOU ACTUALLY ...?
POP
SHE CAN SEE US!
!!
YAHOO!!
A GIRL! HOW'D YOU GET IN HERE?
!
WOOSH
DON'T POP UP BEHIND ME LIKE THAT!!
OH!

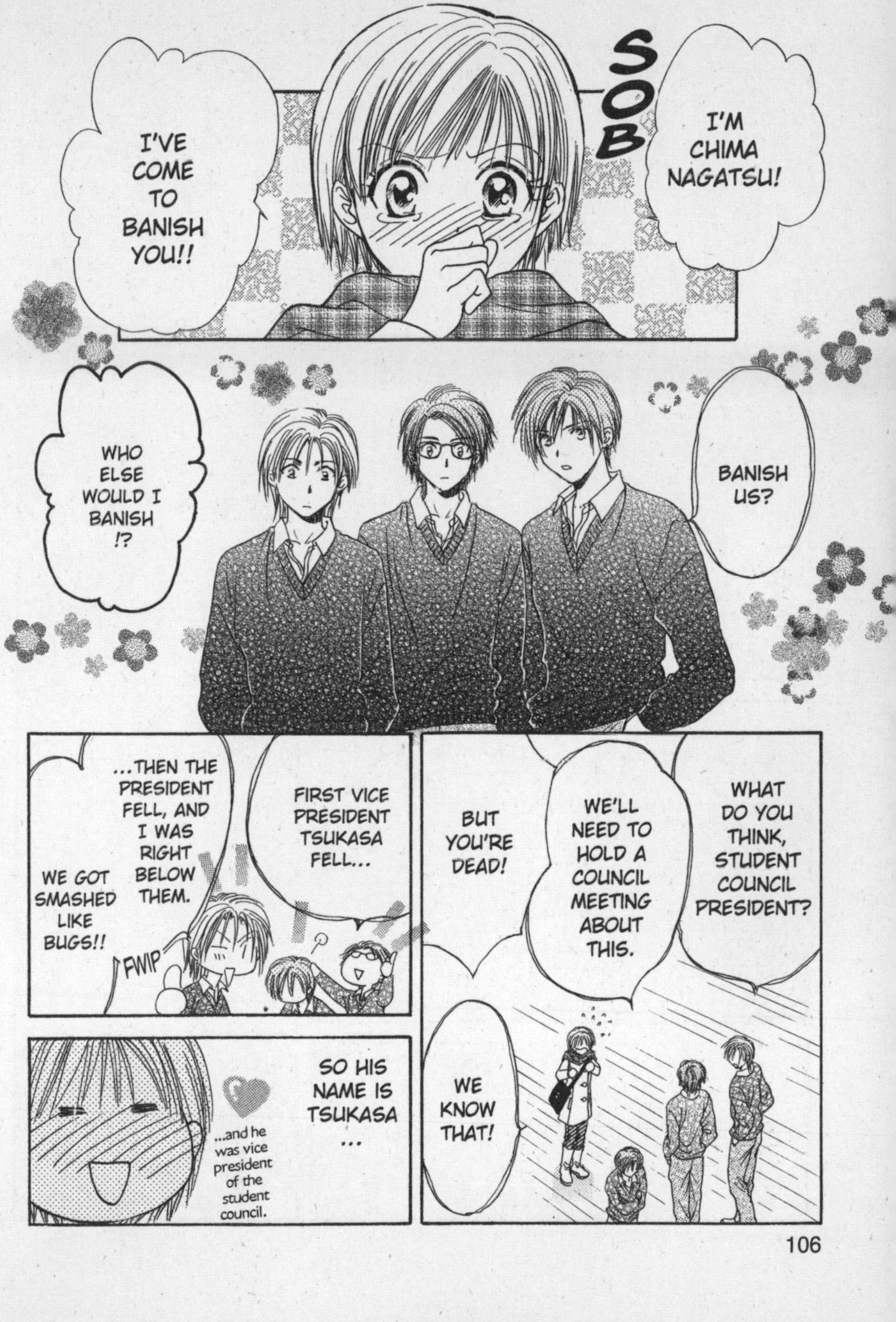
SOB
I'M CHIMA NAGATSU!
I'VE COME TO BANISH YOU!!
BANISH US?
WHO ELSE WOULD I BANISH !?
WHAT DO YOU THINK, STUDENT COUNCIL PRESIDENT?
WE'LL NEED TO HOLD A COUNCIL MEETING ABOUT THIS.
BUT YOU'RE DEAD!
WE KNOW THAT!
FIRST VICE PRESIDENT TSUKASA FELL...
...THEN THE PRESIDENT FELL, AND I WAS RIGHT BELOW THEM.
WE GOT SMASHED LIKE BUGS!!
FWIP
SO HIS NAME IS TSUKASA ...
...and he was vice president of the student council.

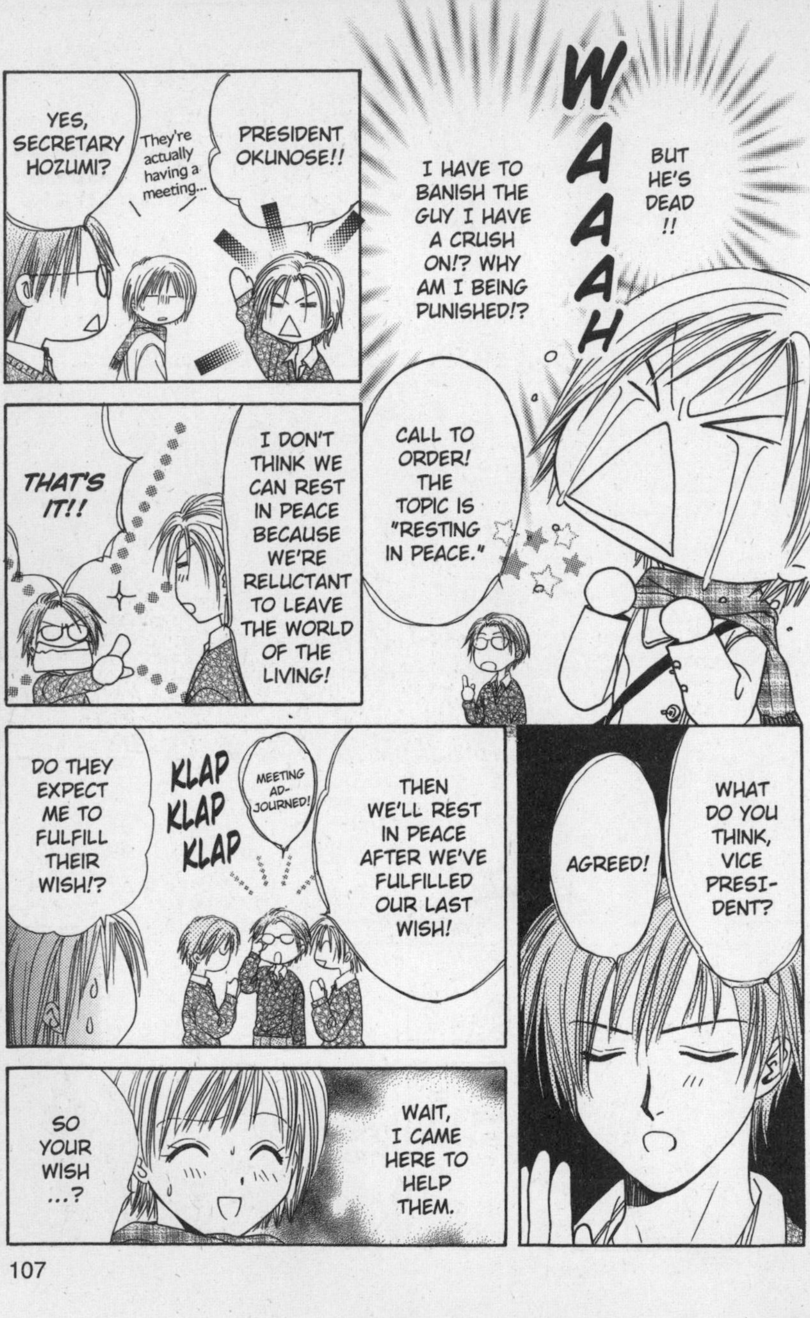
WAAAH
BUT HE'S DEAD!!
I HAVE TO BANISH THE GUY I HAVE A CRUSH ON!? WHY AM I BEING PUNISHED!?
CALL TO ORDER! THE TOPIC IS "RESTING IN PEACE."
PRESIDENT OKUNOSE!!
They're actually having a meeting...
YES, SECRETARY HOZUMI?
I DON'T THINK WE CAN REST IN PEACE BECAUSE WE'RE RELUCTANT TO LEAVE THE WORLD OF THE LIVING!
THAT'S IT!!
WHAT DO YOU THINK, VICE PRESIDENT?
AGREED!
THEN WE'LL REST IN PEACE AFTER WE'VE FULFILLED OUR LAST WISH!
MEETING AD-JOURNED!
KLAP KLAP KLAP
DO THEY EXPECT ME TO FULFILL THEIR WISH!?
WAIT, I CAME HERE TO HELP THEM.
SO YOUR WISH ...?

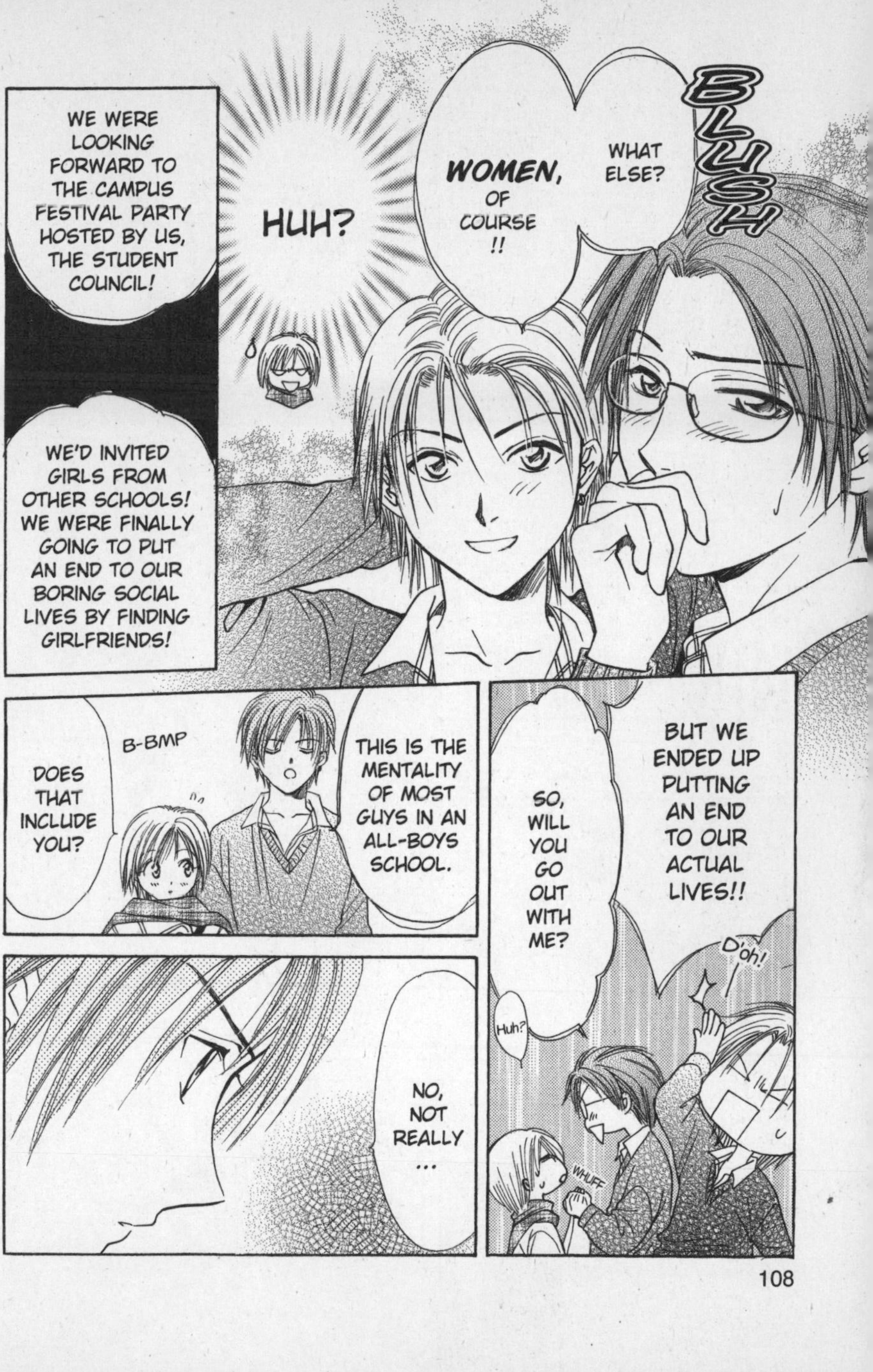
BLUSH
WHAT ELSE?
WOMEN, OF COURSE !!
HUH?
WE WERE LOOKING FORWARD TO THE CAMPUS FESTIVAL PARTY HOSTED BY US, THE STUDENT COUNCIL!
WE'D INVITED GIRLS FROM OTHER SCHOOLS! WE WERE FINALLY GOING TO PUT AN END TO OUR BORING SOCIAL LIVES BY FINDING GIRLFRIENDS!
BUT WE ENDED UP PUTTING AN END TO OUR ACTUAL LIVES!!
SO, WILL YOU GO OUT WITH ME?
D'oh!
Huh?
WHUFF
THIS IS THE MENTALITY OF MOST GUYS IN AN ALL-BOYS SCHOOL.
B-BMP
DOES THAT INCLUDE YOU?
NO, NOT REALLY ...

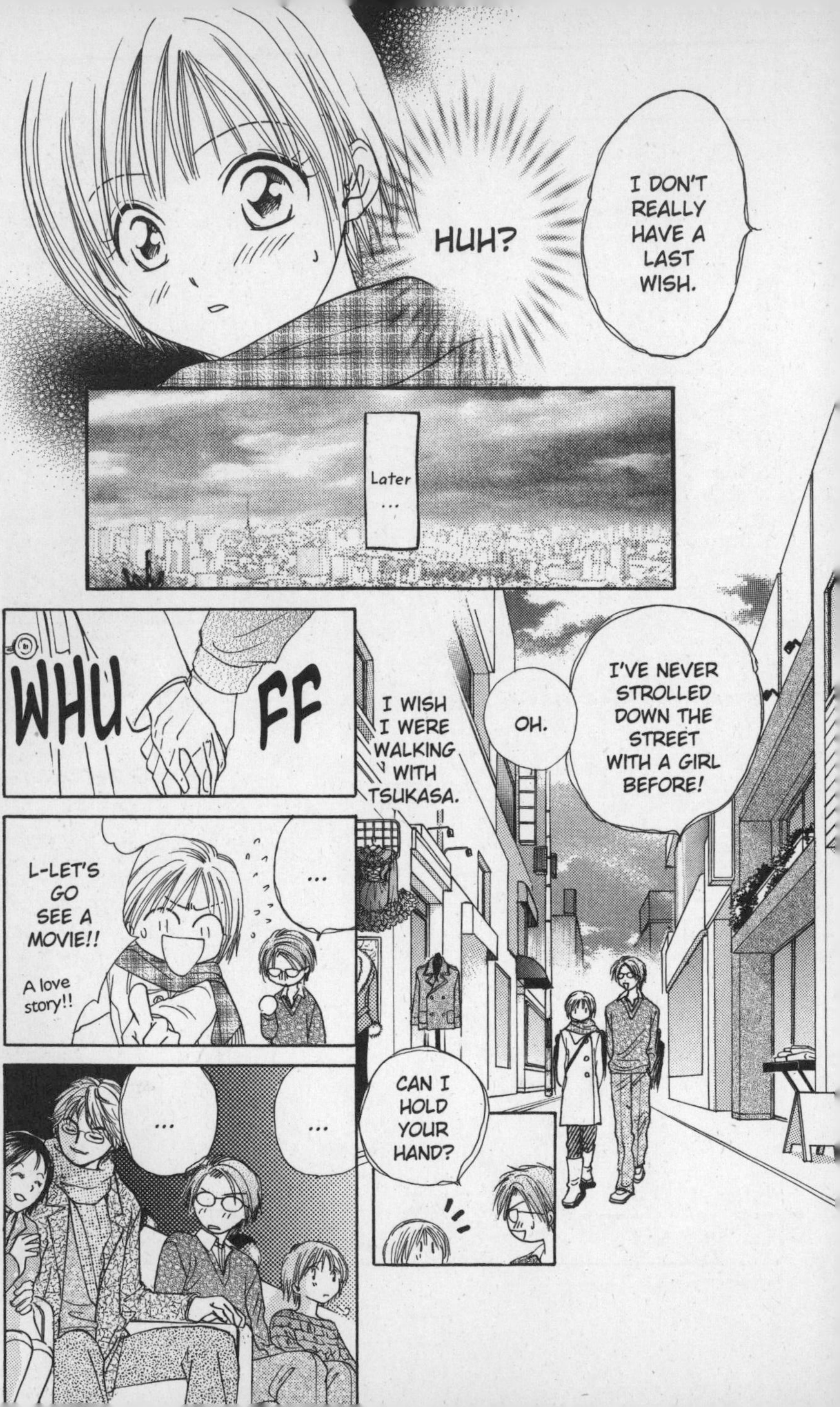
I DON'T REALLY HAVE A LAST WISH.
HUH?
Later...
I'VE NEVER STROLLED DOWN THE STREET WITH A GIRL BEFORE!
OH.
I WISH I WERE WALKING WITH TSUKASA.
CAN I HOLD YOUR HAND?
WHUFF
...
L-LET'S GO SEE A MOVIE!!
A love story!!
...
...

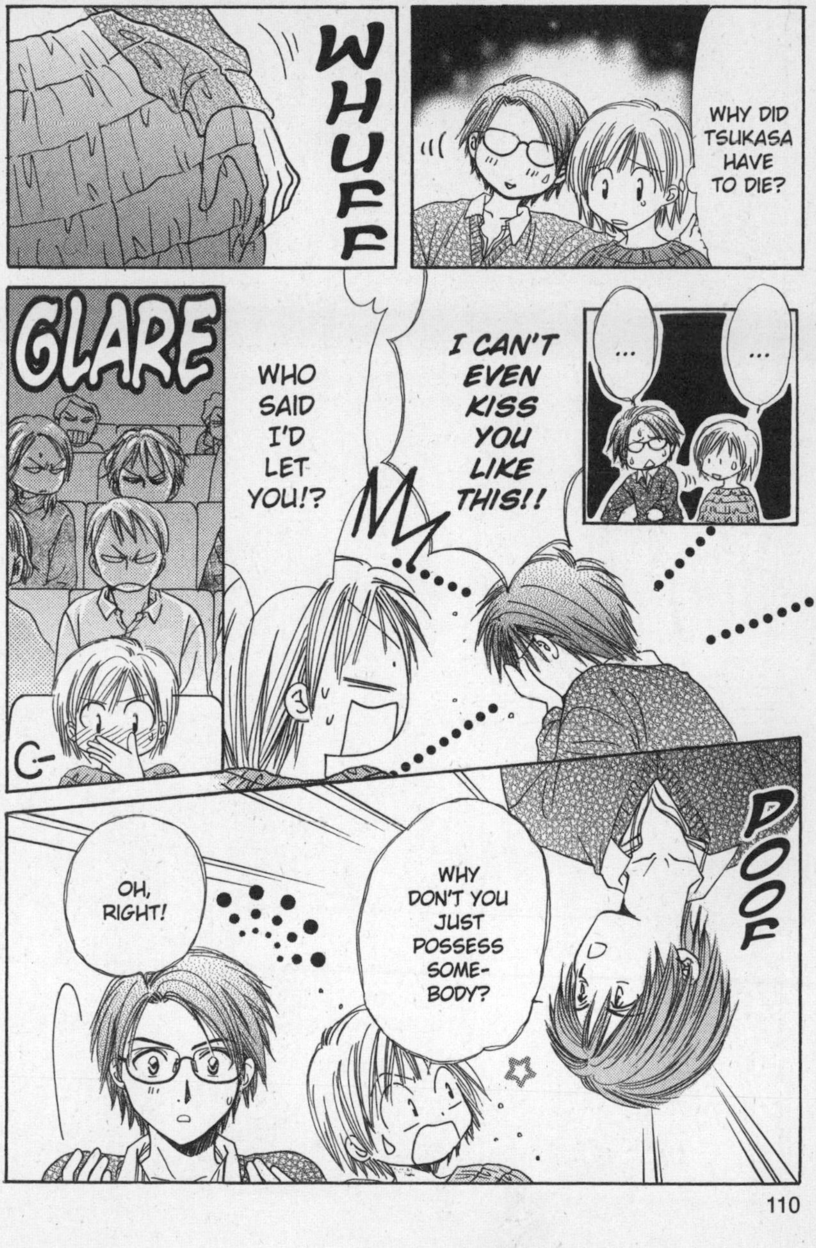
WHY DID TSUKASA HAVE TO DIE?
WHUFF
...
...
I CAN'T EVEN KISS YOU LIKE THIS!!
WHO SAID I'D LET YOU!?
GLARE
DOOF
WHY DON'T YOU JUST POSSESS SOME-BODY?
OH, RIGHT!

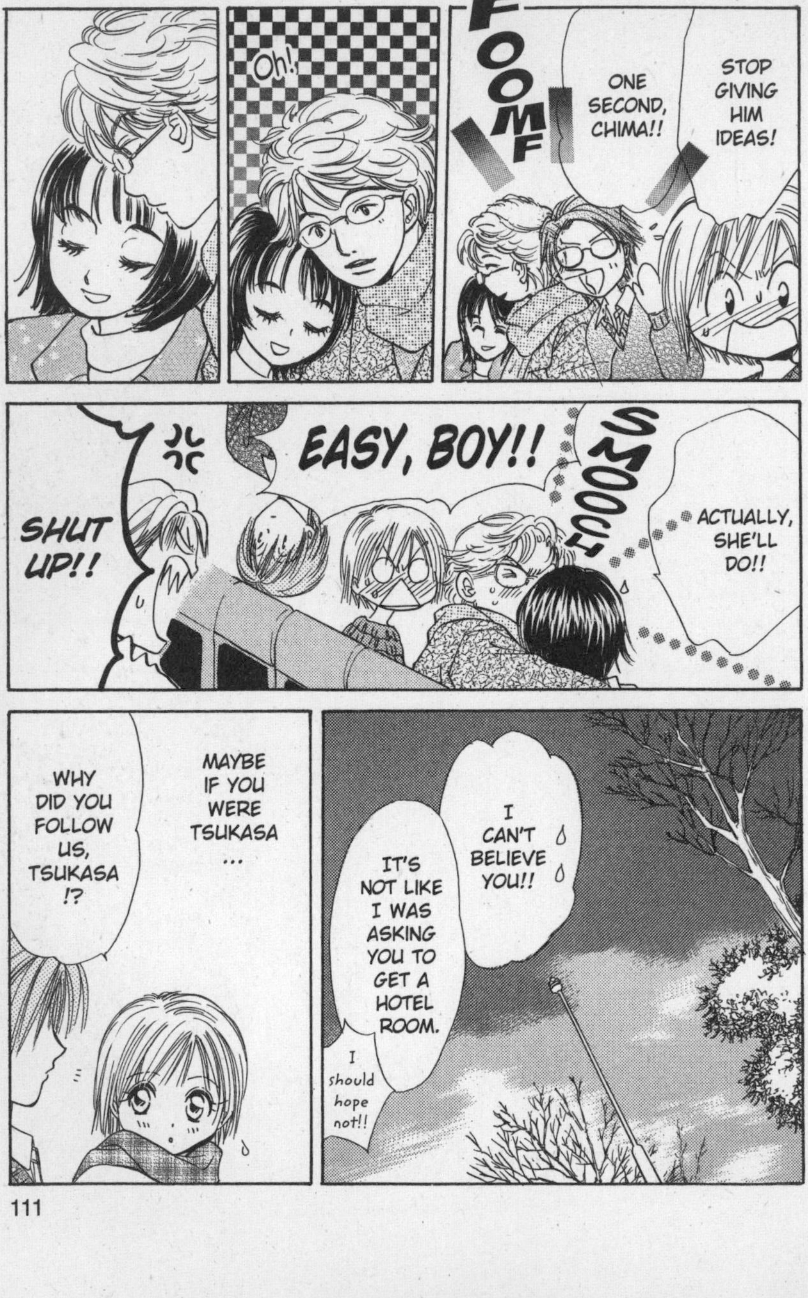
STOP GIVING HIM IDEAS!
ONE SECOND, CHIMA!!
FOOMF
Oh!
ACTUALLY, SHE'LL DO!!
SMOOCH
EASY, BOY!!
SHUT UP!!
I CAN'T BELIEVE YOU!!
IT'S NOT LIKE I WAS ASKING YOU TO GET A HOTEL ROOM.
I should hope not!!
MAYBE IF YOU WERE TSUKASA...
WHY DID YOU FOLLOW US, TSUKASA!?

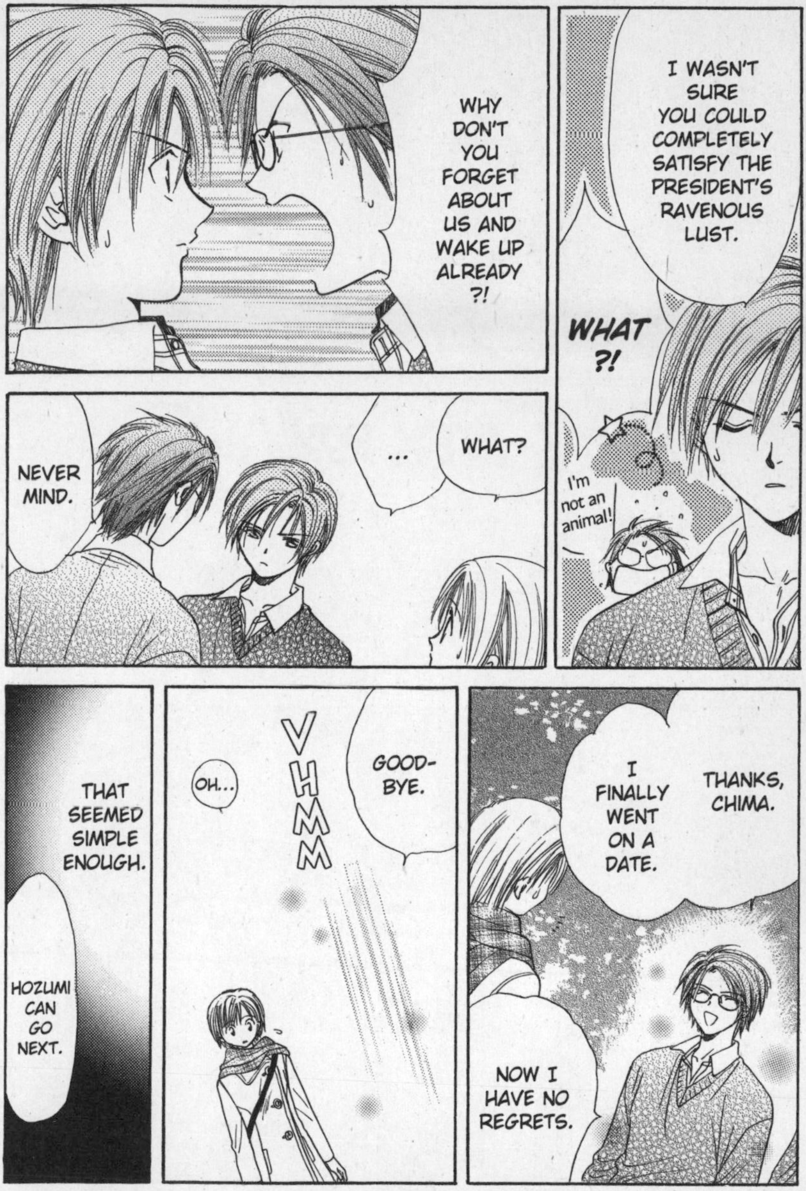
I WASN'T SURE YOU COULD COMPLETELY SATISFY THE PRESIDENT'S RAVENOUS LUST.
WHAT?!
I'm not an animal!
WHY DON'T YOU FORGET ABOUT US AND WAKE UP ALREADY?!
WHAT?
...
NEVER MIND.
THANKS, CHIMA.
I FINALLY WENT ON A DATE.
NOW I HAVE NO REGRETS.
GOOD-BYE.
VHMM
OH...
THAT SEEMED SIMPLE ENOUGH.
HOZUMI CAN GO NEXT.

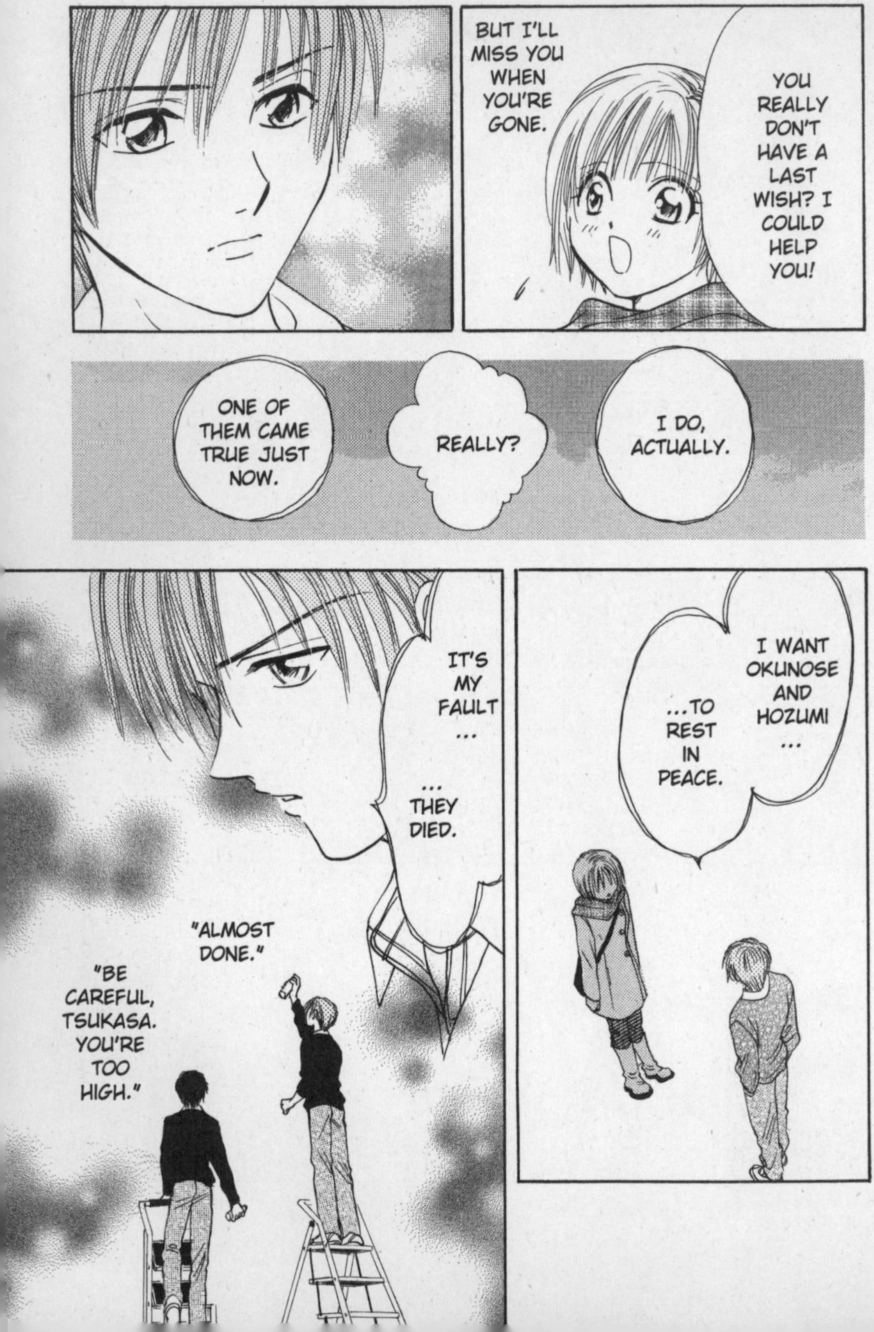
YOU REALLY DON'T HAVE A LAST WISH? I COULD HELP YOU!
BUT I'LL MISS YOU WHEN YOU'RE GONE.
I DO, ACTUALLY.
REALLY?
ONE OF THEM CAME TRUE JUST NOW.
I WANT OKUNOSE AND HOZUMI...
...TO REST IN PEACE.
IT'S MY FAULT...
...THEY DIED.
"ALMOST DONE."
"BE CAREFUL, TSUKASA. YOU'RE TOO HIGH."

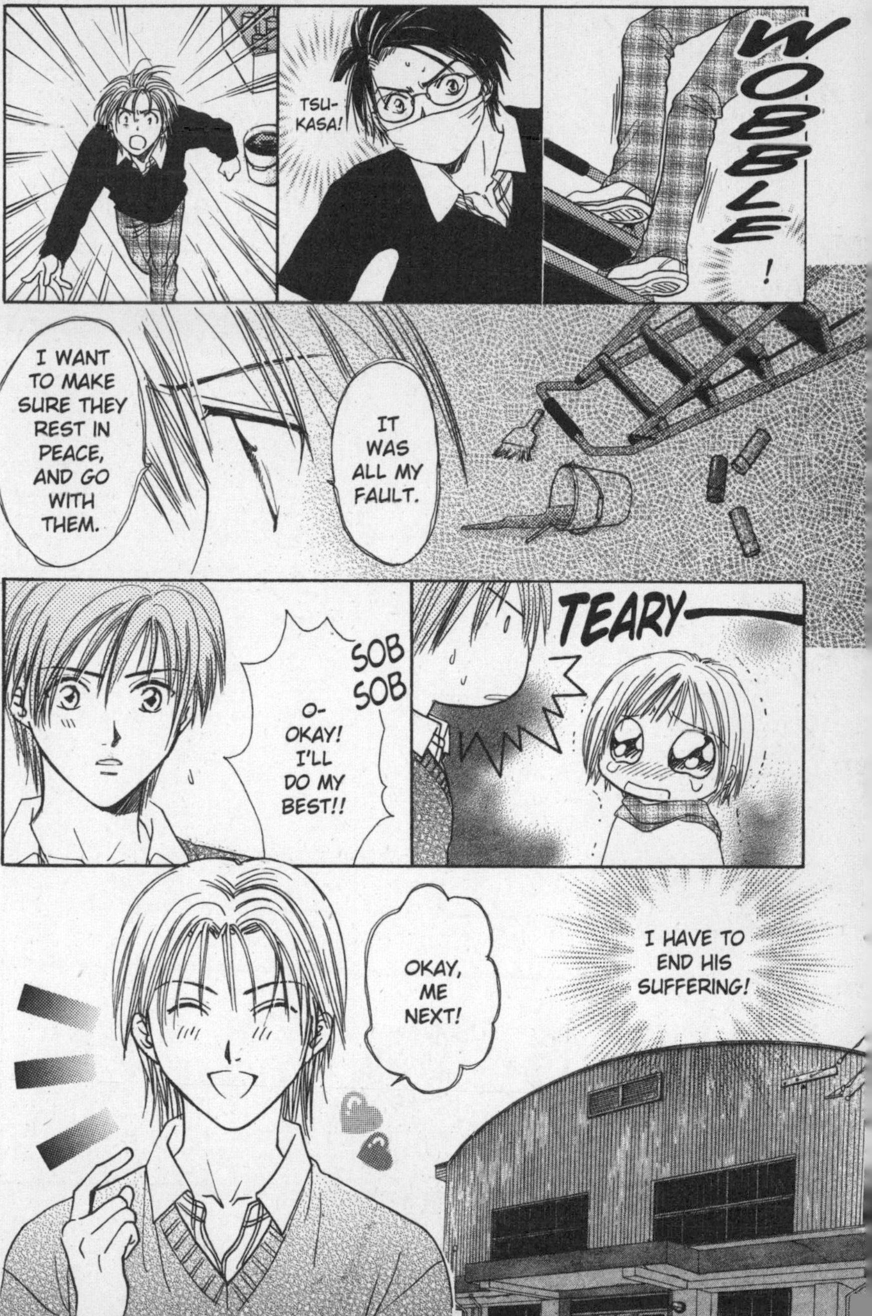
WOBBLE!
TSU-KASA!
IT WAS ALL MY FAULT.
I WANT TO MAKE SURE THEY REST IN PEACE, AND GO WITH THEM.
TEARY
SOB SOB
O-OKAY! I'LL DO MY BEST!!
I HAVE TO END HIS SUFFERING!
OKAY, ME NEXT!

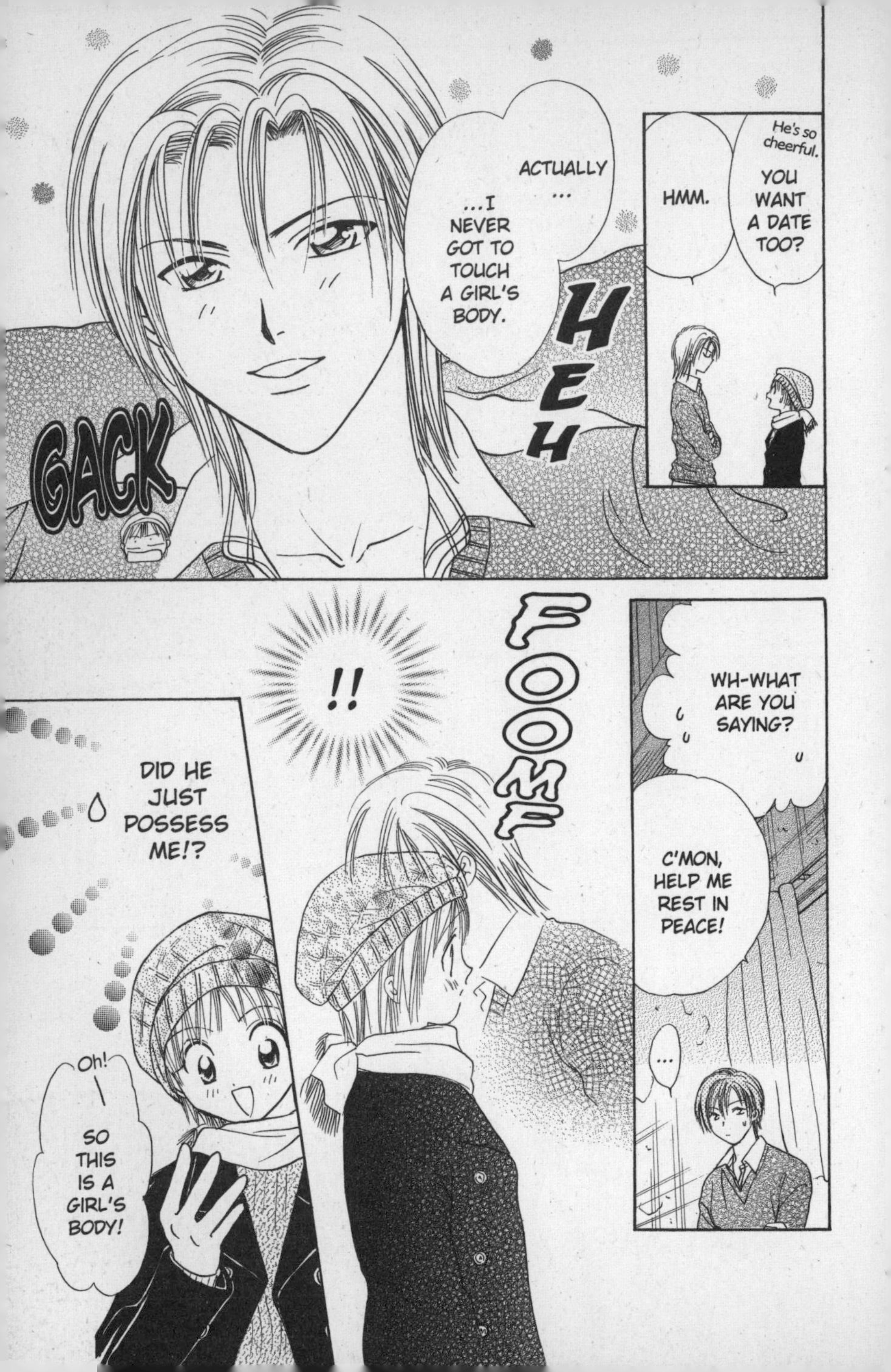
He's so cheerful.
YOU WANT A DATE TOO?
HMM.
ACTUALLY ...
...I NEVER GOT TO TOUCH A GIRL'S BODY.
HEH HEH
GACK
WH-WHAT ARE YOU SAYING?
C'MON, HELP ME REST IN PEACE!
...
FOOMF
!!
DID HE JUST POSSESS ME!?
Oh!
SO THIS IS A GIRL'S BODY!

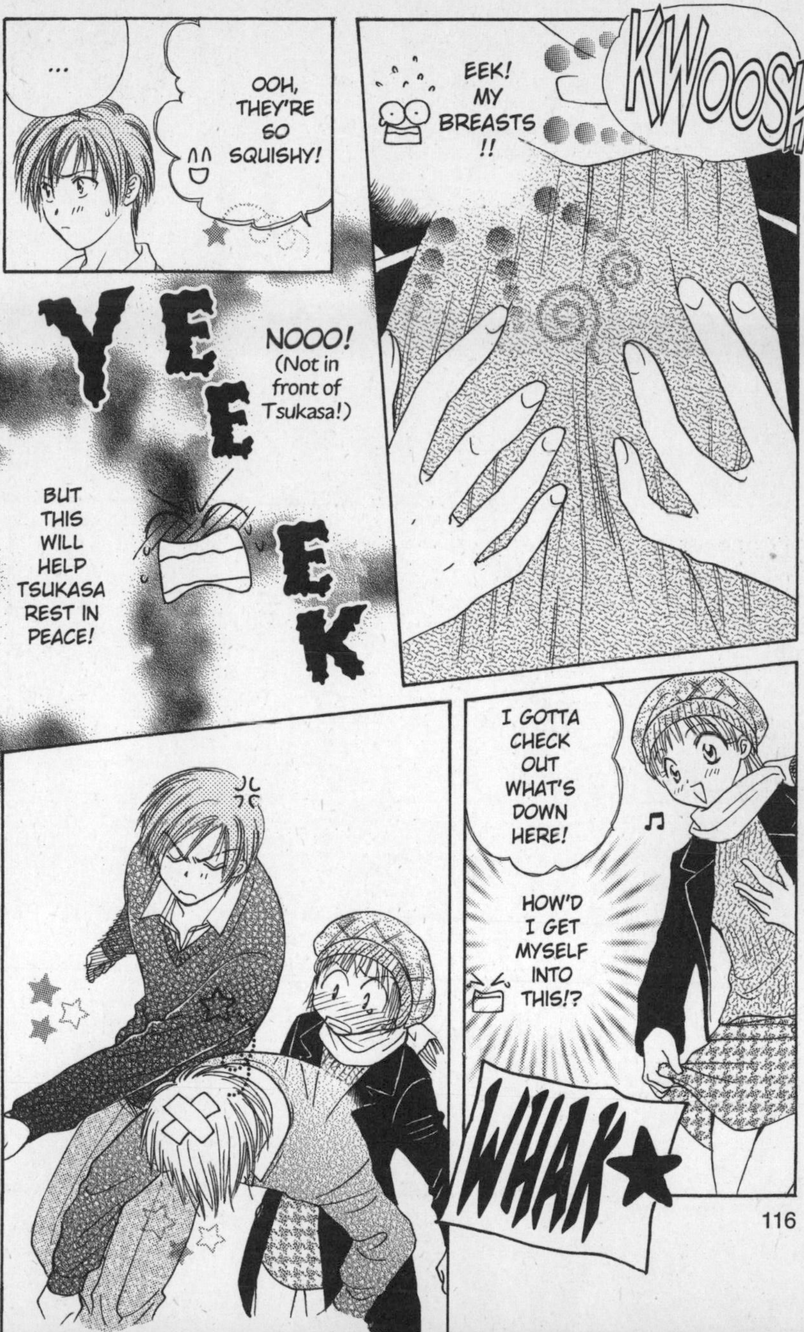
KWOOSH
EEK! MY BREASTS!!
...
OOH, THEY'RE SO SQUISHY!
YEEEK
NOOO! (Not in front of Tsukasa!)
BUT THIS WILL HELP TSUKASA REST IN PEACE!
I GOTTA CHECK OUT WHAT'S DOWN HERE!
HOW'D I GET MYSELF INTO THIS!?
WHAK

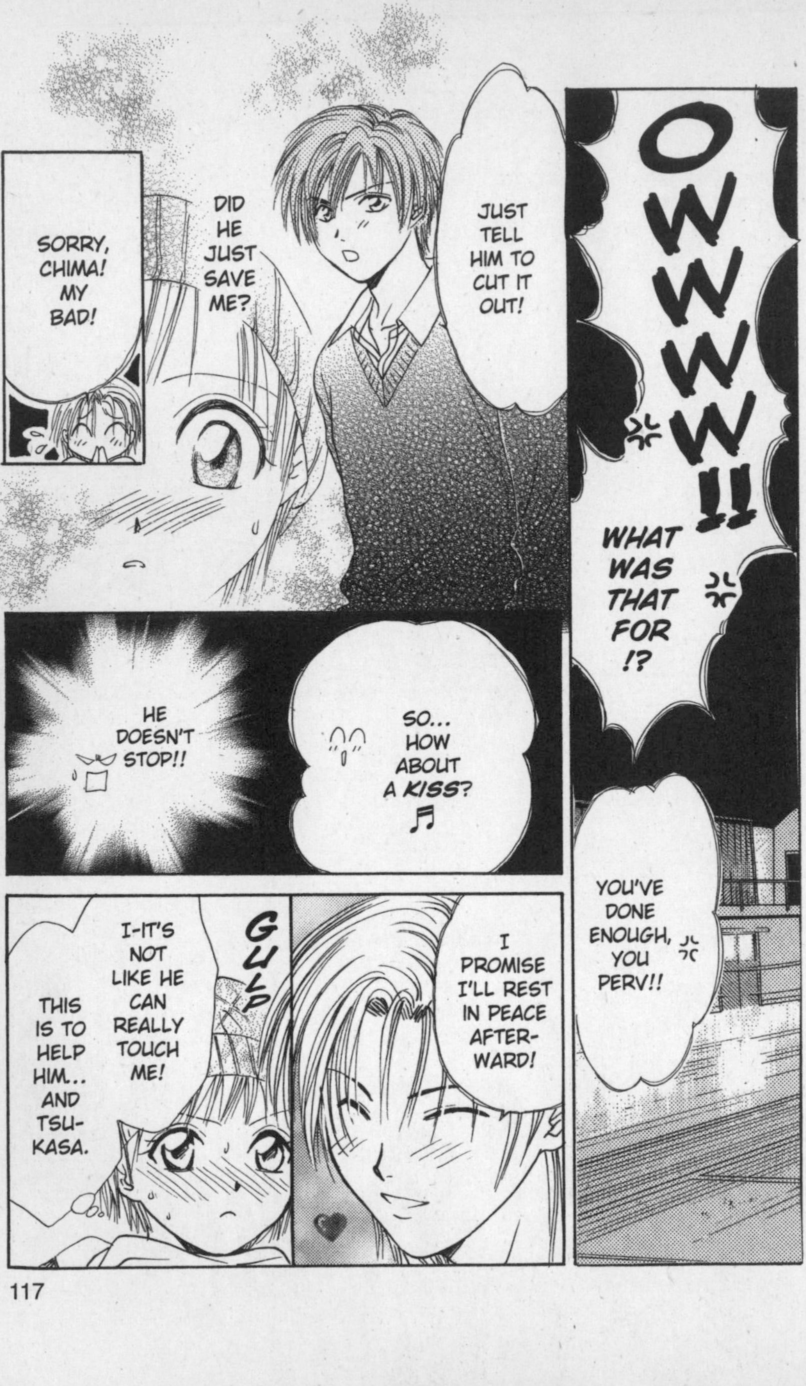

OWWWW!!
WHAT WAS THAT FOR!?
YOU'VE DONE ENOUGH, YOU PERV!!
JUST TELL HIM TO CUT IT OUT!
DID HE JUST SAVE ME?
SORRY, CHIMA! MY BAD!
SO... HOW ABOUT A KISS? ♬
HE DOESN'T STOP!!
I PROMISE I'LL REST IN PEACE AFTER-WARD!
GULP
I-IT'S NOT LIKE HE CAN REALLY TOUCH ME!
THIS IS TO HELP HIM... AND TSU-KASA.

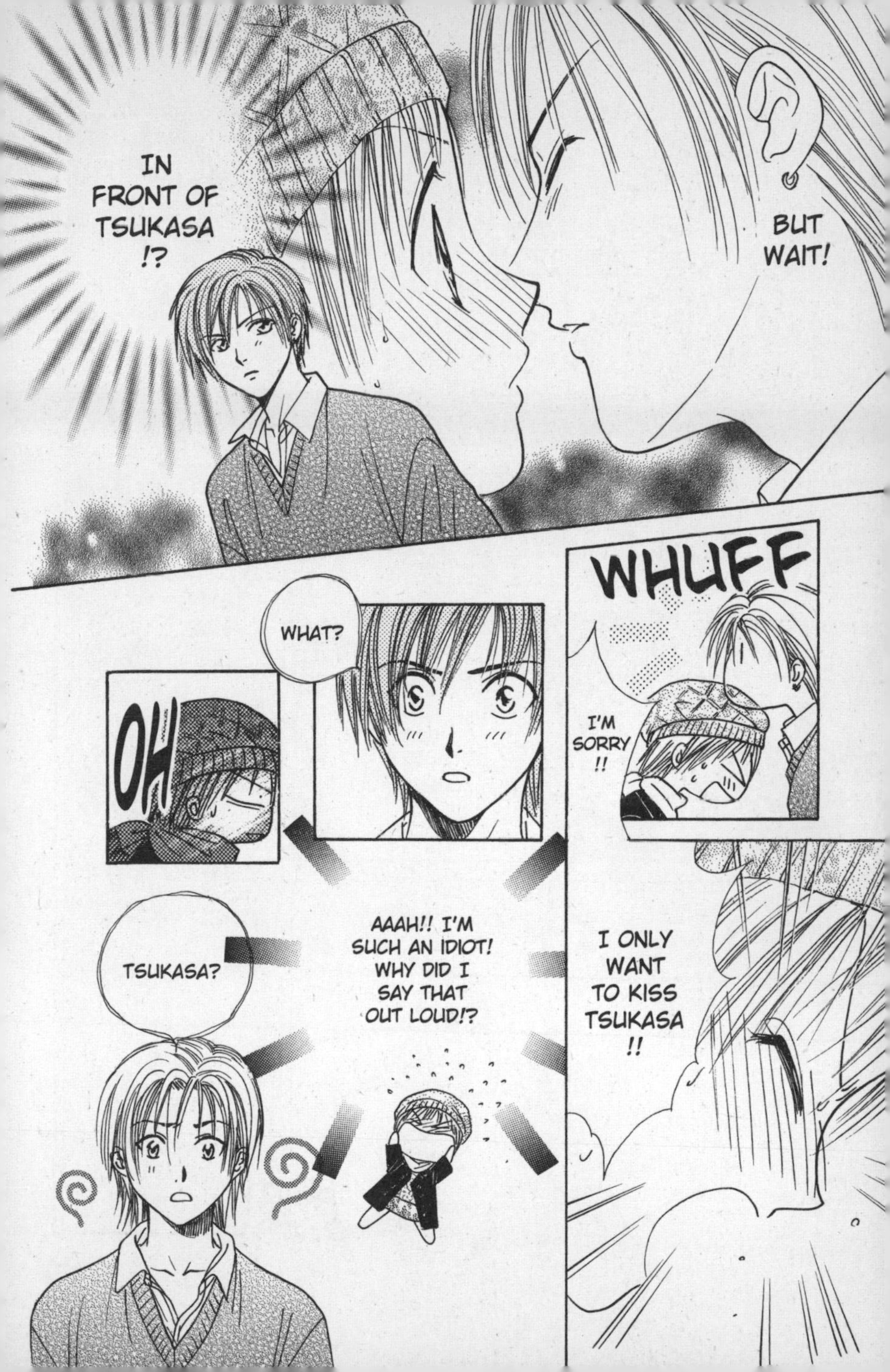

BUT WAIT!
IN FRONT OF TSUKASA !?
WHUFF
I'M SORRY !!
I ONLY WANT TO KISS TSUKASA !!
WHAT?
OH
AAAH!! I'M SUCH AN IDIOT! WHY DID I SAY THAT OUT LOUD!?
TSUKASA?

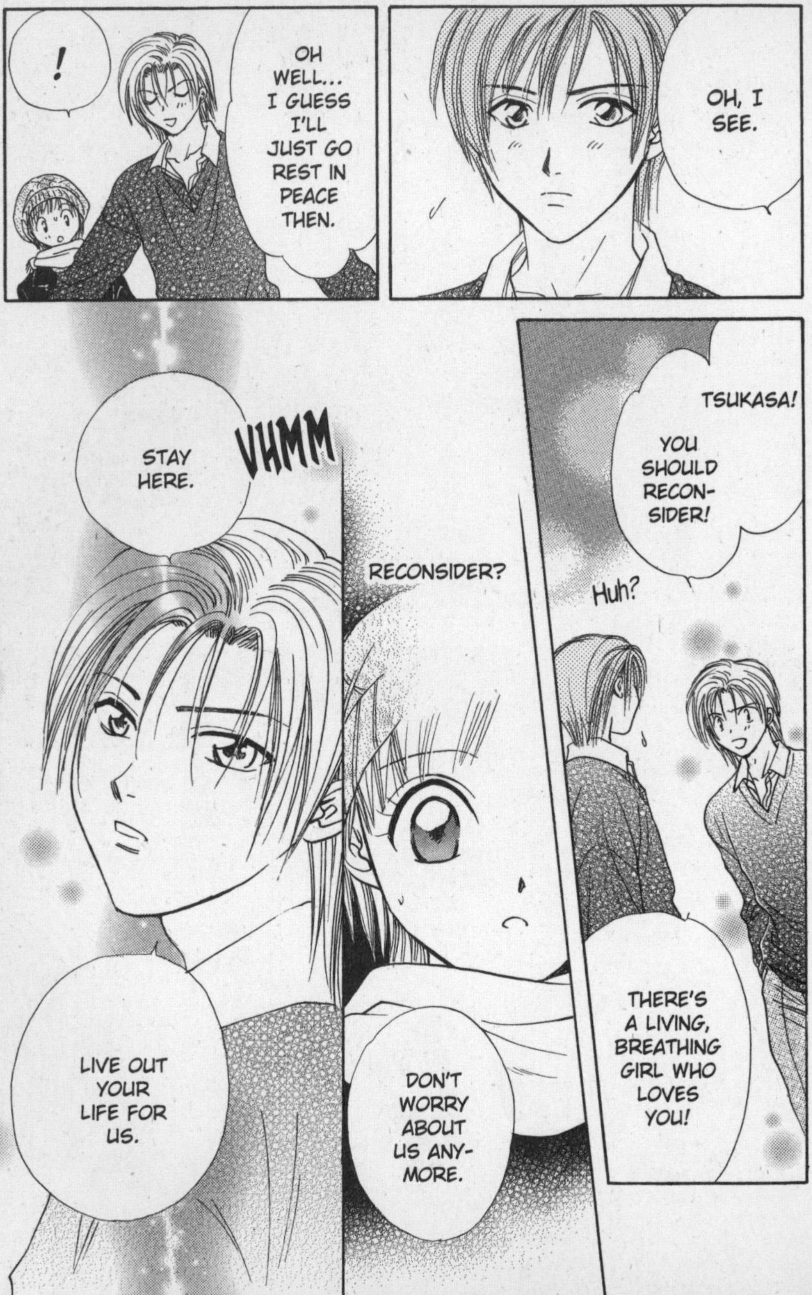
OH, I SEE.
OH WELL... I GUESS I'LL JUST GO REST IN PEACE THEN.
!
TSUKASA!
YOU SHOULD RECON-SIDER!
Huh?
THERE'S A LIVING, BREATHING GIRL WHO LOVES YOU!
RECONSIDER?
VHMM
STAY HERE.
DON'T WORRY ABOUT US ANY-MORE.
LIVE OUT YOUR LIFE FOR US.

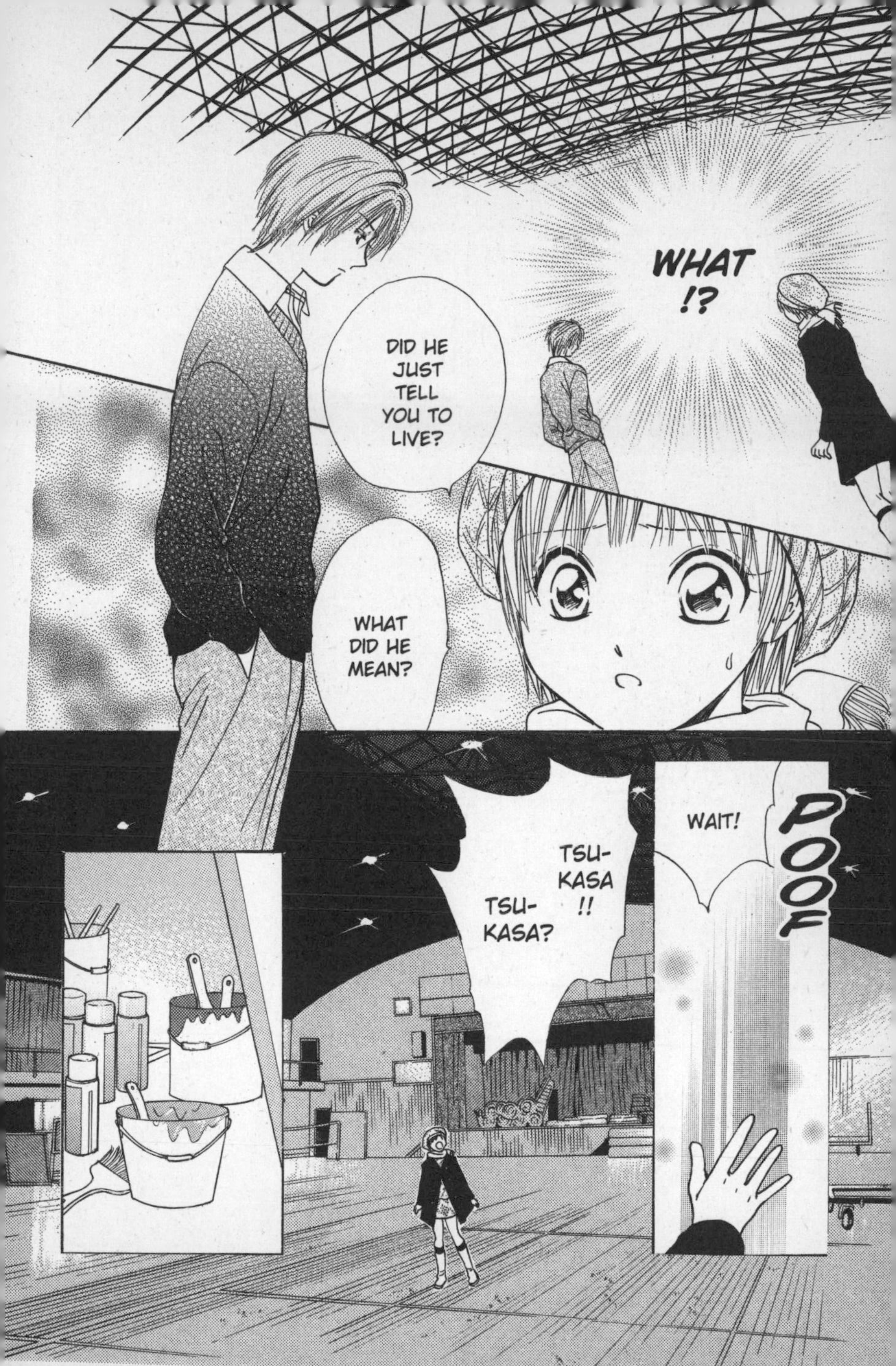
WHAT !?
DID HE JUST TELL YOU TO LIVE?
WHAT DID HE MEAN?
POOF
WAIT!
TSU-KASA !!
TSU-KASA?

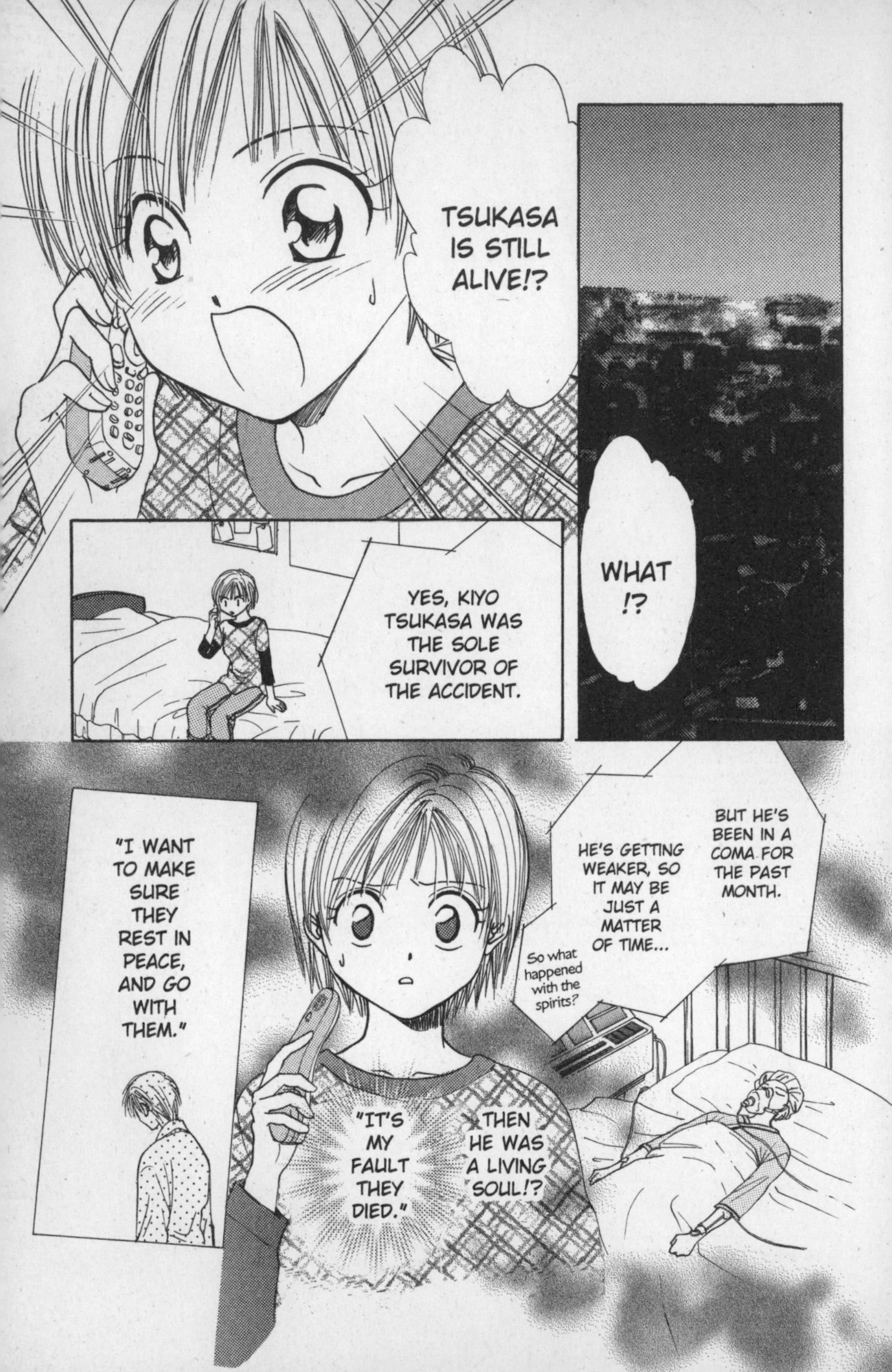
WHAT!?
TSUKASA IS STILL ALIVE!?
YES, KIYO TSUKASA WAS THE SOLE SURVIVOR OF THE ACCIDENT.
BUT HE'S BEEN IN A COMA FOR THE PAST MONTH.
HE'S GETTING WEAKER, SO IT MAY BE JUST A MATTER OF TIME...
So what happened with the spirits?
THEN HE WAS A LIVING SOUL!?
"IT'S MY FAULT THEY DIED."
"I WANT TO MAKE SURE THEY REST IN PEACE, AND GO WITH THEM."

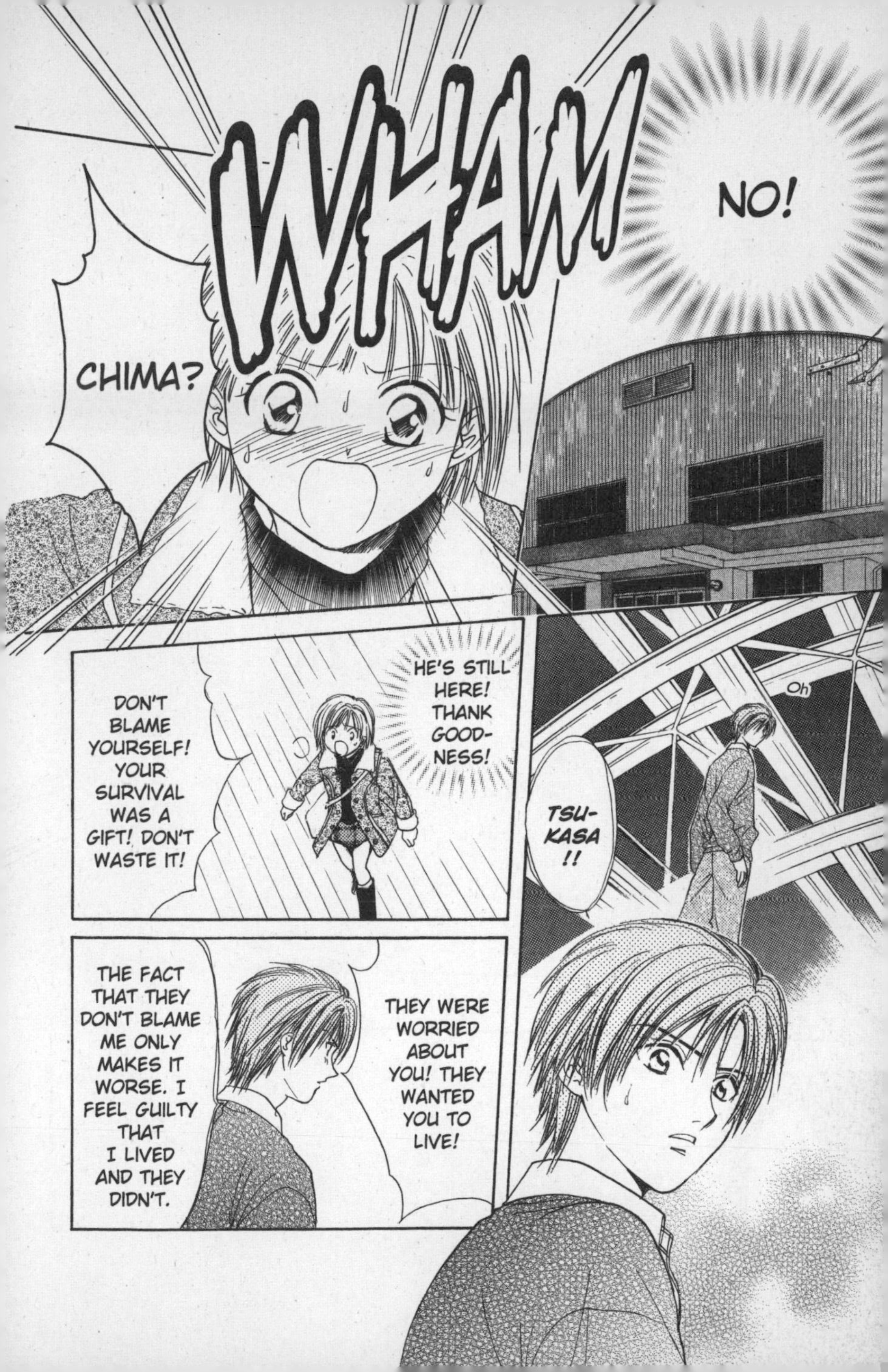
NO!
WHAM
CHIMA?
Oh
TSU-KASA!!
HE'S STILL HERE! THANK GOODNESS!
DON'T BLAME YOURSELF! YOUR SURVIVAL WAS A GIFT! DON'T WASTE IT!
THEY WERE WORRIED ABOUT YOU! THEY WANTED YOU TO LIVE!
THE FACT THAT THEY DON'T BLAME ME ONLY MAKES IT WORSE. I FEEL GUILTY THAT I LIVED AND THEY DIDN'T.

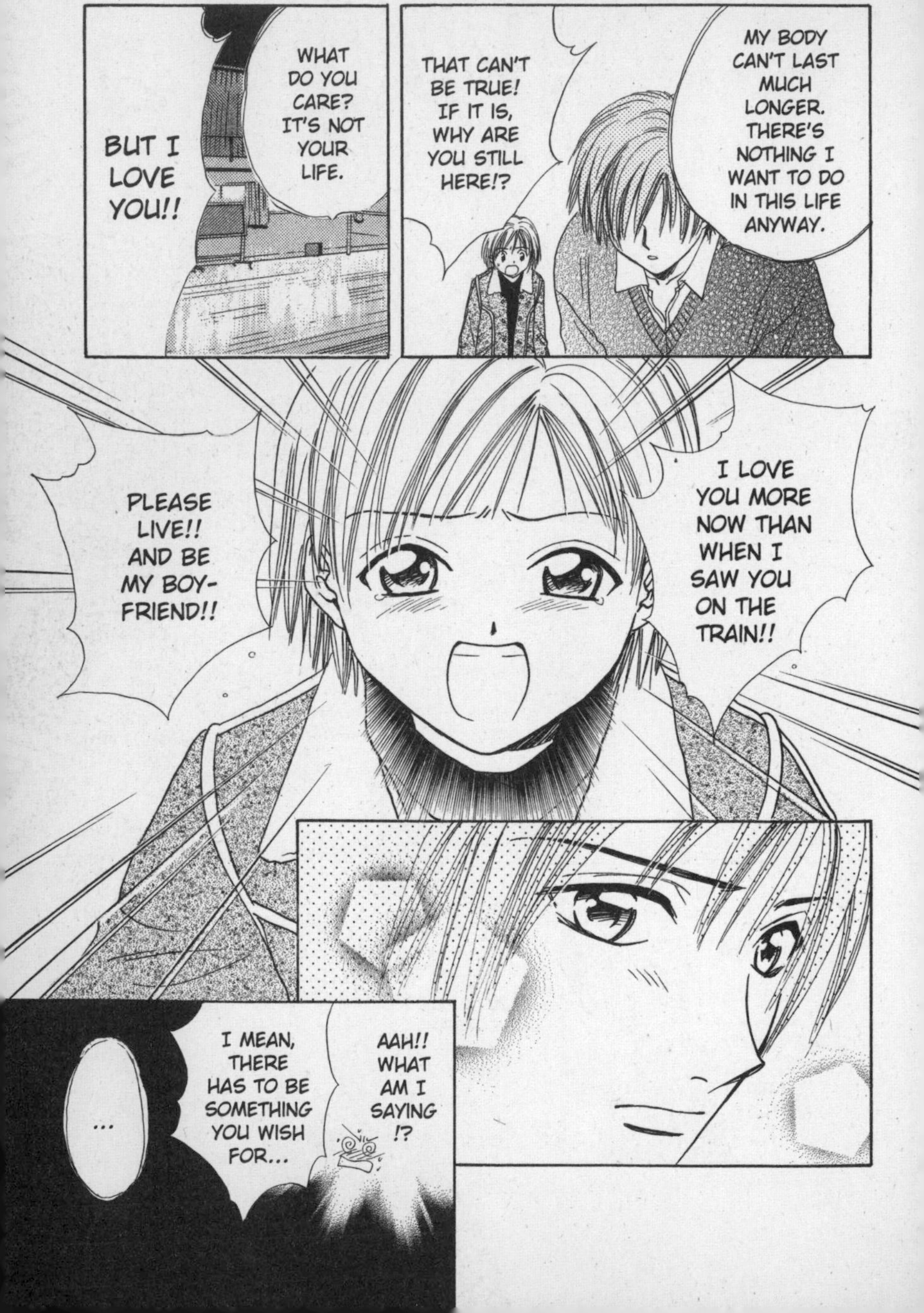
MY BODY CAN'T LAST MUCH LONGER. THERE'S NOTHING I WANT TO DO IN THIS LIFE ANYWAY.
THAT CAN'T BE TRUE! IF IT IS, WHY ARE YOU STILL HERE!?
WHAT DO YOU CARE? IT'S NOT YOUR LIFE.
BUT I LOVE YOU!!
I LOVE YOU MORE NOW THAN WHEN I SAW YOU ON THE TRAIN!!
PLEASE LIVE!! AND BE MY BOY-FRIEND!!
AAH!! WHAT AM I SAYING!?
I MEAN, THERE HAS TO BE SOMETHING YOU WISH FOR...
...

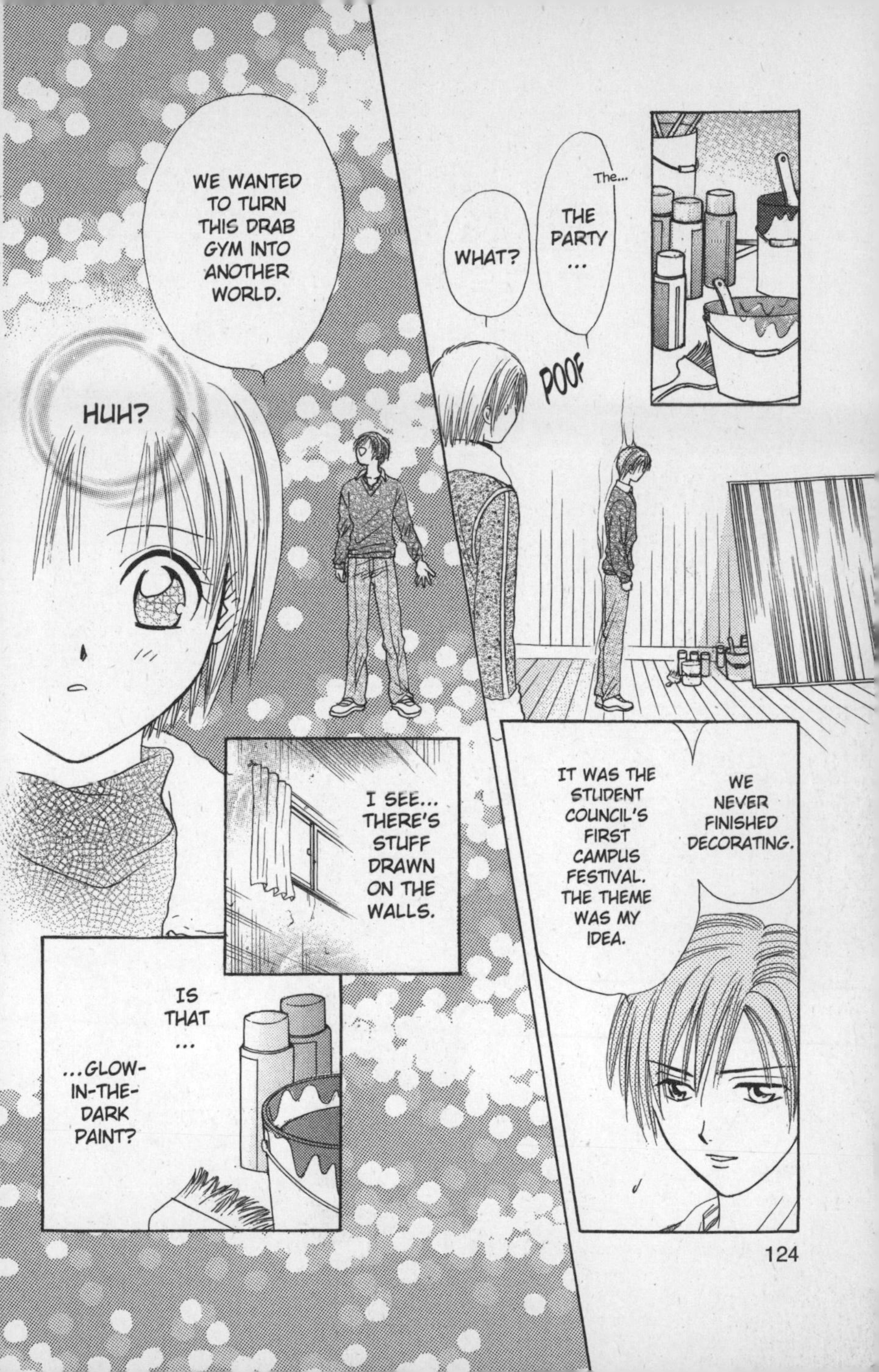

The... THE PARTY ...
WHAT?
POOF
WE NEVER FINISHED DECORATING.
IT WAS THE STUDENT COUNCIL'S FIRST CAMPUS FESTIVAL. THE THEME WAS MY IDEA.
WE WANTED TO TURN THIS DRAB GYM INTO ANOTHER WORLD.
HUH?
I SEE... THERE'S STUFF DRAWN ON THE WALLS.
IS THAT ...
...GLOW-IN-THE-DARK PAINT?

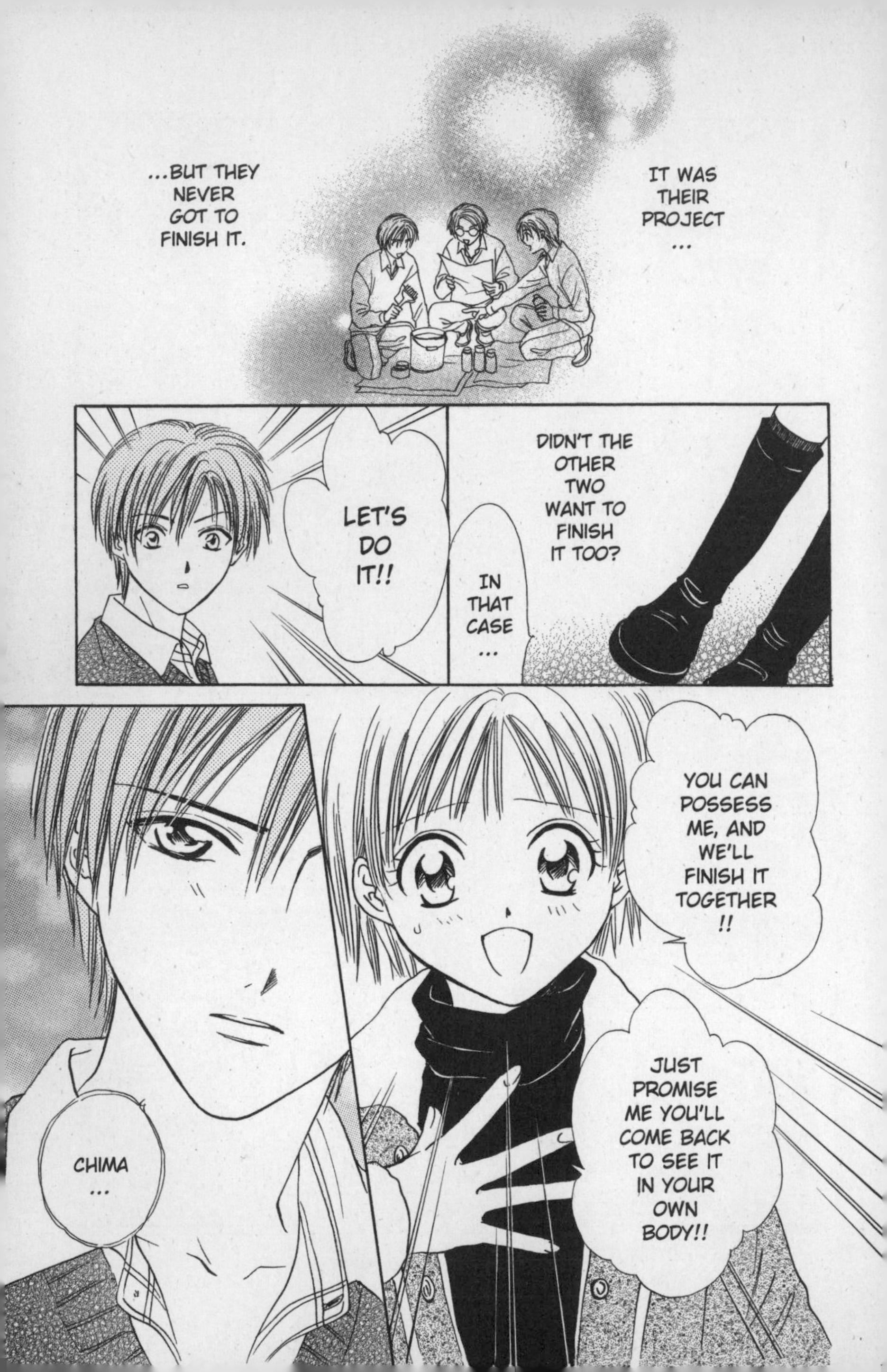
IT WAS THEIR PROJECT ...
...BUT THEY NEVER GOT TO FINISH IT.
DIDN'T THE OTHER TWO WANT TO FINISH IT TOO?
IN THAT CASE ...
LET'S DO IT!!
YOU CAN POSSESS ME, AND WE'LL FINISH IT TOGETHER !!
JUST PROMISE ME YOU'LL COME BACK TO SEE IT IN YOUR OWN BODY!!
CHIMA ...

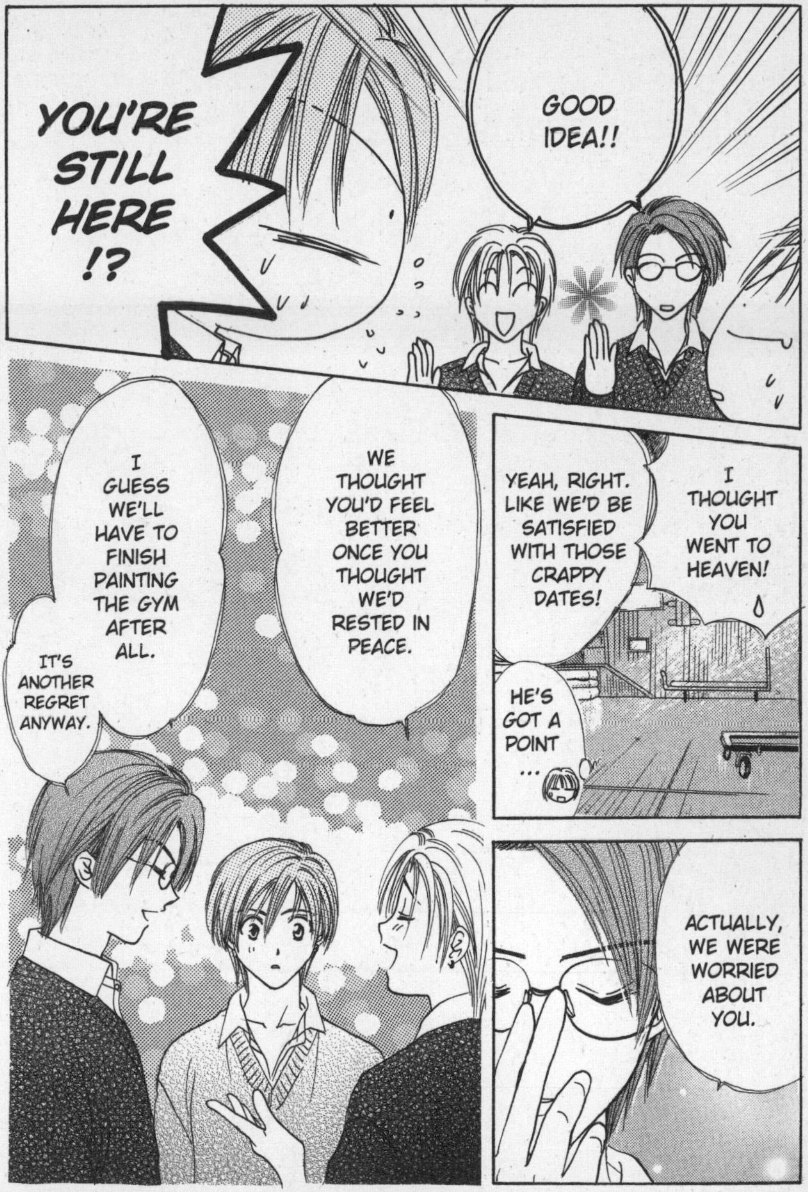
GOOD IDEA!!
YOU'RE STILL HERE !?
I THOUGHT YOU WENT TO HEAVEN!
YEAH, RIGHT. LIKE WE'D BE SATISFIED WITH THOSE CRAPPY DATES!
HE'S GOT A POINT ...
ACTUALLY, WE WERE WORRIED ABOUT YOU.
WE THOUGHT YOU'D FEEL BETTER ONCE YOU THOUGHT WE'D RESTED IN PEACE.
I GUESS WE'LL HAVE TO FINISH PAINTING THE GYM AFTER ALL.
IT'S ANOTHER REGRET ANYWAY.

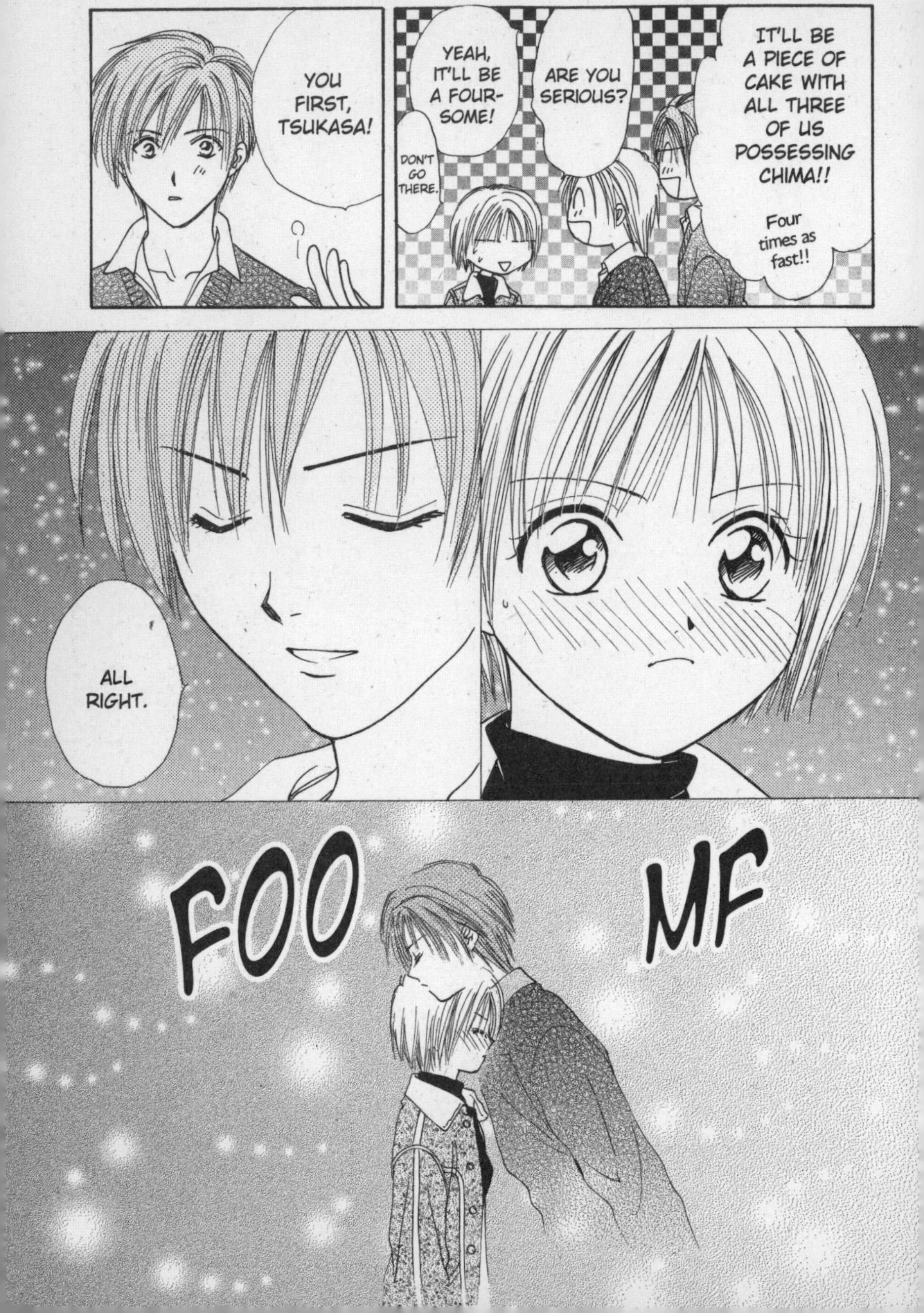
IT'LL BE A PIECE OF CAKE WITH ALL THREE OF US POSSESSING CHIMA!!
Four times as fast!!
ARE YOU SERIOUS?
YEAH, IT'LL BE A FOURSOME!
DON'T GO THERE.
YOU FIRST, TSUKASA!
ALL RIGHT.
FOO MF

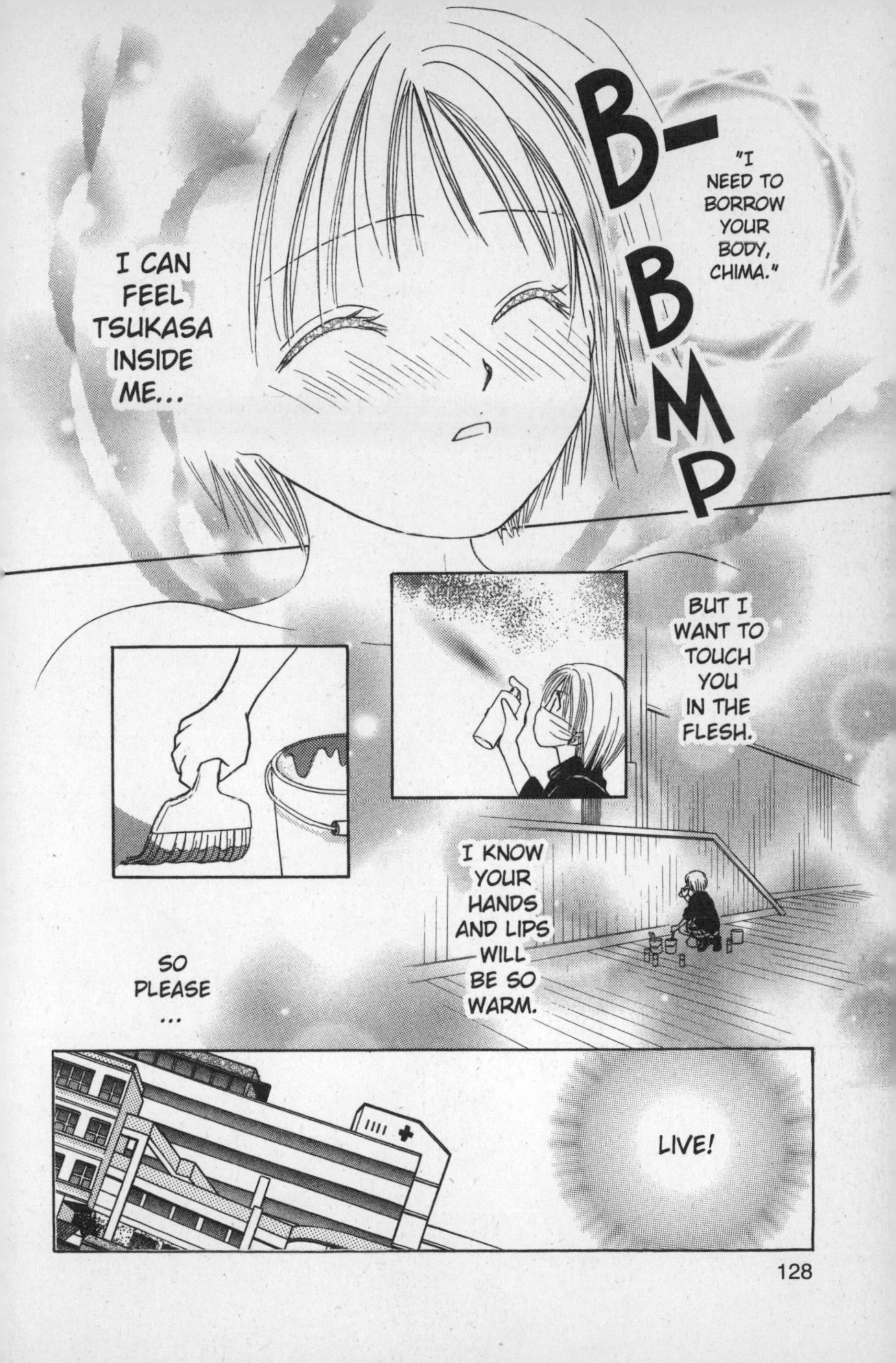
B-BMP
"I NEED TO BORROW YOUR BODY, CHIMA."
I CAN FEEL TSUKASA INSIDE ME...
BUT I WANT TO TOUCH YOU IN THE FLESH.
I KNOW YOUR HANDS AND LIPS WILL BE SO WARM.
SO PLEASE ...
LIVE!

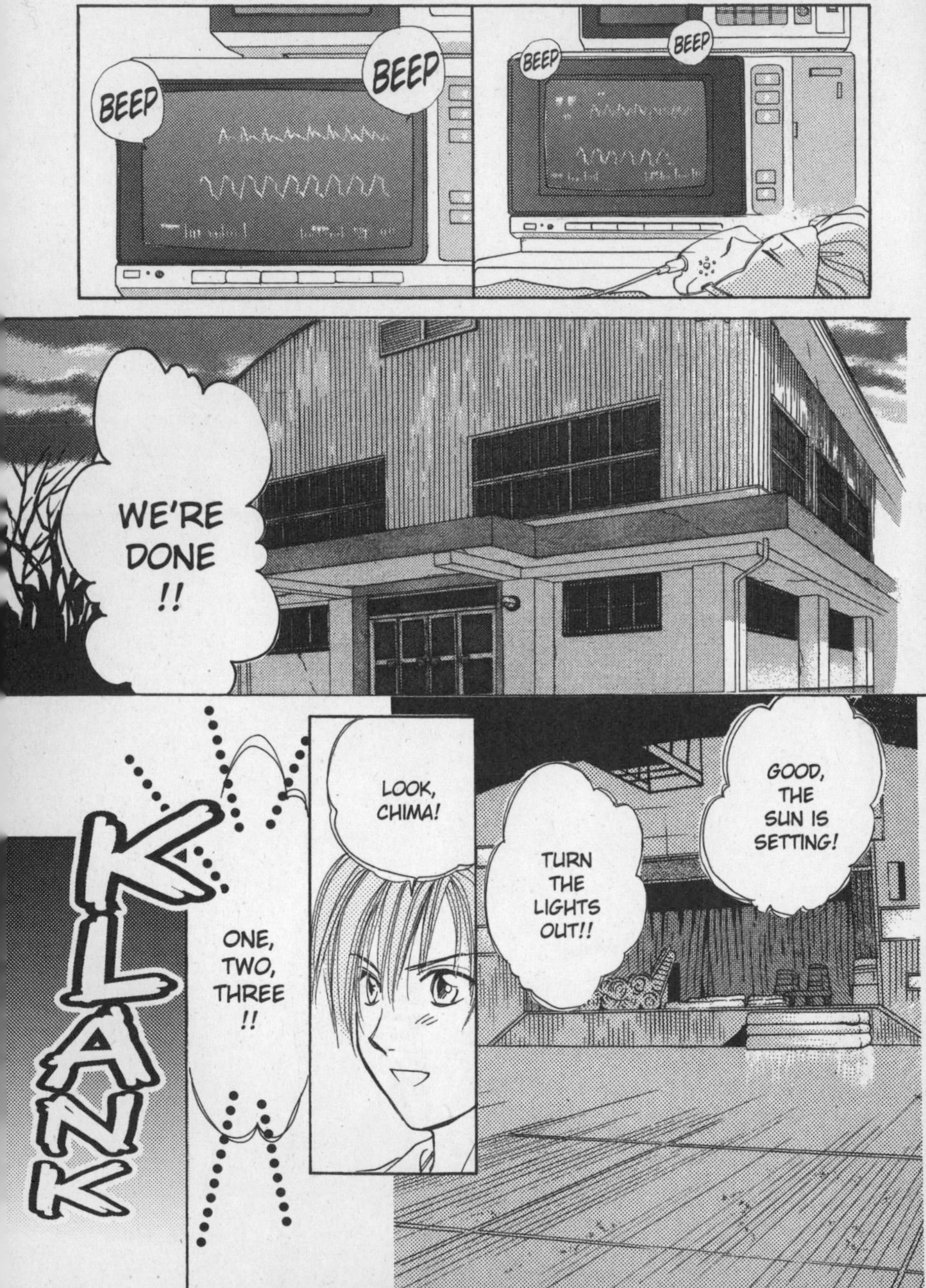
BEEP
BEEP
BEEP
BEEP
WE'RE DONE !!
GOOD, THE SUN IS SETTING!
TURN THE LIGHTS OUT!!
LOOK, CHIMA!
ONE, TWO, THREE !!
KLANK

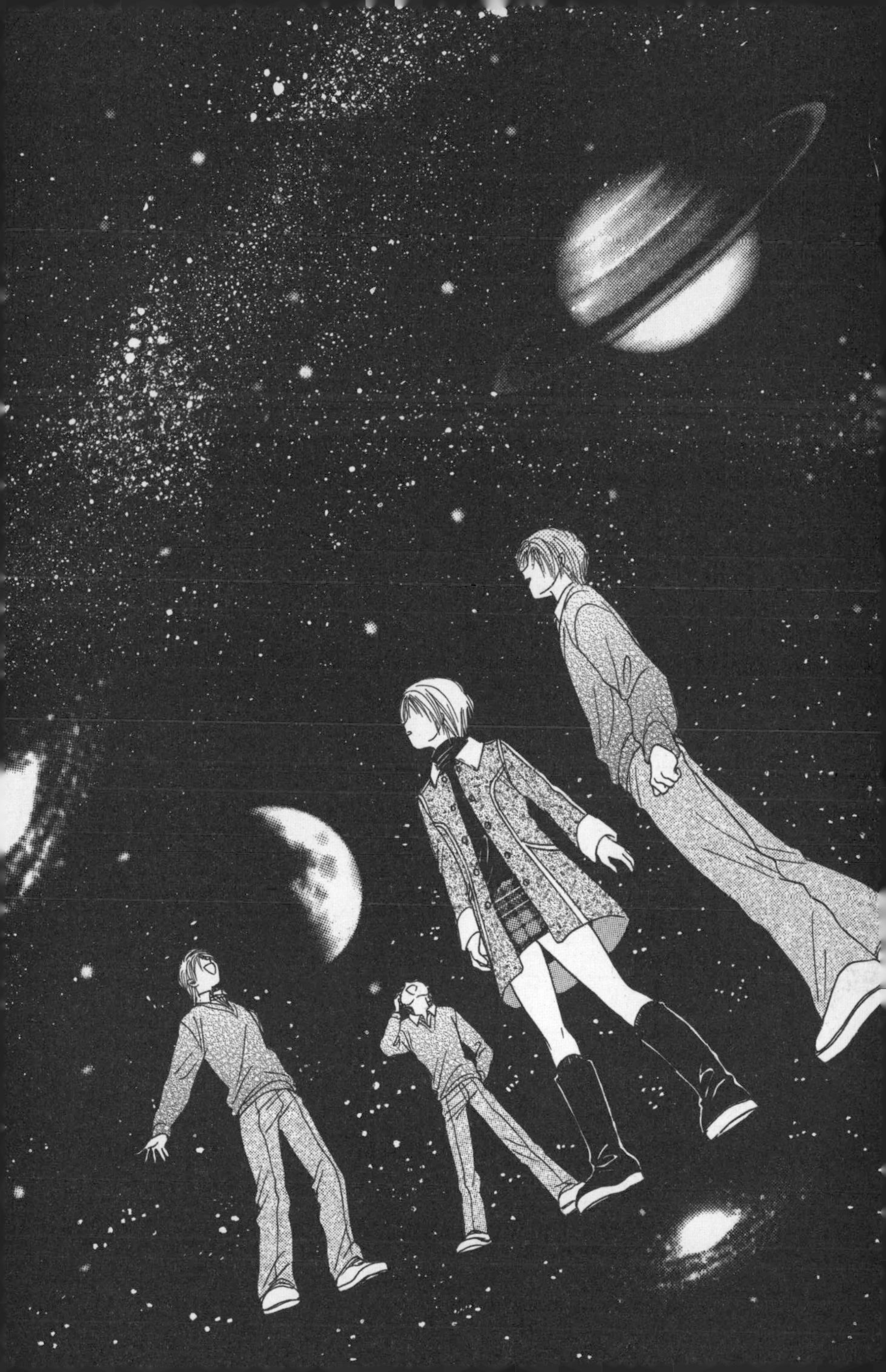

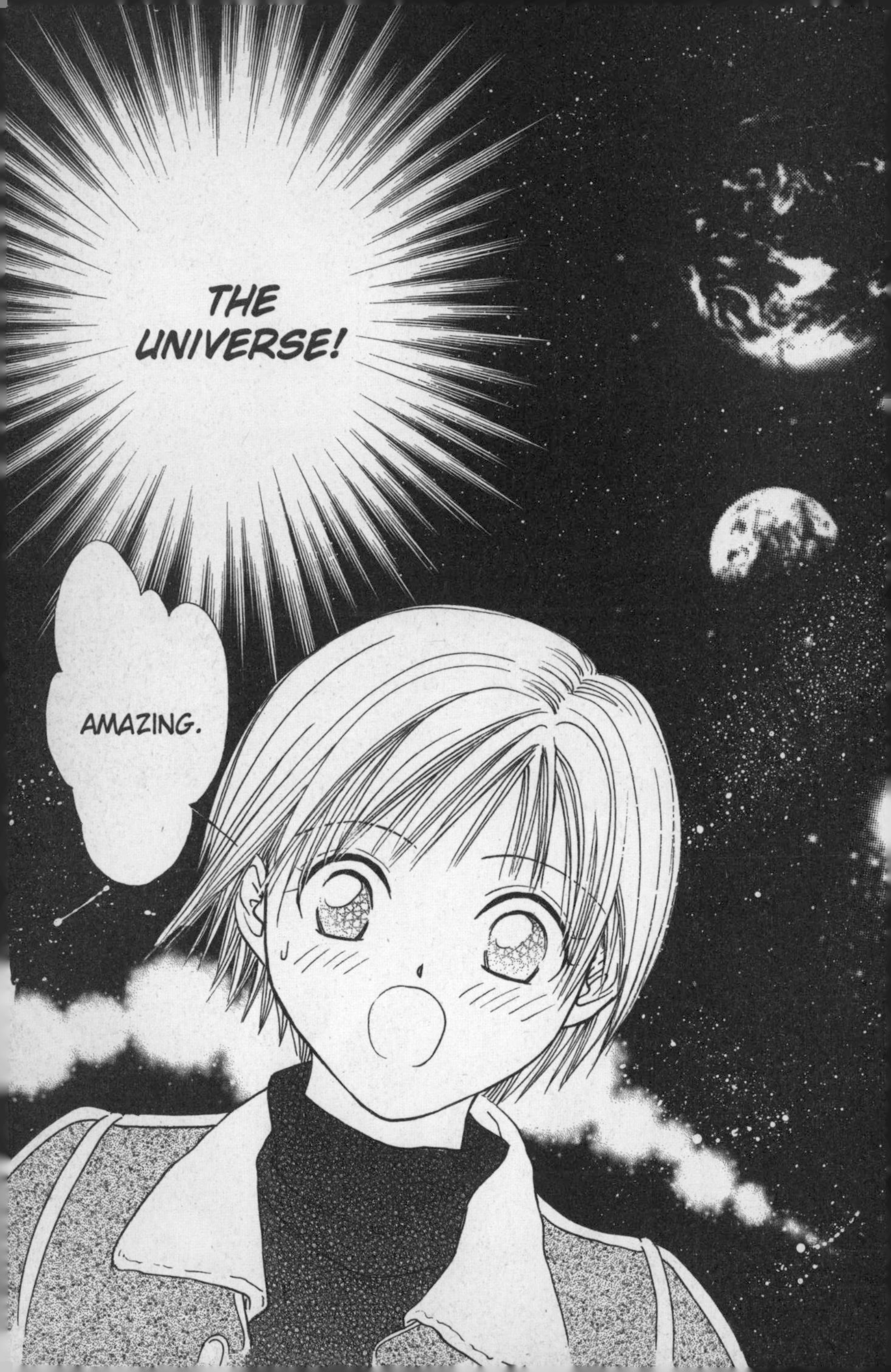
THE UNIVERSE!
AMAZING.

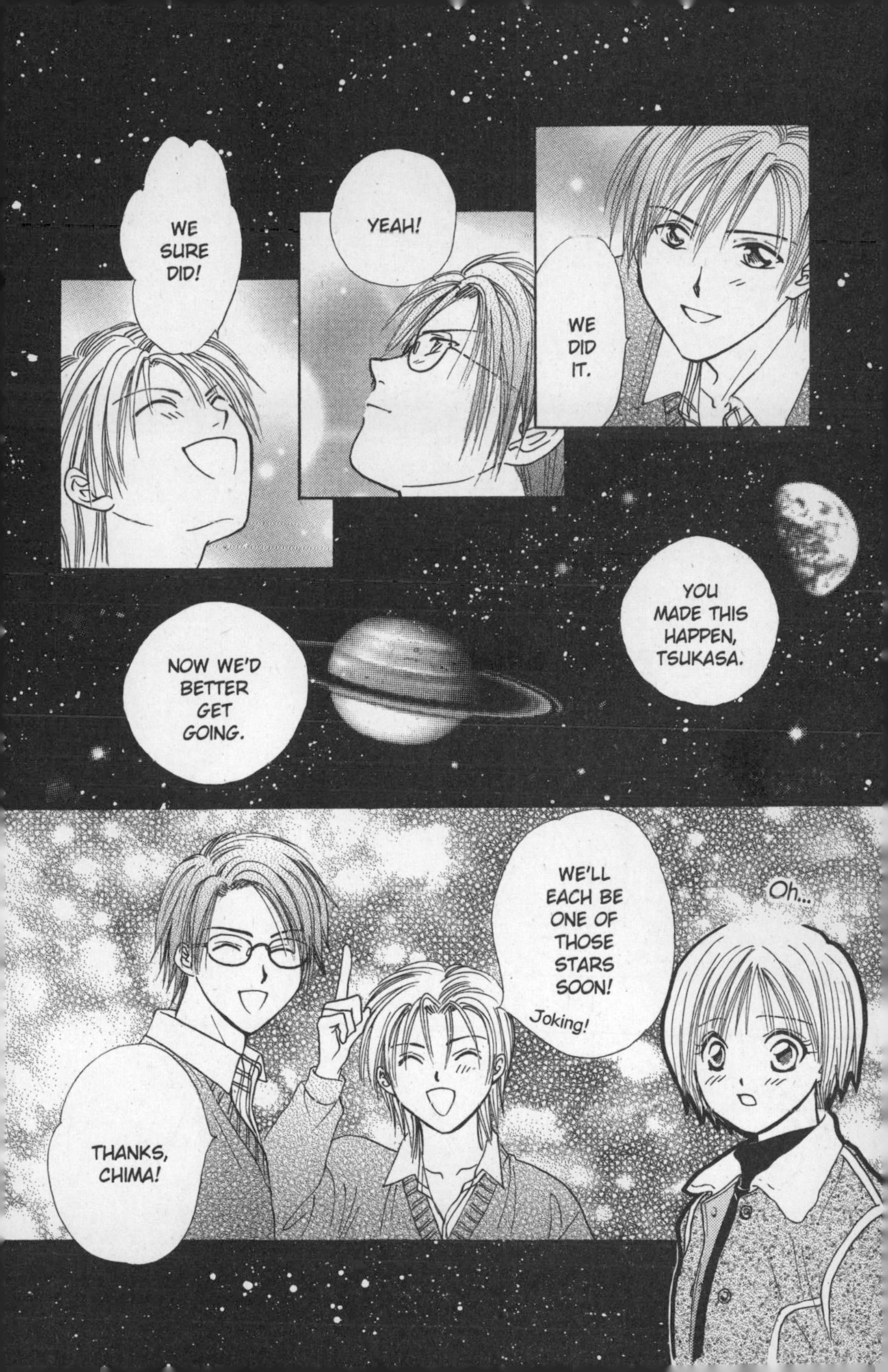
WE DID IT.
YEAH!
WE SURE DID!
YOU MADE THIS HAPPEN, TSUKASA.
NOW WE'D BETTER GET GOING.
Oh...
WE'LL EACH BE ONE OF THOSE STARS SOON!
Joking!
THANKS, CHIMA!

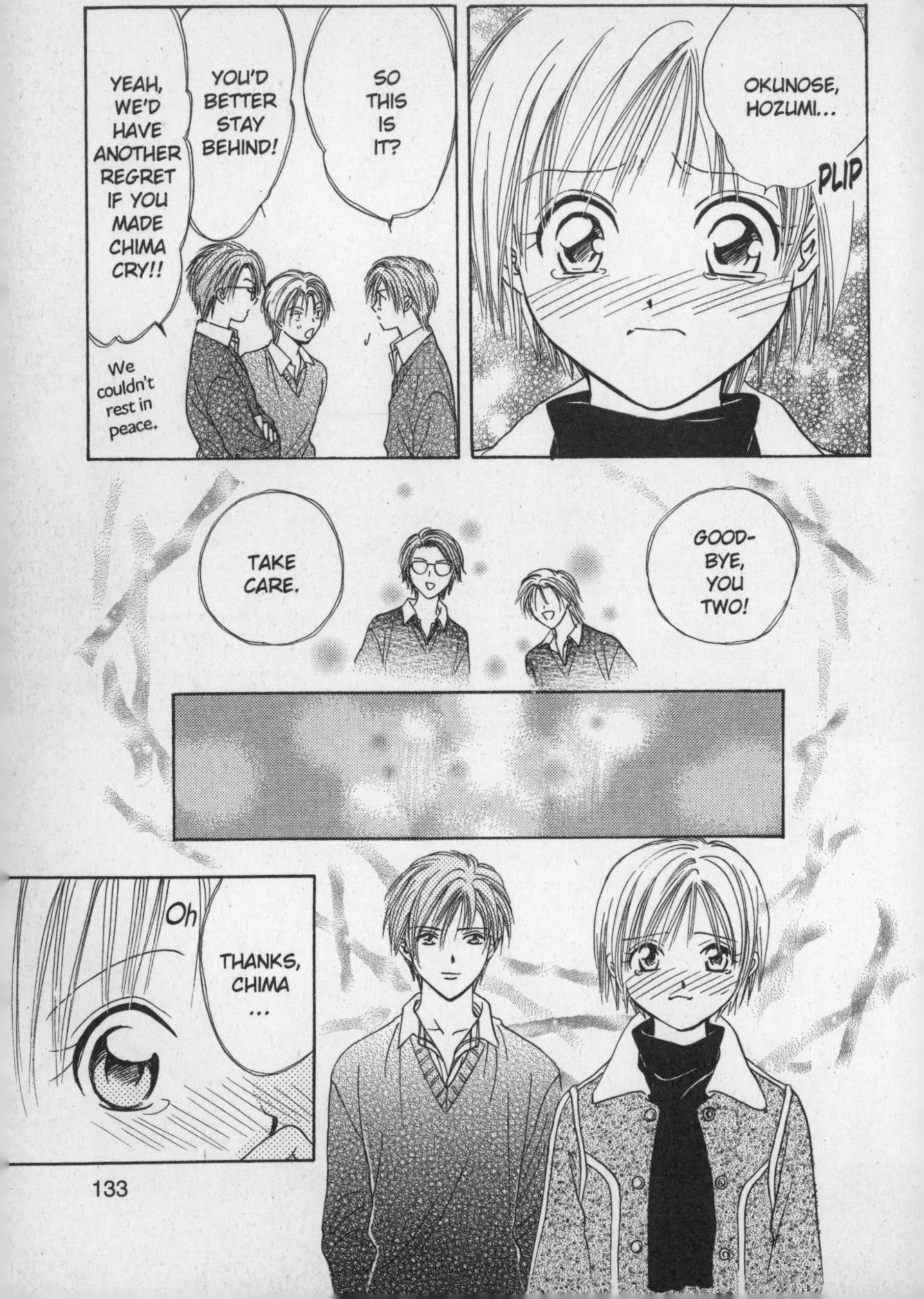
OKUNOSE, HOZUMI...
PLIP
SO THIS IS IT?
YOU'D BETTER STAY BEHIND!
YEAH, WE'D HAVE ANOTHER REGRET IF YOU MADE CHIMA CRY!!
We couldn't rest in peace.
GOOD-BYE, YOU TWO!
TAKE CARE.
Oh
THANKS, CHIMA ...

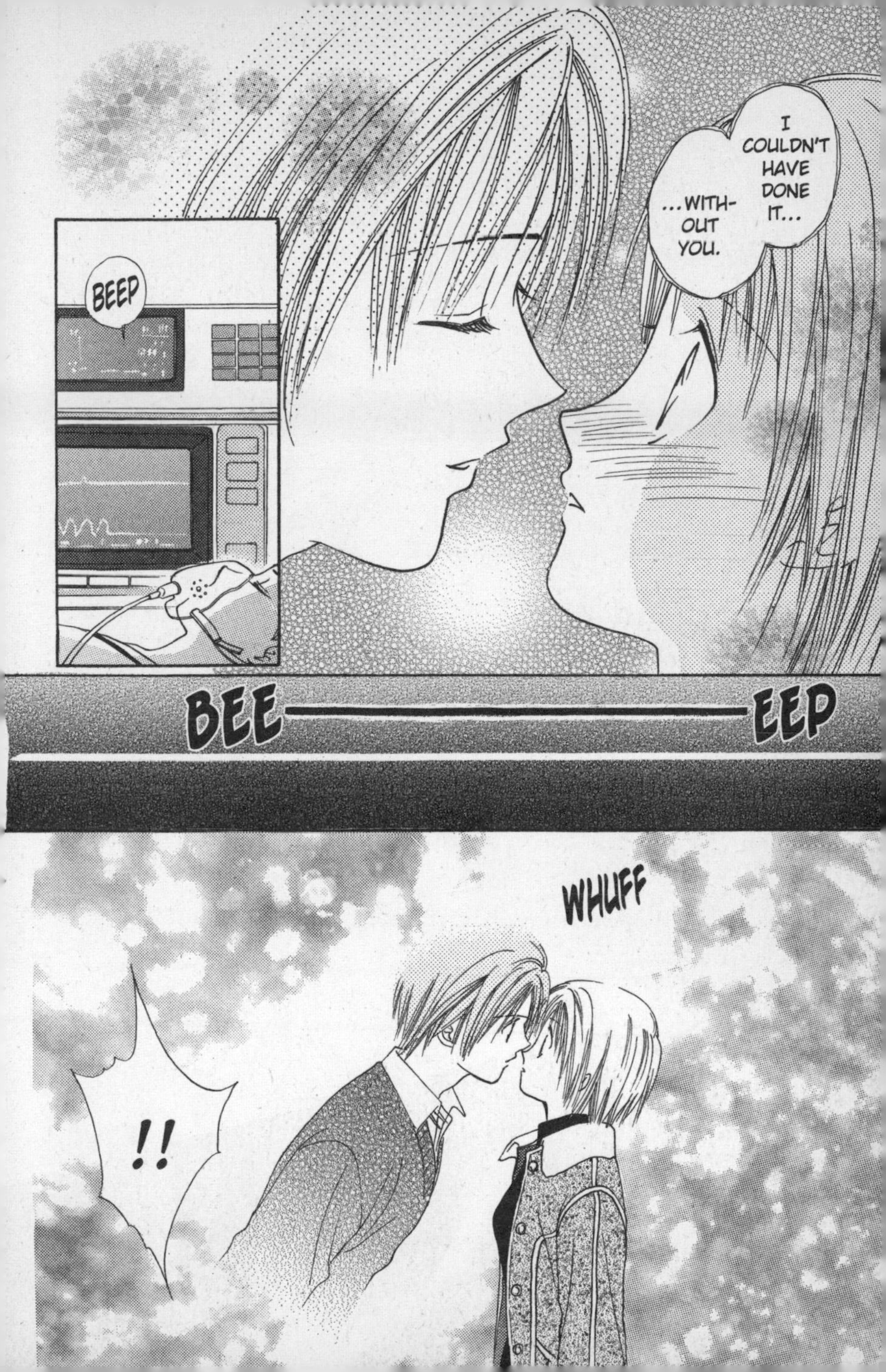
I COULDN'T HAVE DONE IT...
...WITH-OUT YOU.
BEEP
BEE———EEP
WHUFF
!!

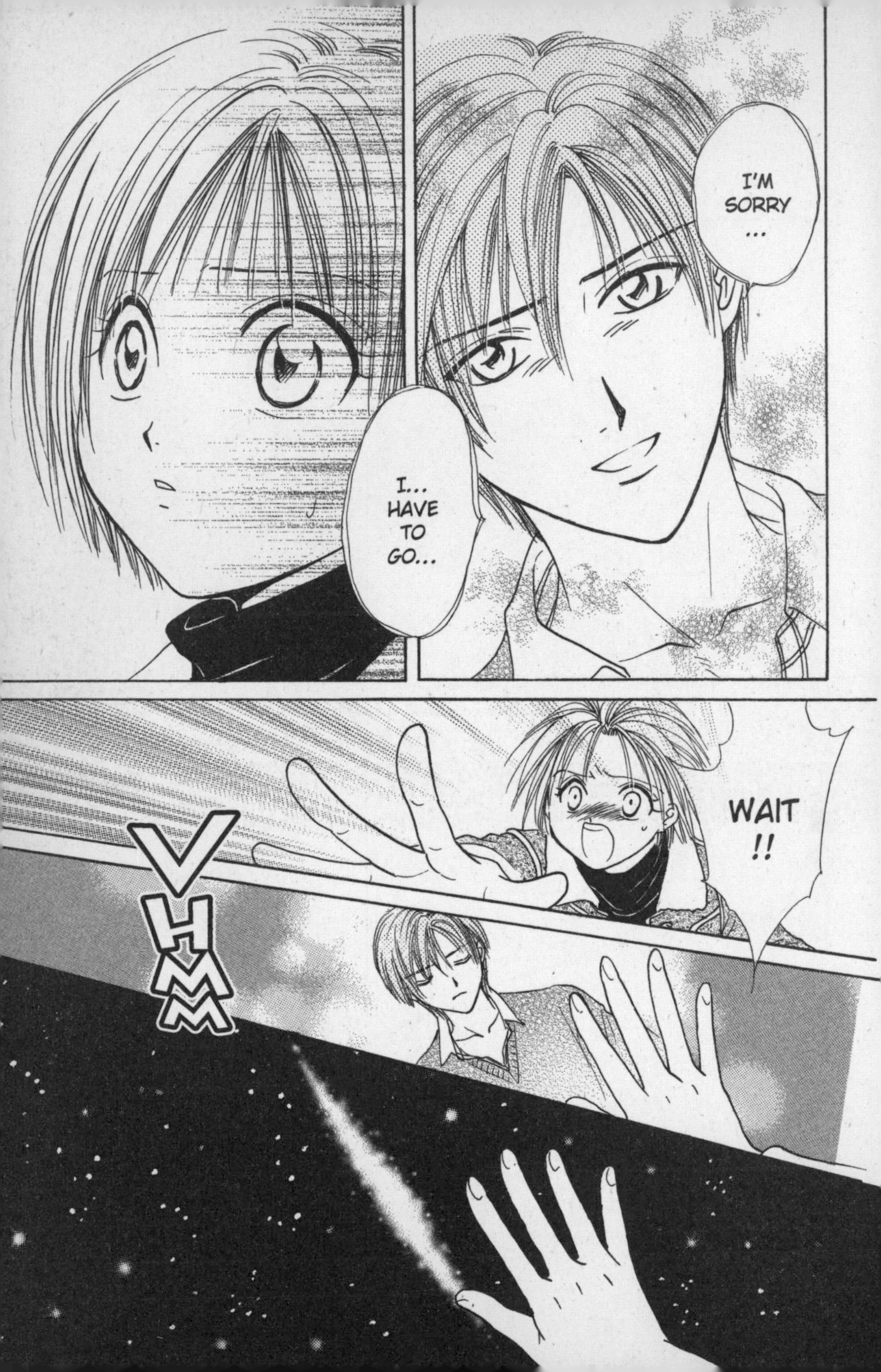
I'M SORRY ...
I... HAVE TO GO...
WAIT !!
VHMM

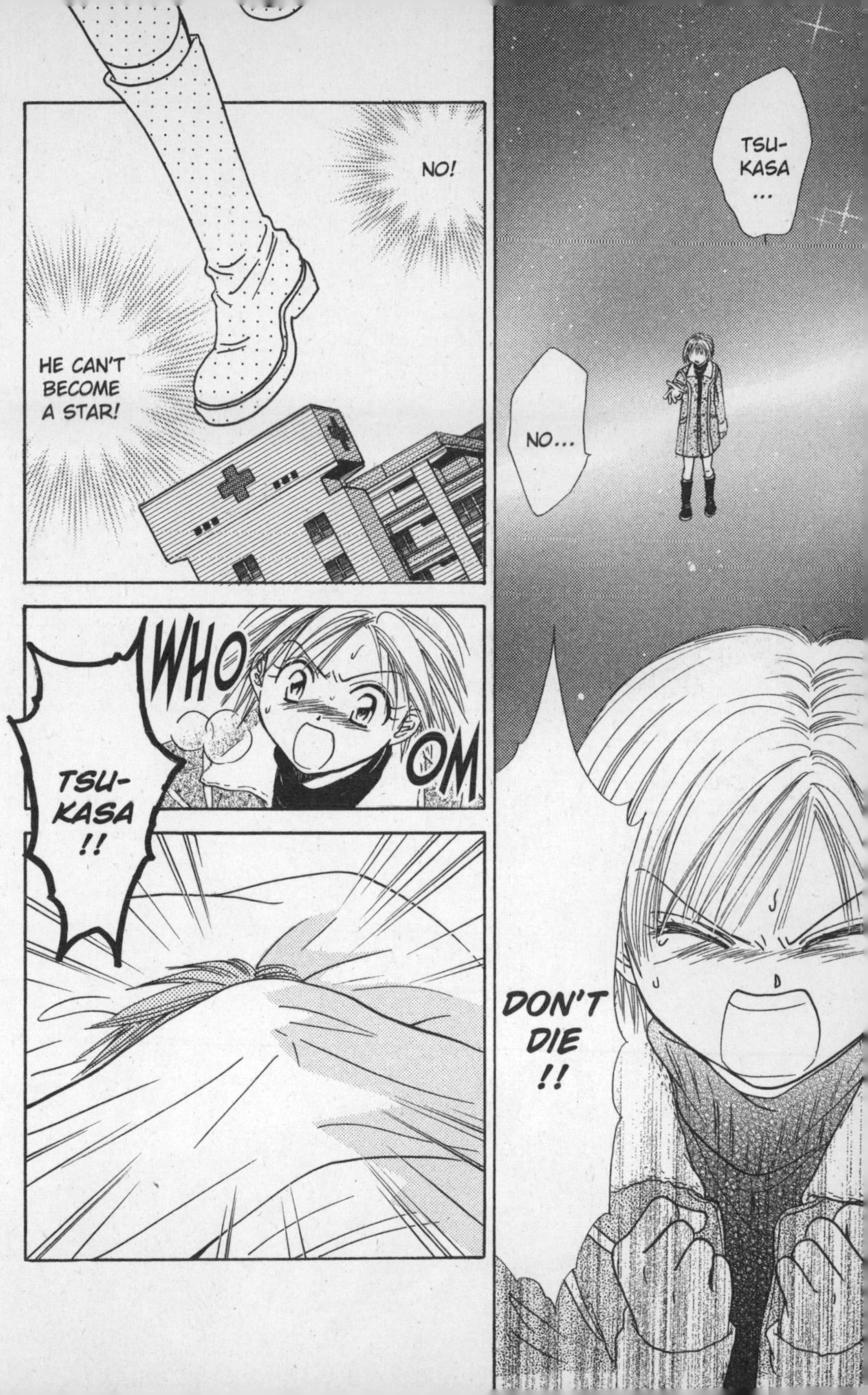
TSU-KASA ...
NO...
DON'T DIE !!
NO!
HE CAN'T BECOME A STAR!
WHOOM
TSU-KASA !!

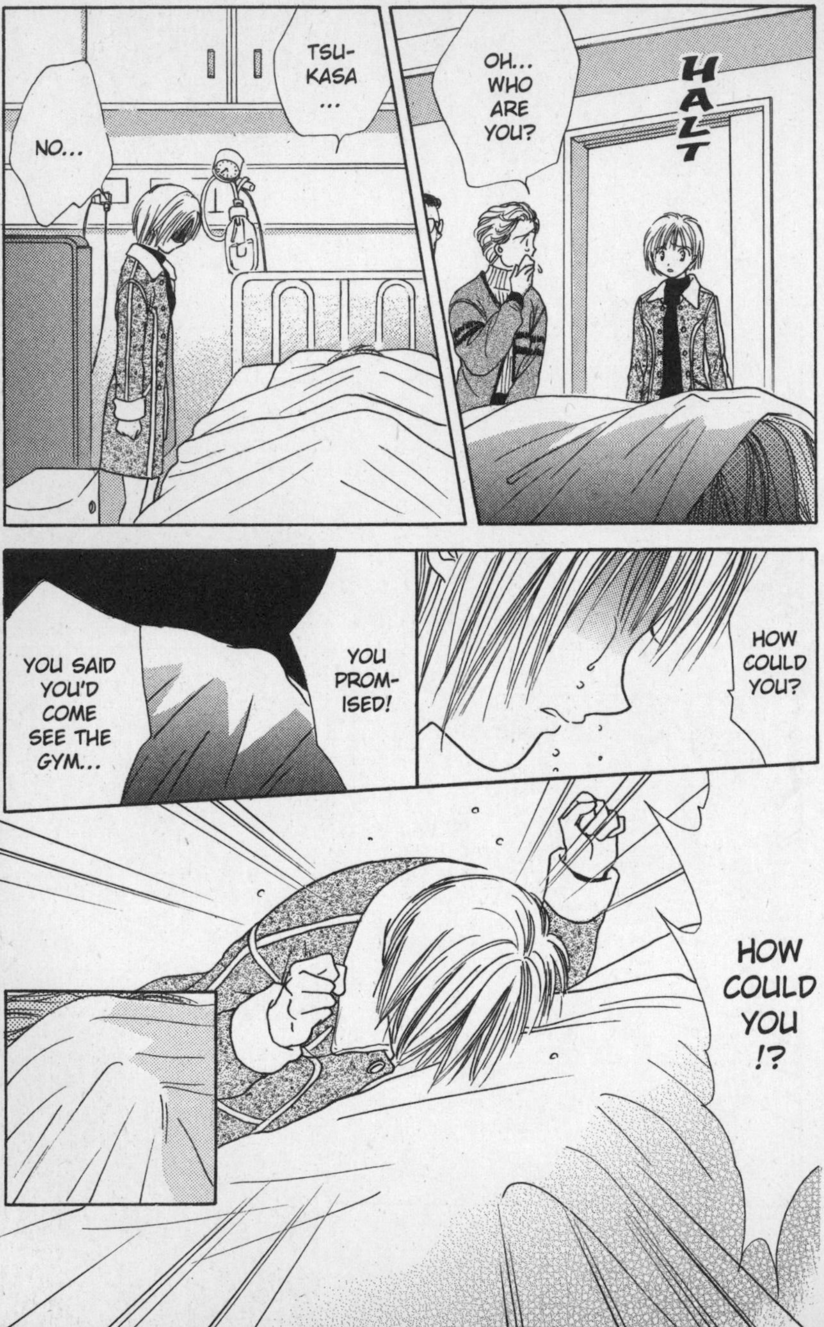

OH... WHO ARE YOU?
HALT
TSU-KASA ...
NO...
HOW COULD YOU?
YOU PROMISED!
YOU SAID YOU'D COME SEE THE GYM...
HOW COULD YOU !?

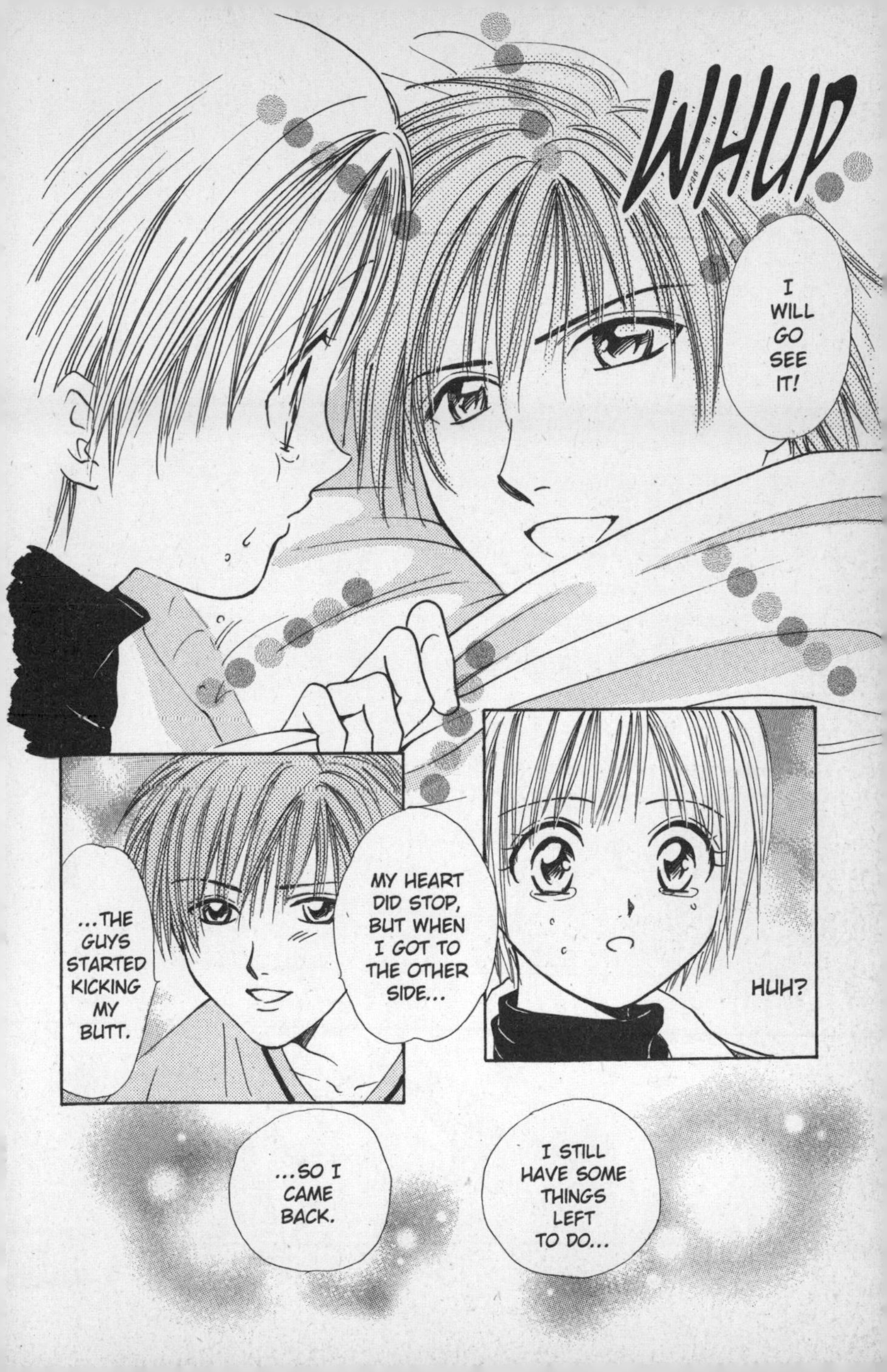
WHUP
I WILL GO SEE IT!
HUH?
MY HEART DID STOP, BUT WHEN I GOT TO THE OTHER SIDE...
...THE GUYS STARTED KICKING MY BUTT.
I STILL HAVE SOME THINGS LEFT TO DO...
...SO I CAME BACK.

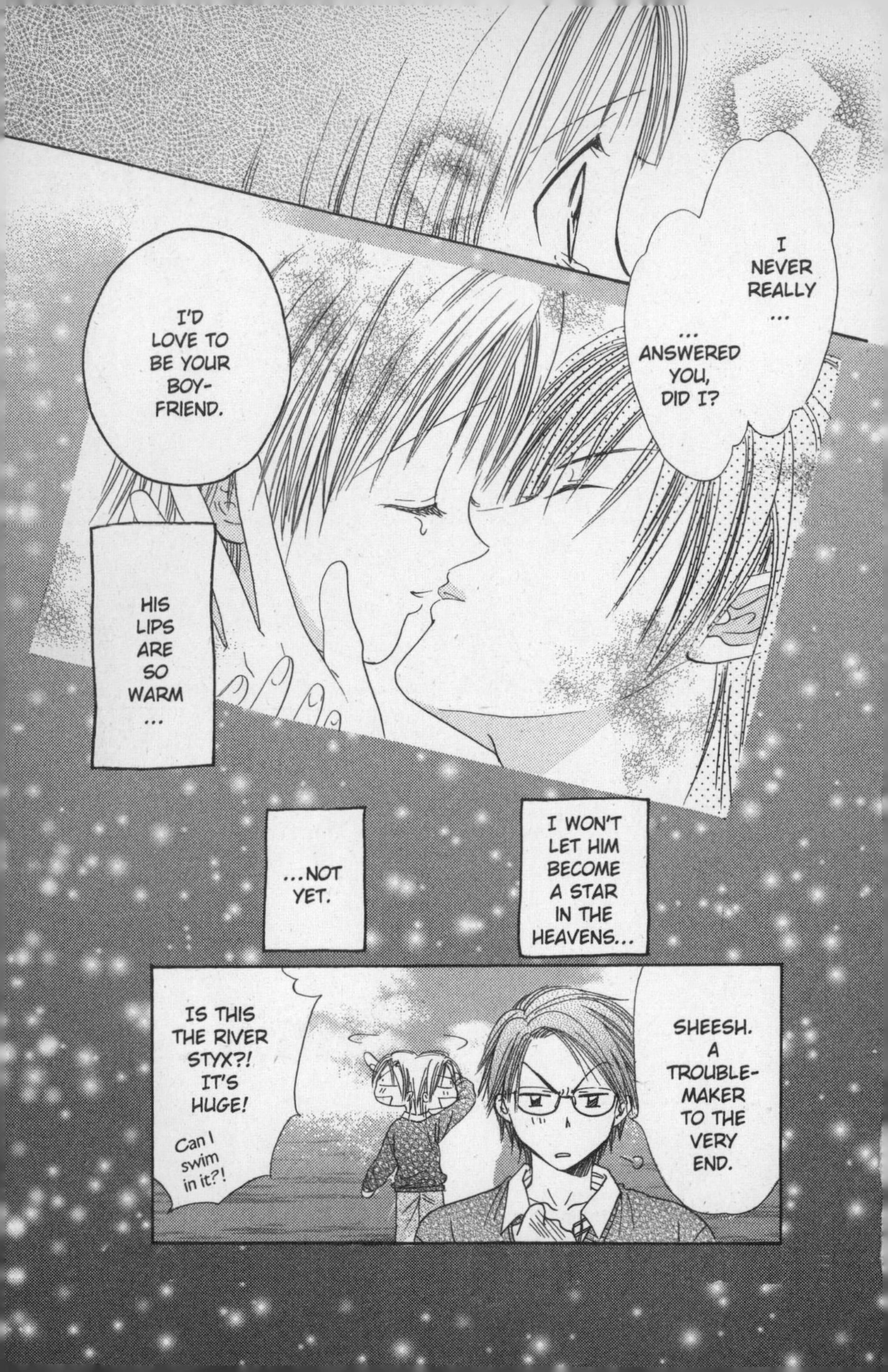
I NEVER REALLY ...
... ANSWERED YOU, DID I?
I'D LOVE TO BE YOUR BOY-FRIEND.
HIS LIPS ARE SO WARM ...
I WON'T LET HIM BECOME A STAR IN THE HEAVENS...
...NOT YET.
SHEESH. A TROUBLE-MAKER TO THE VERY END.
IS THIS THE RIVER STYX?! IT'S HUGE!
Can I swim in it?!

Absolute Boyfriend

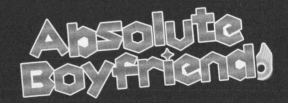

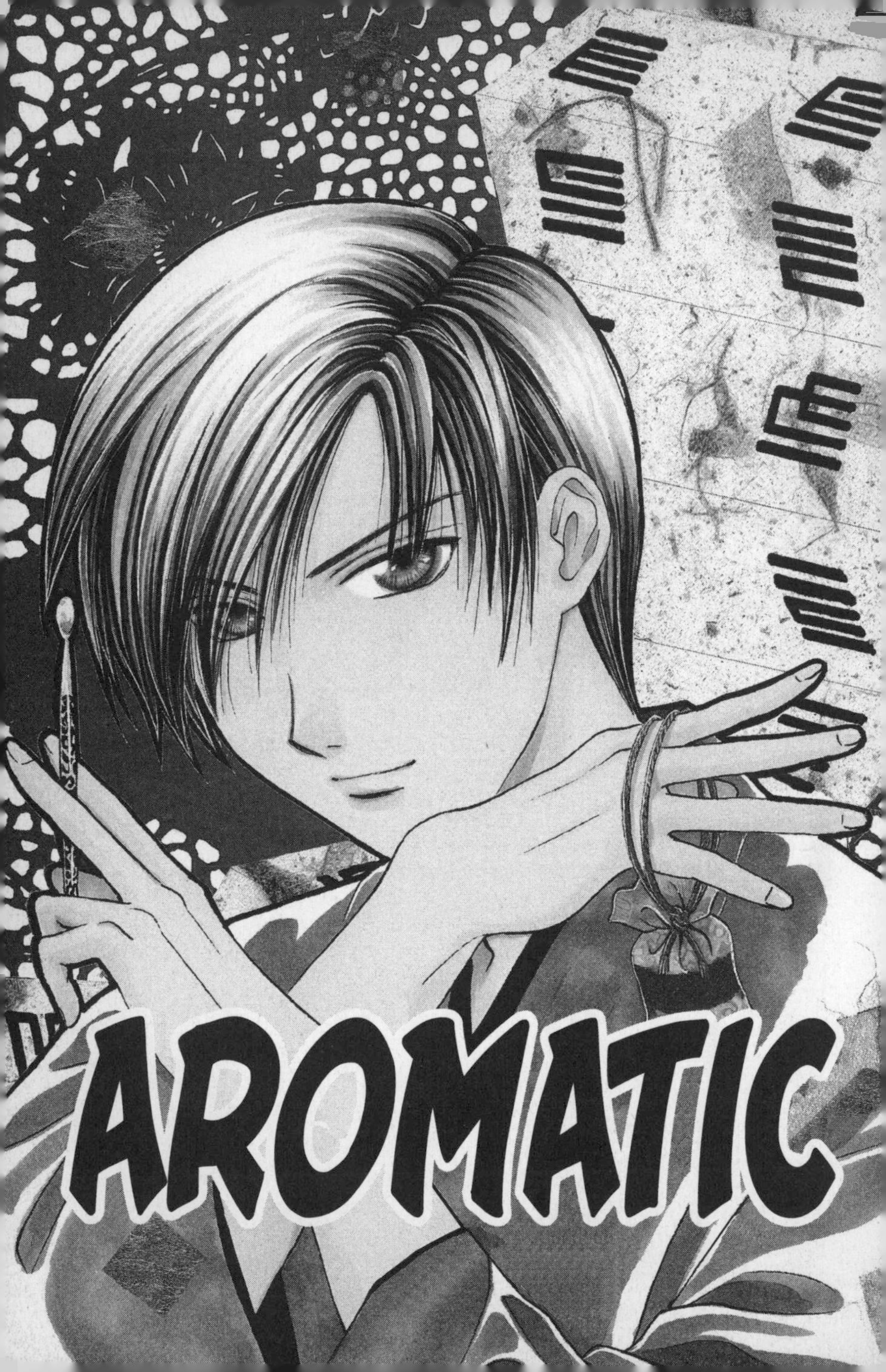
AROMATIC

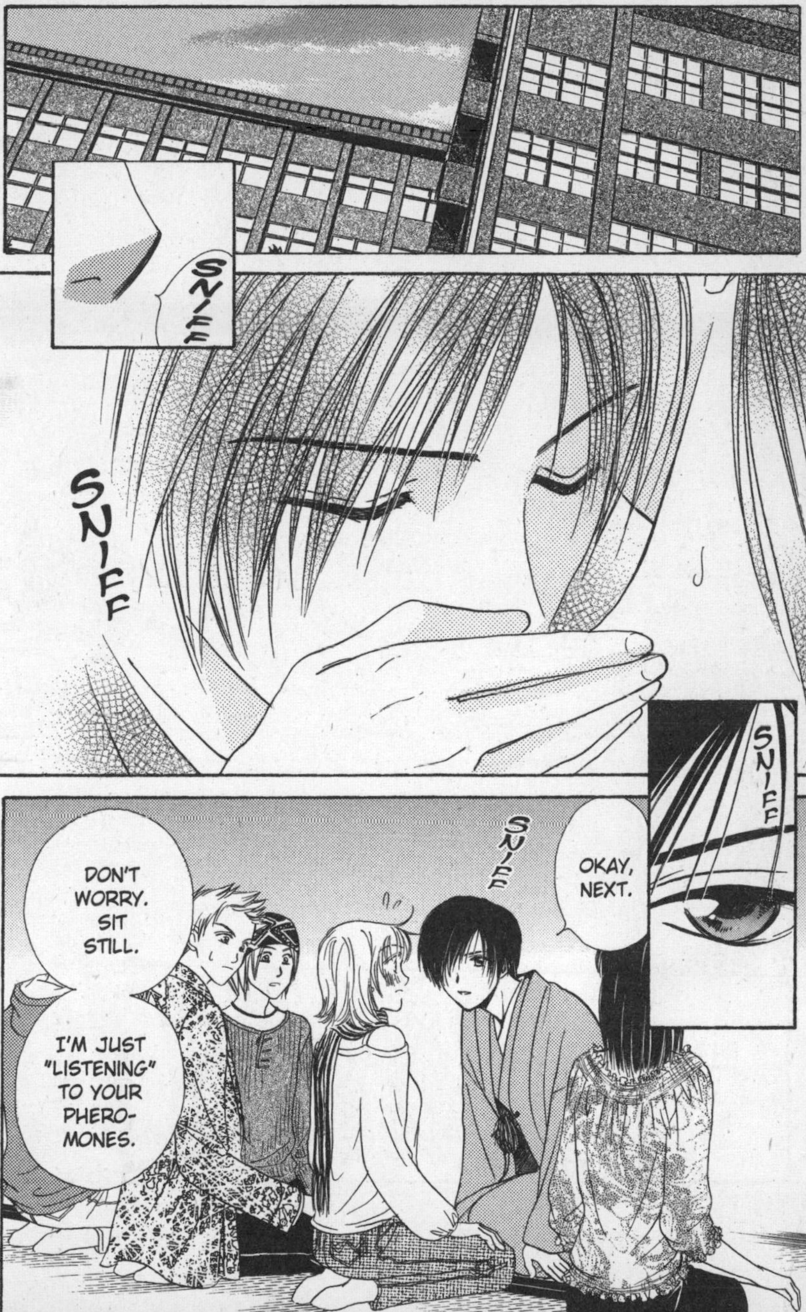
SNIFF
SNIFF
SNIFF
OKAY, NEXT.
SNIFF
DON'T WORRY. SIT STILL.
I'M JUST "LISTENING" TO YOUR PHERO-MONES.

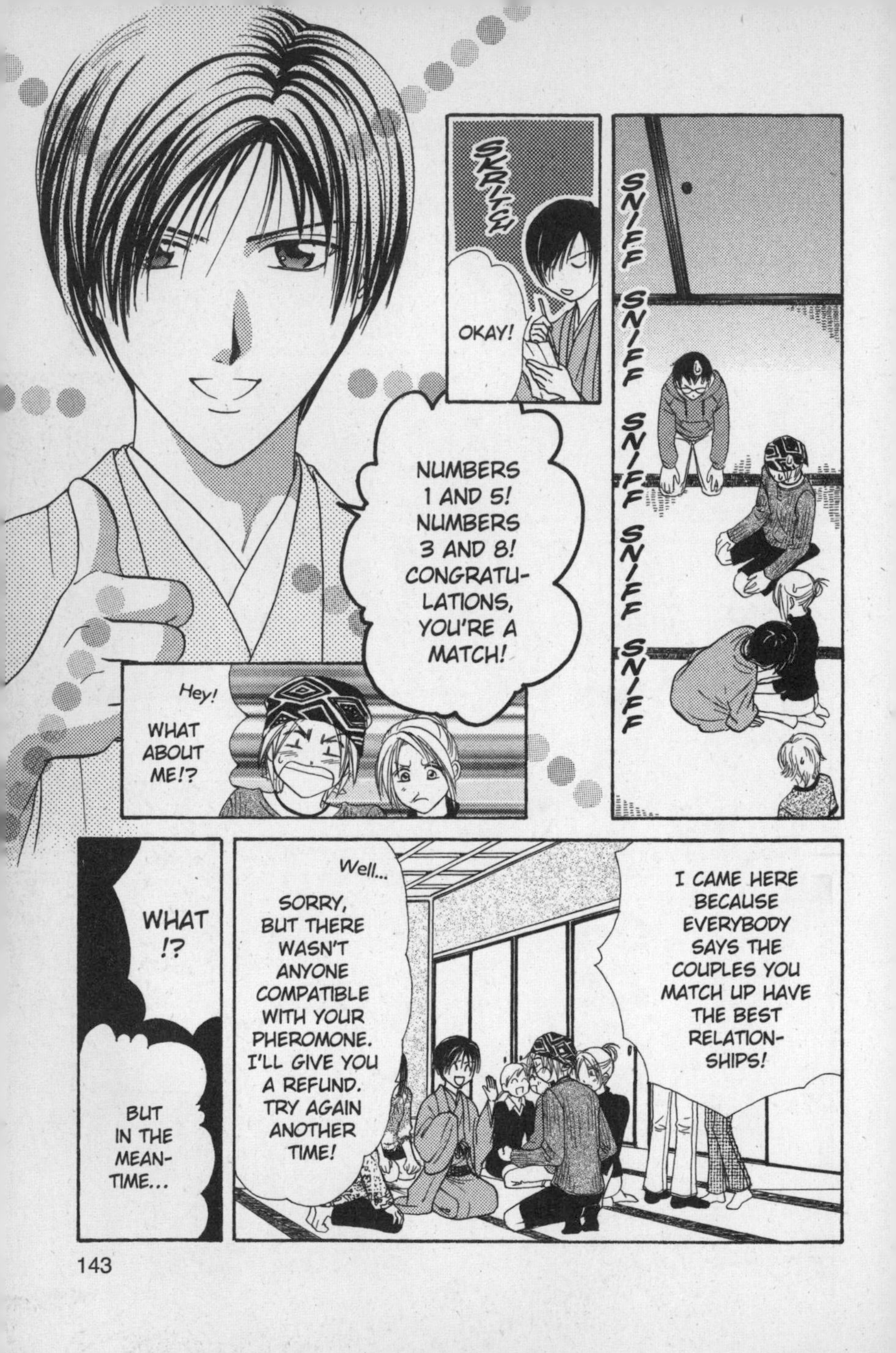
SNIFF SNIFF SNIFF SNIFF SNIFF
SKRITCH
OKAY!
NUMBERS 1 AND 5! NUMBERS 3 AND 8! CONGRATULATIONS, YOU'RE A MATCH!
Hey!
WHAT ABOUT ME!?
I CAME HERE BECAUSE EVERYBODY SAYS THE COUPLES YOU MATCH UP HAVE THE BEST RELATIONSHIPS!
Well...
SORRY, BUT THERE WASN'T ANYONE COMPATIBLE WITH YOUR PHEROMONE. I'LL GIVE YOU A REFUND. TRY AGAIN ANOTHER TIME!
WHAT!?
BUT IN THE MEANTIME...

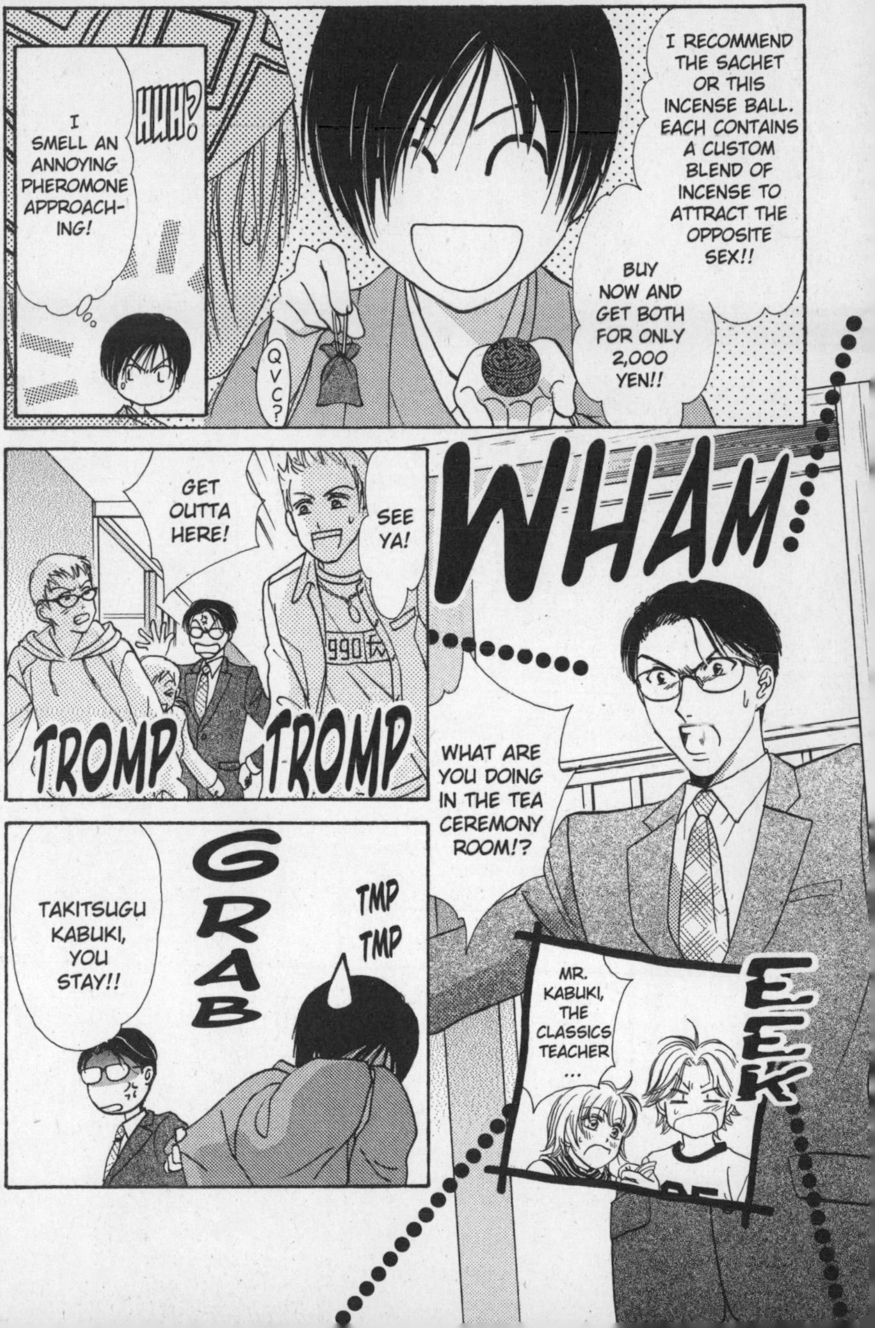
I RECOMMEND THE SACHET OR THIS INCENSE BALL. EACH CONTAINS A CUSTOM BLEND OF INCENSE TO ATTRACT THE OPPOSITE SEX!!
BUY NOW AND GET BOTH FOR ONLY 2,000 YEN!!
QVC?
HUH?
I SMELL AN ANNOYING PHEROMONE APPROACH-ING!
WHAM
WHAT ARE YOU DOING IN THE TEA CEREMONY ROOM!?
EEK
MR. KABUKI, THE CLASSICS TEACHER ...
SEE YA!
GET OUTTA HERE!
TROMP
TROMP
TMP TMP
GRAB
TAKITSUGU KABUKI, YOU STAY!!

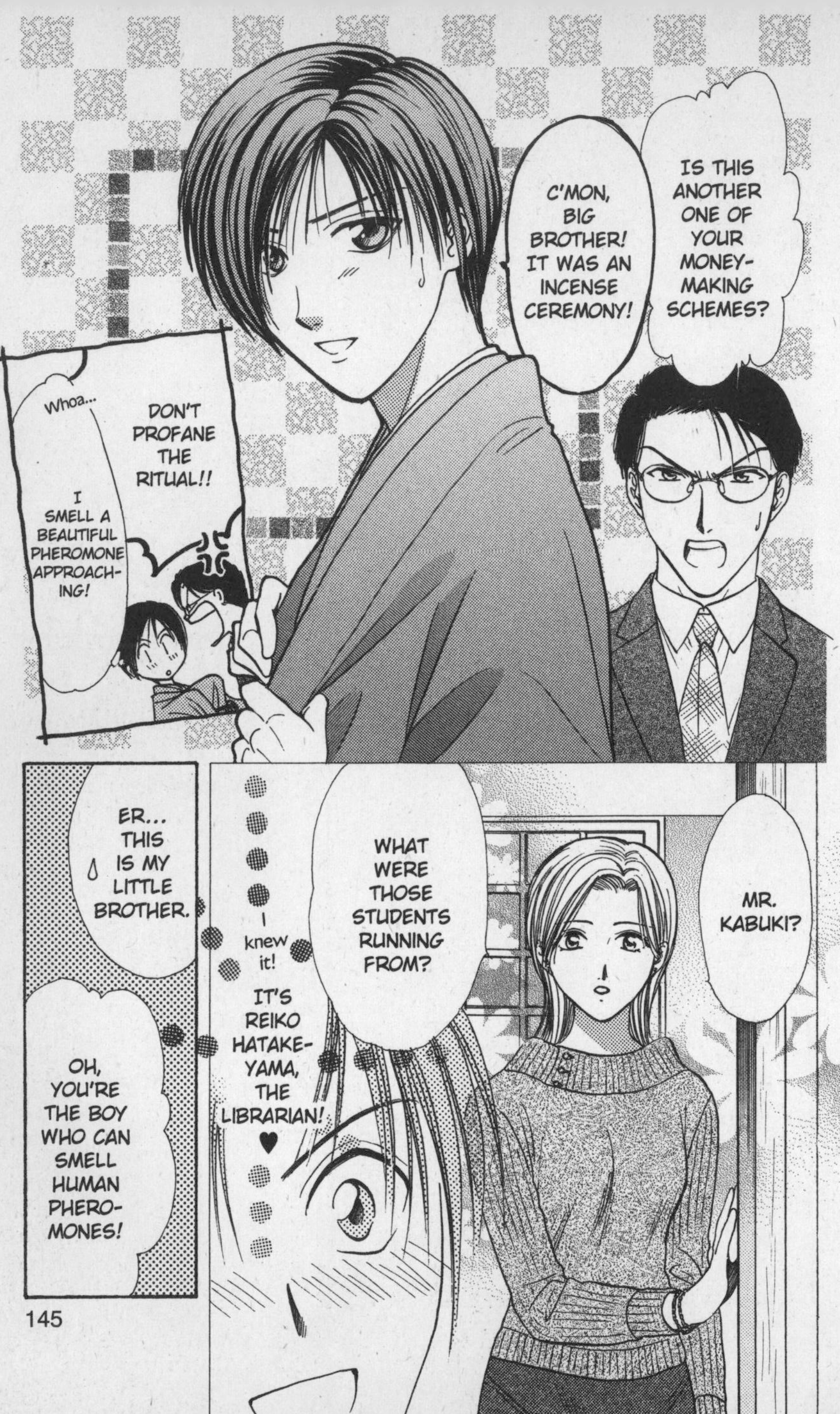
IS THIS ANOTHER ONE OF YOUR MONEY-MAKING SCHEMES?
C'MON, BIG BROTHER! IT WAS AN INCENSE CEREMONY!
DON'T PROFANE THE RITUAL!!
Whoa...
I SMELL A BEAUTIFUL PHEROMONE APPROACHING!
MR. KABUKI?
WHAT WERE THOSE STUDENTS RUNNING FROM?
I knew it!
IT'S REIKO HATAKEYAMA, THE LIBRARIAN! ♥
ER... THIS IS MY LITTLE BROTHER.
OH, YOU'RE THE BOY WHO CAN SMELL HUMAN PHEROMONES!

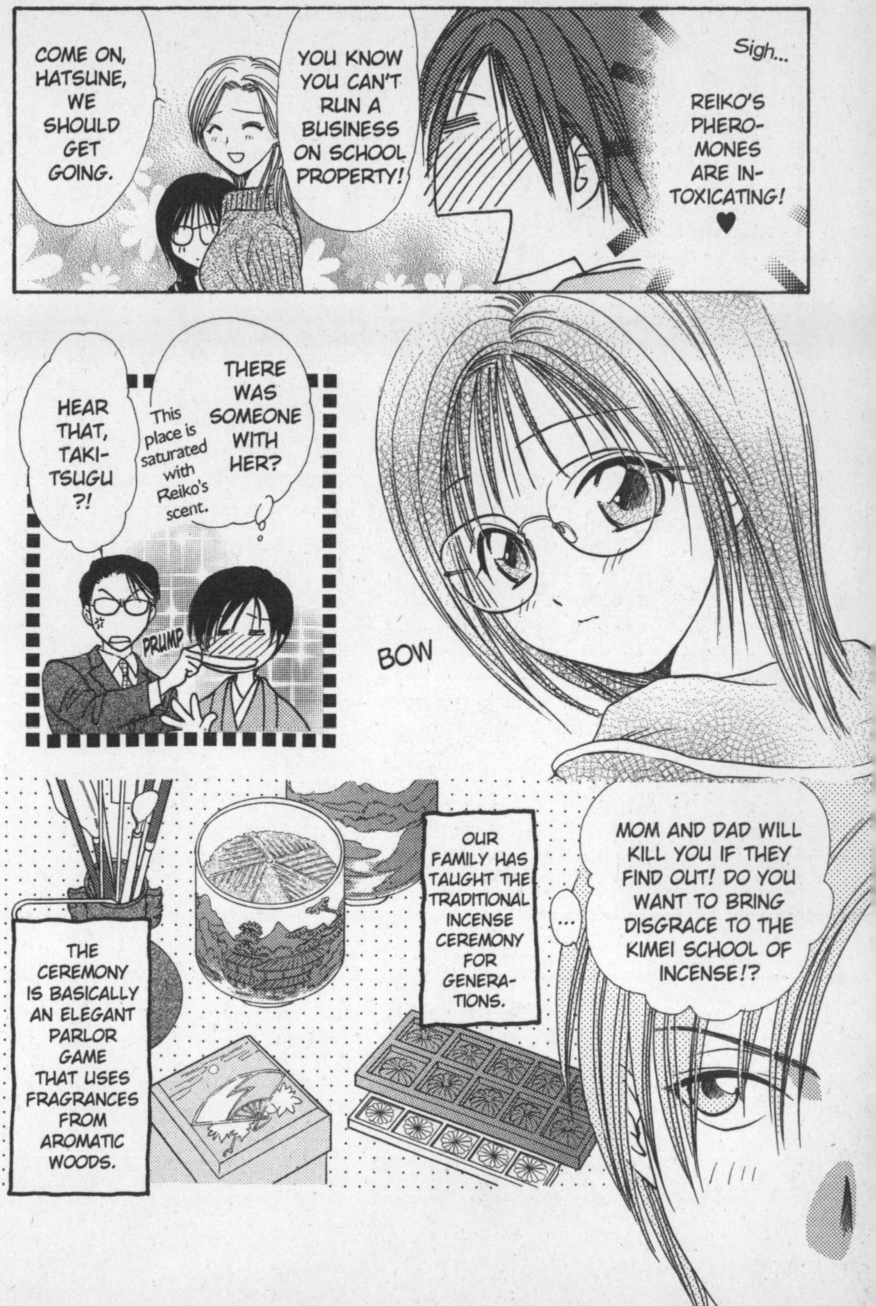
Sigh...
REIKO'S PHEROMONES ARE INTOXICATING! ♥
YOU KNOW YOU CAN'T RUN A BUSINESS ON SCHOOL PROPERTY!
COME ON, HATSUNE, WE SHOULD GET GOING.
BOW
THERE WAS SOMEONE WITH HER?
This place is saturated with Reiko's scent.
HEAR THAT, TAKITSUGU?!
PRUMP
MOM AND DAD WILL KILL YOU IF THEY FIND OUT! DO YOU WANT TO BRING DISGRACE TO THE KIMEI SCHOOL OF INCENSE!?
...
OUR FAMILY HAS TAUGHT THE TRADITIONAL INCENSE CEREMONY FOR GENERATIONS.
THE CEREMONY IS BASICALLY AN ELEGANT PARLOR GAME THAT USES FRAGRANCES FROM AROMATIC WOODS.

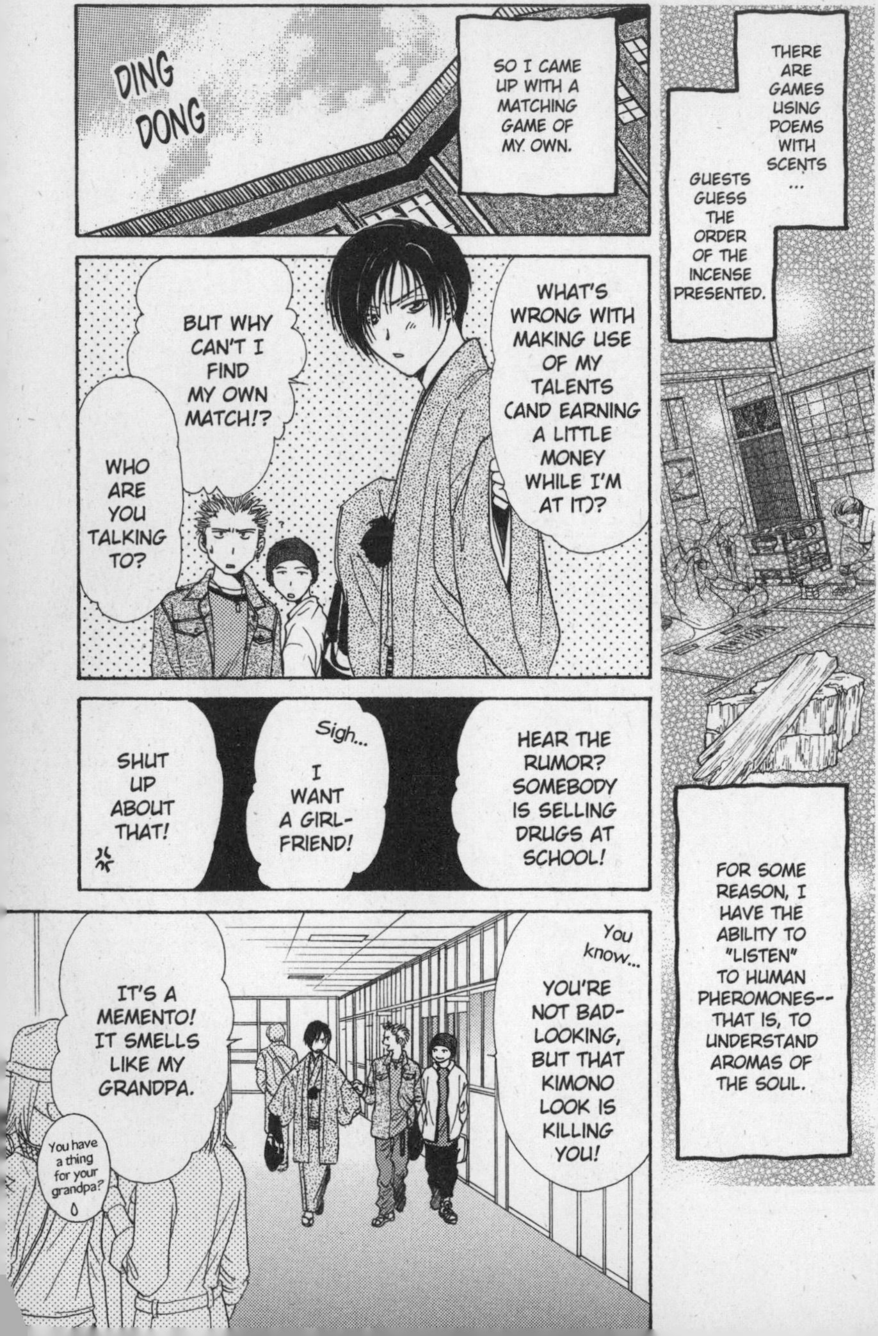
THERE ARE GAMES USING POEMS WITH SCENTS...
GUESTS GUESS THE ORDER OF THE INCENSE PRESENTED.
FOR SOME REASON, I HAVE THE ABILITY TO "LISTEN" TO HUMAN PHEROMONES--THAT IS, TO UNDERSTAND AROMAS OF THE SOUL.
SO I CAME UP WITH A MATCHING GAME OF MY OWN.
DING DONG
WHAT'S WRONG WITH MAKING USE OF MY TALENTS (AND EARNING A LITTLE MONEY WHILE I'M AT IT)?
BUT WHY CAN'T I FIND MY OWN MATCH!?
WHO ARE YOU TALKING TO?
HEAR THE RUMOR? SOMEBODY IS SELLING DRUGS AT SCHOOL!
Sigh...
I WANT A GIRL-FRIEND!
SHUT UP ABOUT THAT!
You know...
YOU'RE NOT BAD-LOOKING, BUT THAT KIMONO LOOK IS KILLING YOU!
IT'S A MEMENTO! IT SMELLS LIKE MY GRANDPA.
You have a thing for your grandpa?

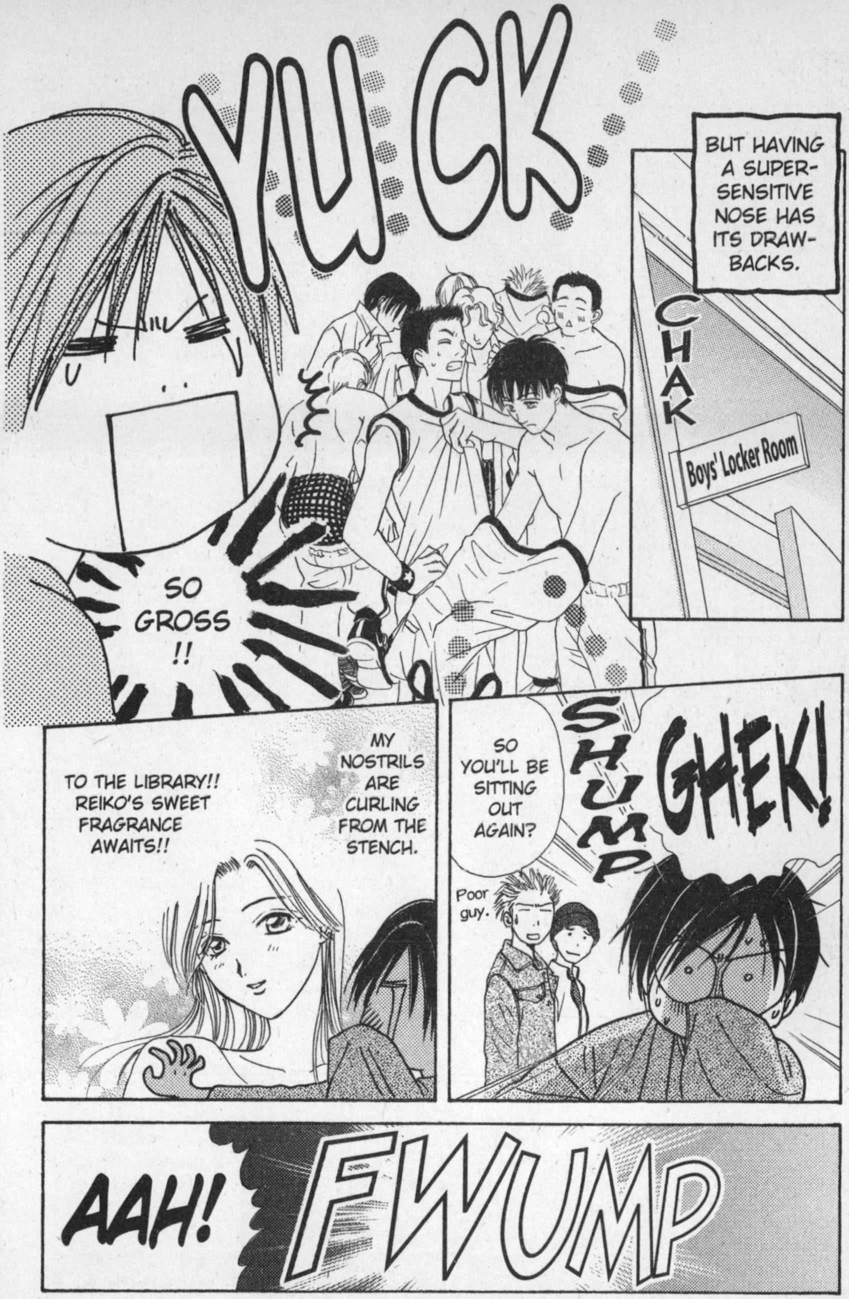
BUT HAVING A SUPER-SENSITIVE NOSE HAS ITS DRAW-BACKS.
CHAK
Boys' Locker Room
YUCK
SO GROSS!!
GHEK!
SHUMP
SO YOU'LL BE SITTING OUT AGAIN?
Poor guy.
MY NOSTRILS ARE CURLING FROM THE STENCH.
TO THE LIBRARY!! REIKO'S SWEET FRAGRANCE AWAITS!!
FWUMP
AAH!

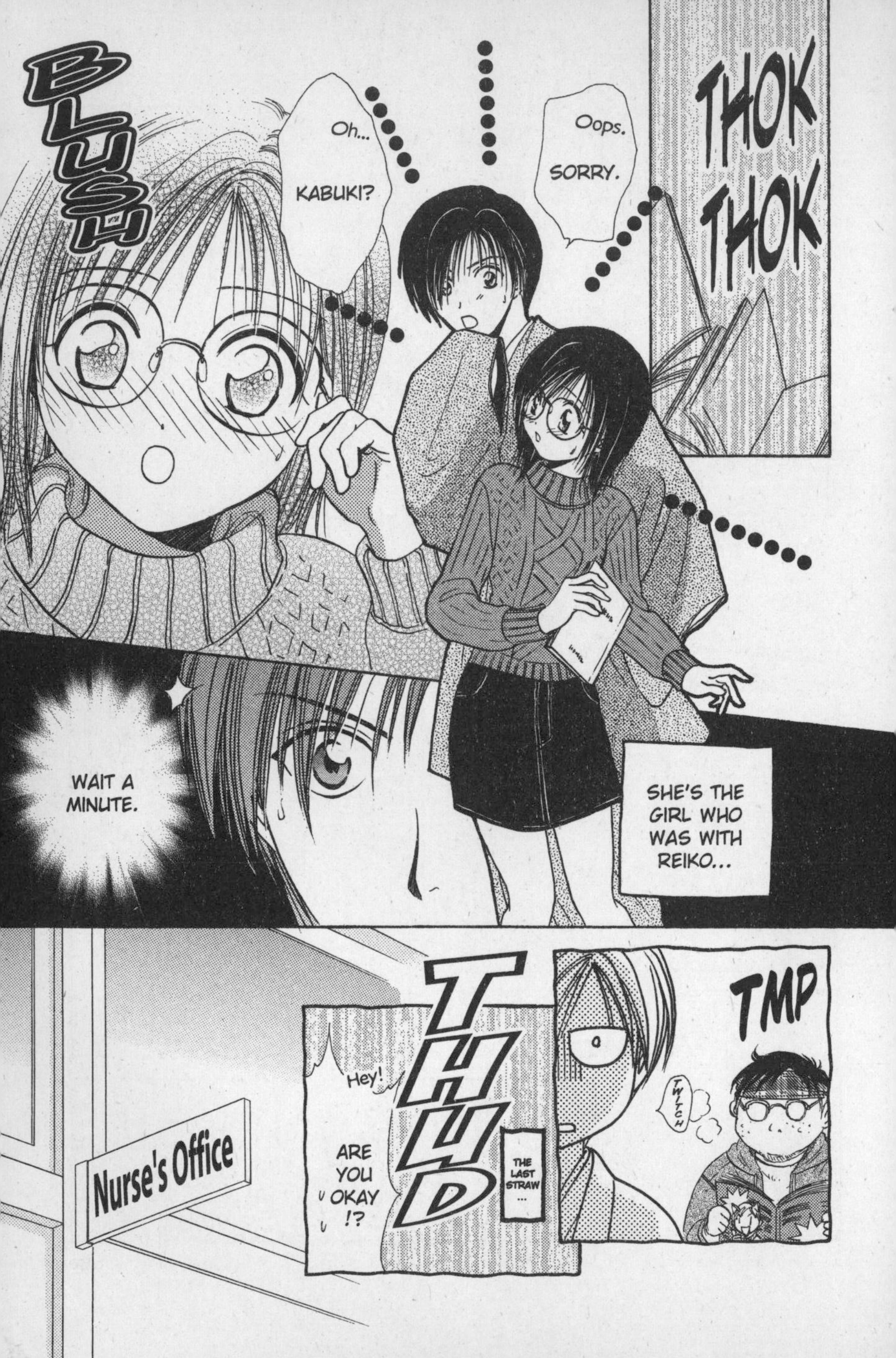
THOK THOK
Oops. SORRY.
Oh... KABUKI?
BLUSH
SHE'S THE GIRL WHO WAS WITH REIKO...
WAIT A MINUTE.
TMP
TWITCH
THE LAST STRAW...
THUD
Hey!
ARE YOU OKAY!?
Nurse's Office

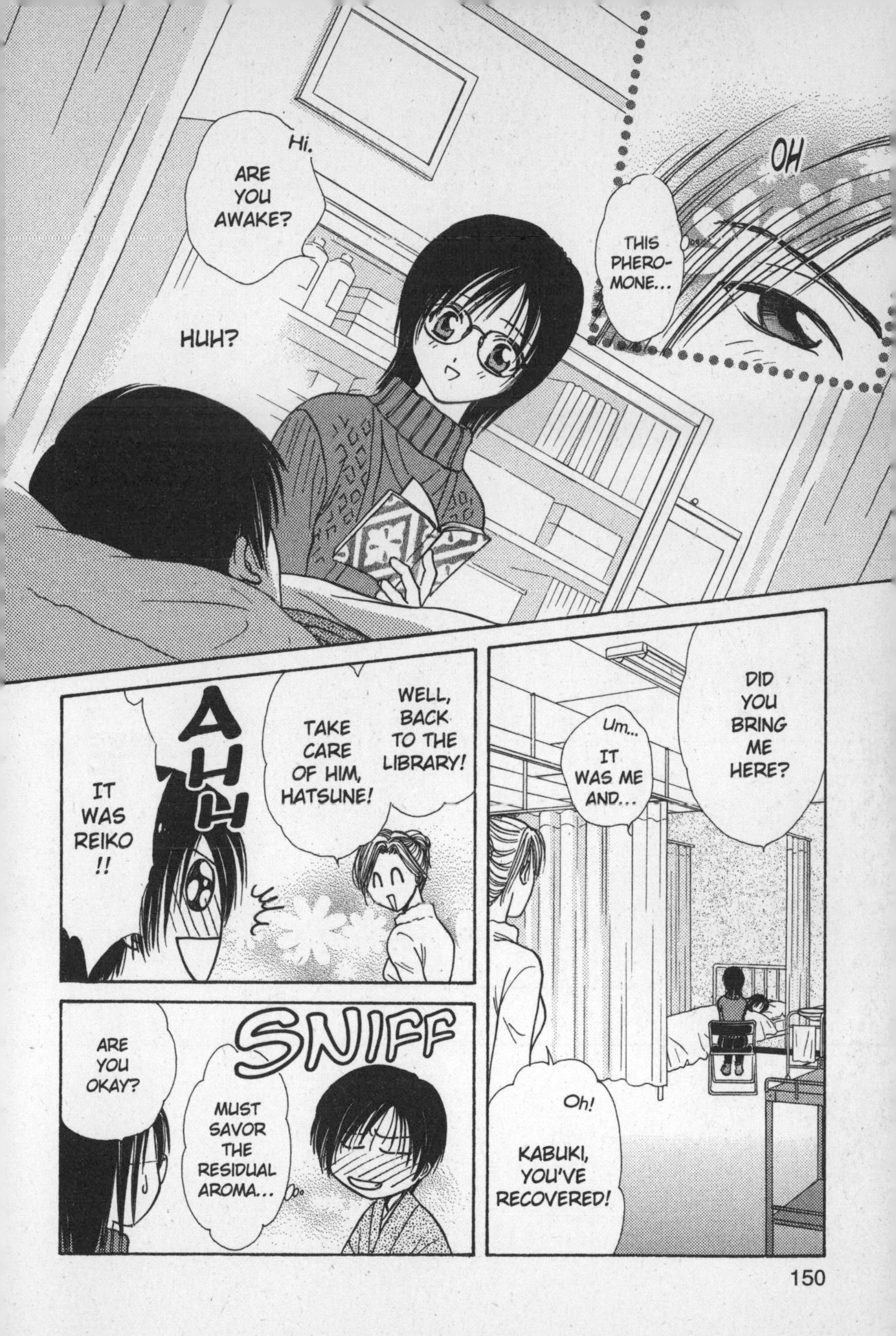
OH
THIS PHEROMONE...
Hi.
ARE YOU AWAKE?
HUH?
DID YOU BRING ME HERE?
Um... IT WAS ME AND...
Oh!
KABUKI, YOU'VE RECOVERED!
WELL, BACK TO THE LIBRARY!
TAKE CARE OF HIM, HATSUNE!
AHH
IT WAS REIKO !!
SNIFF
ARE YOU OKAY?
MUST SAVOR THE RESIDUAL AROMA...

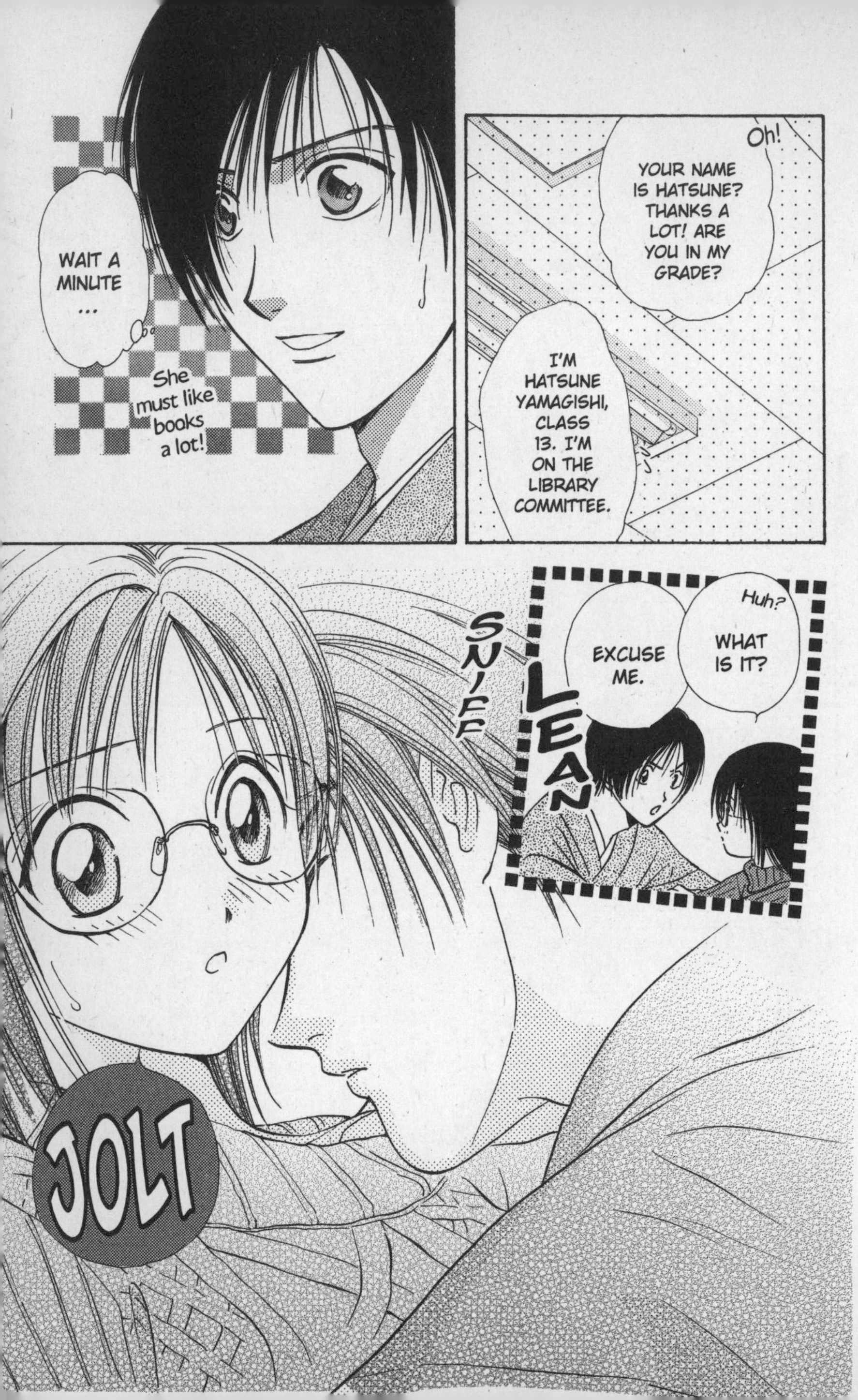
Oh!
YOUR NAME IS HATSUNE? THANKS A LOT! ARE YOU IN MY GRADE?
I'M HATSUNE YAMAGISHI, CLASS 13. I'M ON THE LIBRARY COMMITTEE.
WAIT A MINUTE ...
She must like books a lot!
Huh?
WHAT IS IT?
EXCUSE ME.
LEAN
SNIFF
JOLT

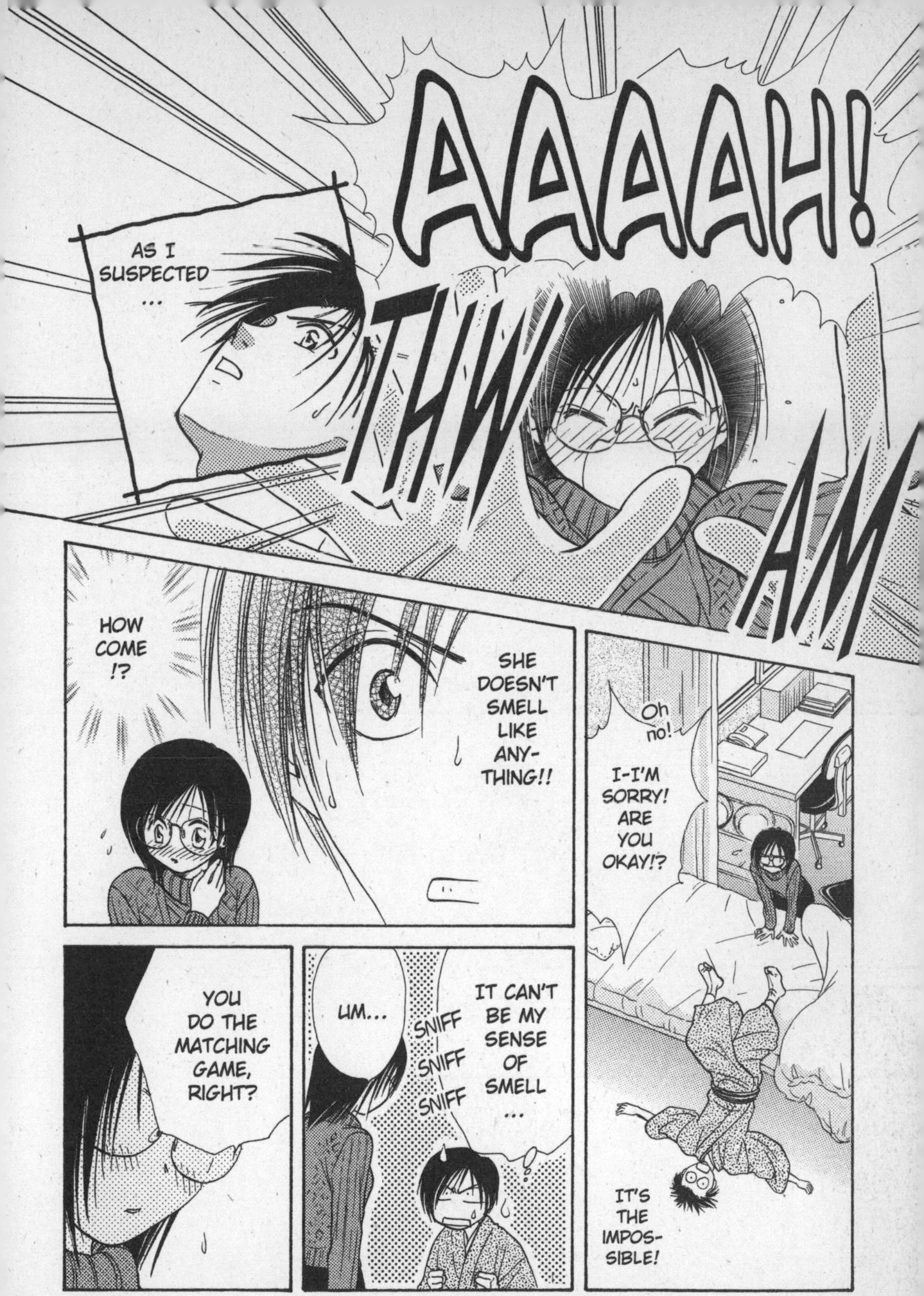
AAAAH!
THWAM
AS I SUSPECTED ...
Oh no!
I-I'M SORRY! ARE YOU OKAY!?
IT'S THE IMPOSSIBLE!
SHE DOESN'T SMELL LIKE ANYTHING!!
HOW COME !?
IT CAN'T BE MY SENSE OF SMELL ...
SNIFF SNIFF SNIFF
UM...
YOU DO THE MATCHING GAME, RIGHT?

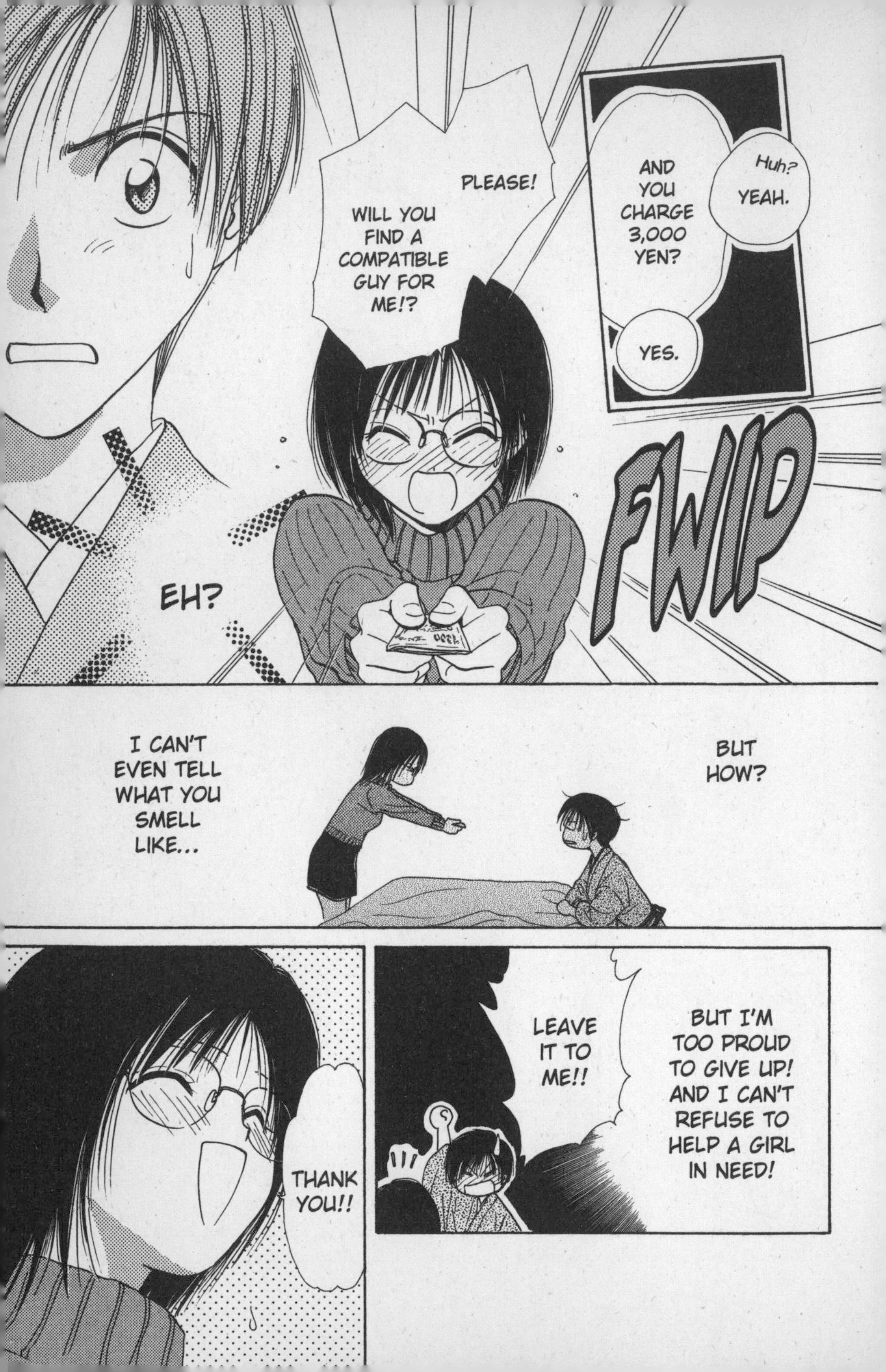
Huh? YEAH.
AND YOU CHARGE 3,000 YEN?
YES.
PLEASE!
WILL YOU FIND A COMPATIBLE GUY FOR ME!?
FWIP
EH?
BUT HOW?
I CAN'T EVEN TELL WHAT YOU SMELL LIKE...
BUT I'M TOO PROUD TO GIVE UP! AND I CAN'T REFUSE TO HELP A GIRL IN NEED!
LEAVE IT TO ME!!
THANK YOU!!

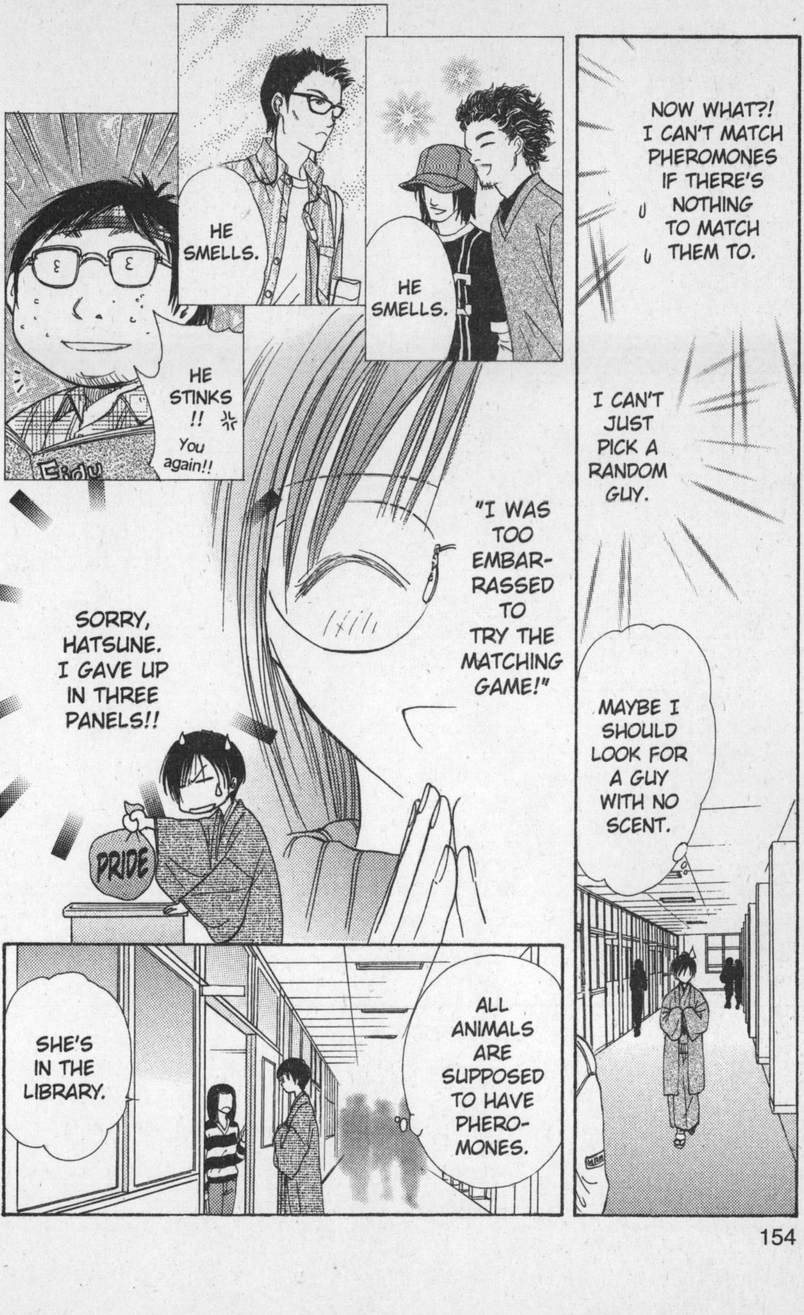
NOW WHAT?! I CAN'T MATCH PHEROMONES IF THERE'S NOTHING TO MATCH THEM TO.
I CAN'T JUST PICK A RANDOM GUY.
MAYBE I SHOULD LOOK FOR A GUY WITH NO SCENT.
HE SMELLS.
HE SMELLS.
HE STINKS!!
You again!!
"I WAS TOO EMBARRASSED TO TRY THE MATCHING GAME!"
SORRY, HATSUNE. I GAVE UP IN THREE PANELS!!
PRIDE
ALL ANIMALS ARE SUPPOSED TO HAVE PHEROMONES.
SHE'S IN THE LIBRARY.

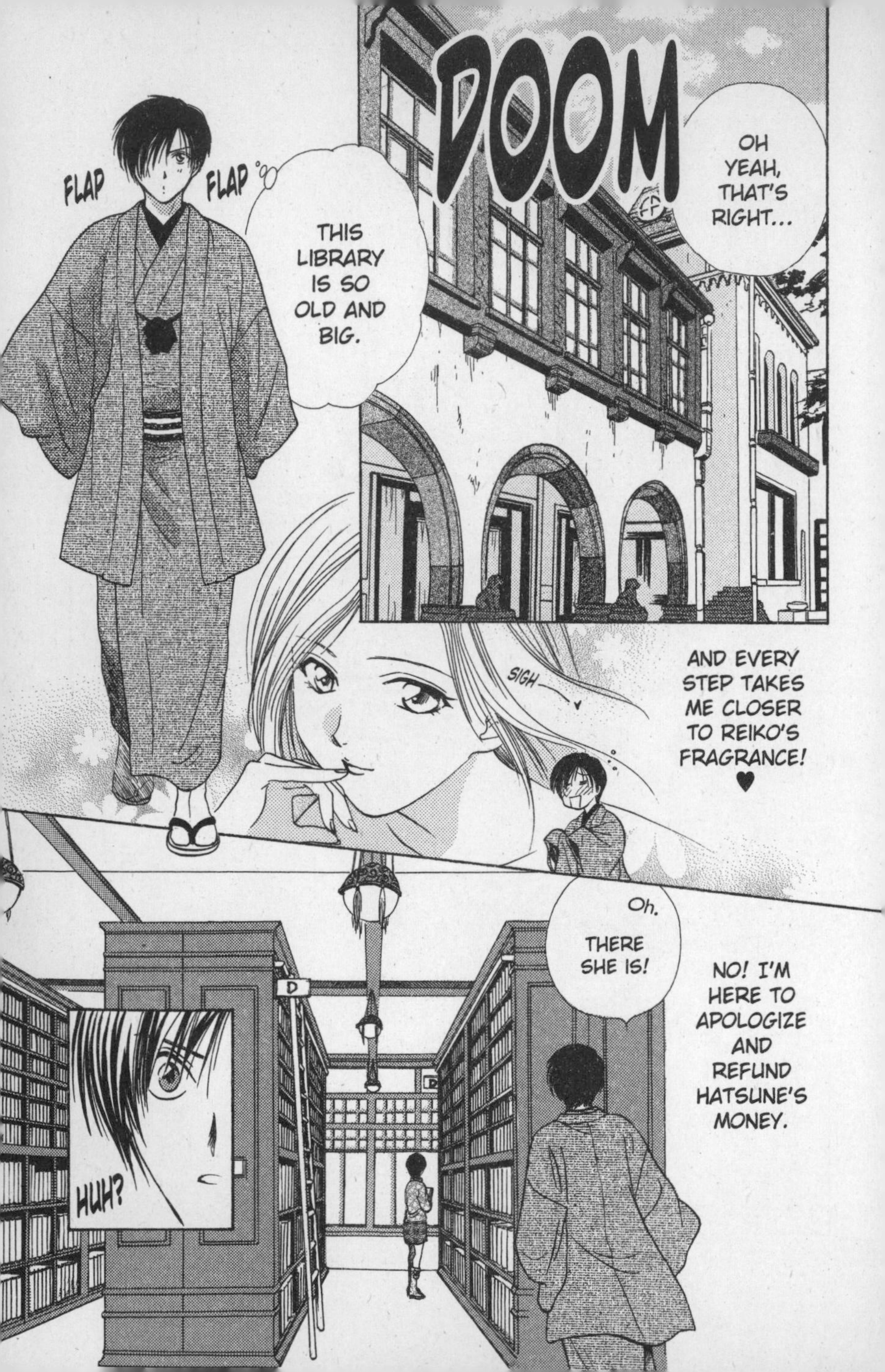
FLAP FLAP
THIS LIBRARY IS SO OLD AND BIG.
DOOM
OH YEAH, THAT'S RIGHT...
SIGH
AND EVERY STEP TAKES ME CLOSER TO REIKO'S FRAGRANCE! ♥
Oh. THERE SHE IS!
NO! I'M HERE TO APOLOGIZE AND REFUND HATSUNE'S MONEY.
HUH?

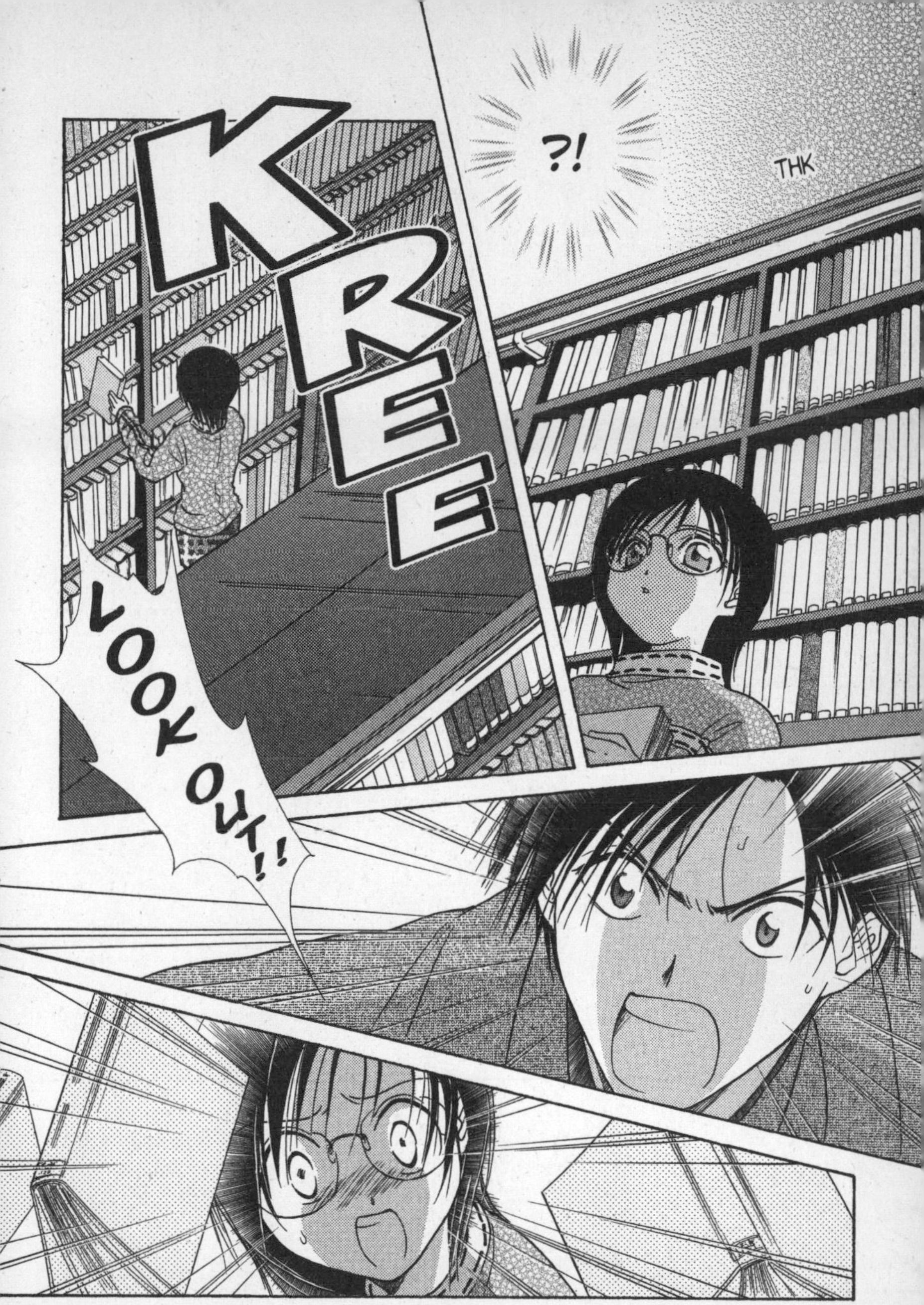
THK
?!
KREE
LOOK OUT!!

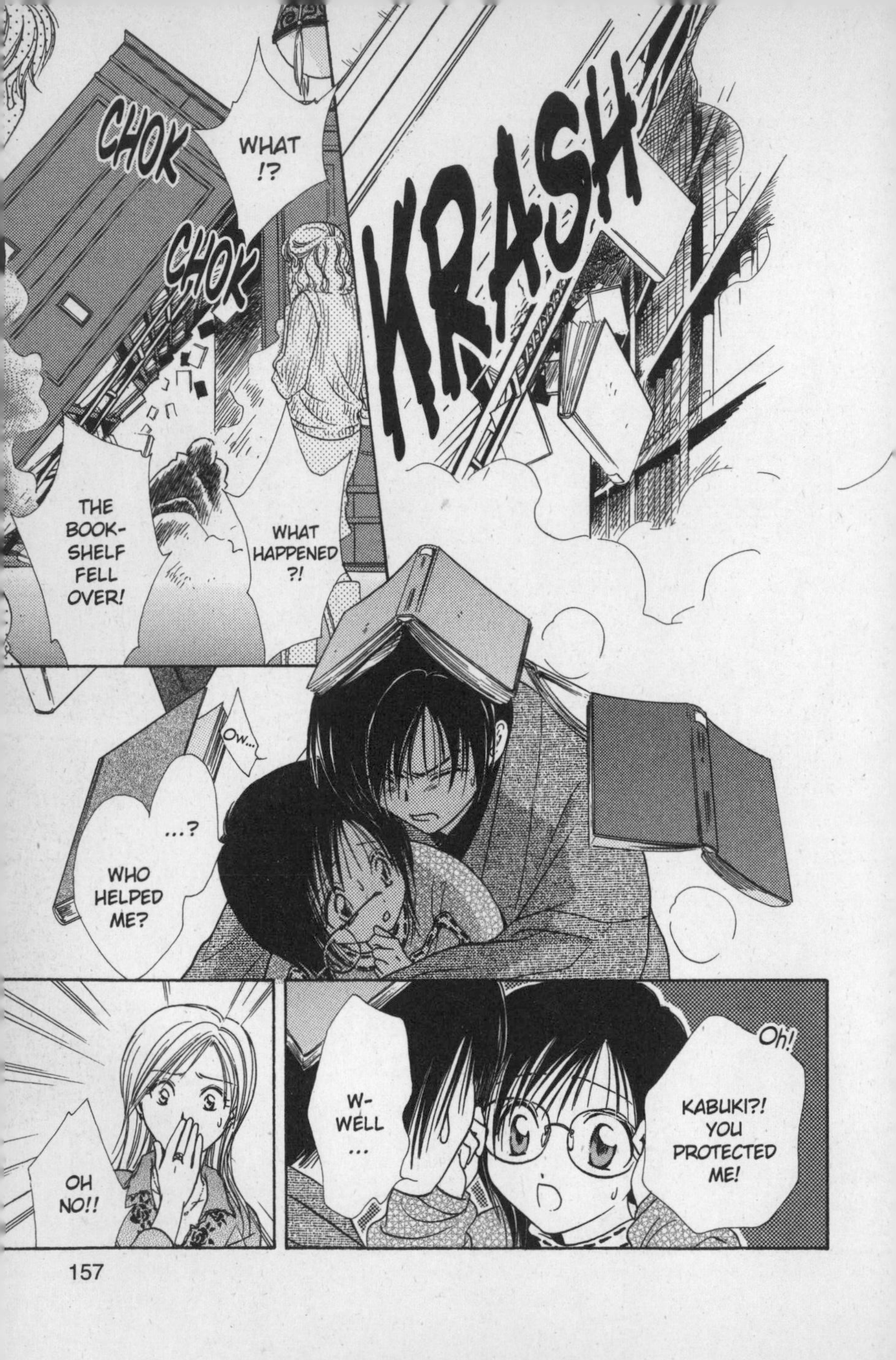
KRASH
WHAT !?
CHOK
CHOK
WHAT HAPPENED ?!
THE BOOK-SHELF FELL OVER!
Ow...
...?
WHO HELPED ME?
Oh!
KABUKI?! YOU PROTECTED ME!
W-WELL ...
OH NO!!

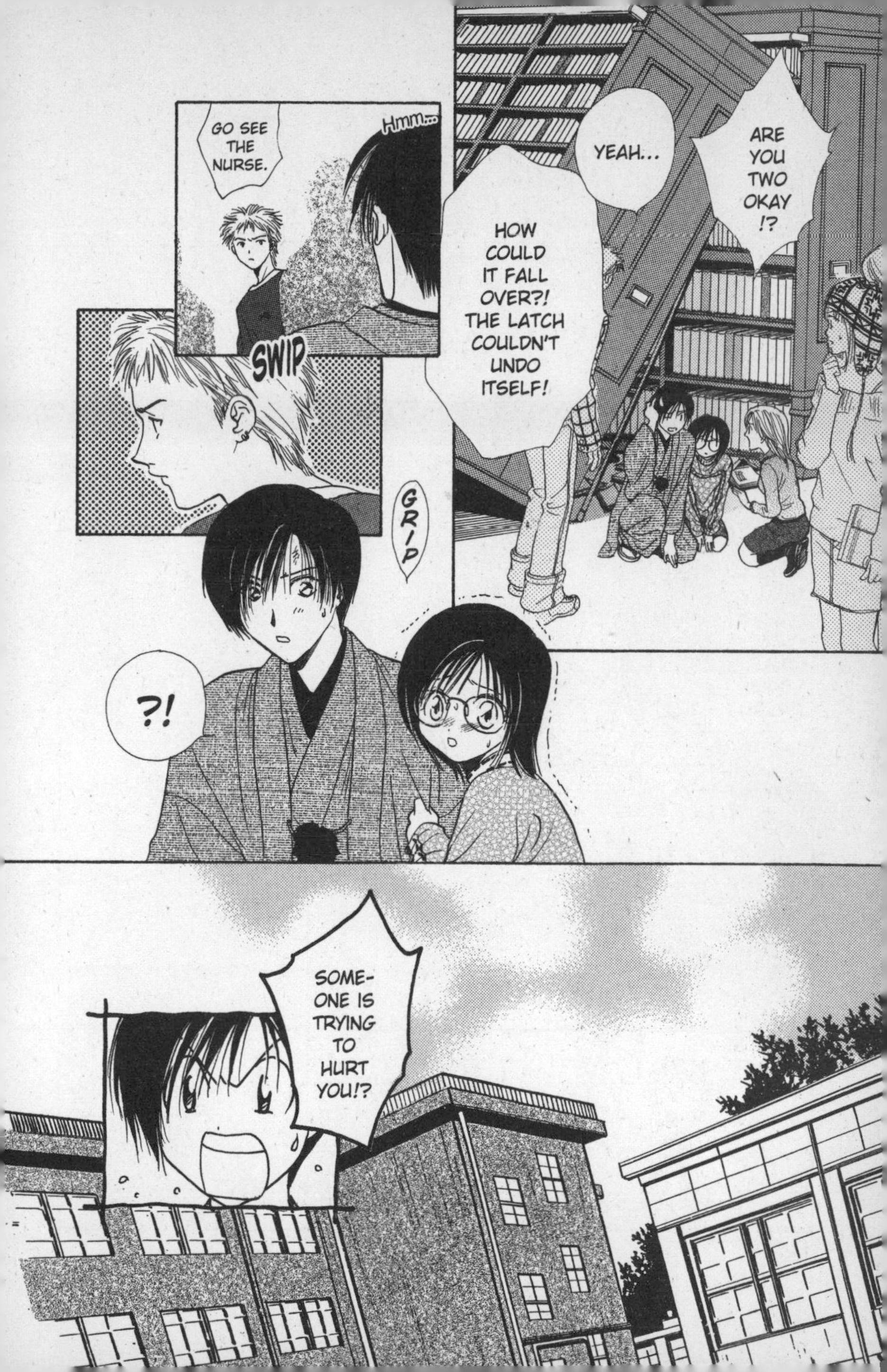
ARE YOU TWO OKAY!?
YEAH...
HOW COULD IT FALL OVER?! THE LATCH COULDN'T UNDO ITSELF!
Hmm...
GO SEE THE NURSE.
SWIP
GRIP
?!
SOME-ONE IS TRYING TO HURT YOU!?

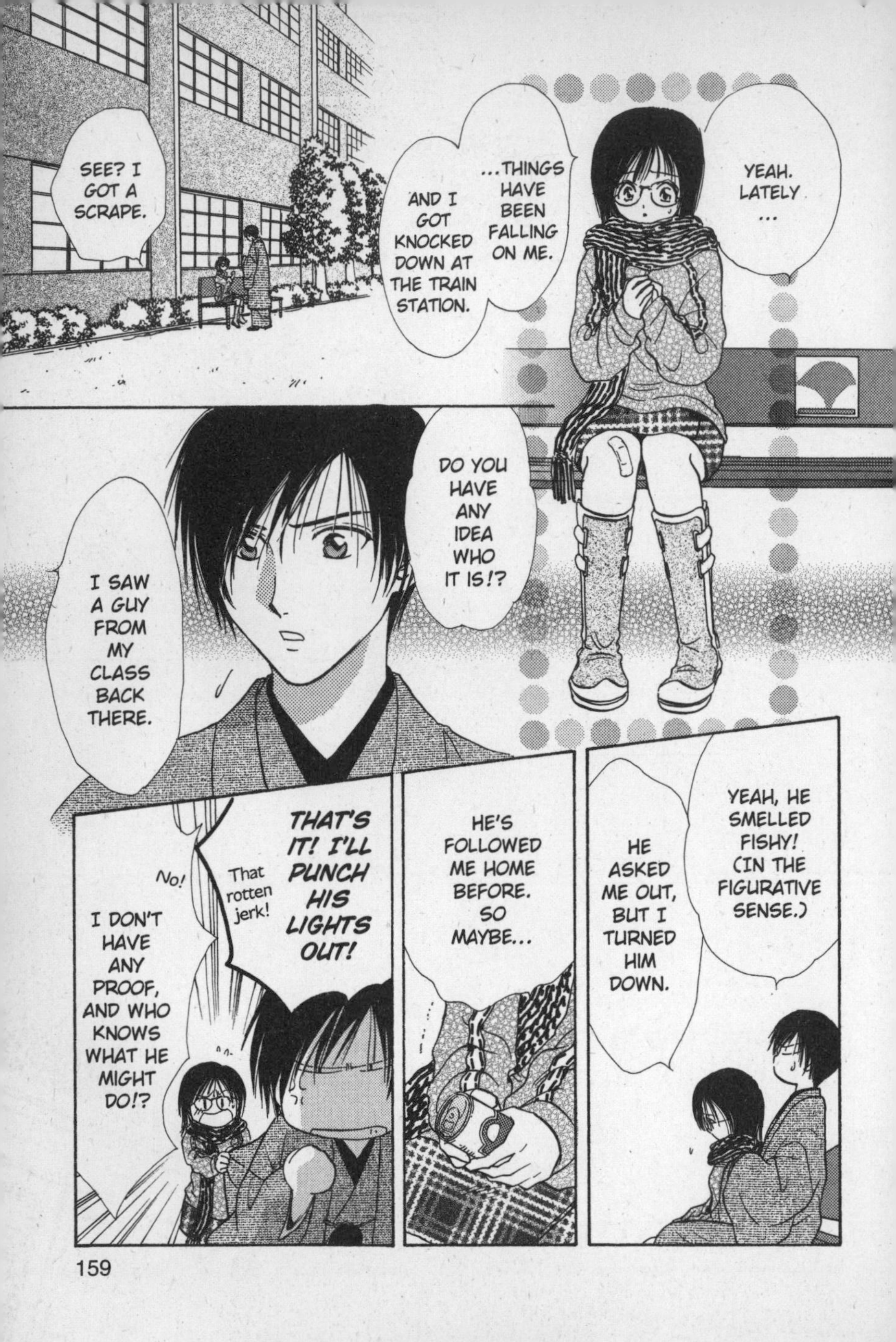
YEAH. LATELY ...
...THINGS HAVE BEEN FALLING ON ME.
AND I GOT KNOCKED DOWN AT THE TRAIN STATION.
SEE? I GOT A SCRAPE.
DO YOU HAVE ANY IDEA WHO IT IS!?
I SAW A GUY FROM MY CLASS BACK THERE.
YEAH, HE SMELLED FISHY! (IN THE FIGURATIVE SENSE.)
HE ASKED ME OUT, BUT I TURNED HIM DOWN.
HE'S FOLLOWED ME HOME BEFORE. SO MAYBE...
THAT'S IT! I'LL PUNCH HIS LIGHTS OUT!
That rotten jerk!
No!
I DON'T HAVE ANY PROOF, AND WHO KNOWS WHAT HE MIGHT DO!?

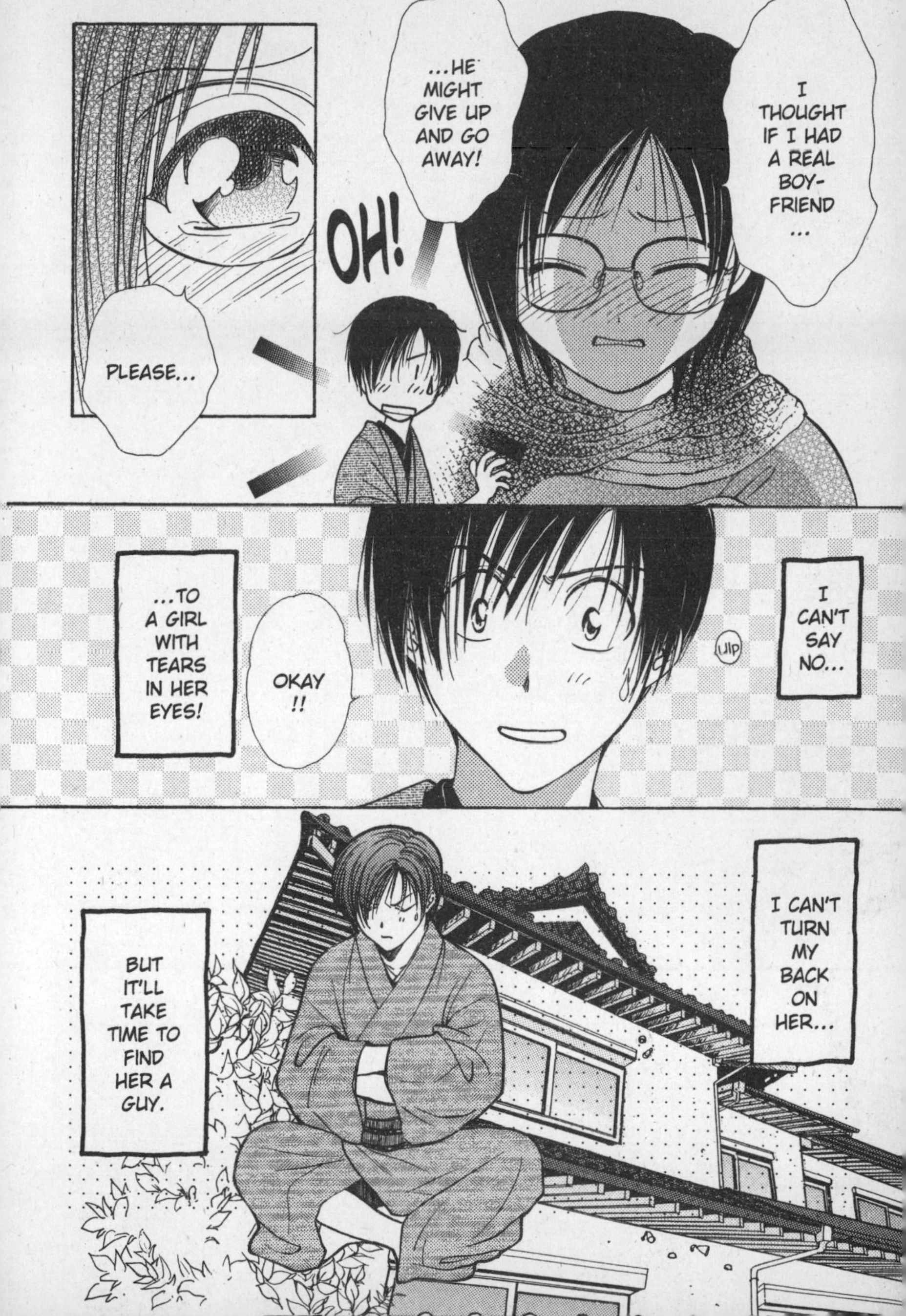
I THOUGHT IF I HAD A REAL BOY-FRIEND ...
...HE MIGHT GIVE UP AND GO AWAY!
OH!
PLEASE...
I CAN'T SAY NO...
ulp
OKAY !!
...TO A GIRL WITH TEARS IN HER EYES!
I CAN'T TURN MY BACK ON HER...
BUT IT'LL TAKE TIME TO FIND HER A GUY.

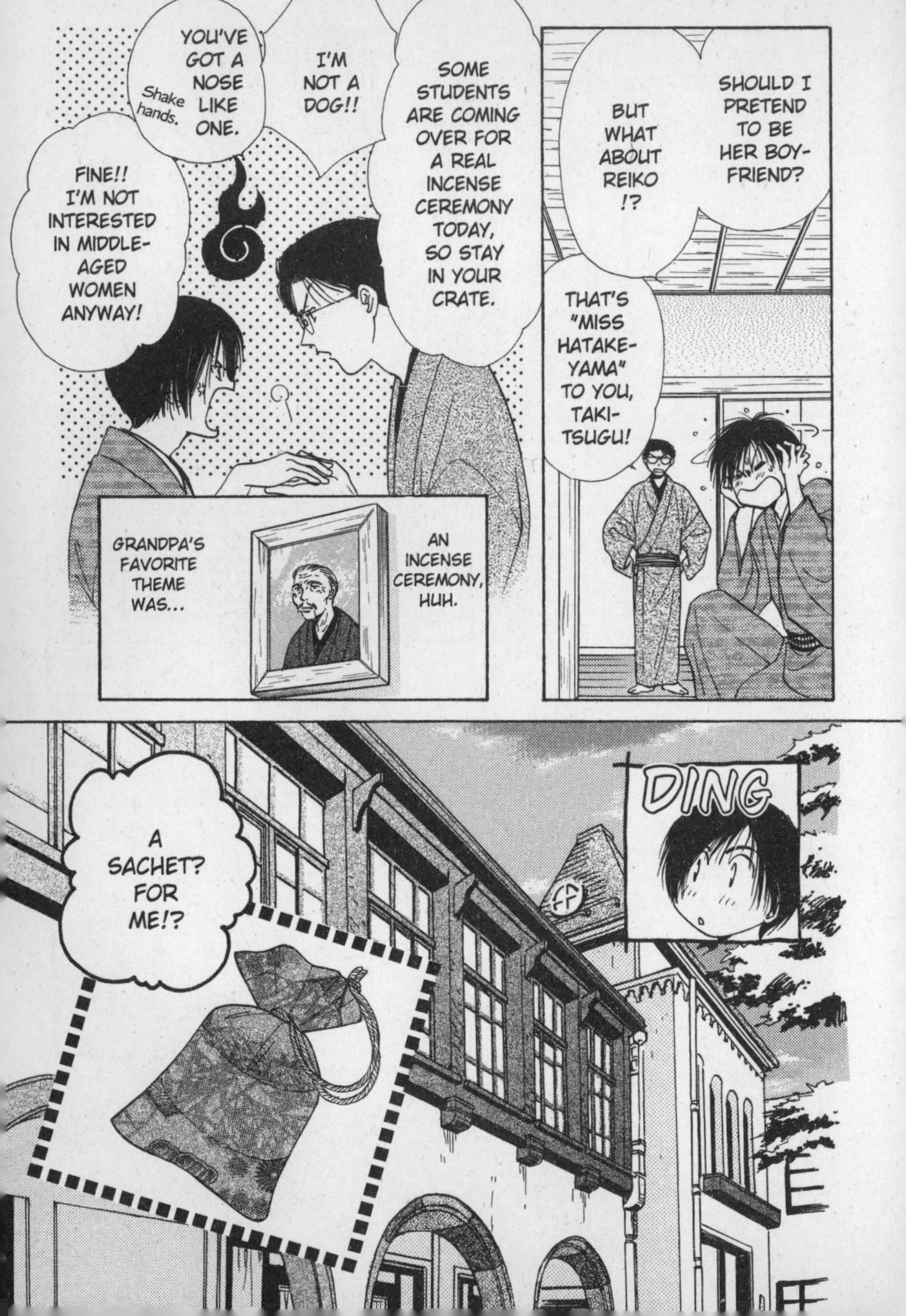
SHOULD I PRETEND TO BE HER BOY-FRIEND?
BUT WHAT ABOUT REIKO!?
THAT'S "MISS HATAKE-YAMA" TO YOU, TAKI-TSUGU!
SOME STUDENTS ARE COMING OVER FOR A REAL INCENSE CEREMONY TODAY, SO STAY IN YOUR CRATE.
I'M NOT A DOG!!
YOU'VE GOT A NOSE LIKE ONE.
Shake hands.
FINE!! I'M NOT INTERESTED IN MIDDLE-AGED WOMEN ANYWAY!
AN INCENSE CEREMONY, HUH.
GRANDPA'S FAVORITE THEME WAS...
DING
A SACHET? FOR ME!?

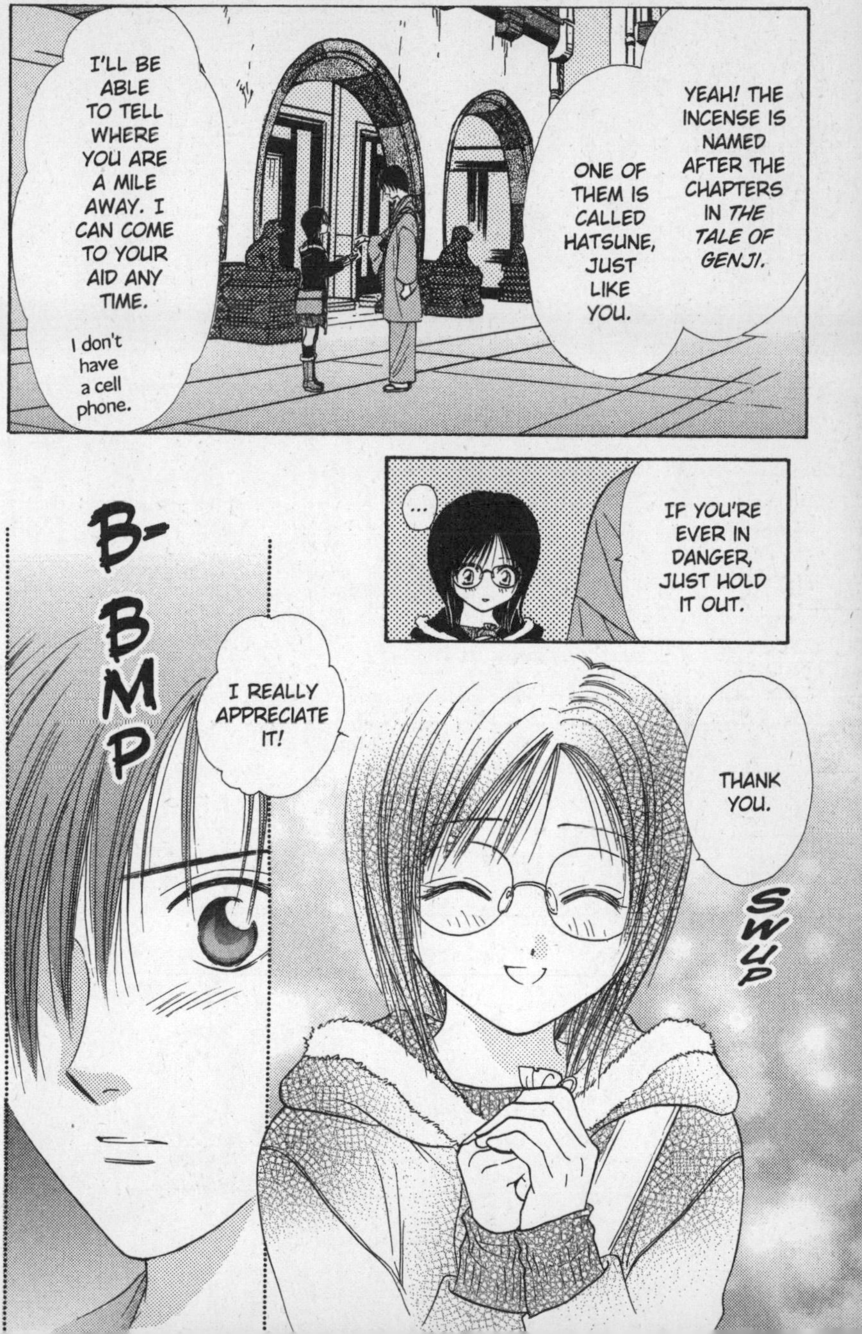
YEAH! THE INCENSE IS NAMED AFTER THE CHAPTERS IN *THE TALE OF GENJI*.
ONE OF THEM IS CALLED HATSUNE, JUST LIKE YOU.
I'LL BE ABLE TO TELL WHERE YOU ARE A MILE AWAY. I CAN COME TO YOUR AID ANY TIME.
I don't have a cell phone.
IF YOU'RE EVER IN DANGER, JUST HOLD IT OUT.
...
THANK YOU.
SWUP
I REALLY APPRECIATE IT!
B-BMP

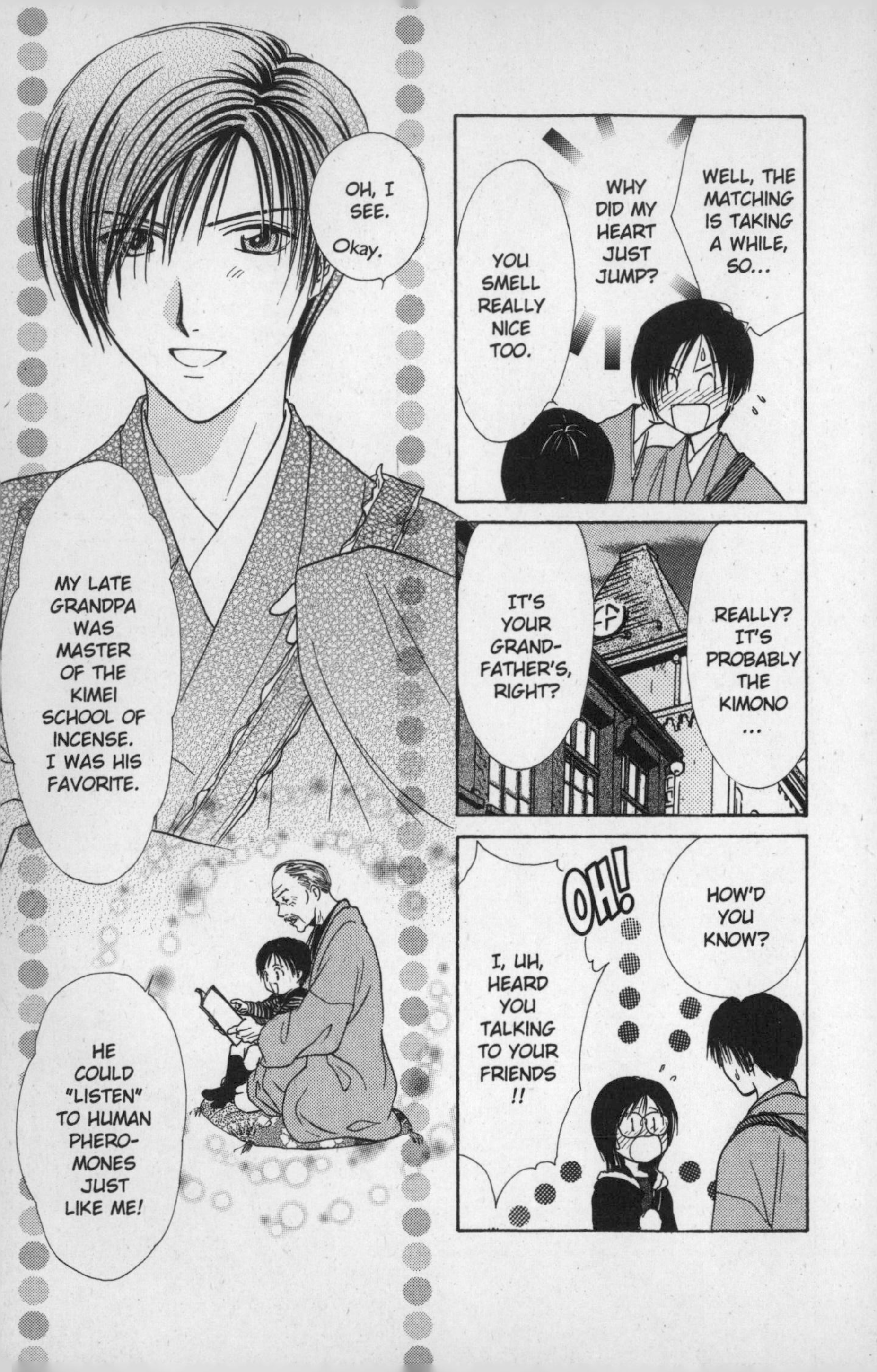

WELL, THE MATCHING IS TAKING A WHILE, SO...
WHY DID MY HEART JUST JUMP?
YOU SMELL REALLY NICE TOO.
REALLY? IT'S PROBABLY THE KIMONO ...
IT'S YOUR GRAND-FATHER'S, RIGHT?
HOW'D YOU KNOW?
OH!
I, UH, HEARD YOU TALKING TO YOUR FRIENDS !!
OH, I SEE.
Okay.
MY LATE GRANDPA WAS MASTER OF THE KIMEI SCHOOL OF INCENSE. I WAS HIS FAVORITE.
HE COULD "LISTEN" TO HUMAN PHERO-MONES JUST LIKE ME!

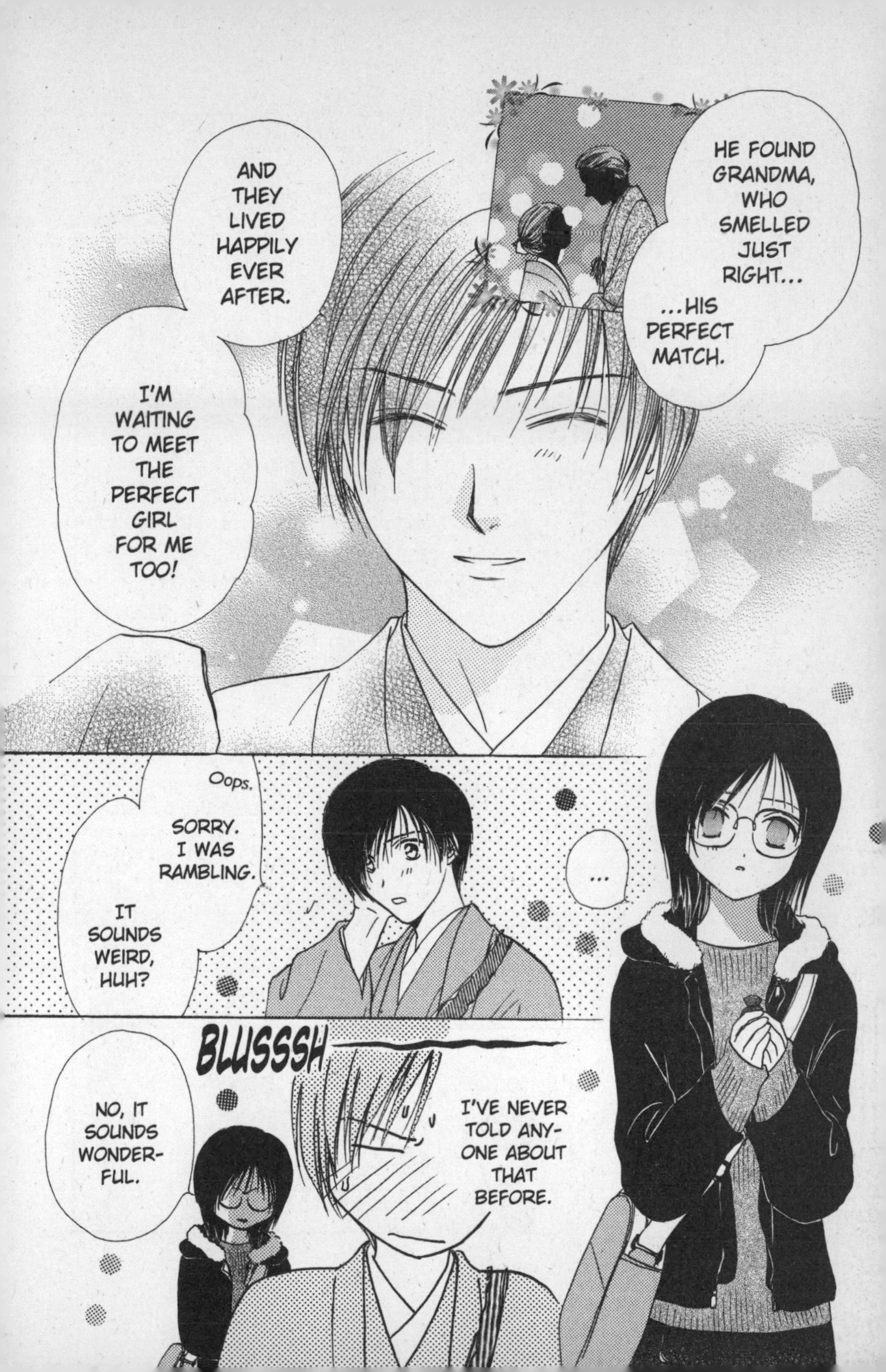
HE FOUND GRANDMA, WHO SMELLED JUST RIGHT...
...HIS PERFECT MATCH.
AND THEY LIVED HAPPILY EVER AFTER.
I'M WAITING TO MEET THE PERFECT GIRL FOR ME TOO!
...
Oops.
SORRY. I WAS RAMBLING.
IT SOUNDS WEIRD, HUH?
BLUSSSH
I'VE NEVER TOLD ANY-ONE ABOUT THAT BEFORE.
NO, IT SOUNDS WONDER-FUL.

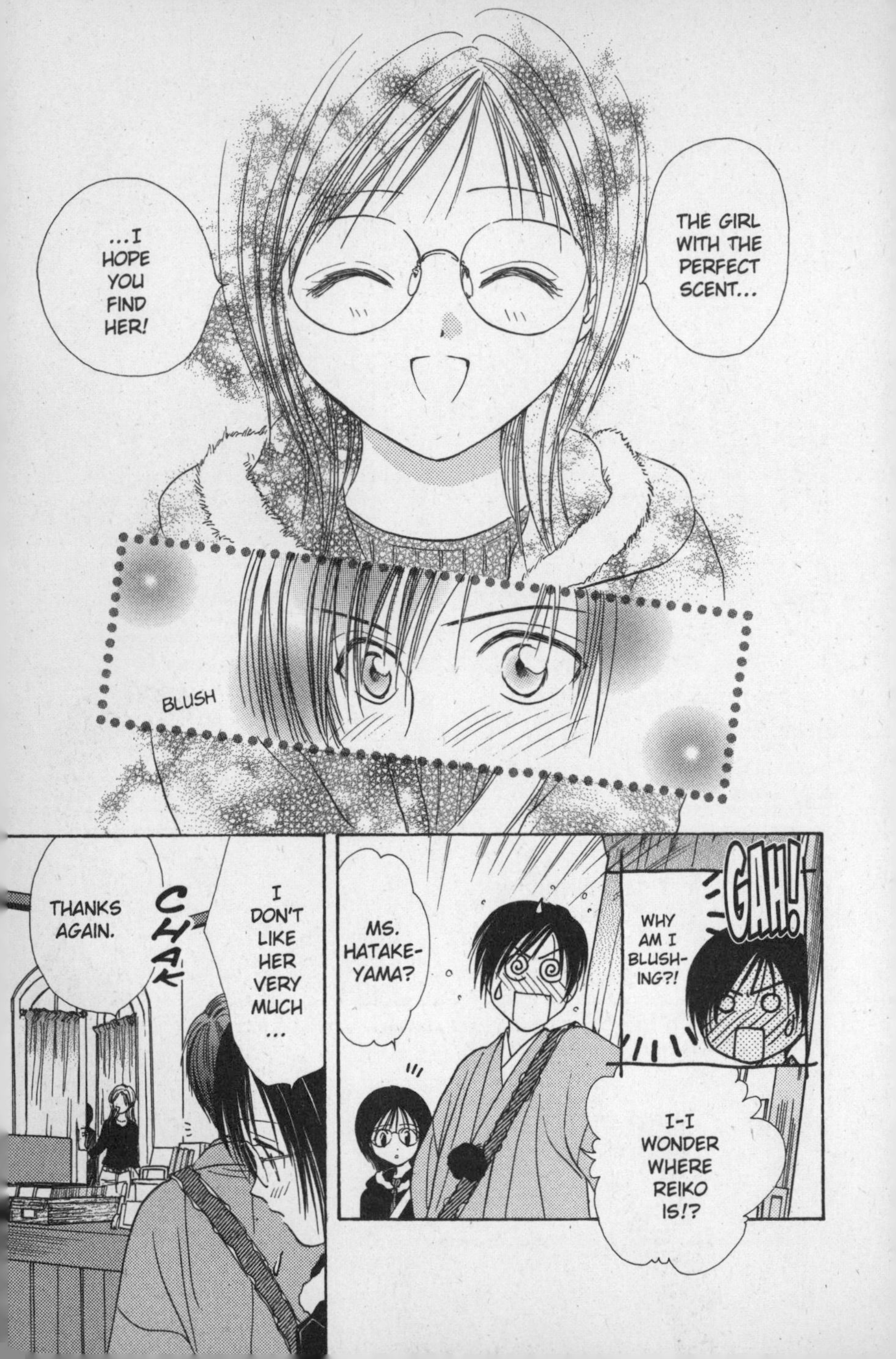
THE GIRL WITH THE PERFECT SCENT...
...I HOPE YOU FIND HER!
BLUSH
GAH!
WHY AM I BLUSH-ING?!
MS. HATAKE-YAMA?
I-I WONDER WHERE REIKO IS!?
I DON'T LIKE HER VERY MUCH...
CHAK
THANKS AGAIN.

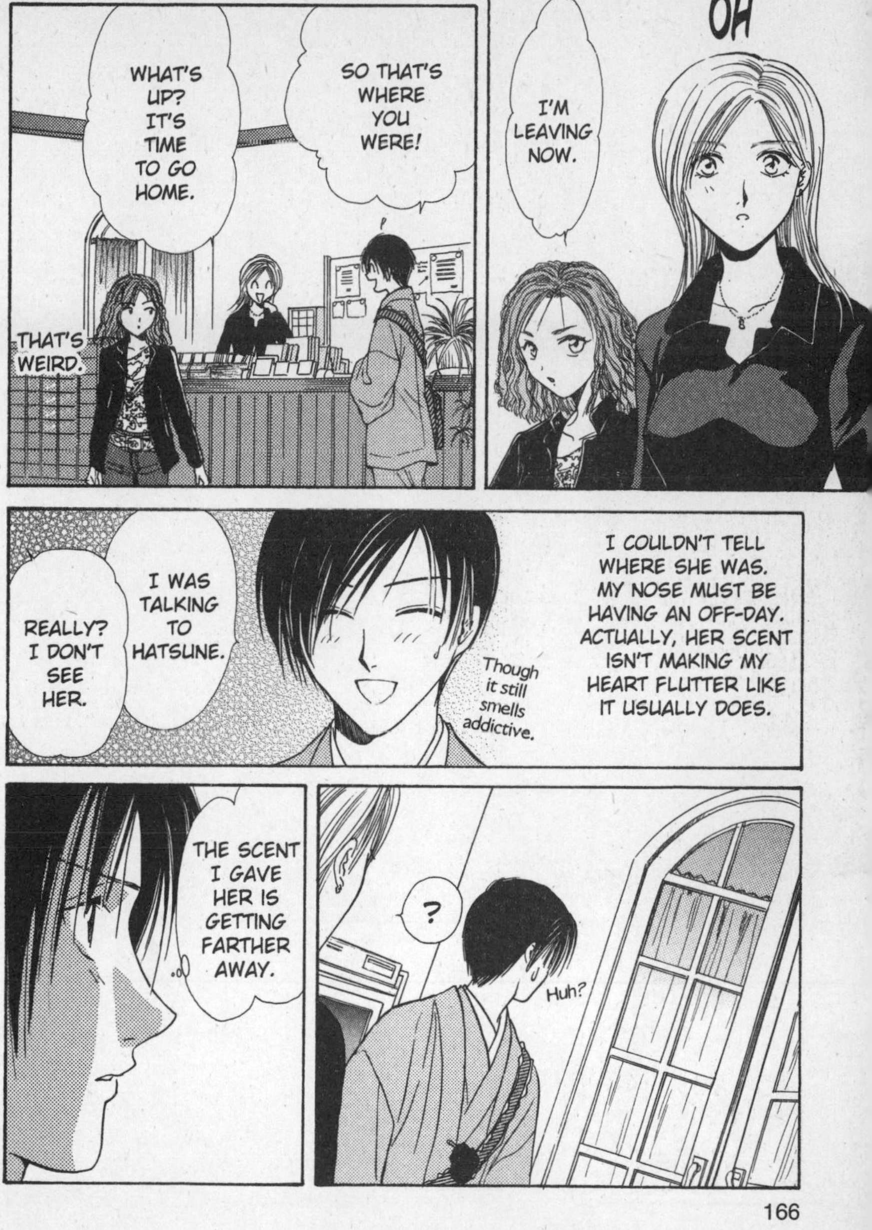
OH
I'M LEAVING NOW.
SO THAT'S WHERE YOU WERE!
WHAT'S UP? IT'S TIME TO GO HOME.
THAT'S WEIRD.
I COULDN'T TELL WHERE SHE WAS. MY NOSE MUST BE HAVING AN OFF-DAY. ACTUALLY, HER SCENT ISN'T MAKING MY HEART FLUTTER LIKE IT USUALLY DOES.
Though it still smells addictive.
I WAS TALKING TO HATSUNE.
REALLY? I DON'T SEE HER.
?
Huh?
THE SCENT I GAVE HER IS GETTING FARTHER AWAY.

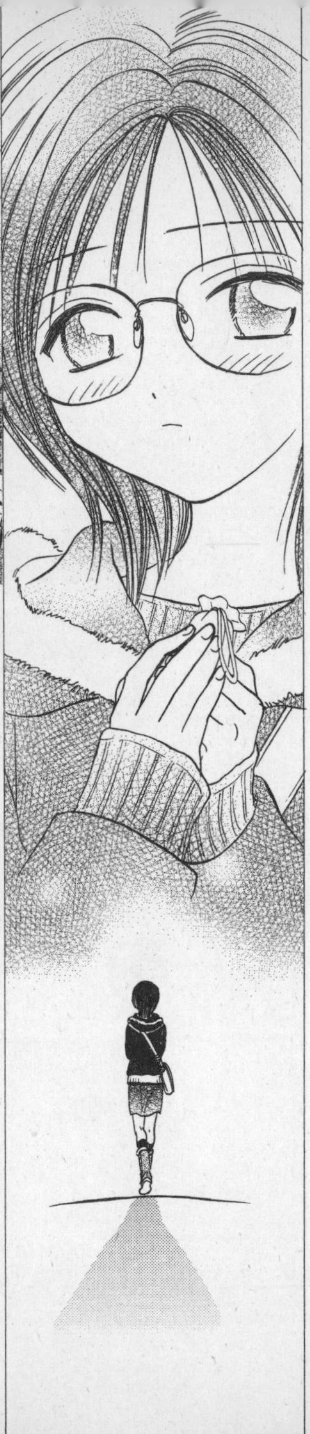

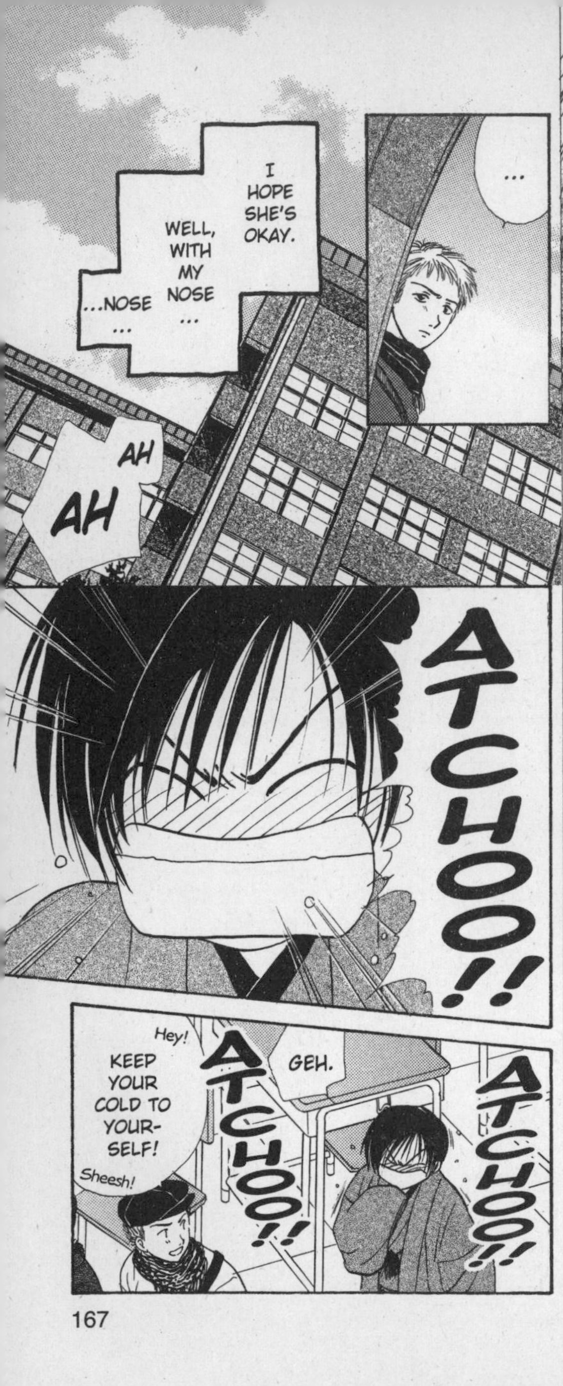
...
I HOPE SHE'S OKAY.
WELL, WITH MY NOSE ...
...NOSE ...
AH AH
ATCHOO!!
ATCHOO!!
GEH.
ATCHOO!!
Hey!
KEEP YOUR COLD TO YOUR-SELF!
Sheesh!

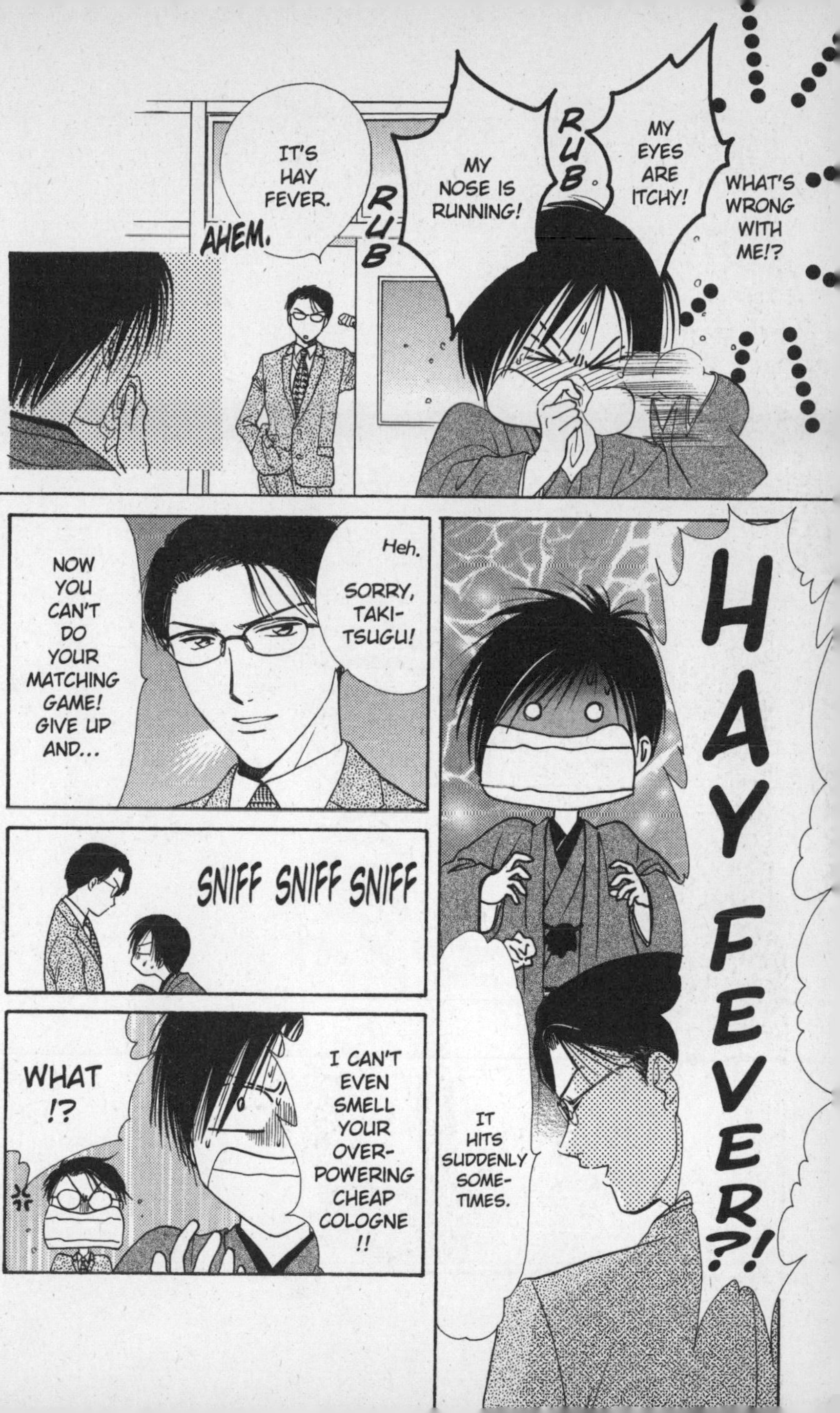
WHAT'S WRONG WITH ME!?
MY EYES ARE ITCHY!
RUB
MY NOSE IS RUNNING!
RUB
IT'S HAY FEVER.
AHEM.
HAY FEVER?!
IT HITS SUDDENLY SOME-TIMES.
Heh.
SORRY, TAKI-TSUGU!
NOW YOU CAN'T DO YOUR MATCHING GAME! GIVE UP AND...
SNIFF SNIFF SNIFF
I CAN'T EVEN SMELL YOUR OVER-POWERING CHEAP COLOGNE !!
WHAT !?

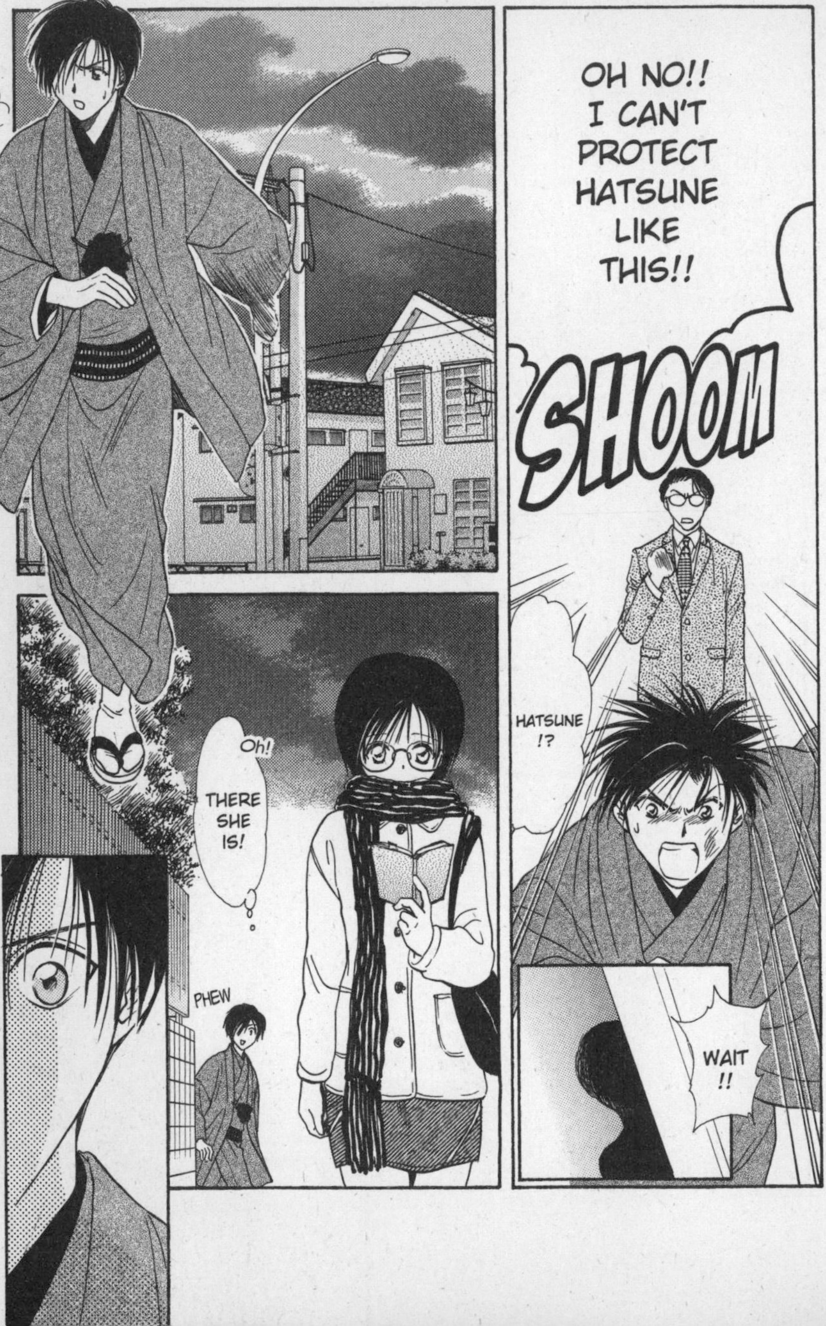
OH NO!! I CAN'T PROTECT HATSUNE LIKE THIS!!
SHOOM
HATSUNE !?
WAIT !!
Oh!
THERE SHE IS!
PHEW

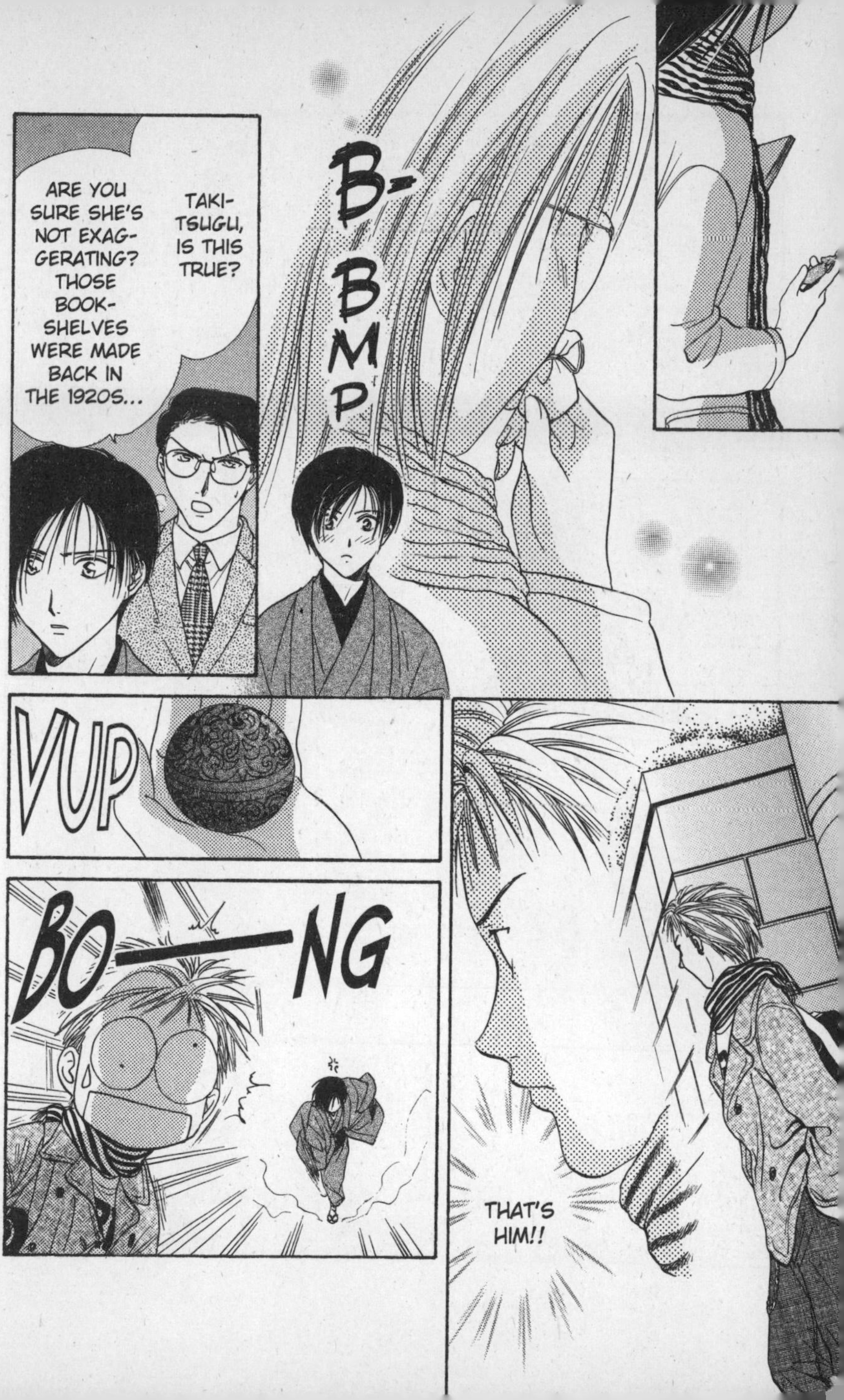
B-BMP
TAKI-TSUGU, IS THIS TRUE?
ARE YOU SURE SHE'S NOT EXAG-GERATING? THOSE BOOK-SHELVES WERE MADE BACK IN THE 1920S...
THAT'S HIM!!
VUP
BO——NG

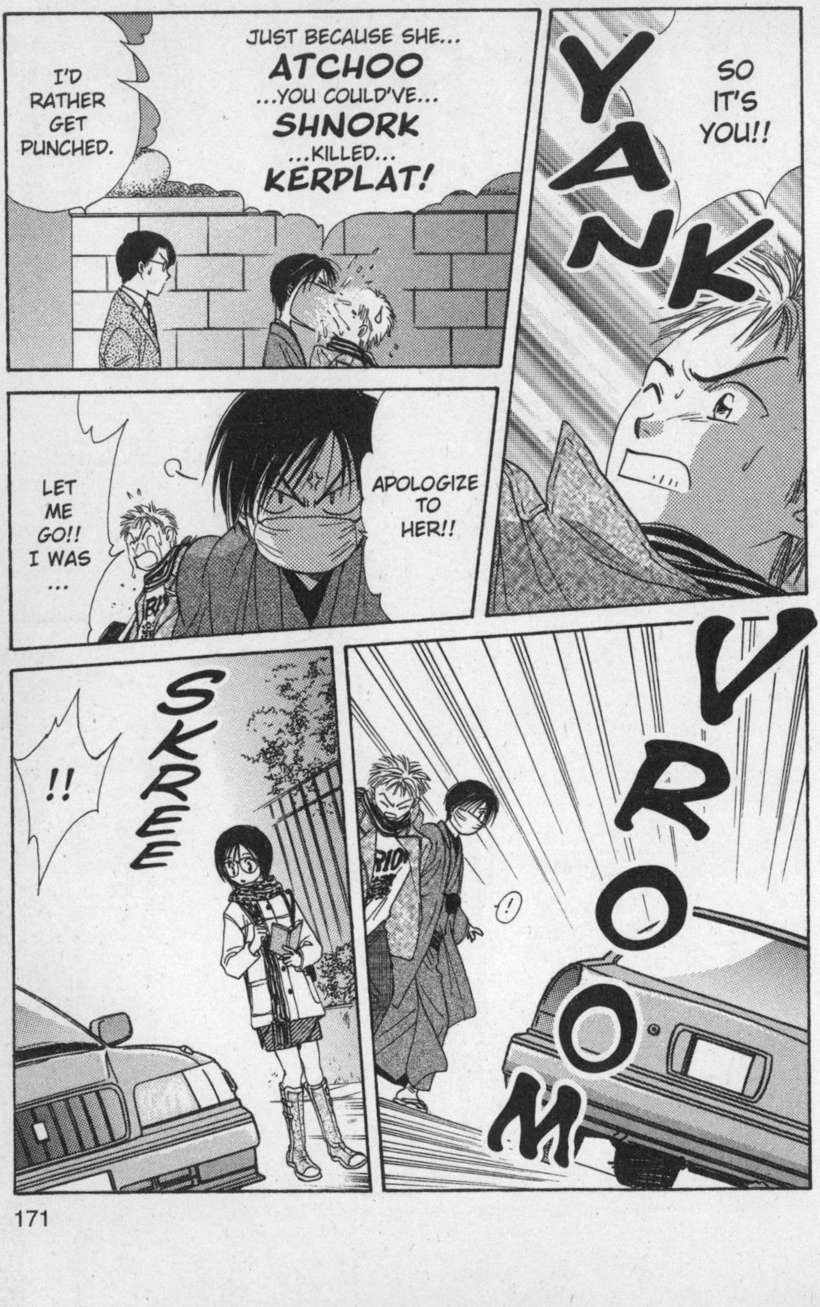
YANK
SO IT'S YOU!!
JUST BECAUSE SHE... ATCHOO ...YOU COULD'VE... SHNORK ...KILLED... KERPLAT!
I'D RATHER GET PUNCHED.
APOLOGIZE TO HER!!
LET ME GO!! I WAS ...
VROOOM
!
SKREE
!!

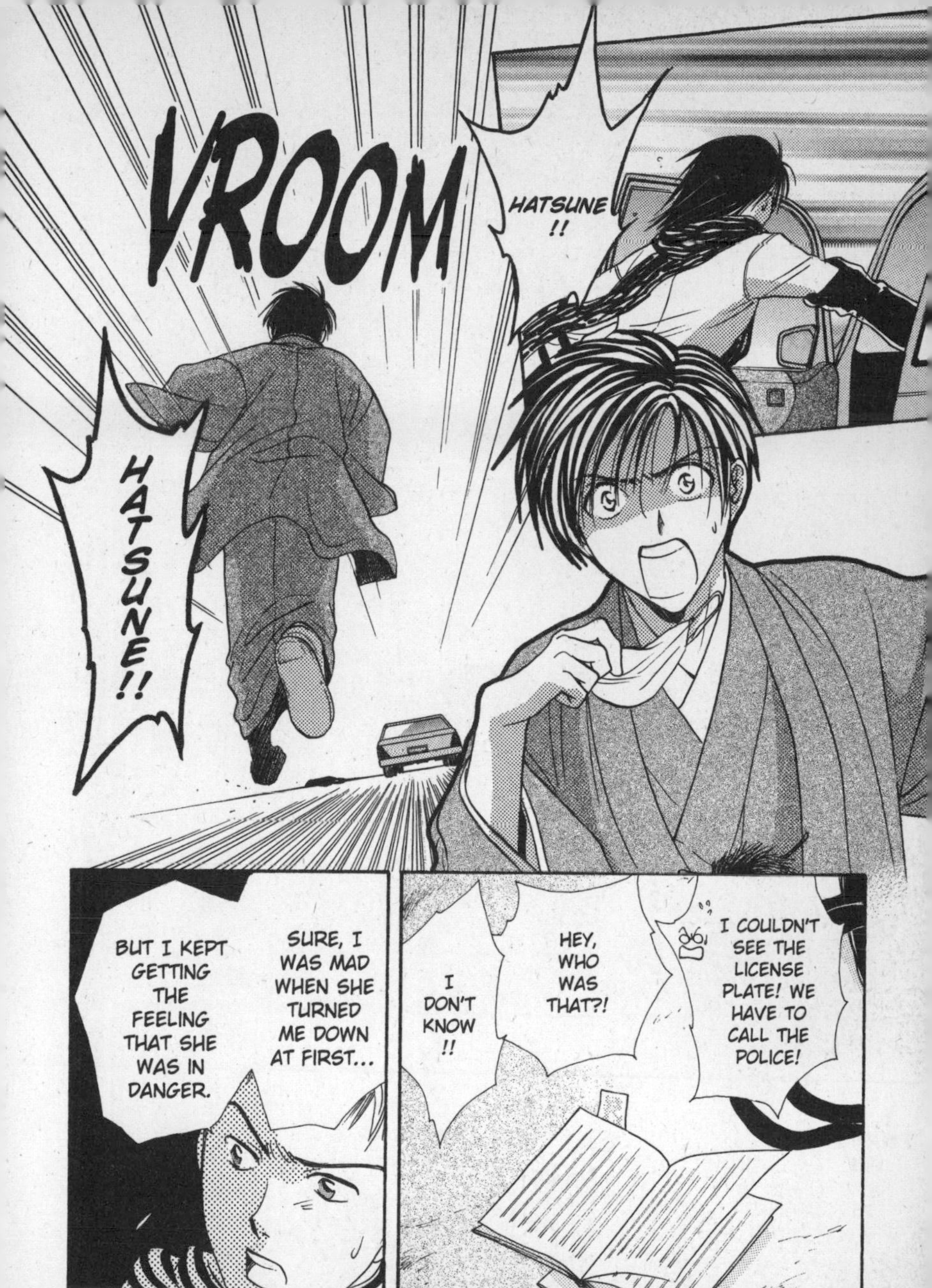
VROOM
HATSUNE !!
HATSUNE!!
I COULDN'T SEE THE LICENSE PLATE! WE HAVE TO CALL THE POLICE!
HEY, WHO WAS THAT?!
I DON'T KNOW !!
SURE, I WAS MAD WHEN SHE TURNED ME DOWN AT FIRST...
BUT I KEPT GETTING THE FEELING THAT SHE WAS IN DANGER.

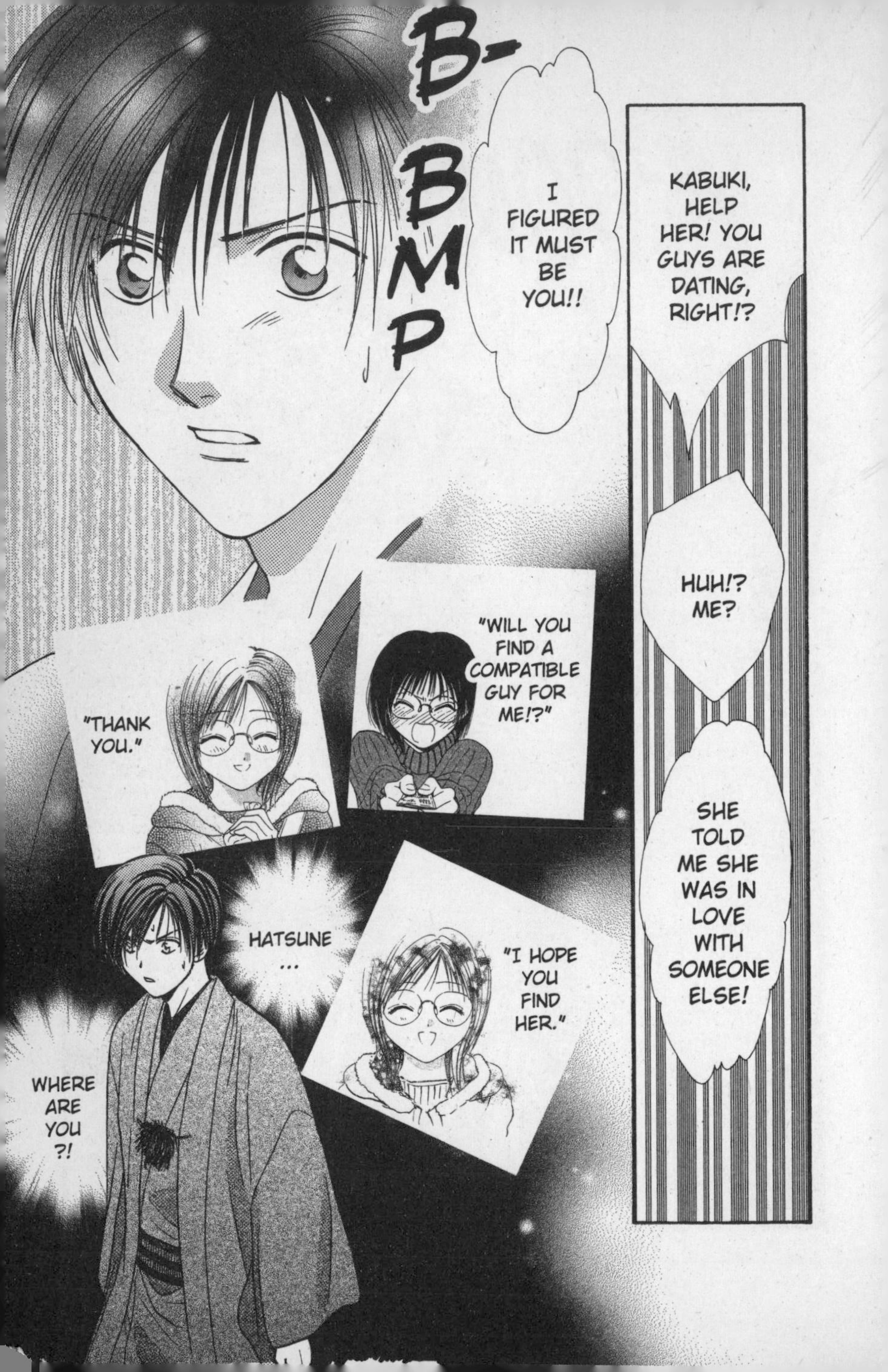
KABUKI, HELP HER! YOU GUYS ARE DATING, RIGHT!?
HUH!? ME?
SHE TOLD ME SHE WAS IN LOVE WITH SOMEONE ELSE!
B-BMP
I FIGURED IT MUST BE YOU!!
"WILL YOU FIND A COMPATIBLE GUY FOR ME!?"
"THANK YOU."
"I HOPE YOU FIND HER."
HATSUNE ...
WHERE ARE YOU ?!

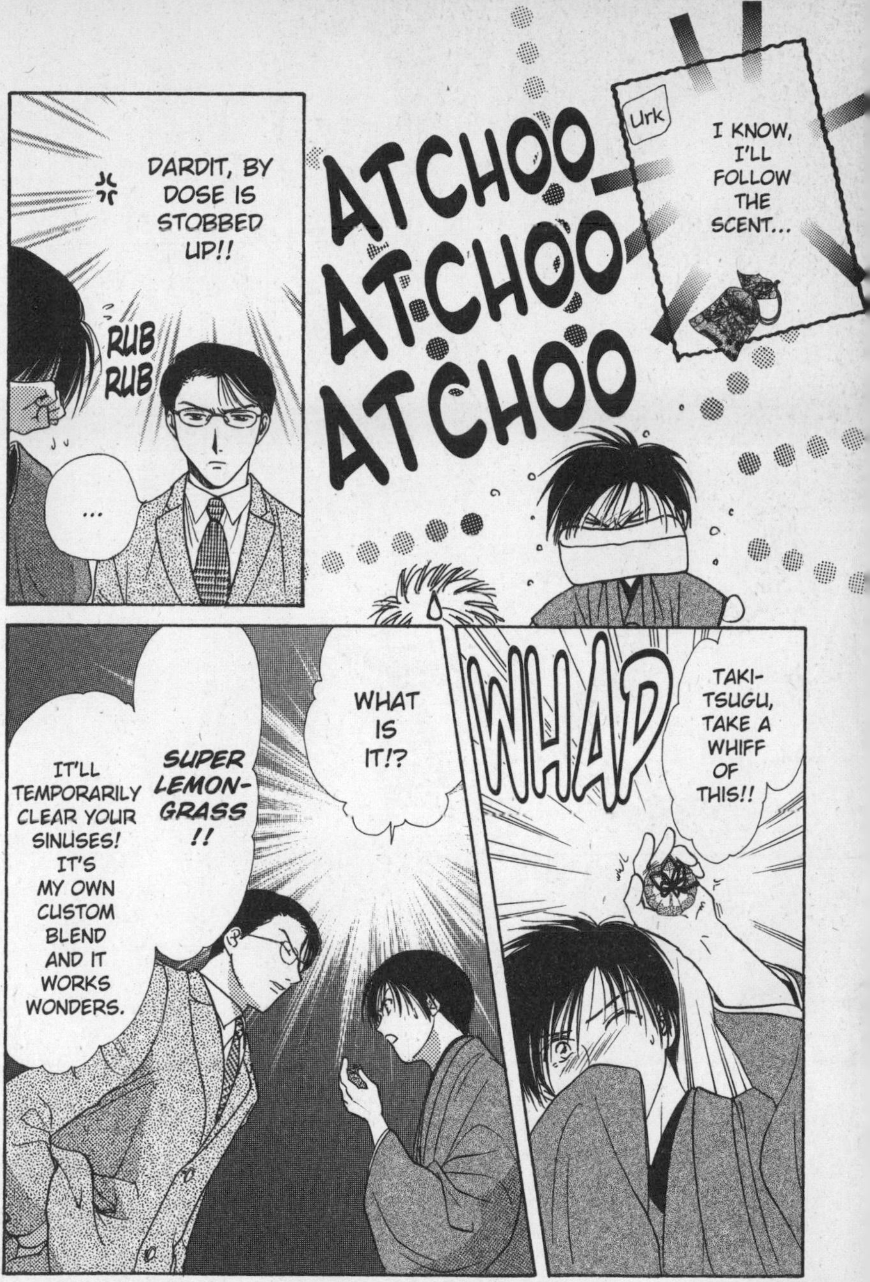
Urk
I KNOW, I'LL FOLLOW THE SCENT...
ATCHOO
ATCHOO
ATCHOO
DARDIT, BY DOSE IS STOBBED UP!!
RUB RUB
...
TAKI-TSUGU, TAKE A WHIFF OF THIS!!
WHAP
WHAT IS IT!?
SUPER LEMON-GRASS!!
IT'LL TEMPORARILY CLEAR YOUR SINUSES! IT'S MY OWN CUSTOM BLEND AND IT WORKS WONDERS.

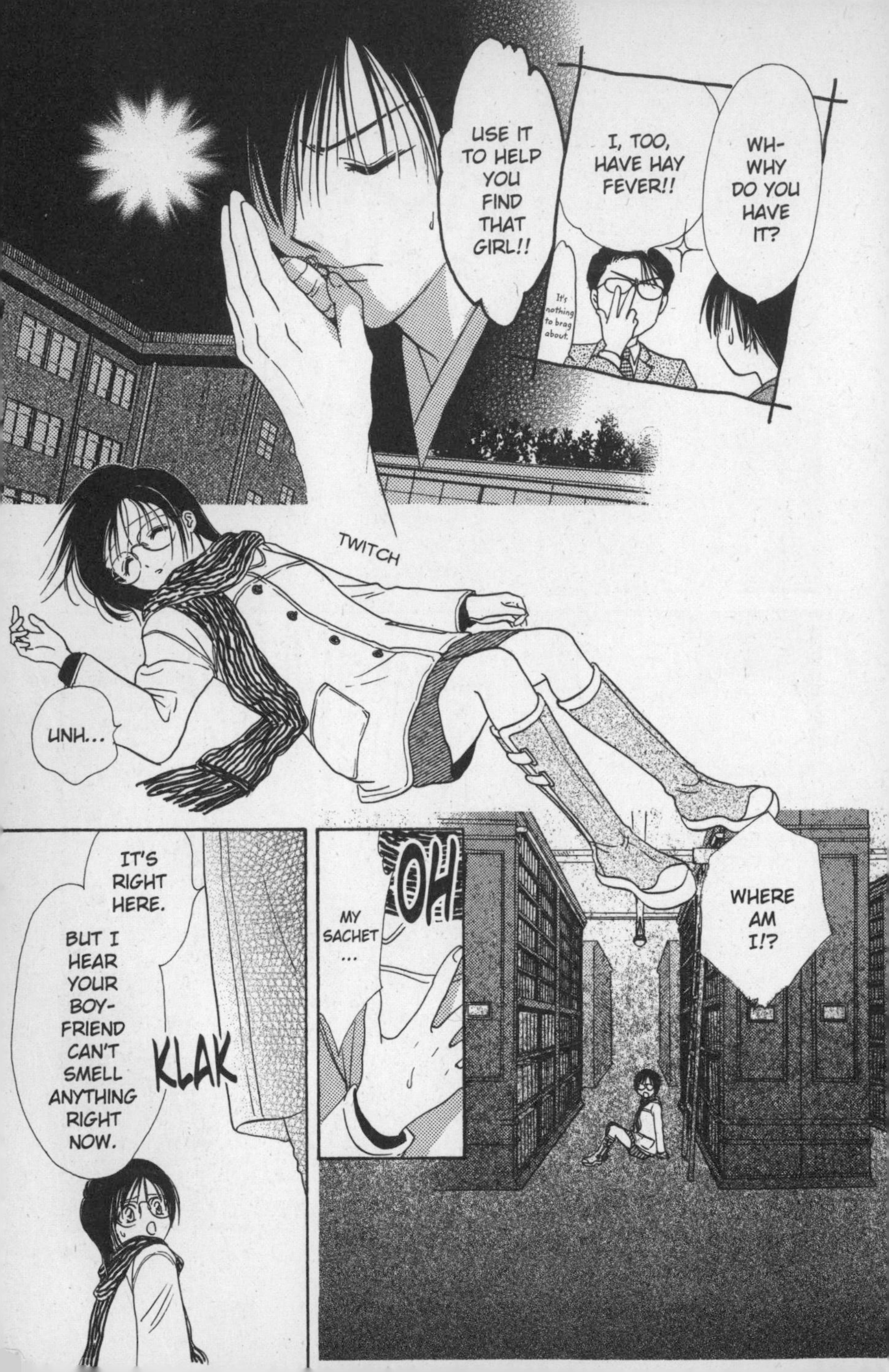
WH- WHY DO YOU HAVE IT?
I, TOO, HAVE HAY FEVER!!
It's nothing to brag about.
USE IT TO HELP YOU FIND THAT GIRL!!
TWITCH
UNH...
WHERE AM I!?
OH
MY SACHET ...
IT'S RIGHT HERE.
BUT I HEAR YOUR BOY-FRIEND CAN'T SMELL ANYTHING RIGHT NOW.
KLAK

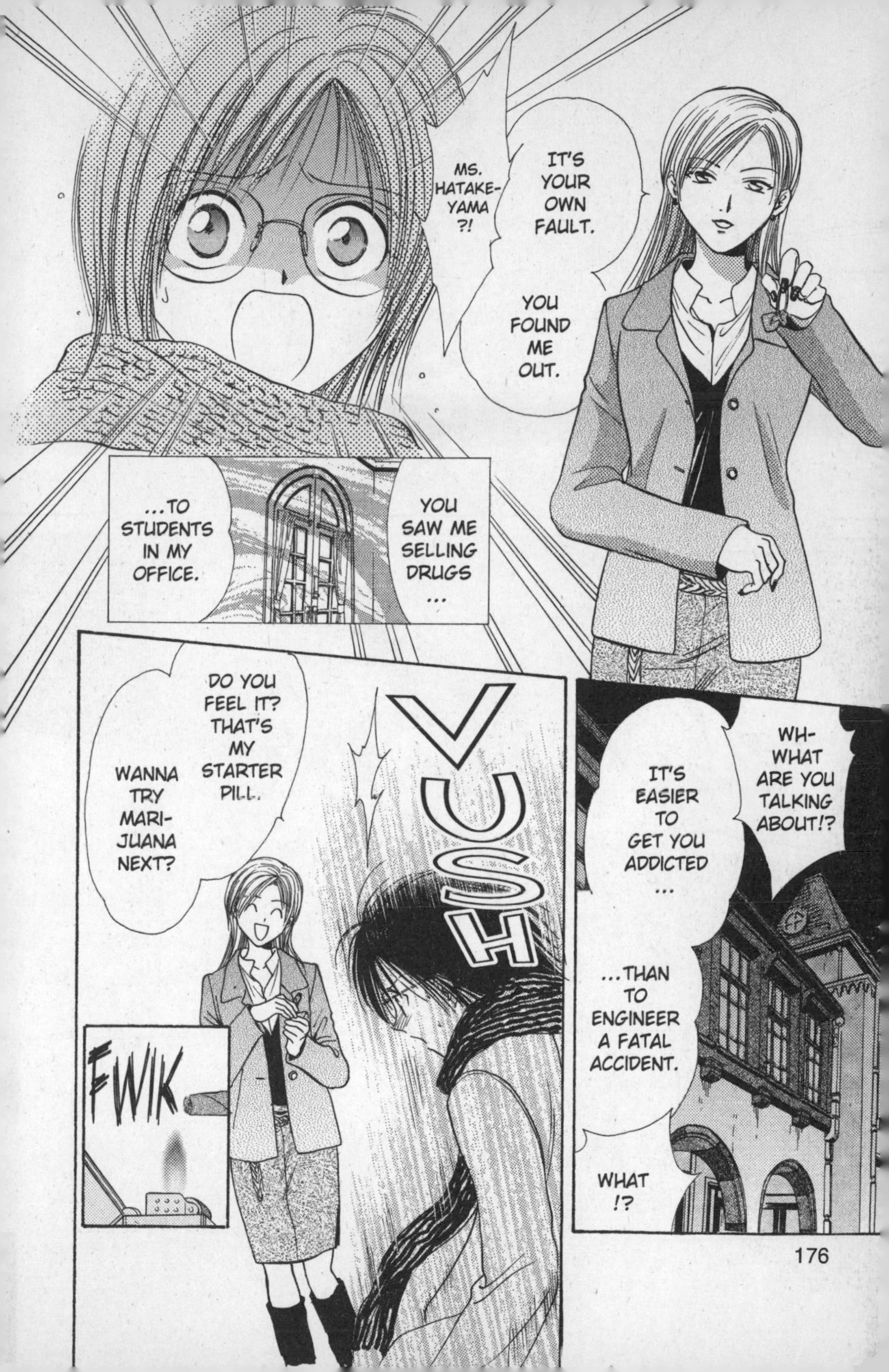
IT'S YOUR OWN FAULT.
MS. HATAKE-YAMA?!
YOU FOUND ME OUT.
YOU SAW ME SELLING DRUGS...
...TO STUDENTS IN MY OFFICE.
WH-WHAT ARE YOU TALKING ABOUT!?
IT'S EASIER TO GET YOU ADDICTED...
...THAN TO ENGINEER A FATAL ACCIDENT.
WHAT!?
VUSH
DO YOU FEEL IT? THAT'S MY STARTER PILL.
WANNA TRY MARIJUANA NEXT?
FWIK

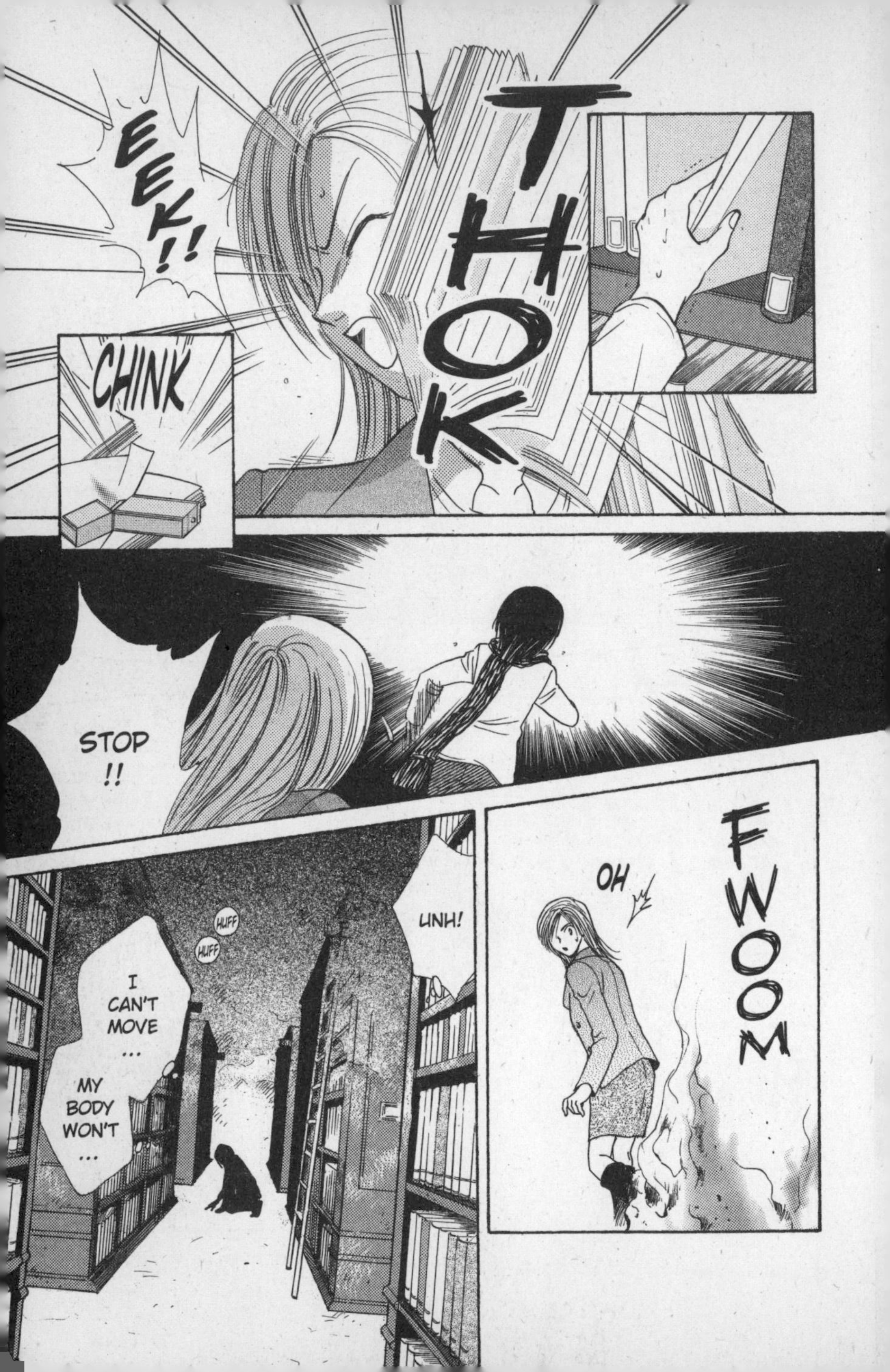
THOK
EEK!!
CHINK
STOP !!
FWOOM
OH
UNH!
HUFF
HUFF
I CAN'T MOVE ...
MY BODY WON'T ...

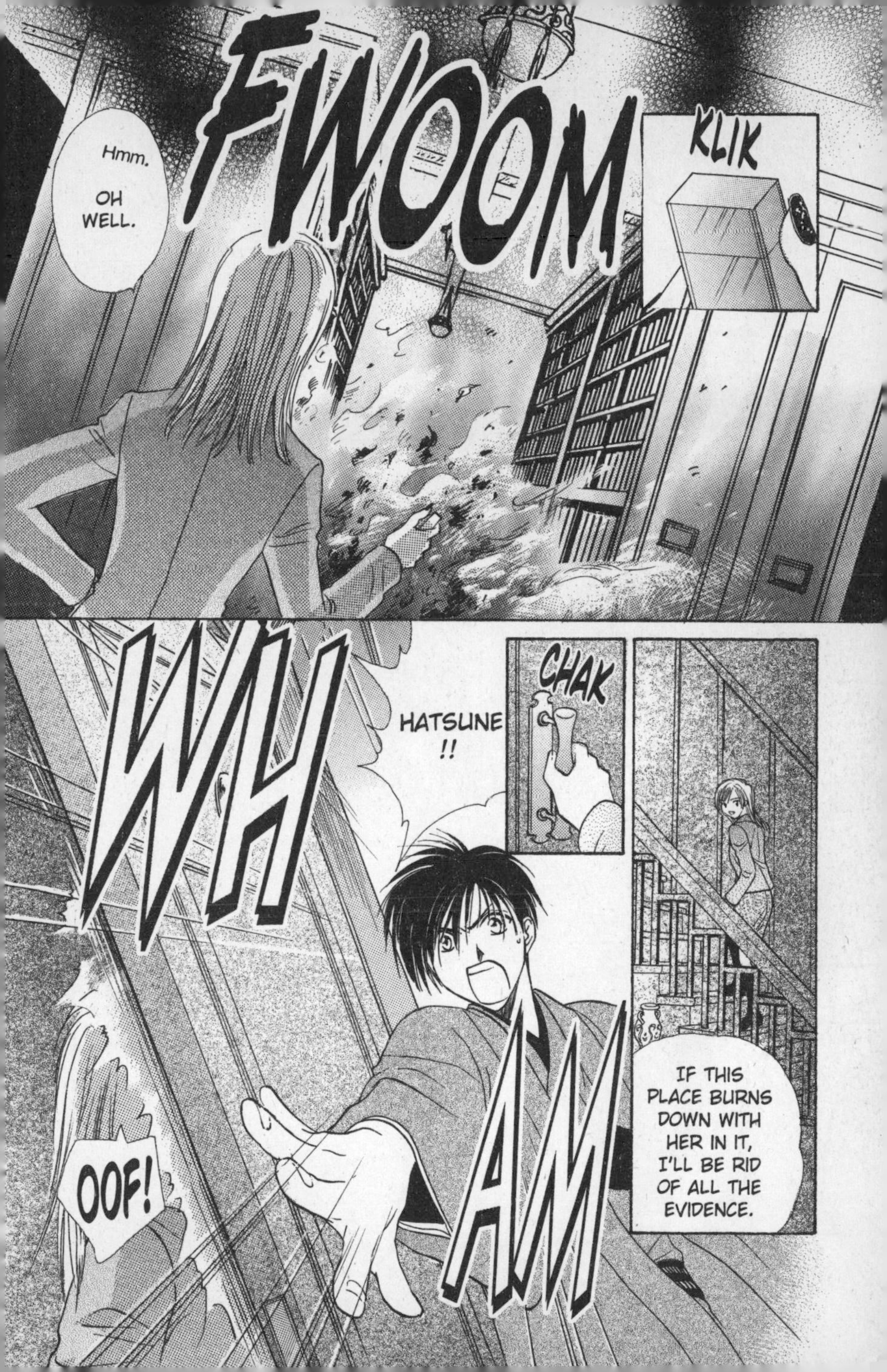
KLIK
FWOOM
Hmm.
OH WELL.
IF THIS PLACE BURNS DOWN WITH HER IN IT, I'LL BE RID OF ALL THE EVIDENCE.
CHAK
HATSUNE !!
WHAM
OOF!

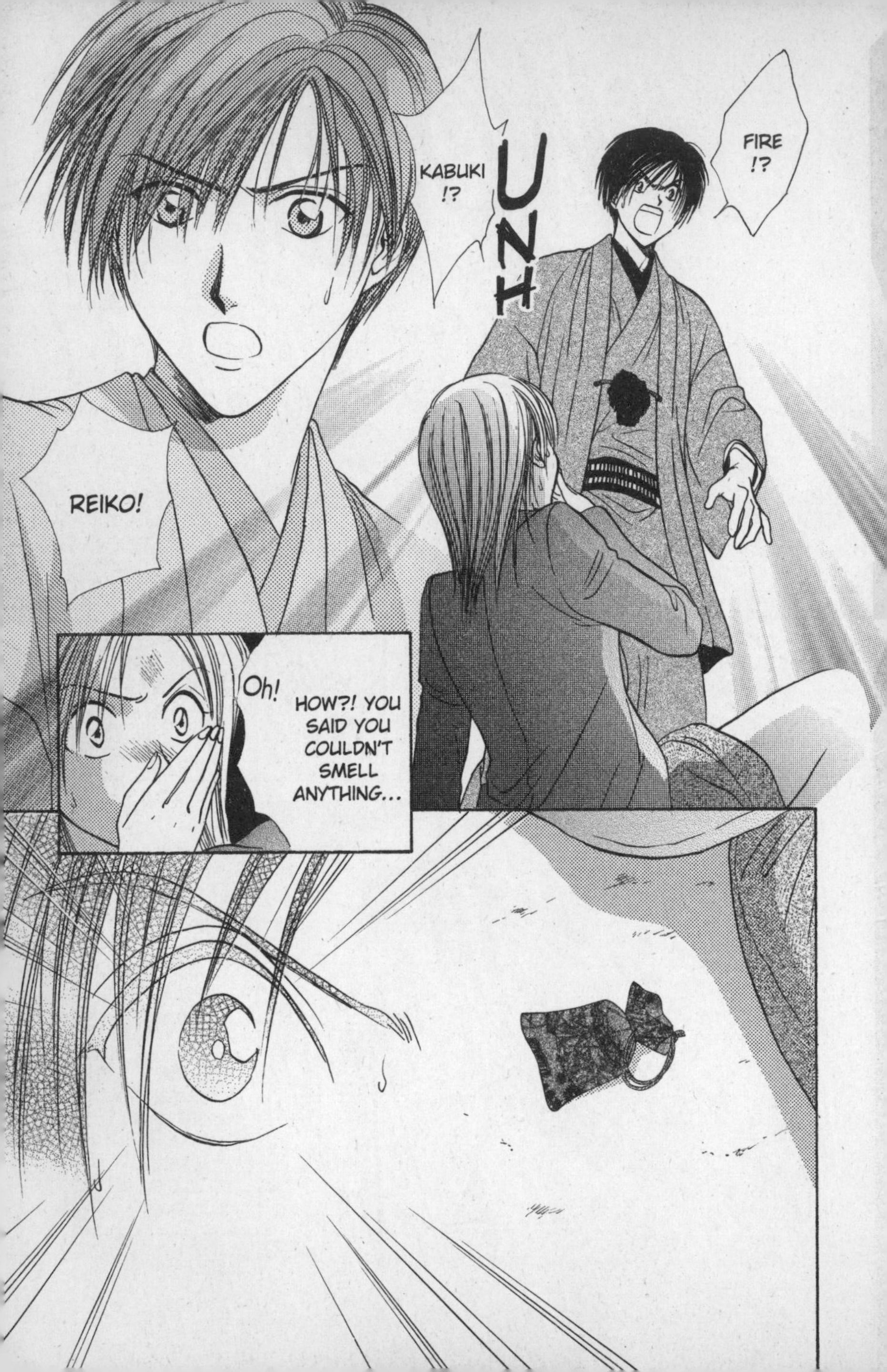
FIRE !?
UNH
KABUKI !?
REIKO!
Oh!
HOW?! YOU SAID YOU COULDN'T SMELL ANYTHING...

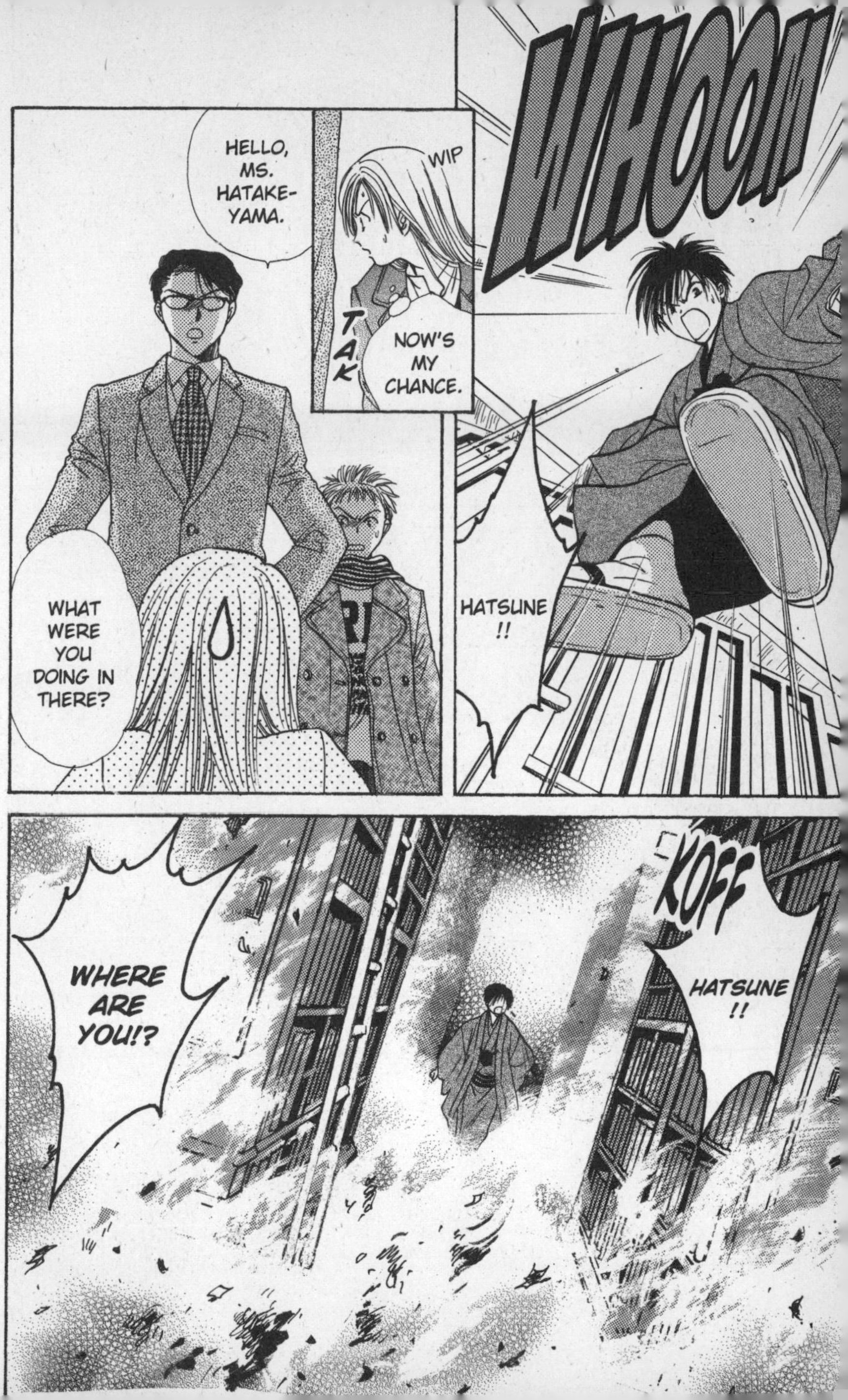
WHOOM
HATSUNE !!
WIP
TAK
NOW'S MY CHANCE.
HELLO, MS. HATAKE-YAMA.
WHAT WERE YOU DOING IN THERE?
KOFF
HATSUNE !!
WHERE ARE YOU!?

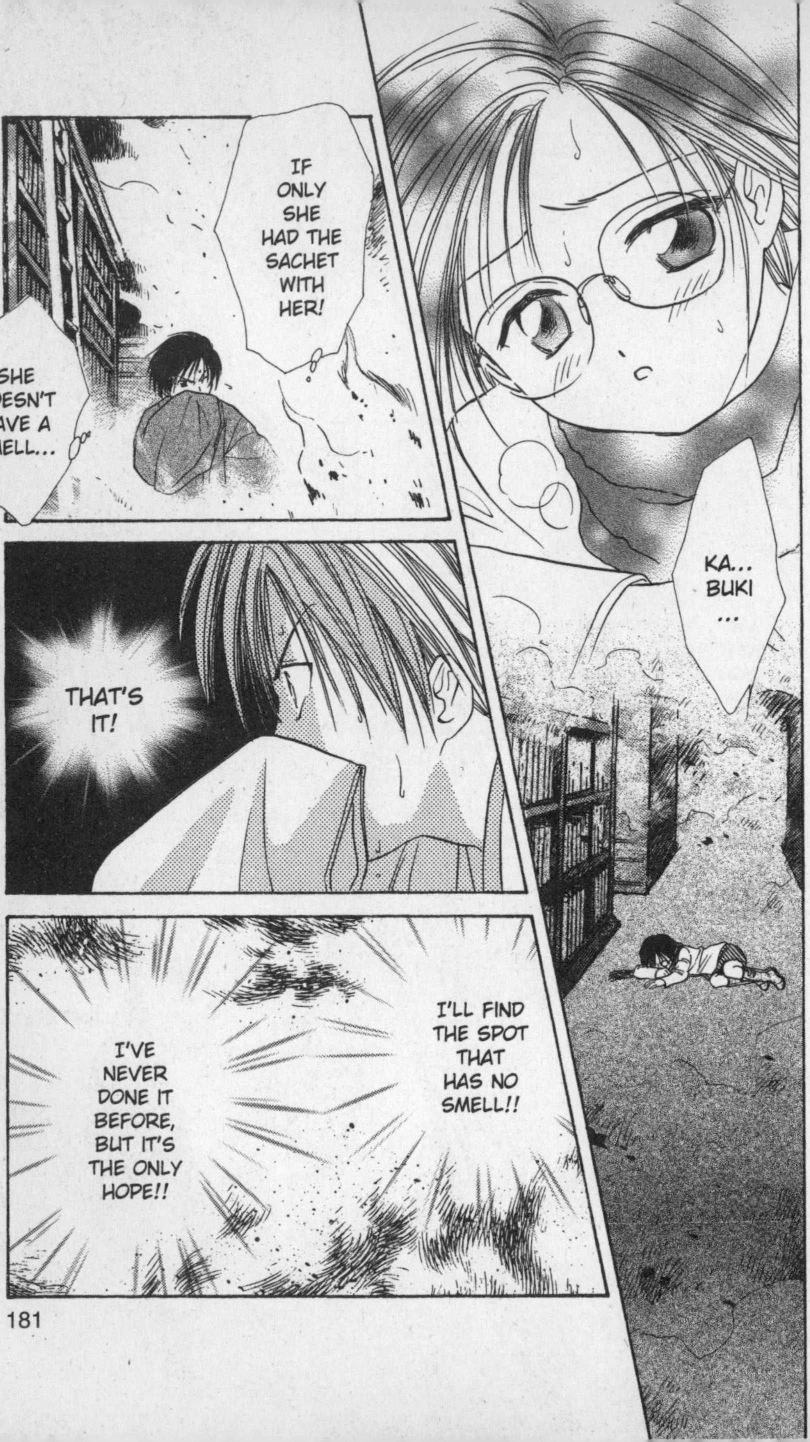
KA... BUKI ...
IF ONLY SHE HAD THE SACHET WITH HER!
SHE DOESN'T HAVE A SMELL...
THAT'S IT!
I'LL FIND THE SPOT THAT HAS NO SMELL!!
I'VE NEVER DONE IT BEFORE, BUT IT'S THE ONLY HOPE!!

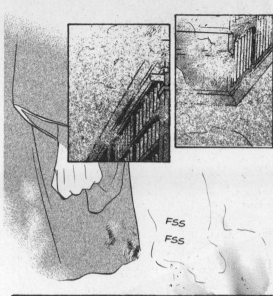

FSS
FSS

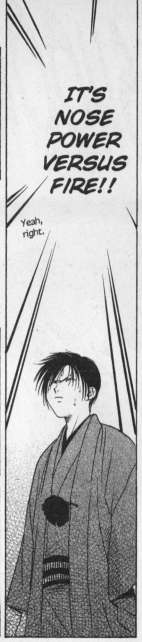

IT'S NOSE POWER VERSUS FIRE!!

Yeah, right.

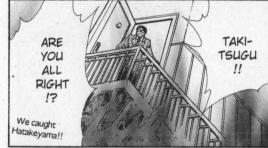

ARE YOU ALL RIGHT!?

We caught Hatakeyama!!

TAKI-TSUGU!!

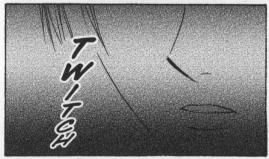

TWITCH

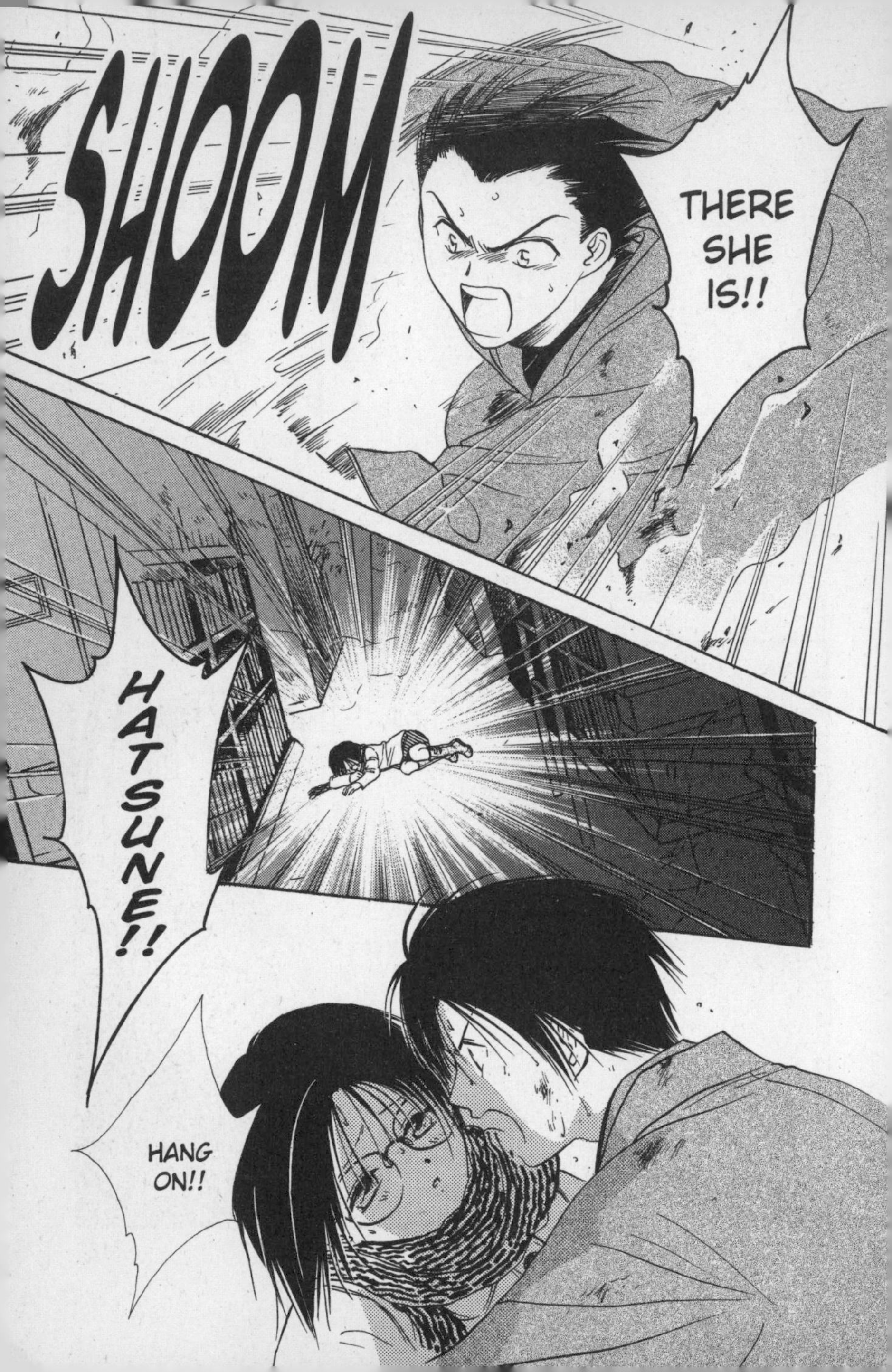
SHOOM
THERE SHE IS!!
HATSUNE!!
HANG ON!!

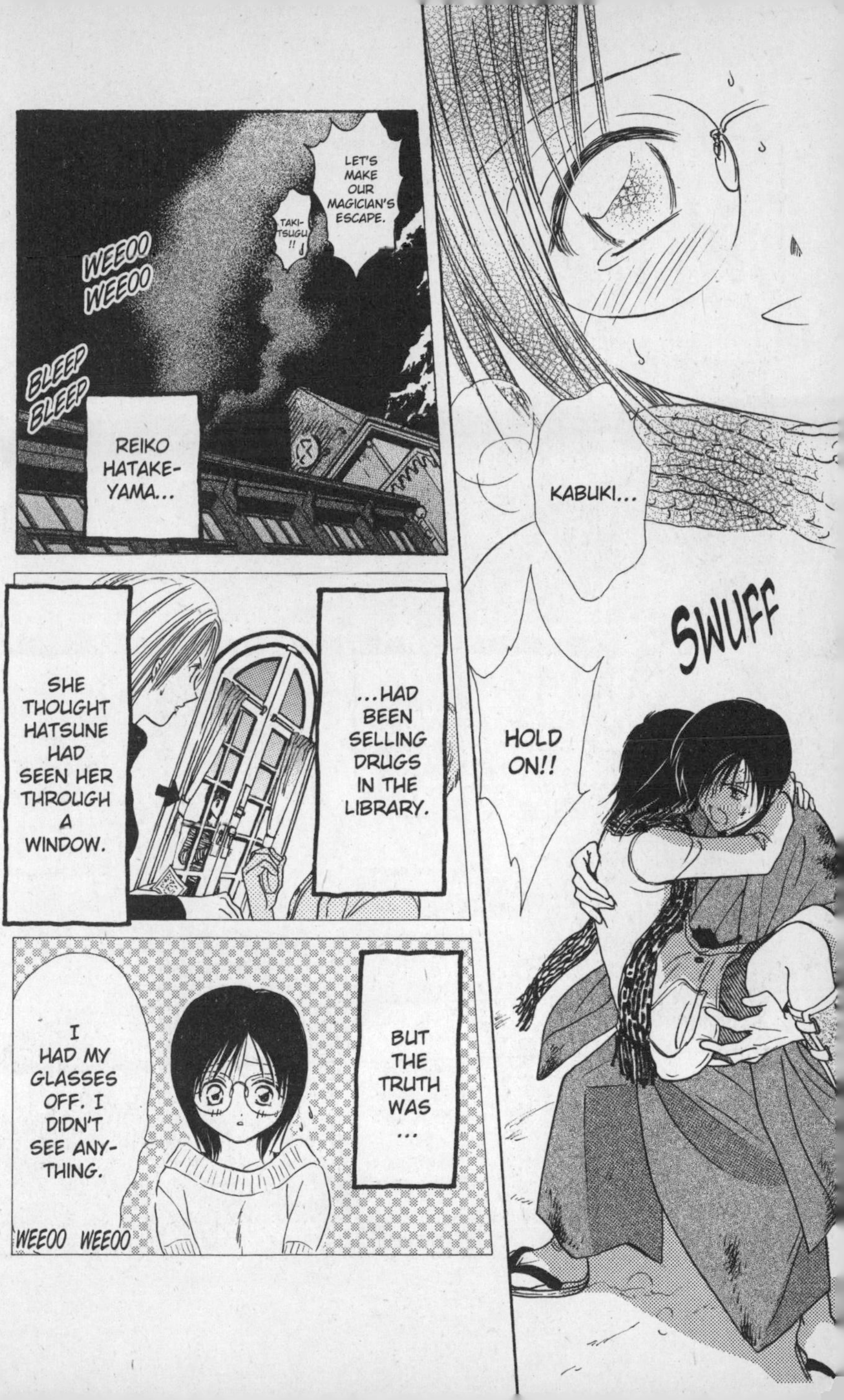
KABUKI...
SWUFF
HOLD ON!!
LET'S MAKE OUR MAGICIAN'S ESCAPE.
TAKI-TSUGU!!
WEEOO WEEOO
BLEEP BLEEP
REIKO HATAKE-YAMA...
...HAD BEEN SELLING DRUGS IN THE LIBRARY.
SHE THOUGHT HATSUNE HAD SEEN HER THROUGH A WINDOW.
BUT THE TRUTH WAS...
I HAD MY GLASSES OFF. I DIDN'T SEE ANY-THING.
WEEOO WEEOO

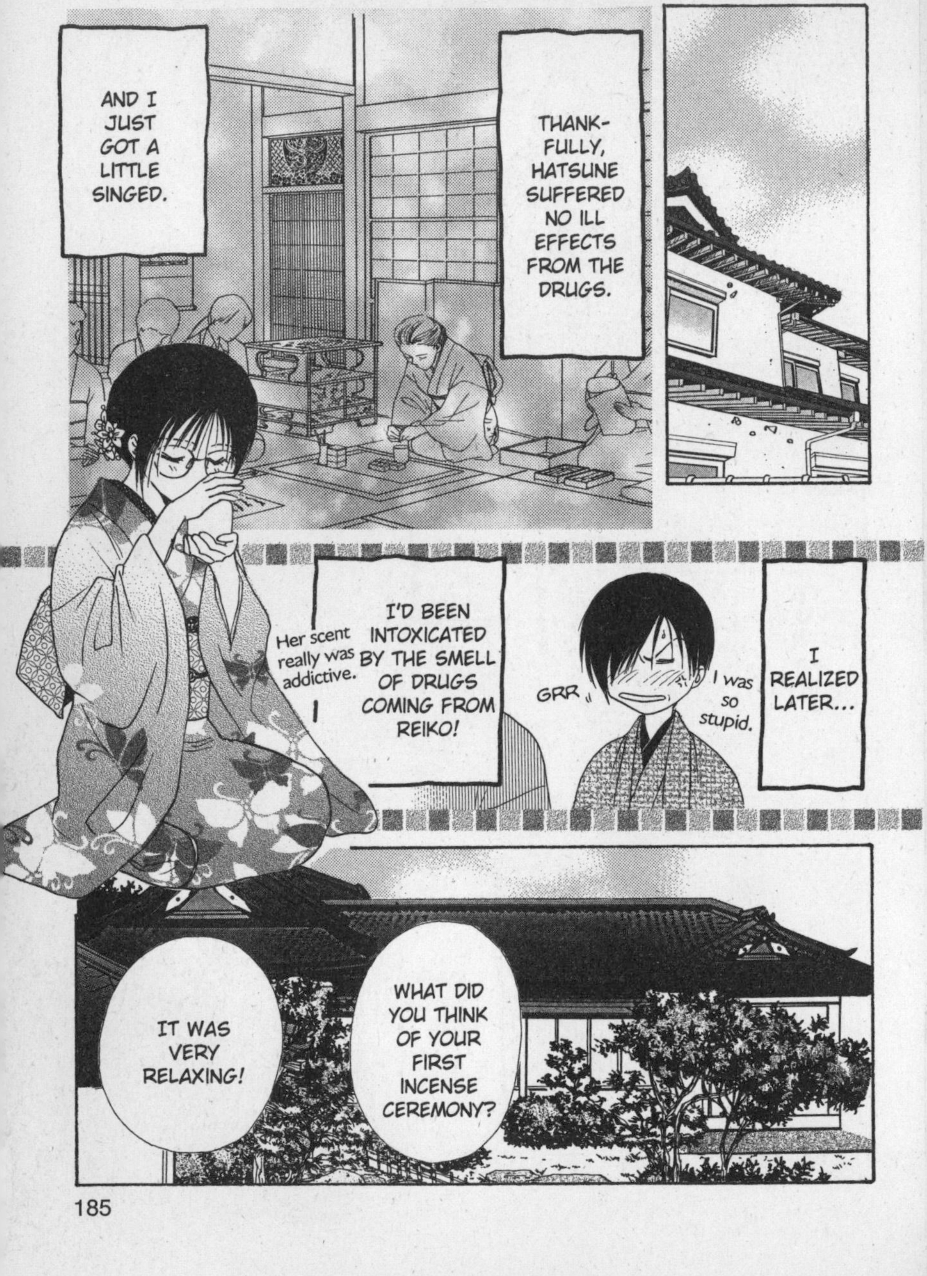
THANK-FULLY, HATSUNE SUFFERED NO ILL EFFECTS FROM THE DRUGS.
AND I JUST GOT A LITTLE SINGED.
I REALIZED LATER...
I was so stupid.
GRR
I'D BEEN INTOXICATED BY THE SMELL OF DRUGS COMING FROM REIKO!
Her scent really was addictive.
WHAT DID YOU THINK OF YOUR FIRST INCENSE CEREMONY?
IT WAS VERY RELAXING!

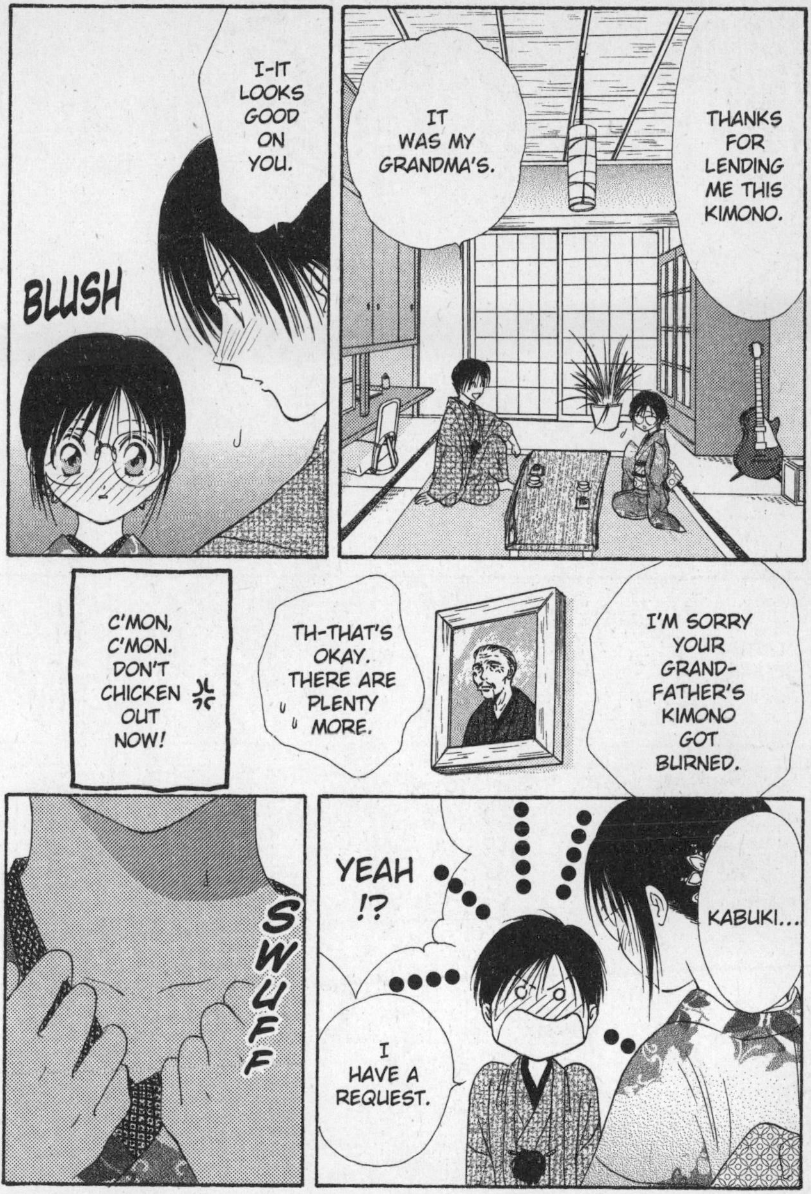
THANKS FOR LENDING ME THIS KIMONO.
IT WAS MY GRANDMA'S.
I-IT LOOKS GOOD ON YOU.
BLUSH
I'M SORRY YOUR GRAND-FATHER'S KIMONO GOT BURNED.
TH-THAT'S OKAY. THERE ARE PLENTY MORE.
C'MON, C'MON. DON'T CHICKEN OUT NOW!
KABUKI...
YEAH!?
I HAVE A REQUEST.
SWUFF

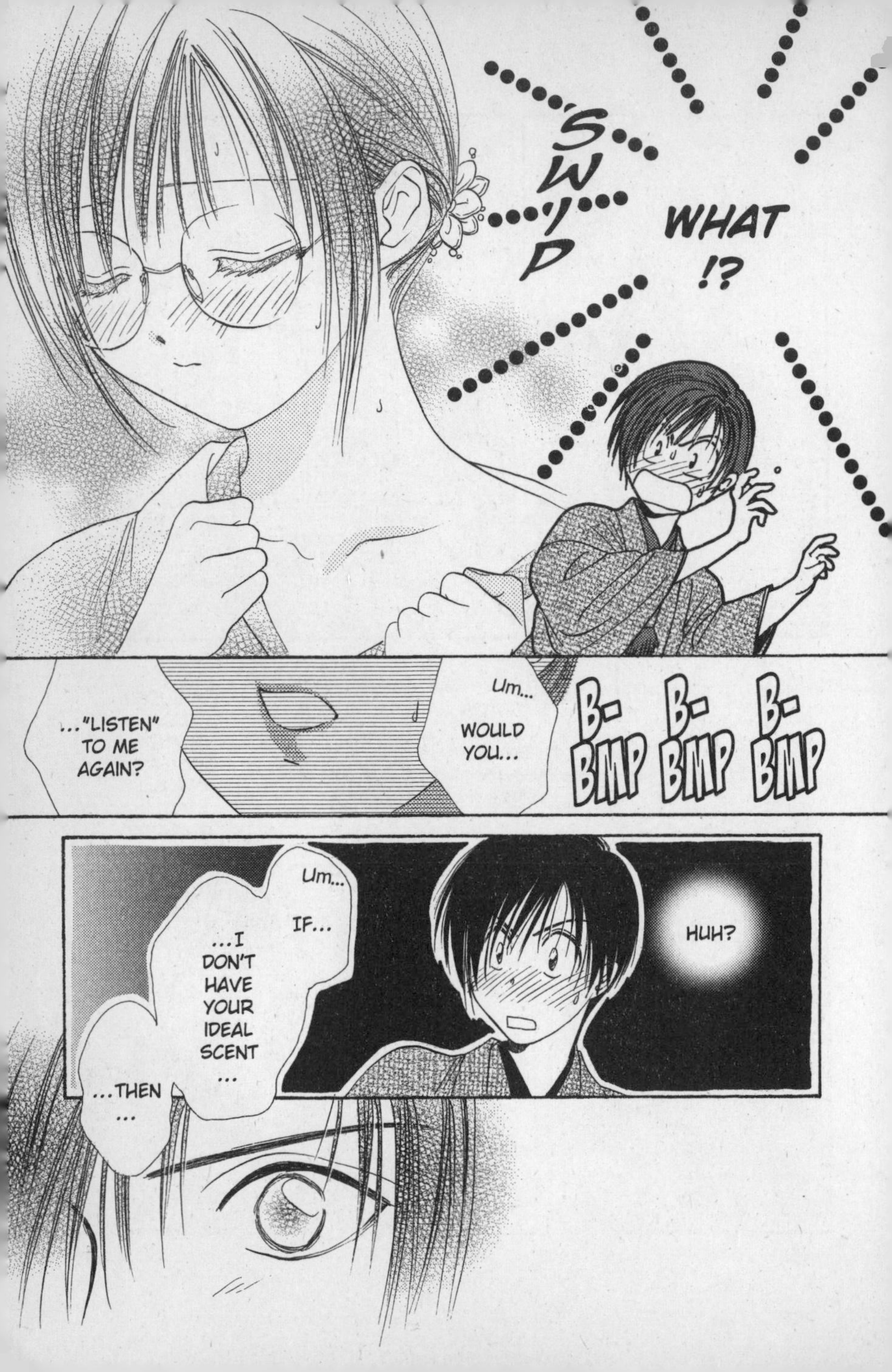
WHAT !?
SWID
B-BMP B-BMP B-BMP
Um... WOULD YOU...
..."LISTEN" TO ME AGAIN?
HUH?
Um... IF...
...I DON'T HAVE YOUR IDEAL SCENT...
...THEN...

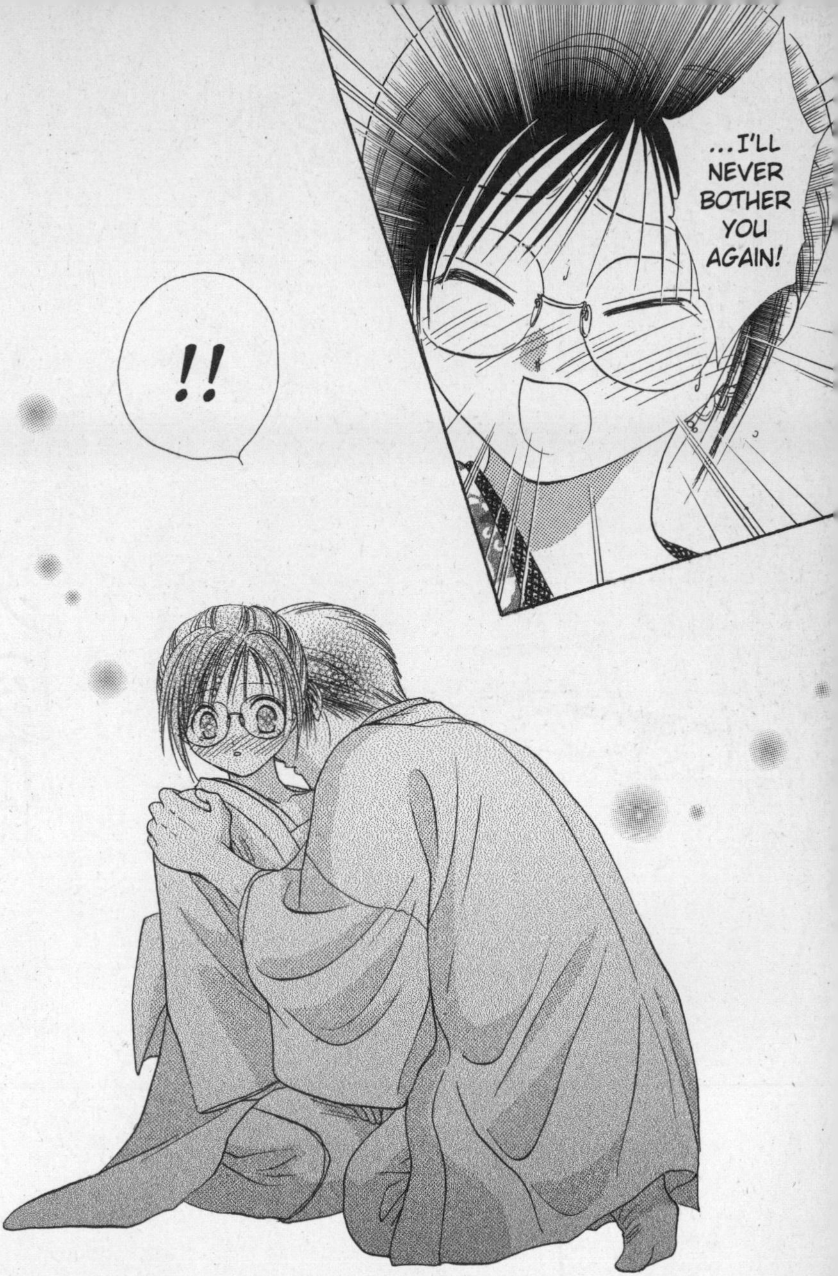
...I'LL NEVER BOTHER YOU AGAIN!
!!

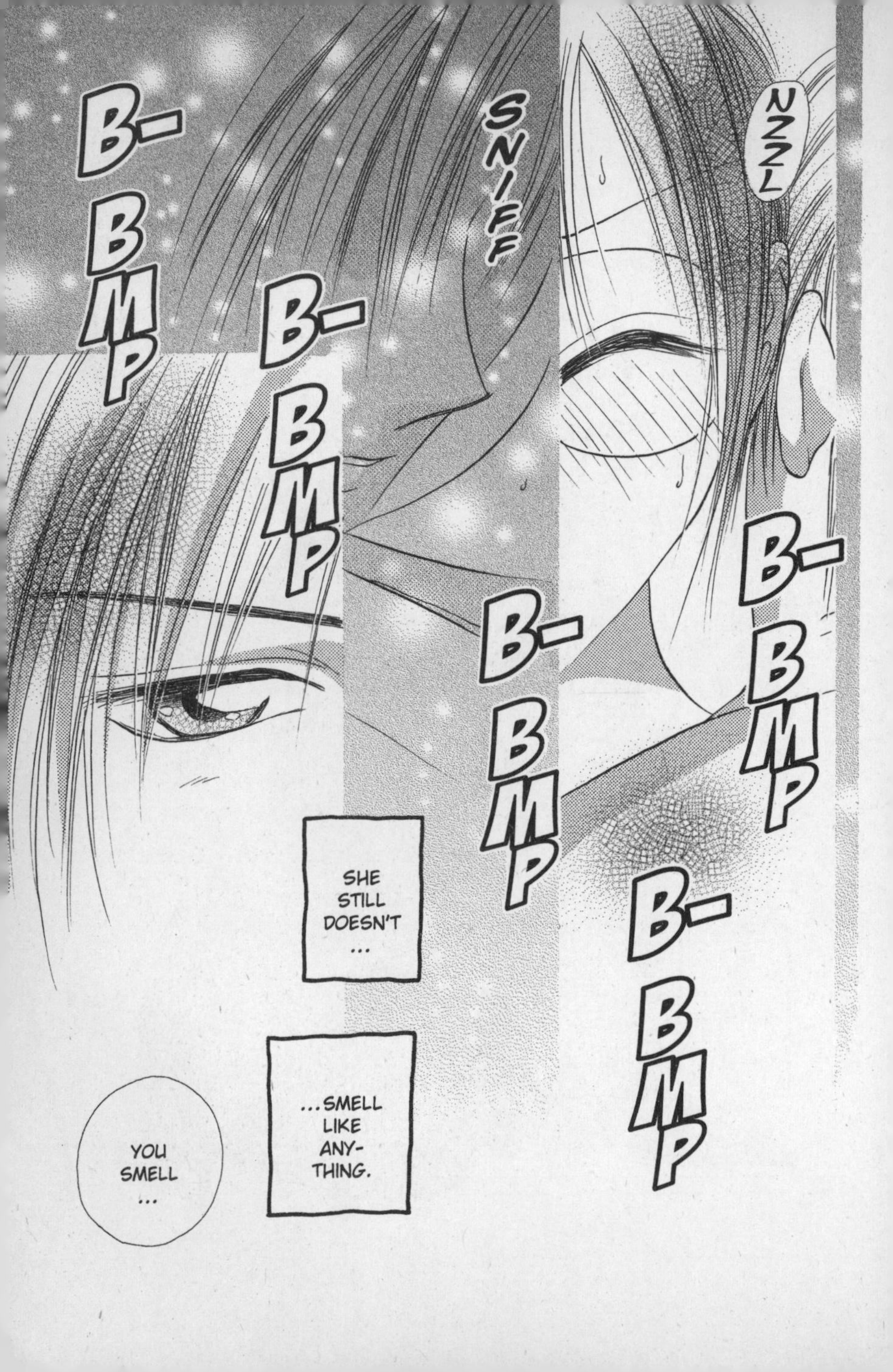

NUZZL
B-BMP
B-BMP
B-BMP
SNIFF
B-BMP
B-BMP
SHE STILL DOESN'T ...
...SMELL LIKE ANY-THING.
YOU SMELL ...

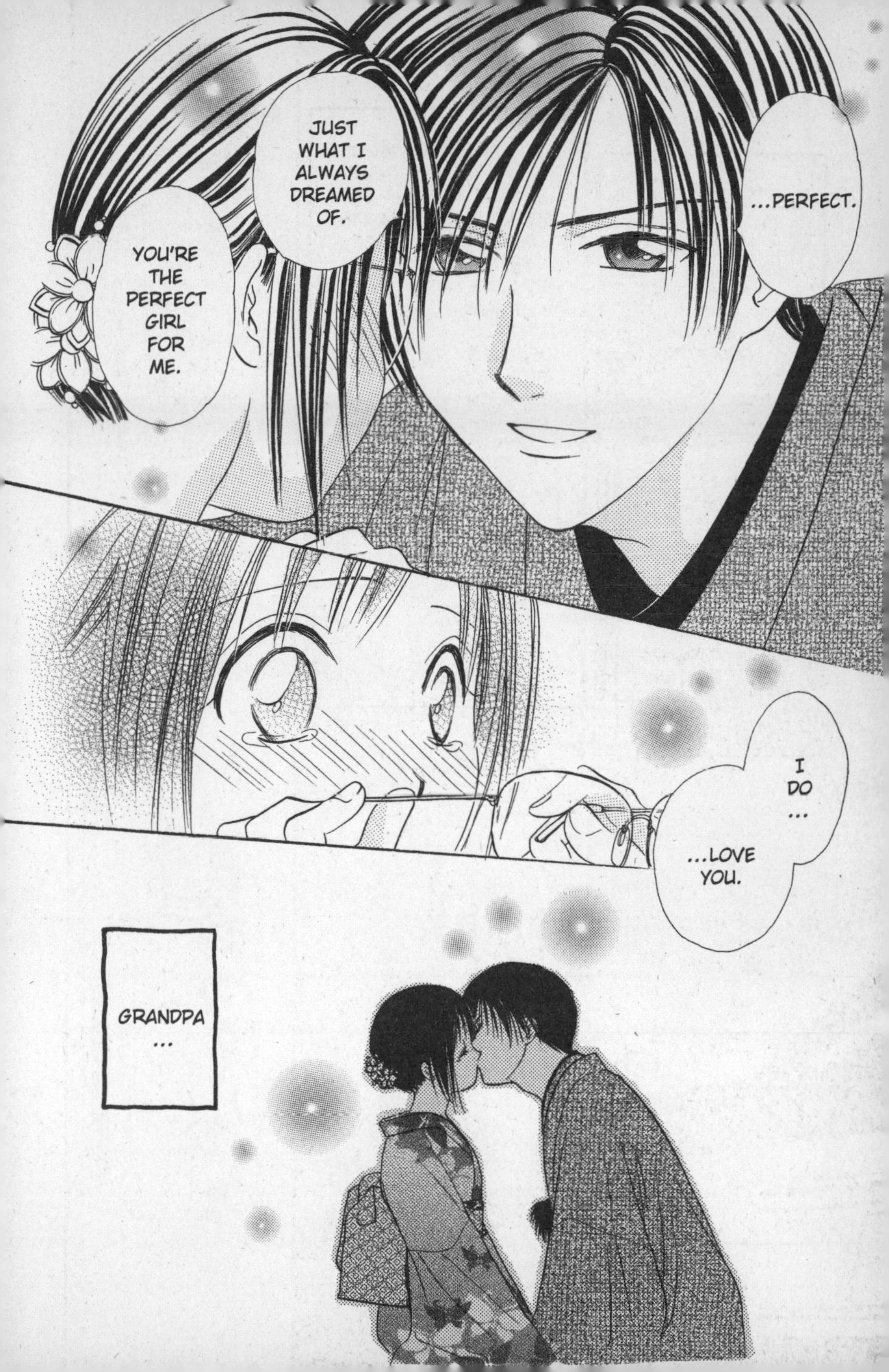
...PERFECT.
JUST WHAT I ALWAYS DREAMED OF.
YOU'RE THE PERFECT GIRL FOR ME.
I DO... ...LOVE YOU.
GRANDPA...

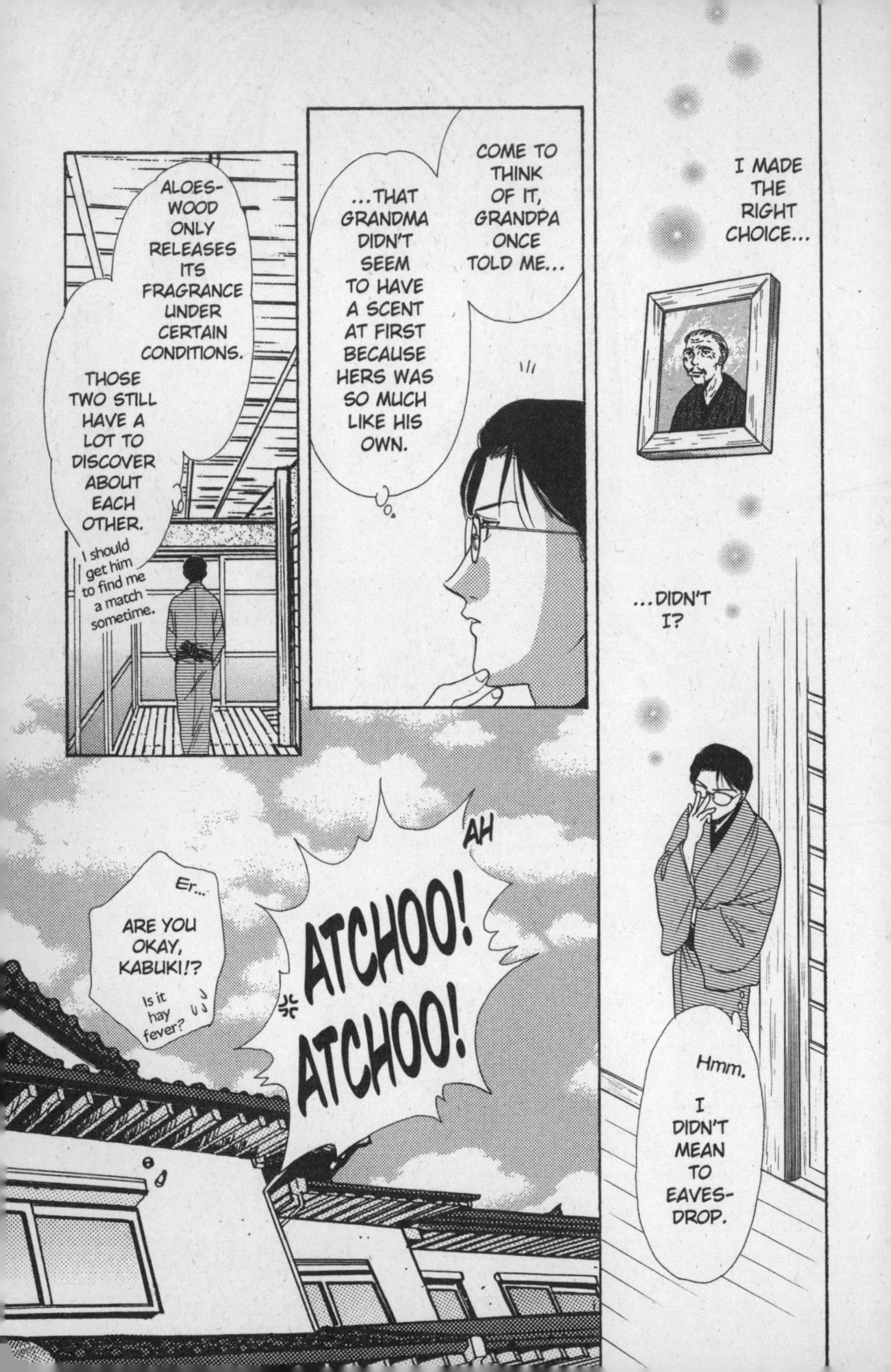

I MADE THE RIGHT CHOICE...
...DIDN'T I?
Hmm.
I DIDN'T MEAN TO EAVESDROP.
COME TO THINK OF IT, GRANDPA ONCE TOLD ME...
...THAT GRANDMA DIDN'T SEEM TO HAVE A SCENT AT FIRST BECAUSE HERS WAS SO MUCH LIKE HIS OWN.
ALOESWOOD ONLY RELEASES ITS FRAGRANCE UNDER CERTAIN CONDITIONS.
THOSE TWO STILL HAVE A LOT TO DISCOVER ABOUT EACH OTHER.
I should get him to find me a match sometime.
AH
ATCHOO! ATCHOO!
Er...
ARE YOU OKAY, KABUKI!?
Is it hay fever?

i've been drinking my wheatgrass juice religiously. it's pretty intense, to say the least! But i can usually handle stuff that makes other people gag. i've offered people medicinal liquors and turmeric, and they usually say, "No way!" But it's important to try new things, and not just foods. You never know what you might be missing. i tend to resist new things myself, so i want to work on that.

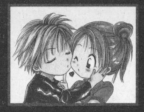

Yuu Watase

Birthday: March 5 (Pisces)

Blood type: B

Born and raised in Osaka.

Hobbies: listening to music, reading. Likes most music besides *enka* (traditional Japanese ballads) and heavy metal. Lately into health and wellness, like massage, mineral waters and wheatgrass juice. But her job is her biggest "hobby"!

Debut title: *Pajama de Ojama* (An intrusion in Pajamas) (*Shojo Comics*, 1989, No. 3)

ABSOLUTE BOYFRIEND
Volume 6
Shojo Beat Edition

Story and Art by
YUU WATASE

© 2003 Yuu WATASE/Shogakukan
All rights reserved.
Original Japanese edition "ZETTAI KARESHI"
published by SHOGAKUKAN Inc.

English Adaptation/Lance Caselman
Translation/Lillian Olsen
Touch-up Art & Lettering/Freeman Wong
Design/Courtney Utt
Editor/Nancy Thistlethwaite

Printed in Canada

Published by VIZ Media, LLC
P.O. Box 77010
San Francisco, CA 94107

10 9 8 7 6 5 4 3
First printing, May 2008
Third printing, September 2011

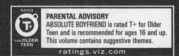
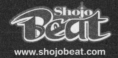

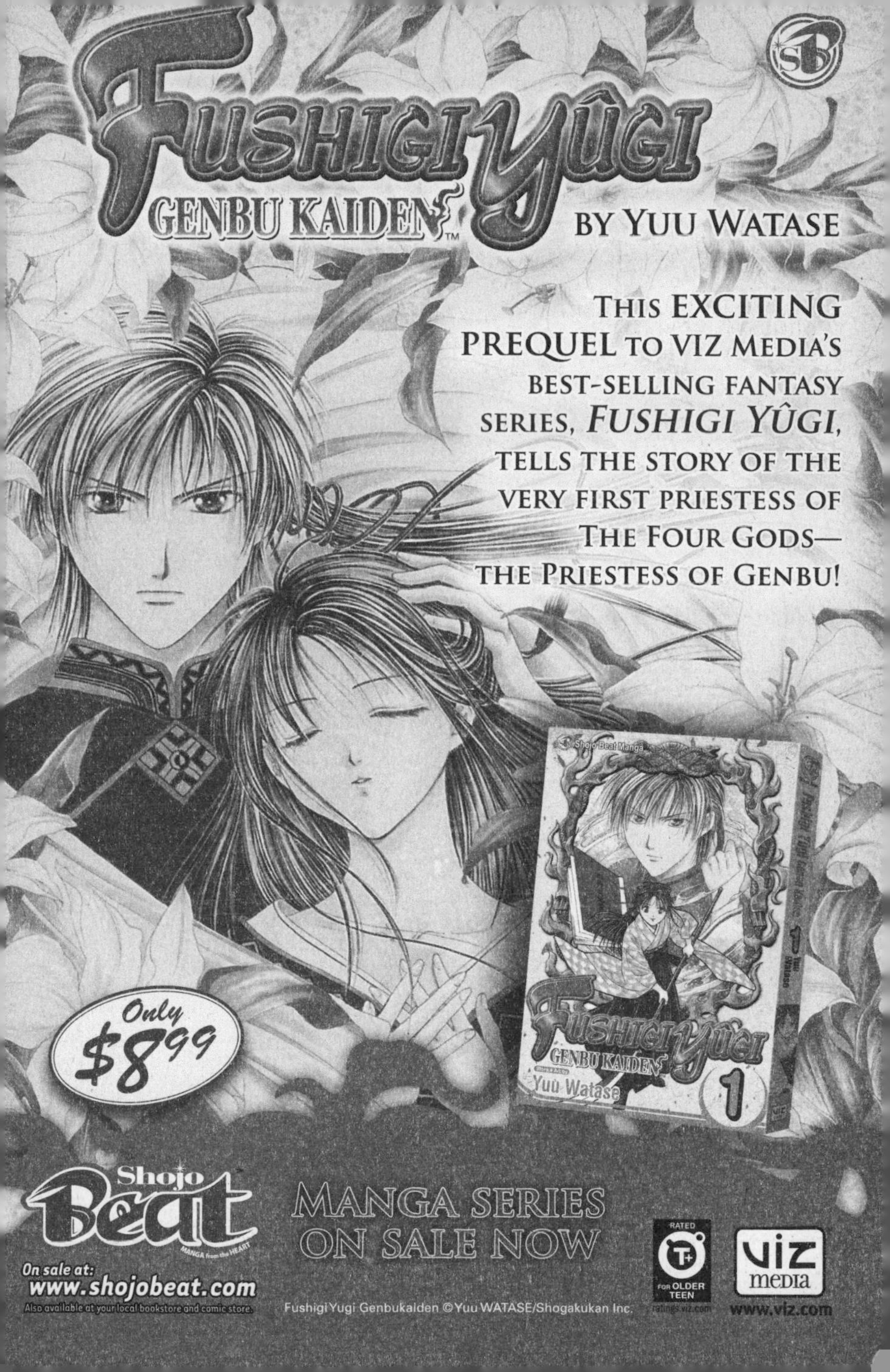

Fushigi Yûgi
Genbu Kaiden™
By Yuu Watase
This EXCITING PREQUEL to VIZ Media's best-selling fantasy series, *Fushigi Yûgi*, tells the story of the very first priestess of The Four Gods—the Priestess of Genbu!
Only $8.99
Shojo Beat Manga
Fushigi Yûgi
Genbu Kaiden
Yuu Watase
1
Shojo Beat
MANGA from the HEART
Manga Series On Sale Now
On sale at:
www.shojobeat.com
Also available at your local bookstore and comic store.
Fushigi Yugi Genbukaiden © Yuu WATASE/Shogakukan Inc.
RATED T+ FOR OLDER TEEN
ratings.viz.com
VIZ media
www.viz.com

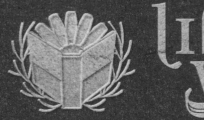
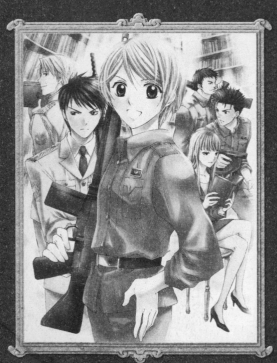

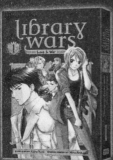

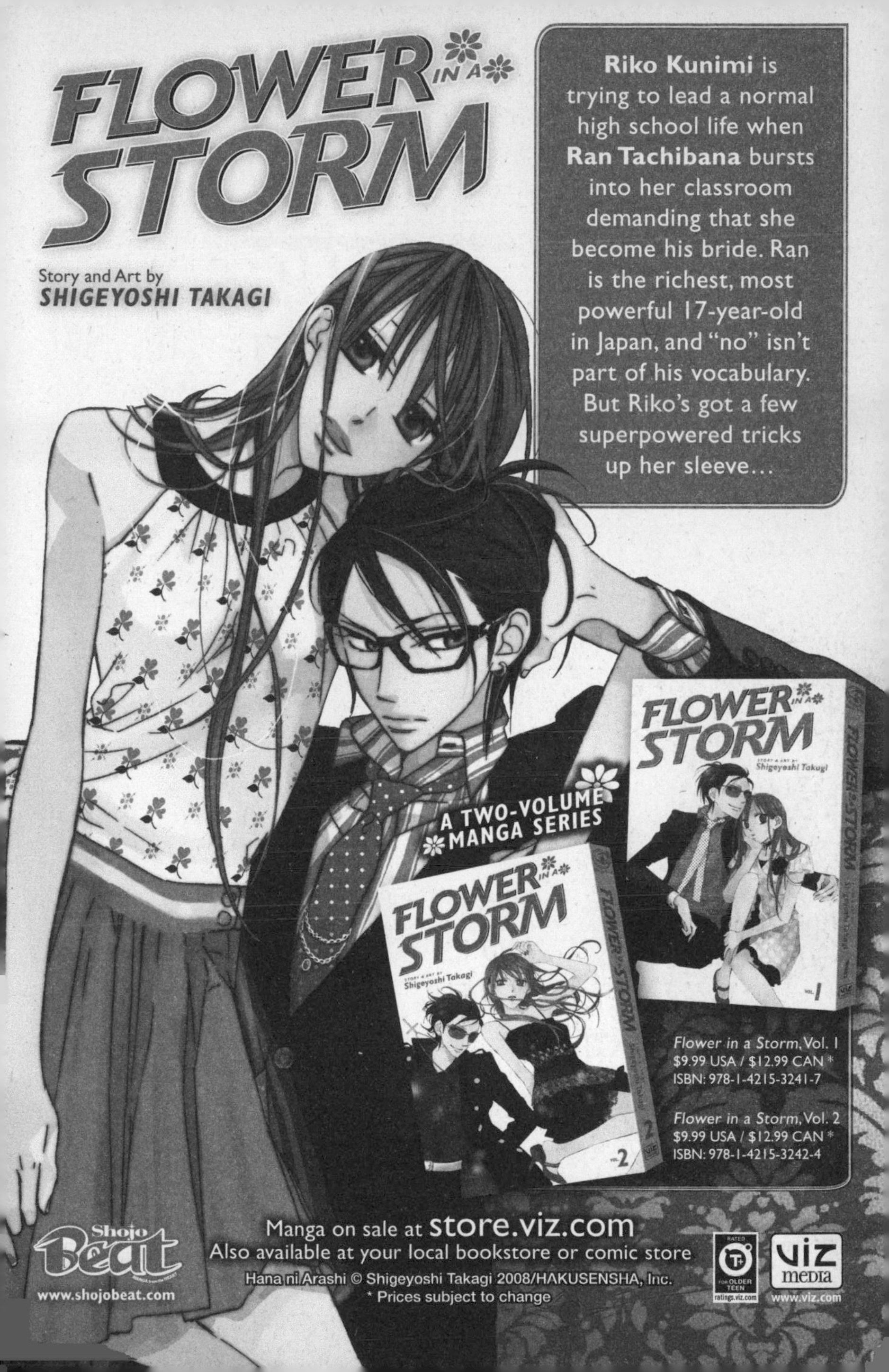
FLOWER IN A STORM
Story and Art by
SHIGEYOSHI TAKAGI
Riko Kunimi is trying to lead a normal high school life when Ran Tachibana bursts into her classroom demanding that she become his bride. Ran is the richest, most powerful 17-year-old in Japan, and "no" isn't part of his vocabulary. But Riko's got a few superpowered tricks up her sleeve...
A TWO-VOLUME MANGA SERIES
Flower in a Storm, Vol. 1
$9.99 USA / $12.99 CAN *
ISBN: 978-1-4215-3241-7
Flower in a Storm, Vol. 2
$9.99 USA / $12.99 CAN *
ISBN: 978-1-4215-3242-4
Manga on sale at store.viz.com
Also available at your local bookstore or comic store
Hana ni Arashi © Shigeyoshi Takagi 2008/HAKUSENSHA, Inc.
* Prices subject to change
Shojo Beat
www.shojobeat.com
RATED T+ FOR OLDER TEEN
ratings.viz.com
VIZ MEDIA
www.viz.com

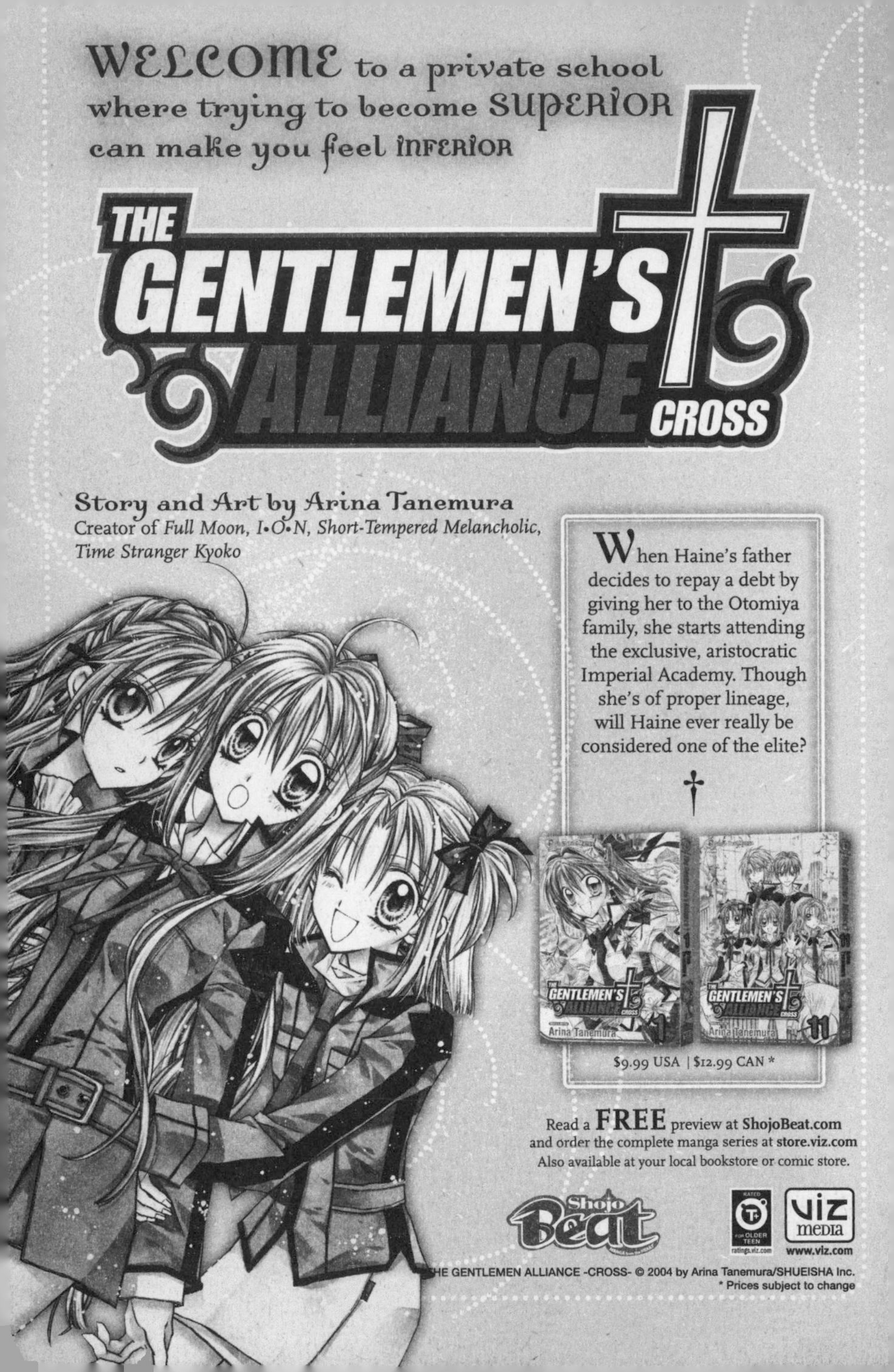
WELCOME to a private school
where trying to become SUPERIOR
can make you feel INFERIOR
THE GENTLEMEN'S ALLIANCE CROSS
Story and Art by Arina Tanemura
Creator of Full Moon, I•O•N, Short-Tempered Melancholic, Time Stranger Kyoko
When Haine's father decides to repay a debt by giving her to the Otomiya family, she starts attending the exclusive, aristocratic Imperial Academy. Though she's of proper lineage, will Haine ever really be considered one of the elite?
THE GENTLEMEN'S ALLIANCE CROSS
Arina Tanemura
1
THE GENTLEMEN'S ALLIANCE CROSS
Arina Tanemura
11
$9.99 USA | $12.99 CAN *
Read a FREE preview at ShojoBeat.com
and order the complete manga series at store.viz.com
Also available at your local bookstore or comic store.
Shojo Beat
RATED T+ FOR OLDER TEEN
ratings.viz.com
VIZ media
www.viz.com
THE GENTLEMEN ALLIANCE -CROSS- © 2004 by Arina Tanemura/SHUEISHA Inc.
* Prices subject to change

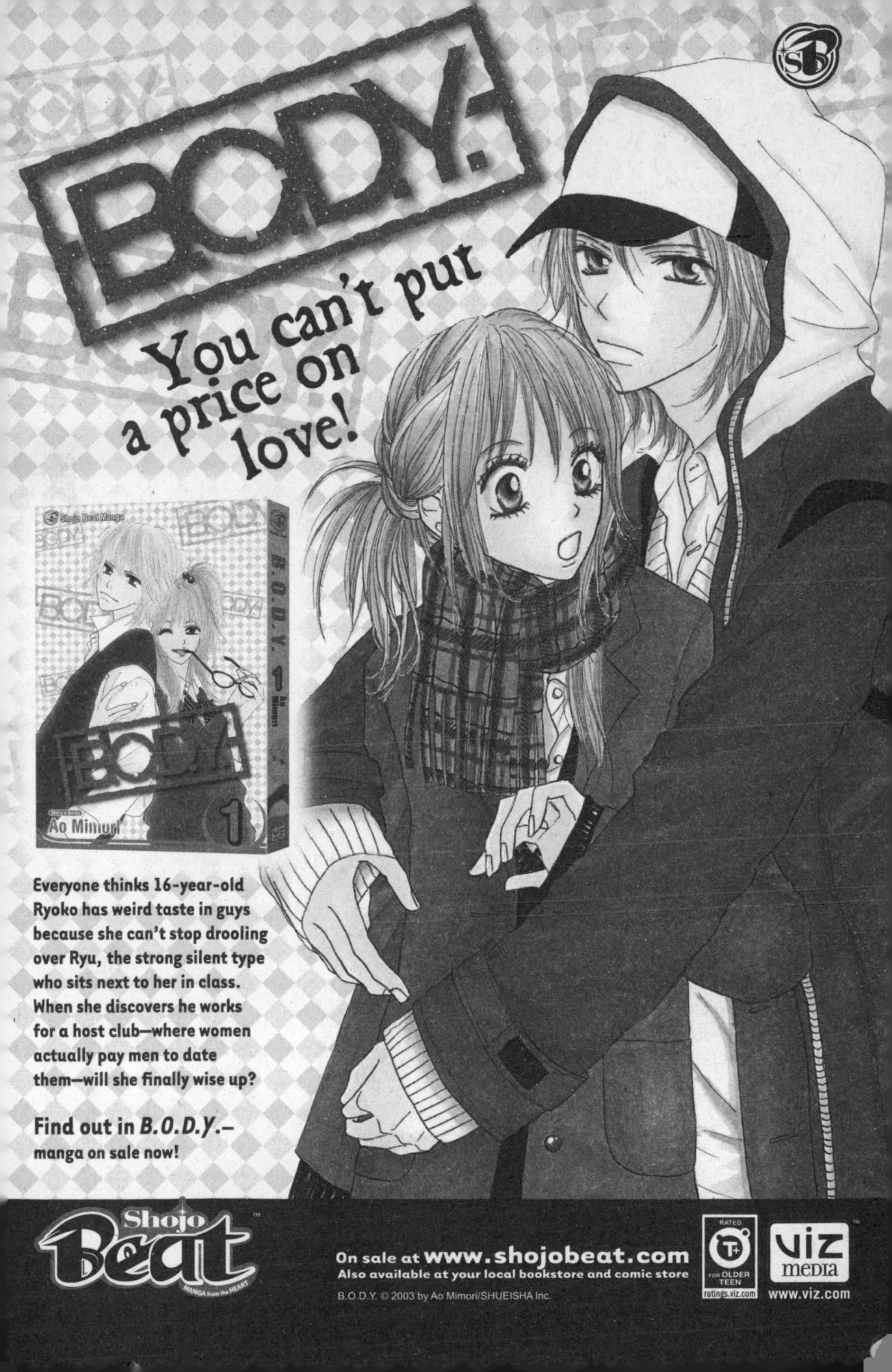
B.O.D.Y.
You can't put a price on love!
Shojo Beat Manga
B.O.D.Y.
1
Ao Mimori
Everyone thinks 16-year-old Ryoko has weird taste in guys because she can't stop drooling over Ryu, the strong silent type who sits next to her in class. When she discovers he works for a host club—where women actually pay men to date them—will she finally wise up?
Find out in *B.O.D.Y.*—manga on sale now!
Shojo Beat
MANGA from the HEART
On sale at www.shojobeat.com
Also available at your local bookstore and comic store
B.O.D.Y. © 2003 by Ao Mimori/SHUEISHA Inc.
RATED T+ FOR OLDER TEEN
ratings.viz.com
VIZ media
www.viz.com

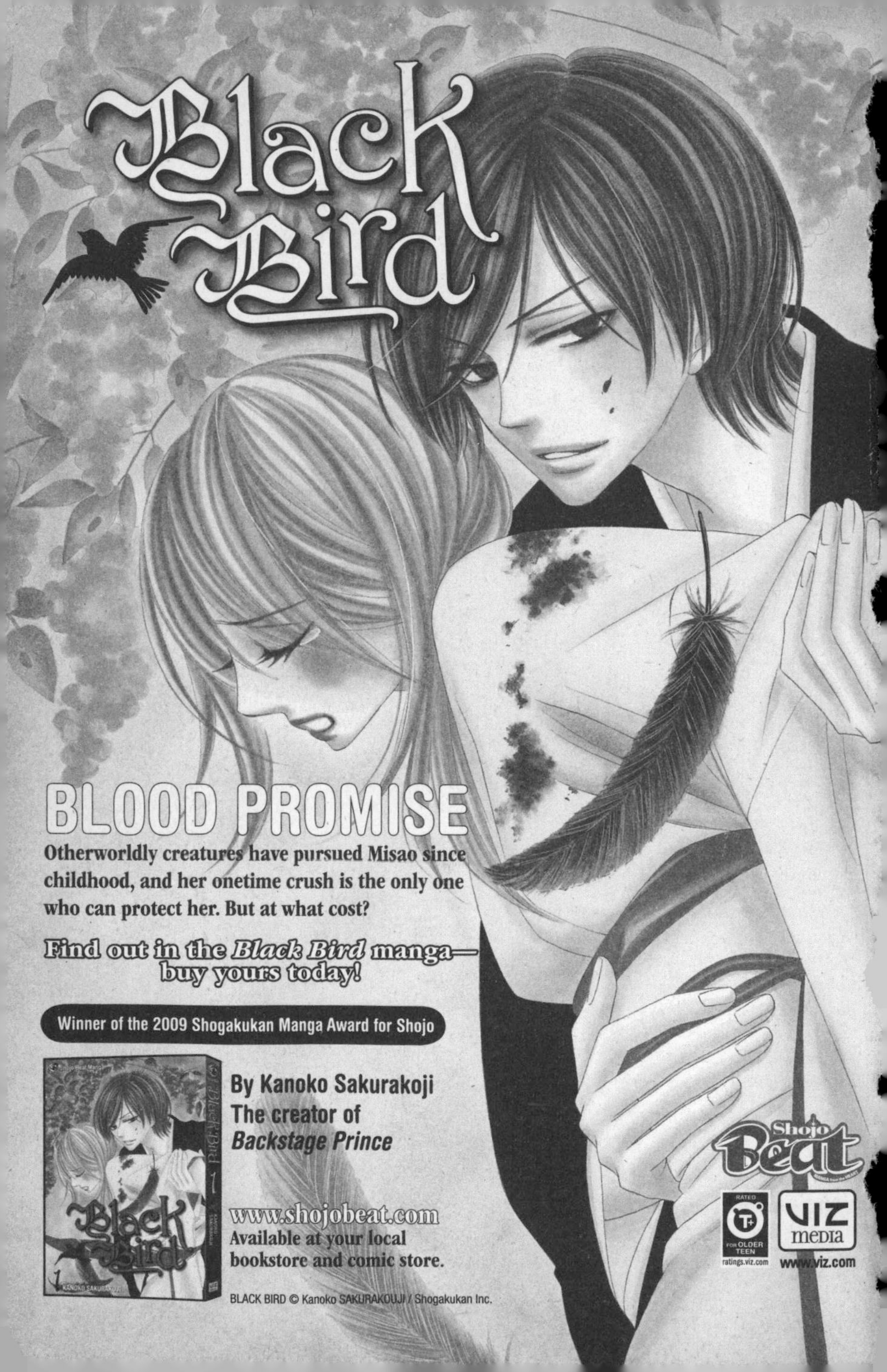
Black Bird
BLOOD PROMISE
Otherworldly creatures have pursued Misao since childhood, and her onetime crush is the only one who can protect her. But at what cost?
Find out in the Black Bird manga—buy yours today!
Winner of the 2009 Shogakukan Manga Award for Shojo
By Kanoko Sakurakoji
The creator of Backstage Prince
www.shojobeat.com
Available at your local bookstore and comic store.
BLACK BIRD © Kanoko SAKURAKOUJI / Shogakukan Inc.
Shojo Beat
RATED T+ FOR OLDER TEEN
ratings.viz.com
VIZ media
www.viz.com

MANGA from the HEART

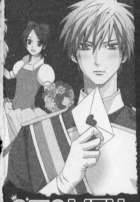
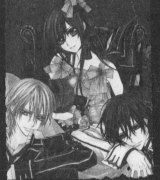
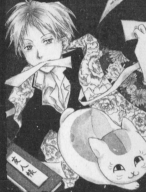

OTOMEN

STORY AND ART BY
AYA KANNO

VAMPIRE KNIGHT

STORY AND ART BY
MATSURI HINO

Natsume's BOOK of FRIENDS

STORY AND ART BY
YUKI MIDORIKAWA

Want to see more of what you're looking for?

Let your voice be heard!

shojobeat.com/mangasurvey

Help us give you more manga from the heart!

www.viz.com